RESPONDING
TO THE
RIGHT

ALSO BY NATHAN J. ROBINSON

Why You Should Be a Socialist

RESPONDING TO THE RIGHT

Brief Replies to 25 Conservative Arguments

Nathan J. Robinson

ST. MARTIN'S GRIFFIN
NEW YORK

First published in the United States by St. Martin's Griffin, an imprint of St. Martin's
Publishing Group

RESPONDING TO THE RIGHT. Copyright © 2023 by Nathan J. Robinson. All rights re-
served. Printed in the United States of America. For information, address St. Martin's
Publishing Group, 120 Broadway, New York, NY 10271.

www.stmartins.com

Designed by Meryl Sussman Levavi

Charts by Mapping Specialists, Ltd.

The Library of Congress Cataloging-in-Publication Data is available upon request.

ISBN 978-1-250-77774-4 (trade paperback)
ISBN 978-1-250-77775-1 (ebook)

Our books may be purchased in bulk for promotional, educational, or business
use. Please contact your local bookseller or the Macmillan Corporate and Premium
Sales Department at 1-800-221-7945, extension 5442, or by email at
MacmillanSpecialMarkets@macmillan.com.

First Edition: 2023

10 9 8 7 6 5 4 3 2 1

To those on the right who are open-minded and thoughtful enough to entertain the idea that they have gotten everything completely wrong

Contents

Introduction

Conservatives have been wildly successful at advancing their talking points. You have certainly heard them. Taxation is "punishing success." Social welfare programs "create laziness and dependence." We need aggressive immigration enforcement to "uphold the law" and "preserve national security." Government is "the problem, not the solution." From the high-volume rage of Fox News and Rush Limbaugh to the (supposedly) more elevated and sophisticated philosophies of Milton Friedman and William F. Buckley,[1] the American right has managed to set the ideological agenda for the past several decades. Ronald Reagan is still the most admired U.S. president according to some polls,[2] and "neoliberal" Democrats like Bill Clinton and Barack Obama felt the need to adopt important parts of right-wing messaging as their own, including talk about personal responsibility, low taxes, and the power of capitalism and markets.[3]

For too long, the left has failed to adequately challenge the conservative framework. Liberals scoff at conservatives as ignorant and callous, but they don't actually spend much time deconstructing right-wing arguments to show how they work. Right-wing books are bestsellers and right-wing talk show hosts are phenomenally popular, yet someone looking for clear refutations of the conservative worldview would struggle to find a comprehensive treatment. This failure to engage with the right has actually contributed to its success: it's common for conservatives to say that the left "has no arguments," in part because we're suspicious of "debate."

In this book, I'll do something that too often on the left, we fail to do: I'll actually deal thoroughly and persuasively with the cases made by pundits like Ben Shapiro, Ann Coulter, Tucker

Carlson, and Jordan Peterson, as well as conservative philosophers and economists like Friedrich von Hayek, Ayn Rand, Thomas Sowell, and Milton Friedman. I'll defend the left's positions on gender, race, wealth inequality, foreign policy, the environment, and more. Combing through the pages of the *Wall Street Journal* op-ed page and books by the right's most popular pundits, plus videos from Prager University and Fox News, I'll explain what the right wants you to believe, and why you shouldn't believe it.

This book is aimed at two different sets of people. First, it's aimed at liberals and leftists who want the "ammunition" necessary to do battle with conservative ideas, whether in public discussions or at the family dinner table. Second, it's aimed at people on the right. Even though it challenges their ideas, it takes them seriously and does not dismiss them as unworthy of a thoughtful response. While it's a blistering critique of the conservative position, it accepts that one cannot trivialize the power of conservative politics or pretend its defenders do not exist.

At *Current Affairs,* the magazine I edit, we have developed a reputation for thorough debunkings of the other side's arguments. Many conservative readers have actually responded well to our work, because few others on the left show the patience necessary to actually read and systematically refute right-wing books. You won't find reviews of the latest Dinesh D'Souza volume in the pages of *The Nation,* because D'Souza is seen as "not worth" dealing with. But you will find such reviews in *Current Affairs,*[4] because I think anyone with a large audience needs to be dealt with. This kind of engagement is healthy, in that it means we break out of our political "bubble." It means we have to consider the other side's position and be able to articulate our reasons for rejecting it, rather than simply ignoring it. It also makes for entertaining reading, as we skewer bad arguments with wit and verve.

I differ from a lot of my comrades on the left in that I find conservative arguments deeply compelling and persuasive. But I don't mean that as a compliment. I mean that I see how they compel and persuade people, and it scares me, because they are wrong. I mean that these ideas are powerful. They lure for a reason. There's something very tempting about ideas like "just respect people's individual choices in a marketplace." In fact, it sounds completely uncontroversial: of course we should respect people's choices! It's only when you actually start to think about the *implications* of these positions that things become more complicated. Conservative talking points are not, as some on the left assume, "self-evidently" absurd. Actually, the problem is that their absurdity is *not* self-evident. On the surface, they often seem like such basic common sense that nobody could disagree with them, which is why conservatives think the left must be loopy, bleeding-heart wackadoodles who let our emotions get the better of our reason. It frequently takes some deep thinking to see where their case goes wrong.

Conservative arguments often sound good when they are just a bunch of words on paper, and it is only when we look at them against the reality of the world that we begin to see the problems with them. Free-market *rhetoric* is extremely appealing. *Leave people alone*: great, hooray! *Don't interfere in contracts*: right! Interference, who wants that? *Don't tamper with prices through regulation*: no, tampering would disrupt the market process, best to *leave it alone*. (There is a libertarian manifesto called *Don't Hurt People and Don't Take Their Stuff*, which sounds so unobjectionable that any disagreement would appear crazy.) But then in practice, what these things mean are: leave *employers* alone to fire people for getting sick, don't interfere in contracts that require employees to let their bosses spy on them twenty-four hours a day,[5] or don't prevent landlords from raising the rent by 500 percent in a single month if they feel like it. What sounds like "common sense" can actually be a rationalization for cruelty.

So I don't think people are stupid for accepting conservative arguments. I think that it's very easy for these perspectives to sound reasonable ("I earned my money, so why should the government get to give it to someone who didn't earn it?"), and it's not until we start really thinking hard about the way the world works that the assumptions behind these bits of rhetoric begin to break down.

Of course, conservatives think we do not listen. They think the left is *emotional*, that we are soft relativists who cannot handle the facts. They believe that because we think they are Evil and we are Good, we are incapable of seeing things as they really are, of accepting the hard and brutal truth of reality. Here's how libertarian economist Deirdre McCloskey puts it:

> The standard take in American politics is that the left is ethical and the right is not. And this is why we have such a hard time talking to each other. Because the left won't listen. "Why should you listen to Hitler?" ... There's this ethical belief the left has that anyone who's not left wing hates the poor and is salaried by the Charles Koch Foundation.[6]

Now, as a matter of fact, the left is not actually insane to think that any given conservative pundit is probably funded by the Koch brothers—the network of Koch-funded scholars and talkers is almost unfathomably vast. (McCloskey herself has indeed been "salaried by the Koch Foundation.")[7] But is it the case that the left refuses to listen to conservative arguments, that the "standard" take is that the left is ethical, and that we do not take seriously conservative ideas because we simply assume they hate the poor?

Perhaps for some. But not for me. I listen to conservative arguments all the time. I listen to right-wing radio, I read the *National Review*, and I have an entire bookcase devoted to conservative "philosophy" from Edmund Burke to Milo Yiannopoulos.[8] I am concerned to treat these arguments fairly and judiciously. This is for reasons of basic intellectual integrity, but also because everyone has a responsibility to hear the other side out carefully in order to determine whether their own beliefs are, in fact, defensible. John Stuart Mill explained this well in *On Liberty*, writing that those who "have never thrown themselves into the mental position of those who think differently from them" do not "know the doctrine which they themselves profess," and if we do not "know [the other side's arguments] in their most plausible and persuasive form" and "feel the whole force of the difficulty which the true view of the subject has to encounter and dispose of," we will never really possess "the portion of truth which meets and removes that difficulty." If I am not closely acquainted with the arguments against mainstream climate science, for instance, I will not know why they are false.

In this book, I intend to show that leftists are fully capable of hearing out conservative arguments, that it is not necessarily because we "refuse to listen" that we find right-wing views abhorrent, but may be because we have listened plenty and been horrified. And while I do not think it is right to say that conservatives "hate the poor," the reason that many leftists think conservatives are *indifferent to* poverty and lack compassion is the frequency with which we hear those on the right trivialize poverty or express their indifference to the fates of others.

For example, consider this passage from the conservative Heritage Foundation:

> For decades, the U.S. Census Bureau has reported that over 30 million Americans were living in "poverty," but the bureau's definition of poverty differs widely from that held by most Americans. In fact, other government surveys show that most of the persons whom the government defines as "in poverty" are not poor in any ordinary sense of the term. The overwhelming majority of the poor have air conditioning, cable TV, and a host of other modern amenities. They are well housed, have an adequate and reasonably steady supply of food, and have met their other basic needs, including medical care.[9]

Now, perhaps this doesn't voice any kind of "hate" for the poor. But it does show an indifference to American poverty. It is saying, in its essence, that the people we call "poor" aren't *really* poor. That they actually have good housing, good medical care, and even luxuries. George Gilder, one of Ronald Reagan's favorite writers, echoed the sentiment, saying that "poor people in America live better than the middle class in most other countries in the world" and "the so-called 'poor' are ruined by the overflow of American prosperity. What they need is Christian teaching from the churches."[10] If you share these writers' beliefs, you're not going to think addressing poverty is a very urgent question—after all, for the most part it doesn't even exist! Here is a very clear divide between the left and right perspectives: The left looks at the lives of the least well-off in the United States and we see an urgent and unfair situation. The right thinks this is a complaint about nothing.

We will get into the question of who is correct on this later on, but note that we're starting to see what the nature of the divide between right and left is, at least on economic issues. The right accepts existing unequal distributions of power and wealth, while the left thinks they are intolerable. The right believes that "American capitalism" has produced wonders, the left believes that it produces unnecessary deprivation and misery and thinks there must clearly be a better way.[11]

How do we decide who is right? In part, it takes a patient examination of the arguments and the evidence. We have to ask serious questions, first philosophical and then empirical. What does it mean to be "deprived"? What kind of poverty, if any, is "acceptable" in a society? How should we judge whether our economic system is succeeding or failing? Once we have a standard, we can evaluate the reality we see: Is it really the case that the condition of America's least well-off is acceptable? Is it really the case that capitalism has given us "the best of all possible worlds"? If we believe things could be different, don't we have an obligation to try to change the present situation rather than making excuses for it?

We're going to go through a lot of different arguments here, and you'll see that I have very little in common with the conservative position. In fact, I find it repugnant. But I also believe in taking it seriously, because it's so influential, and in deconstructing these points carefully to see where they go wrong. My hope is that you will leave this book with a better understanding not only of why conservative points of view in particular are wrong and shallow but how political argumentation works generally. It will hopefully make you a more thoughtful and critical person who is less susceptible to being hoodwinked by propaganda. As you will see, there are many ways to trick people with rhetoric, and I hope you'll come to see through some of the most transparent tactics. At the end of the day, it's crucial to understand what the other side is doing and why it's working if we are to offer a powerful and persuasive alternative.

I will not go into much detail about that alternative in this particular book, but I have thought and written about it before. In my previous book, *Why You Should Be a Socialist,* I have given the *positive* case for left-wing political beliefs. Here, I am taking a negative stance, debunking the other side's talking points. Please do not think, then, that I am solely a critic, with no political framework of my own to offer. I have one, you just have to buy another book in order to hear it. (And if you have already bought it, thank you!)

A Quick Note on Terminology

This book is about "right-wing" or "conservative" political beliefs. But what makes someone "right-wing" or "conservative"? The arguments in this book include both free-market libertarian arguments and socially conservative arguments. There is sometimes tension between libertarian and socially conservative viewpoints— libertarians are all about "not telling people what to do" while social conservatism is highly prescriptive. Do these tendencies really belong together?

I believe they do, because both of them have in common an

opposition to some of the core principles of left politics. They both contain defenses of inequality and social hierarchy against the claims of progressive movements. It is true that a Christian conservative might be anti-abortion, and a libertarian conservative might believe abortion is fine (although libertarian-leaning senator Rand Paul has said he "will always support legislation that would end abortion or lead us in the direction of ending abortion.")[12] It is also true that progressives sometimes find their goals overlapping with those of libertarian conservatives, who tend to be similarly skeptical of the excessive deployment of American military muscle overseas.

Furthermore, in the United States, there has been a great deal of convergence on the right. The late twentieth century's most prominent conservatives, like William F. Buckley and Ronald Reagan, combined free-market economics with socially conservative opposition to abortion, gay rights, and drug use.[13] *National Review*'s Charles C. W. Cooke uses the term "conservatarianism" to describe the mixture of social conservatism and free-market economics that characterizes much of the contemporary right.[14] It is true that there has been hostility between libertarian and socially conservative camps—free-market economist Friedrich von Hayek once wrote an essay called "Why I Am Not a Conservative," and Buckley's *National Review* published an infamously withering review of Ayn Rand's *Atlas Shrugged* that all but accused her of wanting to gas the underclass.[15] But the defense of "traditional values" and "free markets" can be found on Fox News, the *Wall Street Journal* op-ed page, *The Rush Limbaugh Show*, *Breitbart*, and in the books of both "libertarians" like Rand Paul and social conservatives like Ted Cruz. Even if, however, any given person on the right subscribes to only a portion of the 25 specific arguments I discuss here, each one of these is nevertheless an argument that frequently comes from the right, and I want to prepare you to deal with them when and where they crop up.

PART I

How Conservative Arguments Work
and Why They Seem More Powerful
than They Really Are

Conservatism versus Rationality

Three distinct types of critiques, the perversity, futility, and jeopardy arguments, have been leveled unfailingly, if in multiple variants, at three major "revolutionary," "progressive," or "reform" moves of the last two hundred years. . . . A general suspicion of overuse of the arguments is aroused by the demonstration that they are invoked time and again almost routinely to cover a wide variety of real situations. . . . The arguments have considerable intrinsic appeal because they hitch onto powerful myths. . . . In view of these extraneous attractions, it becomes likely that the standard reactionary theses will often be embraced regardless of their fit.

—Albert O. Hirschman, *The Rhetoric of Reaction*

In *The Rhetoric of Reaction*, Albert Hirschman combed through the history of conservative responses to social reform. Hirschman showed that in every generation, "reactionary" politics tends to sound similar, no matter what the issue is. There are a few categories of argument that recur over and over. Hirschman called these "perversity, futility, and jeopardy." Perversity means that a proposed reform will have disastrous unintended consequences. Futility means that a proposed reform will accomplish nothing. And jeopardy means that the reform will undermine its own goals, jeopardizing the precious progress we have made so far.

Hirschman showed that these arguments are made regardless of the facts of any given situation. They do not *need* the facts, because they already know what they will think. Conservatism is always pessimistic about the prospects for bettering society, whether what's being proposed is universal suffrage or the Green New Deal.[1] That makes sense given the conservative starting position. Michael Oakeshott, one of the right's deepest thinkers, said that to be conservative was "to prefer the familiar to the unknown, to prefer the tried to the untried, fact to mystery, the actual to the possible, the limited to the unbounded, the near to the distant, the sufficient to the superabundant, the convenient to the perfect, present laughter to utopian bliss."[2] Oakeshott's conservatism is a temperament or preference, a belief that we should stick with what we have because the "untried" carries risk.

Personally, I sympathize with that kind of "fear of change"—I, too, like familiar things and am of a cautious nature. But it's easy to see how this kind of *feeling* could subconsciously affect assessment of the *facts*. Hirschman shows that in many historical cases, the conservative objections were clearly unfounded, that they were ideological rather than rational—that is, they were the product of seeing the facts through the lens of the preexisting conservative worldview rather than conducting an open-minded empirical investigation. Here, for instance, is an 1840s reactionary talking about the perils of letting everybody vote:

> The word freedom sounds rich and beautiful, but no one should talk about it who has not seen and experienced slavery under the loud-mouthed masses, called the "people," seen it with his own eyes, and endured civil unrest. . . . I know too much history to expect anything from the despotism of the masses but a future tyranny, which will mean the end of history.[3]

Universal suffrage will mean the end of history! Over a hundred years later, similar arguments could be found in the pages of William F. Buckley's *National Review,* which argued that the preservation of "civilized standards" required white Southerners to disenfranchise Black people. Buckley wrote that "the claims of civilization supersede those of universal suffrage," and that "the South does not want to deprive the Negro of a vote for the sake of depriving him of the vote" but because extending the franchise would be "socially atavistic."[4]

This looks ludicrous, and deeply racist, in retrospect. No serious person today, even on the Trumpian right, makes the explicit argument that the franchise should be revoked from people of color to preserve social order,[5] and Buckley himself wisely retreated from the position after the success of the civil rights movement. But what we should notice is that the right's arguments never change. Propose something that challenges the social or economic status quo and they will loudly scream that it will never work, that it will hurt the very people it is trying to help, that it will be the death of civilization.

Hirschman made clear that he wasn't saying conservative objections were *never correct*. Some reforms do, indeed, fail, and harmful unintended consequences are not uncommon. His point, however, was that conservative arguments of this kind were always *suspect*, because they were likely to be the same regardless of whether they had any factual support. Indeed, one common feature of conservative arguments, as we will see throughout this book, is that they often *sound* extremely persuasive, and can even masquerade as "rationality," "just the facts," or "common sense"— yet when we think about them carefully and examine the underlying facts, the arguments swiftly crumble.[6]

Some on the left believe conservative ideas are, for the most part, best explained as rationalizations of the status quo pushed by those who benefit from it. Political theorist Corey Robin, in *The Reactionary Mind,* said that conservatism is "a meditation on— and theoretical rendition of—the felt experience of having power, seeing it threatened, and trying to win it back." Robin stresses conservatism as *reaction*, being horrified by movements like trade unionism, feminism, anti-racism, socialism. "When the conservative looks upon a democratic movement from below," Robin writes, "this (and the exercise of agency) is what he sees: a terrible disturbance in the private life of power."[7]

There is certainly something to this. When I see billionaires giving arguments for why the capitalist system is great and socialism will destroy the country, for instance, I cannot help but think that their arguments have *something* to do with the fact that the system is great *for them* and their critics threaten their wealth and power. The Home Depot cofounder Ken Langone released a book called *I Love Capitalism!* in which he warns that the populist policies of Bernie Sanders pose a threat.[8] But it is fair to assume that Langone's love of capitalism is a bit like a king's love of monarchy. *Of course* he loves capitalism. It's the system that gave him a billion dollars.

But it is also very difficult to psychoanalyze people and discover their "real" motivations, so I do not think it is possible to make a statement like "conservative ideas are manufactured by the powerful to defend their power."[9] At the very least, if we are to try to make such a statement, we ought to first show that the ideas are wrong or irrational. If the ideas are correct, after all, then the motivations of those who hold them are of less interest. Furthermore, if we focus on the identity or motivations of the person offering an idea, we have little to say when those ideas are voiced by someone who clearly doesn't share that identity or motivation—plenty of people hold right-wing views who are not wealthy white men.

In this book, I will therefore focus on addressing the substance of the right's ideas, rather than speculating about why people believe them or whose interests they serve. If I can show that most right-wing talking points are ignorant and fallacious, and that left-wing beliefs are far more sensible and humane, then this should end the discussion: the reasonable reader is obliged to come and join the left. I am interested in the question of which ideas hold up under scrutiny and which do not. Once I have shown that the right's core beliefs cannot be maintained by a rational human being, then we can enter into a discussion about the sociological and psychological reasons why people might hold such mistaken beliefs.

The Terror of Having to Think

One of the great things about being a conservative is that when a decision has to be made—for example, is hiding your spinach under your dinner plate and then trying to feed it to the dog right or wrong?—facts can be consulted. Does it violate the Ten Commandments? Is it a cardinal sin? A venial sin? Against the law? Or you can just ask Mom. Radicals have to work everything through de novo. Radicals have ideas about sin, law, and motherhood. And the more obscure the ideas, the more difficulty in feeding them to the dog.

The great moral principles of conservatism, if not self-evident, have at least been entered into evidence by thousands of years of human experience. And the great political principles of conservatism are simple. . . . "Mind your own business and keep your hands to yourself."

—P. J. O'Rourke, "The Unthinking Man's Guide to Conservatism" in *Why I Turned Right*

"'But what will become of men then . . . without God and immortal life? All things are permitted then, they can do what they like?'"

—Fyodor Dostoyevsky, *The Brothers Karamazov*

We can see why conservative beliefs are extremely appealing. First, fixed political ideologies in general are incredibly useful things, because they prevent us from having to engage in the terrifying and painful exercise of thinking things through for ourselves. All I need to do is check what the rules say. How do I know that criminals deserve their sentences? Because they broke the law. *If* *you can't do the time, don't do the crime.* Immigrants who came to our country illegally violated the rules. I don't need to ask whether the rules are *fair,* and whether deporting them is a proportional punishment to their moral offense. All I need to know is that rules are rules. Political psychologist Jonathan Haidt has argued that conservatism is distinguished in part by the emphasis it places on *authority* and *tradition* as part of its core moral foundations.[1] In practice, this can mean demanding that the will of those in charge be respected because they are the ones in charge.

If you believe in enforcing the rules because they are the rules, it is very easy to evade otherwise sticky moral dilemmas. The judicial doctrine of "originalism" is meant to do this: instead of forcing a judge to think about questions of justice, it insists the judge's job is simply to apply the original meaning of a law's drafters, even if those drafters had been bigoted and irrational. So, for a judge in a capital case, the question of whether to impose the death penalty would be about what the "law" says, rather than what was right or wrong. In Supreme Court chief justice John Roberts's view, his job is comparable to that of the "umpire," who merely says what the law *is* rather than saying what it ought to be.[2]

It is very comforting to have a rule book that can just tell us the right answers to questions. A "rule book" can come in many different forms. It can be a statute that a judge applies rigidly, regardless of the human consequences of doing so. Or it can be something like Milton Friedman's dictum that "the social responsibility of business is to increase its profits."[3] This is a very helpful rule for business executives, because it keeps them from having to ask hard questions about the morality of their conduct. The CEO of a tobacco company does not need to introspect on whether it is moral to try to get people to buy a product that will kill them. *The social responsibility of business is to increase its profits.* So long as the CEO is serving their shareholders, they are fulfilling their duties toward fellow human beings.

These cheap formulas can be very persuasive. But they also

lead to calamity. A drug manufacturer that accepts Friedman's formula for "social responsibility" might conclude that there is nothing wrong with trying to get people hooked on opiates—after all, if it's good for business, it's good for society, by definition.[4] To protect their profits, fossil fuel companies spent decades casting doubt on climate science and trying to convince the public that the factual question was more unsettled than it actually was,[5] but executives could tell themselves that there was nothing unethical about this. Protecting profit is socially responsible by definition.

Many conservatives have written intelligently about how rigid left-wing ideologies, like Marxism at its crudest, can provide ready justifications for mass murder. But anti-communism and free-market ideology are also capable of rationalizing atrocities. During the 1960s and '70s, the United States pursued a hideous campaign of bombing and terror in Vietnam, Laos, and Cambodia, out of a belief that blowing these poor countries to smithereens would protect them from the scourge of communism. Millions of Southeast Asian civilians died during the Vietnam War (as well as nearly fifty thousand U.S. military personnel) but the fog of ideology kept many Americans from seeing the ongoing crime as what it was.[6] Likewise, decades later, the Bush administration's post-9/11 ideology led to a catastrophically disproportionate response. Instead of narrowly pursuing and destroying the criminal network that had orchestrated the attacks, Bush waged an open-ended global "war on terror" that drew from "clash of civilizations" rhetoric. Two entire countries, Afghanistan and Iraq, were destabilized as a result, and there were massive violations of civil liberties and human rights, including torture and indefinite detention.[7]

Common Tendencies in Conservative Arguments

Let's go through and classify some common argumentative tropes and techniques. Hirschman's formula of "perversity, futility, and jeopardy" captures a good deal of the core of conservative arguments, and when you start looking for these tendencies, you will see them everywhere. *Raising the minimum wage will hurt low-wage workers* is an example. Conservative *Wall Street Journal* writer Jason Riley has a book called *Please Stop Helping Us,* which argues that attempts to help Black Americans through social policy actually have the effect of hurting them. We will discuss why these arguments are substantively incorrect. But it is important first to notice just how much of conservative argumentation reduces to fearmongering about hypothetical terrible consequences of various reforms. Thus, the first common tendency is:

Speculative Fiction

Much of the power of conservative arguments comes from storytelling rather than evidence. Think about some common conservative arguments. More immigration will destroy the social fabric of the country, and the immigrants will take jobs. Medicare for All will bankrupt hospitals, raise your taxes, and destroy the quality of American healthcare. Police reform will lead to an explosion of crime. Expanded welfare benefits will produce dependency and sloth. Public housing will inevitably be shoddily built and crime-infested. A wealth tax will destroy innovation and slow down economic growth.

Each of these is an appeal to fear rather than fact. Each sounds like something that certainly *might* happen in theory, and we can tell a story about how it would. We can imagine Medicare paying hospitals too little, and those hospitals cutting their staff. We can conjure a slothful person in our minds, who lives on government checks. We can tell a story about a hypothetical country that expanded the vote to everyone, and then a mob destroyed everything worthwhile by using its vote unwisely. But the stories in themselves are not facts. The stories are just stories. To figure out whether they're facts, we have to look very closely at the world and carefully determine whether they are grounded in reality. This does not just mean plucking random anecdotes or a single convenient statistic. This means doing deep research and observation. The stories on their own are "prejudices," in the literal sense of being prejudgment, judgment before looking at the factual reality.

The question is not whether we can imagine these things. It's whether they're actually likely. We do not live in the world of hypotheticals, we live here on earth. Conservative arguments often work because they tell stories that are genuinely terrifying, and nobody wants to run the risk that the stories come true, but we need to think carefully about whether the stories have any basis beyond vague, irrational fear. Take, for instance, immigration. We can tell a tale about how immigration destroys the "social fabric" of the country. But what actually happens? Well, in reality, the places with the highest levels of immigration in the United States, like Los Angeles and New York, are enriched by their ethnic diversity. It is in areas with the fewest immigrants that there is the most anti-immigrant sentiment,[2] because that sentiment is grounded in apprehension more than experience. Those who encourage Americans to fear immigration suggest that the country will "no longer be America" if its borders are porous. But as libertarian economist Bryan Caplan notes, the United States has had "open borders for centuries," and a large amount of our population growth over the years has been due to immigration, "yet the country remains recognizably American."[3]

The same is true on the left's proposals for healthcare. Around the world, there are models of successful government-run healthcare programs that actually outperform the United States' system.[4] A rational assessment of the data shows that "socialized medicine" is both common and popular, because having healthcare provided as a government service is just like having firefighting provided as a government service. We will see this in more detail in Argument #8, "Socialized Medicine Will Kill Your Grandma." Right-wing scare stories about how socializing a service will turn the U.S. into Venezuela, then, are often not based on evidence, but are mere storytelling.

Much of free-market economics, as we shall see, is more like speculative fiction than social science. "Companies will not exploit their workers, because if they do, their workers will quit," or "in a free market, businesses will not refuse to serve Black people, because if they did, they'd be losing customers" are not descriptions of reality (companies do exploit workers and plenty of discrimination occurs in free markets). They are tales about how things work in a hypothetical world that operates in accordance with various assumptions about what humans "will" do, even if the evidence shows that this is not in fact what they actually do. They tell you that something is true, and it sounds like it *could* be true, but the evidence for it is thin. Free-market economics frequently depends on stories about what humans are supposed to do in this or that situation (e.g., a rational businessman *will* sell to all customers regardless of race, because they want to make as much money as possible, thus the market *will* reduce racism).[5] Here is an example from the Heritage Foundation's Romina Boccia:

> Increasing Social Security's payroll tax rate is a bad idea that would increase every worker's taxes, regardless of income. On the employer side, the payroll tax increases would result in higher labor costs, which would discourage hiring and encourage employers to move overseas or automate more production

processes. This would especially hurt younger and low-wage workers, who would have fewer job opportunities available in a highly competitive global economy. Older workers could also face fewer opportunities and be pushed to retire earlier than they would otherwise choose.[6]

This is a story about what Boccia predicts will happen. But will it? Is there evidence to support this, or is it just a hypothesis? (No evidence is actually cited.)

Or consider this warning from the editorial board of the *Wall Street Journal,* who tell us that meeting targets for reducing carbon emissions will have terrible negative consequences:

> To keep the world from warming more than 1.5 degrees Celsius, global energy consumption would have to fall 7% over the next decade, according to the International Energy Agency (IEA). That means no air conditioning or cars for sub-Saharan Africa. A solar farm the size of the world's current largest solar park would have to be installed roughly every day. That would reduce farmland.[7]

The passage paints a picture of what will happen if energy use is reduced and more solar power is used: Africans will not have air-conditioning and there will be fewer farms. The *Journal* editors don't offer any support for these predictions, or answer the most obvious questions. For instance: Why would reductions in energy use need to come from poor Africans not having air-conditioning, rather than reductions in the carbon-intensive lifestyles of the global rich?[8] And while the implication of "solar will reduce farmland" is that we face a choice between continued use of fossil fuels and starving people to death, is that actually true? (Once you do a bit of research, you find out that "solar farms could supply the world's electricity demands if they covered just 1% of global farmland," that a far bigger threat to farmland comes from developers, and that there is now an entire technique—"agrivoltaics"—of *combining* solar farming and agriculture in one place.)[9] The *Wall Street Journal* passage does not cite any academic studies, and it's obvious why. The moment you start to learn the first thing about the actual issues, you immediately realize that all of these dire predictions are coming from the *Journal's* desire to defend existing fossil fuel use, *not* from a fair-minded examination of the facts.

So: be sure you always demand proof that what the right-winger says "will" happen is not just what will happen in their imagination, but what *does* happen in reality. If you do even a small amount of research, you will frequently find that the predictions are based on gut feelings rather than an actual understanding of how the world works.[10]

Saying Things Rather than Proving Things

This is related but a little distinct. Speculation about the future is a common tendency, but so is making totally unsubstantiated statements about the present. *Wall Street Journal* op-eds are often guilty of this. Frequently, they cite no sources for their claims, and posit cause-and-effect relationships that *should* require mountains of historical and economic data. Consider the following paragraph:

> Central America is poor because over the centuries our laws have obstructed capital formation. In recent decades foreign "experts" and foreign aid have often made matters worse. The Moscow-sponsored Sandinista revolution in Nicaragua and the U.S.-engineered land reform experiment in El Salvador are perhaps the most vivid examples of how foreign bureaucrats have the power to impose ruinous policies on small countries.[11]

This is, once again, a story about what *might* have happened, but you, the skeptic, cannot possibly be persuaded by a paragraph like this that has no evidence. Making a case about the factors underlying the economic history of an entire region should require a vast wealth of data. The questions here are ones that need rigorous social scientific analysis: Does foreign aid make things worse? Is Central American poverty really the result of particular laws that obstruct capital formation? Was the Sandinista revolution imposed by "foreign bureaucrats"? Instead of doing the hard work of investigating these questions, however, it is far easier to just confidently give your preferred answer. And because the assertions *might* be true, and tell a compelling story, the op-ed has the power to persuade despite offering an imaginary version of history. These arguments are often effective because they appeal to people's *preexisting* understandings of how the world works. If you hate bureaucrats, and think their decisions tend to be ruinous, then you likely won't demand much evidence when a particular writer says that some problem was caused by ruinous bureaucrats. It's the sort of thing that fits with your understanding of what tends to happen, so you will be easily persuaded that it *did* happen.

If you're *truly* shameless, you can just claim that there is "irrefutable evidence" or "no evidence" for some proposition or another, and ignore the actual evidence available on the subject. For instance, here is Ben Shapiro:

> The idea behind the transgender civil rights movement is that all of their problems would go away if I would pretend that they were the sex to which they claim membership. That's nonsense. The transgender suicide rate is 40%. And according to the Anderson School at UCLA . . . it makes virtually no difference statistically as to whether people recognize you as a transgender person or not. . . . It has nothing to do with how society treats you. . . . The normal suicide rate across the US is 4%. The suicide rate in the transgender community is 40%. The idea that 36% more transgender people are committing suicide is ridiculous. It's not true and it's not backed by any science that anyone can cite. It's pure conjecture. It's not even true that bullying causes

suicide. . . . There's no evidence whatsoever that the suicide rate in the transgender community would go down in any marked way if people just started pretending that men were women and women were men.[12]

I looked up the study I think Shapiro must have be referring to,[13] and it directly contradicted his assertions. Leaving aside the fact that he's conflated suicide *attempts* with completed suicides, the study concluded that "a higher than average prevalence of lifetime suicide attempts was consistently found among . . . respondents who reported that they had been harassed, bullied, or assaulted in school by other students and/or teachers due to anti-transgender bias" and "the prevalence of suicide attempts was elevated among respondents who reported experiencing rejection, disruption, or abuse by family members or close friends because of anti-transgender bias." Another study found that "social support, reduced transphobia, and having any personal identification documents changed to an appropriate sex designation were associated with large relative and absolute reductions in suicide risk."[14] So when Shapiro says there's "no evidence" that being affirmed in their identities reduces suicide risk for trans people, *the evidence is right there in the study he cites.* He is relying on his audience not reading his source materials, and the trick of saying things emphatically instead of actually proving them.

Extrapolating from Narrow Examples

We have seen that "futility" is a common trope in conservative arguments. Frequently, this shows up in the form of gloomy predictions based on narrow historical examples. For instance, the Soviet economy is often used to discredit all "central planning" by governments. But this is an error, because it overlooks the many successful examples of "central planning" by both public and private institutions, from Asian countries' industrial policies to the French TGV high-speed rail system to the United States interstate highways.[15] In fact, we need to be very careful about drawing conclusions about the future from examples of the past because the past might offer only a very limited guide. Conservatives frequently extrapolate from what has happened during human history to make conclusions about the limits of human nature or inevitabilities we face. Human beings *have* always been violent, thus they *will* always be violent. One proponent of Argument #13, for instance, posits that because no society has ever escaped poverty without child labor, no society *could* ever escape poverty without child labor.

The same arguments are made about public housing: *Public housing projects in the twentieth century were poorly maintained and became hotbeds for violent crime, thus public housing will always be poorly maintained and create hotbeds for crime.* For example, *City Journal's* Howard Husock, in "We Don't Need Subsidized Housing," makes a Hirschmanian "futility" argument about government housing projects:

> Four generations of attempts to provide subsidized housing built to higher standards than the poor could afford on their own in the private market have proved that this idea just doesn't work. Each generation has seen the same depressing pattern: initial success followed by serious decline and ultimately by demands for additional public funds to cover ever-rising costs.[16]

To support this, Husock cites a number of examples of failed American public housing projects. But an intelligent person asks: Are the failings of twentieth-century public housing actually inevitable? The answer is no: from Singapore to Vienna, other countries have introduced comfortable and affordable public housing.[17] U.S. public housing projects were essentially, in the words of housing policy expert Saoirse Gowan, "designed to fail."[18] They were low quality and segregated. European social housing, on the other hand, is designed thoughtfully and carefully, and succeeds.

So we must consider the possibility that what is described as "inevitable" is actually just a *risk*. The worst U.S. housing projects do not show that good public housing cannot be built. They show that when cheap, slapdash housing is built by indifferent bureaucracies, without democratic input from residents, it will not satisfy the needs of the people expected to live in it. That's an argument for democratic planning, not an argument against public housing.

Be careful, because this tendency is everywhere: some absurd and ill-advised environmental rule will be used to indict "environmentalism" generally. Remember that anecdotes are no substitute for data, but it's easy to use them to inflame people emotionally.

The Substitution of Lofty Abstractions for Actual Thought

Here is a quote from Andrew Sullivan's *The Conservative Soul*:

> A free society's deeper asset is its restless, spiritual core. . . . Nothing is more important in that freedom than the ability to take the mystery of life and make something of it, to explore the destiny of one's soul and risk it at every moment. . . . [A] conservative understands that in the face of great and constant loss, in the teeth of disorienting change, there is always the challenge of not knowing for sure. The only peace we will ever really know is the peace that comes from accepting such doubt and turning it into living. We may not know for sure where we came from or where we're going; but we can defend the lucky inheritance of our freedom, be proud of it—and live it.[19]

This is rather poetic. You might even find it inspiring. But what does it really mean? What are its implications for environmental policy? For family leave? For minimum wage? For nuclear non-proliferation? Humility is certainly a virtue, and all of us have our doubts, but why should this make one politically conservative? Sullivan is giving us entrancing poetry, but politics involves concrete questions about how power is going to be wielded and by whom. Be careful not to succumb to the temptation of thinking there is meaning to be found in passages like this. They may be pretty but they shouldn't be persuasive.

Roger Scruton, the preeminent British conservative philosopher and tobacco industry spokesman,[20] gives a warm account of the sentiment underlying right-wing political beliefs in this passage from his *How to Be a Conservative*:

> Conservatism starts from a sentiment that all mature people can readily share: the sentiment that good things are easily destroyed, but not easily created. This is especially true of the good things that come to us as collective assets: peace, freedom, law, civility, public spirit, the security of property and family life, in all of which we depend on the cooperation of others while having no means singlehandedly to obtain it. In respect of such things, the work of destruction is quick, easy and exhilarating; the work of creation slow, laborious and dull. . . . The conservatism I shall be defending tells us that we have collectively inherited good things that we must strive to keep. In the situation in which we, the inheritors both of Western civilization and of the English-speaking part of it, find ourselves, we are well aware of what those good things are. The opportunity to live our lives as we will; the security of impartial law, through which our grievances are answered and our hurts restored; the protection of our environment as a shared asset, which cannot be seized or destroyed at the whim of powerful interests; the open and enquiring culture that has shaped our schools and universities; the democratic procedures that enable us to elect our representatives and to pass our own laws—these and many

other things are familiar to us and taken for granted. All are under threat. And conservatism is the rational response to that threat.[21]

This all sounds quite lovely. I can see one would find it alluring. I even agree with much of what Scruton says here: it's true that we've inherited things we have to keep, and that we shouldn't destroy. Some of this is almost specific enough to have meaning, too: protecting the environment, keeping democratic procedures, etc. But note that a lot of it is abstract, and it remains unclear what the actual *implications* are. In politics, we are asking questions like: Will we transform our energy infrastructure to avert catastrophic climate change? Will we raise the minimum wage so that people can afford to live on it? Will we enact public health measures that will control the spread of a deadly virus? Will we build public transit systems and schools and libraries that people deserve? You may be lured into the conservative camp by its talk of security, freedom, civility, etc., but beneath the appealing abstractions and platitudes are often repugnant beliefs and actions. Scruton, for instance, once wrote that "a concern for social continuity prompts us to view not only promiscuity but also homosexuality as intrinsically threatening."[22] When you inquire into the *substance* of the "cultural inheritance" to be conserved by conservatism, you often find it to be comprised of the set of prejudices traditionally held by members of the author's class, sex, and race.

My friend and erstwhile *Current Affairs* colleague Pete Davis has said of American pundits in general that they tend to be "empirically starved," by which he means "that they've never really touched the wounds of American life—they've never really taken the time to see what it's like in a prison or an eviction court, an underpaid late shift or a free clinic, a border or a war zone." This is doubly true of right-wing pundits. The rhetoric about liberty can be stirring, but we have to remain attuned to the realities of low-wage work, climate change, nuclear proliferation, and mass imprisonment. The poetry about tradition and family and inheritance is all very nice, and can make one feel snug, but it is said that we "govern in prose."[23] The political left and political right are divided on questions like "should we build more public housing?" Do not get distracted by tributes to the collective spiritual inheritance of the West.

The Rhetoric of Reason, Fact, Knowledge

> Knowledge is the food of the soul; and we must take care, my friend, that the Sophist does not deceive us when he praises what he sells, like the dealers wholesale or retail who sell the food of the body; for they praise indiscriminately all their goods, without knowing what are really beneficial or hurtful.
>
> —Plato, *Protagoras*

Watch out for sophistry. Sophistry looks a lot like philosophy, but it isn't. It's easy to mistake the one for the other because they can superficially seem the same, and the sophist goes to great lengths to disguise themselves as a philosopher. Those on the right often put on the trappings of philosophy and science—Ben Shapiro's motto is "facts don't care about your feelings," and there is a constant effort to paint leftists as preferring emotion to logic. But *saying* that your position is logical and factual is not the same as it *being* logical and factual, and when we actually scrutinize conservative claims, we frequently find that they use the *rhetoric* of reason rather than actually reasoning carefully.[24]

> A careful definition of words would destroy half the agenda of the political left and scrutinizing evidence would destroy the other half.
>
> —Thomas Sowell, *The Thomas Sowell Reader*

Sowell says that valuing evidence and precision of language would destroy the political left's agenda. I think the opposite is the case, that Sowell selectively presents evidence and uses loaded language that obscures reality. It can be difficult for a casual observer to know who is right. It is important to be scrupulous, then, in examining conservative claims to see if they *are* really based in "facts," or if they are just cleverly disguised "feelings." Go to the endnotes, check the sources, think hard about the reasoning, spot fallacies and vague terms and unrepresentative anecdotes. Do not confuse the rhetoric of reasonableness for the real thing.

Assumptions about Human Nature

Right-wing storytelling is often grounded in the conservative view of "human nature," which sees people as irreparably flawed and efforts to better our condition as inherently futile. Consider the following quote from the German economist Adam Müller, cited by Hirschman:

> The history of the French Revolution constitutes a proof, administered continuously over thirty years, that man, acting by himself and without religion, is unable to break any chains that oppress him without sinking in the process into still deeper slavery.[25]

Here, the French Revolution, a single historical event, is taken to provide proof of a certitude about the possibilities for bettering human society. That does not, of course, follow logically. In fact, humans have not always sunk into "deeper slavery" when trying to improve themselves. There have been many victories. The labor movement fought for the eight-hour day and the weekend and won them.[26] (Though we are now regressing somewhat on that front, as anyone who works multiple jobs can attest.) Women and people of color fought for suffrage and won it. Pessimism about human nature is thoroughly unwarranted; in fact, we are a naturally cooperative species despite our bloody history.[27]

But the right, which wishes to stymie progressive efforts to alter existing social structures, often comes up with explanations for why those structures are *natural* and *unavoidable,* and tries to discourage any effort to tamper with them, warning that—whether it is tax increases on the rich, same-sex marriage, or a government health insurance plan—any proposal by egalitarians to adjust things will result in Terrible Unintended Consequences that may take us down the Road to Serfdom or cause the Decline of the West.

The appeals to "nature" often involve what looks something like science. Charles Murray, for instance, says that he believes "the genomic and neuroscientific revolutions [will] give us undeniable evidence that differences in personality, abilities, and social behavior exist across individuals and groups alike and that those differences cannot be much reduced by the kinds of public policy changes that are available to us," and we must let an "acceptance of the constraints imposed by human nature . . . guide the administration of the civil and criminal justice systems, the regulation of business, the powers granted to bureaucrats—the operations of just about every social, cultural, economic, and political institution."[28] What he means by this is that human beings are *unequal by nature,* and instead of trying to address this with policy we should treat it as unavoidable.

Murray has become notorious for arguing that racial differences in IQ test scores are partly an unchangeable result of genetics. He is a racist in the most literal sense (I have refuted his racial theories elsewhere),[29] but he is careful to make it appear as if his conclusions are simply facts about human nature derived from scientific research. They aren't—in fact, his argument often boils down to something like: *If U.S. public policy since the 1960s has not managed to fix inequality, then inequality is clearly ineradicable, a product of human nature that must be accepted.*[30] This is absurd, because

U.S. public policy has never made a serious attempt to produce egalitarian outcomes, and several decades in a single country are worthless in producing general conclusions about human nature in all circumstances from the present to the far future.[31] But what is actually wild conjecture is presented as Merely Confronting Hard Truths.

Appeals to nature can look beyond human beings. Here is Jordan Peterson, talking about how social arrangements among lobsters can offer insights into the human propensity for hierarchy:

> So these creatures engage in dominance disputes. . . . [It is] the toughest lobster that wins. . . . We separated from those creatures on the evolutionary timescale somewhere between 350 and 600 million years ago and the damn neurochemistry is the same [because lobsters and humans both have serotonin] and so that's another indication of just how important hierarchies of authority are. I mean, they've been conserved since the time of lobsters, right? There weren't trees around when lobsters first manifested themselves on the planet. And so what that means is these hierarchies that I'd be talking about . . . those things are older than trees. And so one of the truisms for what constitutes real from a Darwinian perspective is that which has been around the longest period of time, right? Because it's had the longest period of time to exert selection pressure. . . . [S]o the idea that human beings, that the hierarchy is something that has exerted selection pressure on human beings is I don't think that's a disputable . . . Exactly what that means we can argue about but, like, that sort of biological continuity is just absolutely unbelievable.[32]

Peterson told the U.K.'s Channel 4 News that the study of lobsters is fruitful because "it's inevitable that there will be continuity in the way that animals and human beings organize their structures."[33]

Now, it is tempting to reply to Peterson that just because something is *natural* doesn't mean it's *good*, and that we shouldn't be taking moral cues from crustaceans. But this would be the wrong approach because Peterson would agree. He's not making the case that things *should* be like this. Instead, he is offering a classically conservative view that no matter what we think things *ought* to be like, this is what they *are* like. He emphasizes the timescale in order to make us believe that social hierarchies are going to be very, very difficult to eradicate. They are all over the natural world and they have been with us for a very long time.

Peterson is not actually interested in a fair-minded examination of the research on how common hierarchies are; he has chosen lobsters because they match his prejudices about what is natural, but one could equally well construct stories from the animal kingdom about the importance of egalitarian cooperation.[34] And if he was interested in anthropology, he would discover that the variety of human societies across time has been tremendous, and hierarchy has *not* been some fixed and inevitable feature.[35] But more importantly, *even* if strict social hierarchies had been present for all of human history, and all of animal history, this *still* would not tell us much about the limits of the possible, any more than pointing out the ubiquity of rape across races and species would prove that rape must be accepted as ineradicable. We do not know what is possible, and attempts to define fixed boundaries for human nature are mostly speculative.

Ludicrous Hyperbole and Big Scary Words

> American Marxism exists, it is here and now, and indeed it is pervasive, and its multitude of hybrid but often interlocking movements are actively working to destroy our society and culture, and overthrow the country as we know it.
>
> —Mark R. Levin, *American Marxism*

It is ironic that the motto of Ben Shapiro is "facts don't care about your feelings" considering how much of conservative discourse is based on *incredibly* strong emotions, virtually hysteria. Leftist social democrats are treated as waging war on sacred values, trying to undo the social fabric. We *hate* America and want to destroy it.

There are, of course, the Big Scary Words that are designed to turn off your brain. Government. Bureaucrats. Regulation. Washington. Nanny state. Cronyism. Radicals. Anarchists. A large part of conservative "thought" focuses on bogeymen, using words that conjure up pictures of evildoers in the mind and trigger an emotional response. The militant feminist who sees everything as a microaggression. The lazy immigrant who comes to sponge off welfare benefits. They are generally not people with names. They are cartoons of people, who are assumed to be out there somewhere. Most of these monsters are created in the mind, though.

Often, when examined, the actual *arguments* fall apart completely. For example, Shapiro and Rand Paul have both argued that if "healthcare is a right," this means that "doctors are slaves."[36] Thus, the left is trying to enslave doctors. The reasoning appears to be that if something is a right, it is absolutely guaranteed. And if it is absolutely guaranteed, then if nobody was willing to provide it voluntarily, the state would have to coerce people into providing it. This is a silly view of what a "right to healthcare" means. First, a right is not "absolutely" guaranteed. A right is a statement of an aspiration, a belief that people are morally entitled to something. It is not a promise that everyone will always be able to have that thing even if we have to commit mass murder to do it. There are, after all, situations in which rights conflict, and if it was true that there simply were not enough doctors to provide everyone with healthcare without the use of forced labor, well, some people wouldn't get healthcare, because there is also a right not to be enslaved. Fortunately, in practice, the extreme situation will never arise because the way a government gives people guaranteed healthcare is to *pay* doctors, not to enslave them. This is, after all, the way the government fulfills the right to education: It hires teachers. It does not conscript them at gunpoint. We can see from countries that do guarantee a right to healthcare that the idea is ridiculous, because it *is not what happens.*

The idea that a "right to healthcare is slavery" is therefore stupid. It is one of the most unintelligent arguments ever made. A child could see through it. But if stated confidently and aggressively, it may carry emotional force. Fight back against this kind of hyperbole. Laugh at it.

Dismissal of Expertise

> Many of the great disasters of our time have been committed by experts.
>
> —Thomas Sowell[37]

One difficulty about arguing with conservatives is that you won't get very far by citing the authority of experts on a subject because conservatives tend to have a belief that experts do not know what they are talking about. In Sowell's books like *Intellectuals and Society* and *The Vision of the Anointed,* "intellectuals" are seen as a class of people arrogantly and ignorantly trying to impose their views and thwart "common sense." Saying that 97 percent of climate scientists believe in human-caused climate change, then, is not going to persuade opponents on the right.[38] In some ways, this is actually a healthy view. After all, it's true that "appeals to authority" should not be very persuasive, and the fact that 97 percent of experts in a field believe something does *not*, in fact, make it true. But the distrust of experts means that, for example, it is not worth citing the authority of the American Medical Association in a discussion about the legitimacy of transgender people's medical needs. This is just proof the AMA has been co-opted by the radical left.[39] During the COVID-19 pandemic, conservatives frequently treated public health authorities as totalitarian bureaucrats,[40] meaning that it was worthless to cite the consensus in the field of public health as evidence conservatives were wrong. The conservative dismissal of expertise makes it very hard to argue on topics in which you are not yourself an expert, because it means any sources you cite can be waved away as irrelevant.

Just Throwing Out Some Statistics

There's a book called *How to Lie with Statistics* by Darrell Huff that everyone ought to read because you will be far better prepared to respond to conservative arguments if you know the common ways in which a useless or misleading piece of information can be dressed up as an illuminating piece of quantitative data.

If you put numbers on something, it helps you seem like you are being empirically rigorous, even if the numbers are all-but-meaningless without other information. For example, here is Sally C. Pipes, a commentator who mostly argues against progressive healthcare reforms, in a book chapter entitled "The Horrors of Single-Payer Insurance—Financial Costs":

> [The British National Health Service (NHS)] costs more than £5,000 per household each year. That per household cost is up 75 percent since 2000. And this figure will likely climb sharply. A report from two British think tanks determined that every British household would need to pay £2,000 more each year to keep the NHS running as the country's population ages.... When the government runs things, politicians make the decisions about how much money every family must devote to health care—whether they like it or not.[41]

These numbers are, of course, useless without context. What do British households *get* for their £5,000 a year? How much do Americans pay? If British households did pay another £2,000, over what time period would that be? If British households did pay another £2000, would it still leave them paying less than other countries? Is government decision-making about spending saving households money they would otherwise be spending? Pipes is interested in none of this, but any serious person who wants to perform a comparative analysis of healthcare systems must care about more than the fact that £7,000 a year seems like a lot of money.[42]

Always beware of conservative statistics. One that gets recycled over and over, and has been cited by Heather Mac Donald, Charlie Kirk, and Candace Owens, is *a police officer is 18.5 times more likely to be shot by a Black man, than an unarmed Black man is to be shot by a cop*. It's a completely meaningless number (using the same data, a cop was 77 times more likely to be killed by a *white* man than an unarmed white man is to be killed by a cop, but that doesn't mean white men are on a nationwide rampage against the police). But it sounds like quantitative analysis that disproves Black Lives Matters's claim that the police are racist. So they keep using it.[43]

Sometimes the process of manufacturing bogus statistics is elaborate. I once happened upon a *very* shady statistic in a PragerU video on why rideshare companies shouldn't have to treat their drivers as full-time employees.[44] The PragerU commentator quoted a study from the Berkeley Research Group, which supposedly found that "forcing app-based delivery and rideshare drivers to become employees would result in eliminating 900,000 jobs, reducing the number of drivers needed in California by 80 to 90 percent." That number seemed extreme (nearly *all* workers will lose their jobs?), so I tried to figure out where it was coming from. But PragerU's sources took me only to what appeared to be a brief summary of a report, without a link to the actual report or an explanation of how the conclusion was arrived at.

I then found a press release touting the statistic on the web page for Yes on 22, a campaign funded by Uber and Lyft, which (successfully) tried to overturn California's rule requiring the companies to treat drivers as full-time workers. That, too, only contained a link to a two-page summary, without a detailed report. But it contained contact information, so I emailed Yes on 22's press person as well as one of the authors of the report. I asked how I could find the actual report. The Yes on 22 person said I should talk to the report coauthor, William Hamm, while Hamm told me I should talk to the Yes on 22 person.

Eventually Hamm and I spoke on the phone. Without my asking, he told me that while he was being paid by Yes on 22, his analysis was completely independent. This was interesting, because in the press release, it did not say that the research had been funded by the campaign (and thus by the rideshare industry).[45] It was presented as if it was independent research. A pretty huge conflict of interest not to note.

I asked Hamm how he arrived at the conclusion that 90 percent of all rideshare jobs in California would be lost if AB5 was put in effect. He reiterated the claim from the published material, that prices would go up as a result and jobs would be lost. This, of course, does not answer the question, and I asked him how specifically he estimated the change in demand for rideshare services that would occur. He said that in the report they use an estimate of "demand elasticity" from a report on rideshare economics by the New School's Center for New York City Affairs. But while he gave me an account of the abstract theory of how it would happen, he did not tell me the actual math that led him to conclude 90 percent of drivers would lose their jobs.[46] It wasn't very easy to assess the claims being made without being able to scrutinize the actual model and figure out where the numbers were coming from, so I asked Hamm to send me the report. He refused, saying that the full report was the property of the Yes on 22 campaign, for whom it had been prepared. So I replied to the Yes on 22 spokesperson and asked him for the report. I never heard back.

No serious person would cite a statistic whose origins are this dubious. But we can see why PragerU did: it confirms the conservative story that government regulation will destroy jobs. It's impossible to know whether the statistic is true, but figuring out how it was made is nearly impossible. Still, we can see why it would be tremendously helpful for a corporation to have such a statistic from a credible-sounding organization. But beware: just because someone has a statistic doesn't mean they have anything true or valuable to say.

The Question They Think You Can't Answer

Sometimes prevailing style conservatives pose questions that they think the left "can't answer" or "doesn't want to answer." Usually, they just haven't looked up any of the many writings by leftists answering these very questions.

We are simultaneously supposed to gasp in awe at teachers' raw dedication and be forced to listen to their incessant caterwauling about how they don't make enough money. Well, which is it? Are they dedicated to teaching tomorrow's future or are they in it for the money? After all the carping about how little teachers are paid, if someone enters the teaching profession for the big bucks, aren't they too stupid to be teaching our kids?

—Ann Coulter, *Godless, the Church of Liberalism*

What is the standard to which we think incomes or other benefits should be aligned? Is the person who has spent years in school goofing off, acting up, or fighting—squandering the tens of thousand of dollars that the taxpayers have spent on his education—supposed to end up with his income aligned with that of the person who spent those same years studying to acquire knowledge and skills that would later be valuable to himself and to society at large?

—Thomas Sowell, *The Thomas Sowell Reader*

ASK "COMPARED TO WHAT"? One way to start might be to ask [leftists] more regularly and more assiduously, "Compared to what?" When people attempt to sum up our societies today as monstrous, racist, sexist, homophobic, transphobic patriarchies the question needs to be asked. If this hasn't worked or isn't working, what is the system that has worked or does work?

—Douglas Murray, *The Madness of Crowds*

Socialists claim to be in favor of equitable redistribution of income and wealth, but who determines what is equitable and does the actual redistribution?

—Dinesh D'Souza, *The Big Lie*

How precisely is diversity our strength? Since you've made this our new national motto, please be specific as you explain it.

—Tucker Carlson

[If] a universal supervision of private conduct is not meant, then there comes the question—Where, between this and no supervision at all, lies the boundary up to which supervision is a duty? To which question no answer can be given.

—Herbert Spencer, *Social Statics*

These questions are meant to be "gotchas" that will stump the left. This often does work in flummoxing an interlocutor in a live debate, because the questions can have complex and nuanced answers that require time and thought to come up with. But it is not *impossible* to answer them.

To Coulter, the answer is "both." People can both be dedicated to their jobs and also desire a living wage.

To Sowell, the answer is that people do not necessarily need to all earn the *same* income, but that the income is that everyone should be able to live reasonably well, and inequalities should not be so great that there are vast differences of power that produce a class system.

To Murray, the answer is that it is okay to compare the present to hypothetical futures rather than things that have already existed. For instance, in a condition where slavery was ubiquitous, if someone said: "But what alternative system has worked or does work?" the answer would be that a different system may not *have* existed, but the change is nevertheless worth trying to make. We can believe that there are plausible systems different from anything that has existed in the past.

To Carlson, the answer is that diversity makes a culture richer and less boring, that artistic, culinary, literary, and even scientific innovations are more likely when people come from many different perspectives.[47]

To D'Souza, the answer is that what is "equitable" is a matter debated through a democratic process, because lots of people have different ideas of what fairness is.

Spencer was pulling the same tricks all the way back in 1851. In the quoted passage he is arguing against public health measures, writing that if it is the job of the state to protect public health, then there is no principled limit to what the state could do in order to make the population healthy. Could it prescribe individuals diets? Tell them how long they had to sleep? How invasive could the government be in the name of making people healthy? No answer, he thought, could be given. But of course an answer *can* be given, which is that those things are more unpleasant infringements on freedom than other, more basic public health measures, and thus in those cases, the value of freedom outweighs the additional health benefit in ways it doesn't when the infringement on liberty is more trivial.

The answers are not always *satisfying*. They may raise more questions. (Okay, what kind of process is democratic?) But the questions do not "destroy" the left position. When they come at you with what they think is an unanswerable question, be ready to answer it!

Be Prepared

The classic go-to gotcha question is: **"Where do you draw the line?"** It's easy to get people with this because strict line drawing is inherently tricky and often arbitrary.[48] It is used in abortion debates (where do you draw the line where a baby begins?), gun control (where do you draw the line in terms of which weapons should be allowed?), taxes (where do you draw the line in terms of how much income people should be allowed to keep?), and countless other issues. Make sure you are ready for it, even if your answer is: line drawing is difficult and while it's obvious that some cases fall on one side and some on the other, it's not always obvious exactly where the boundary falls.

The Gish Gallop

Let us consider a paragraph of conservative rhetoric:

Finally, what's behind the current flavor of multiculturalism for some hardcore leftists is hatred of Judeo-Christianity and rejection of its God. This is evident not only in their treatment of observant Christians and Jews (especially their views on Israel, as [Ben] Shapiro notes), but in their attack on science and truth. In the absence of an absolute, there is no "truth"; there is only "power" and "personal narrative." Thus does good become bad, wrong become right, ugliness come to be hailed as beauty. A human baby in utero is "just a clump of cells." Killing it becomes a "human right." Teaching small children how to perform sex acts becomes "education." A man becomes a woman (and vice-versa) by proclaiming that (s)he feels like one.[49]

When I read a passage like this, I find it hard to know where to begin. There is a debating technique called the "Gish gallop" (named after a creationist who used it successfully in arguing against evolution), which involves making many points in rapid succession without much elaboration. Does one start with the fact that we don't hate Judeo-Christianity? The question of abortion? The distortion of postmodern philosophy? The idea that teaching safe sex is a result of postmodern values? The insistence that trans people are not the gender they say they are? One can easily be overwhelmed.

Are you ready for another? How about this doozy from Sean Hannity's *Live Free or Die: America (and the World) on the Brink*:

> Democrats have become the party of socialism, open borders, sanctuary cities, the elimination of Immigration and Customs Enforcement (ICE), underfunding the military, abortion on demand, infanticide, environmental extremism, gun confiscation, higher taxes, radical identity politics, suppression of free speech and religious expression, and among some Democratic members of Congress, undisguised anti-Semitism. They're also the party of intolerance, smears, lies, character assassination, besmirchment, and fake Russian dossiers.

Where do you start? Every single one of these things requires a long debate. Some are true but defensible (ICE should be abolished and abortion should be provided on demand); some are false, but there's so much packed into the statement that there is no practical way to reply effectively to this.

Let us go into a couple of examples of sophistry in more detail, scrutinizing particular statements closely so we can see how the deceptions are occurring.

The Use of Analogies That Sound Persuasive but Don't Work at All

One of the most commonly used tactics of the conservative de-bater is the use of analogies that can sound powerful to those who do not think about them very hard, but collapse quickly under minimal logical scrutiny. Consider this anti-immigrant passage from Harvard professor and "clash of civilizations" theorist Sam-uel Huntington:

> If each year a million Mexican soldiers attempted to invade the United States and more than 150,000 of them succeeded, es-tablished themselves on American territory, and the Mexican government then demanded that the United States recognize the legality of this invasion, Americans would be outraged and would mobilize whatever resources were necessary to expel the invaders and to establish the integrity of their borders. Yet an illegal demographic invasion of comparable dimensions occurs every year.[50]

Neoconservative writer Douglas Murray calls this a "striking analogy." But it is also a very silly one. What is the difference between the situation we are in and the situation described by Huntington? Well, soldiers are armed and directed by a state. They are trying to violently convert a territory from being ruled by one govern-ment to being ruled by another government. One reason a giant invasion of Mexican soldiers would be met with such resistance is that it would be an attempt by the Mexican government to transfer sovereignty over U.S. territory to Mexico.[51]

Unauthorized immigrants from Mexico have not yet attempted to hand control over the United States government to the Mexi-can government. Instead, they tend to work in meatpacking facil-ities or kitchens, on construction sites and in hotels. Their hourly wages are 42 percent lower, on average, than the wages of U.S.-born workers.[52] Most have no health insurance and their unauthorized status means they are constantly at risk of deportation.[53] They do not have many of the basic constitutional rights that U.S. citizens have. They do not even have the status of "second-class citizens." Instead, they are a fully disenfranchised population.

Huntington's analogy to an invasion, then, is ludicrous. He wants us to find it curious that while Americans *would* oppose a military invasion by Mexico, we do not oppose the peaceful presence of Mexican nationals working at landscaping companies and on food trucks. Since both involve large numbers of Mexican people coming without legal authorization from Mexico to the United States, Huntington wants us to think the two should both be classified as "invasions." But this is like saying that since both the American Revolution and the 1960s "British Invasion" involved English people being sent here to influence our way of life, the Beatles should have been met with the same armed resistance as eighteenth-century redcoats were.

Huntington's blunder is making a "false analogy," one in which the common properties of two things are emphasized in order to make them seem similar, when it is the *differences* between them that matter. Another obvious argument is the "taxation is slavery" argument. Slavery involves people performing work for which they do not receive compensation. Taxation also involves people performing work for which they do not receive compensation, *if* we think of earnings accruing over the course of a workday or a year and treat some of that time as the time spent paying off one's tax burden. (I don't think this is a helpful way to think about taxes, as later explained in the "Taxation Is Slavery and/or Theft" section, but for right now let's assume it's fine.) Thus: taxation and slavery are both unjust appropriations of people's labor.

Why is this a false analogy? Because it leaves out all of the ways in which taxation and slavery are nothing alike, which are hugely relevant for evaluating whether taxation is unjust in the same way that slavery is. Compare the life of a slave to the life of even a heavily taxed billionaire and see if it makes any sense to classify them as being on the receiving end of the same kind of injustice. An enslaved person can be physically punished for not performing hard labor. A dentist or lawyer, on the other hand, is not forced to labor, but if they *choose* to work at a profession that pays them a large amount of money, they must pay a portion of their income to the government.

Once you start to notice bad analogies, you will see them constantly in conservative talking points. "The Nazis Were Socialists" (Argument #11) often goes something like: Hitler believed in Big Government. Democrats believe in Big Government. Thus, Democrats and Hitler have similar political philosophies. But a large part of Hitler's political philosophy, the part people tend to object to most strenuously, was the desire for global military domination and the extermination of Jews, Black people, LGBT people, and communists.

Or try this one: Cars cause many more deaths each year than guns. Thus, if people shouldn't be allowed to own guns, they shouldn't be allowed to own cars. The argument here singles out one single property that guns and cars have in common (causing deaths). But it doesn't consider any of the ways in which guns and cars might be different in ways that matter for evaluating the desirability of restrictions on their use. (You can, for instance, significantly affect the number of deaths caused by cars through better urban planning and better automotive design, but guns must be designed to be lethal. Cars might also have benefits that outweigh their costs, in a way that guns don't.)

If you use abstract language, you can make two extremely different things look like very similar things. For instance, Adolf Hitler can be said to have believed in "collectivism" because he spoke about the interests of a particular collective group. Martin Luther King Jr. also spoke about the interests of a particular group, namely African Americans. King might therefore also be said to have believed in collectivism. This does not, however, mean that King and Hitler believed in a comparable ideology.

Frequently, conservative arguments use a kind of linguistic drift, where mild behavior is lumped into a category that makes it seem a more extreme behavior. We will see in Argument #20 how the criticism of Christianity becomes a "war" on Christianity. We can also see this tendency in the way that those on the right compare "cancel culture" to the authoritarianism of Joseph Stalin or Mao Zedong. Consider the following passage comparing leftists on social media to Maoists during the Chinese Cultural Revolution of the '60s and '70s:

> Today America is going through its own Cultural Revolution, though thankfully much more genteel than that in China. In America the loony mob of left-wing purists seeking to cleanse the revolution is usually virtual. Victims still are expected to grovel and beg, but without the dunce cap. . . . So self-righteous mobs demand that anyone with unpopular thoughts be denied publication, disciplined by employers and professional associations, and fired from their jobs. Those targeted are expected to engage in the online version of self-criticism sessions during the Cultural Revolution. . . . Of course, reeducation, directed by well-compensated, mostly white professionals who make a living selling such nonsense as "white guilt" and "white fragility" is mandatory. Even then, those deemed as insufficiently obsequious are targeted for personal destruction. Campus pseudo-revolutionaries, likely unconsciously, have adopted the Maoist Red Guards as their model.[54]

I hear comparisons like these a lot. Today's American leftists, who "mob" people on social media with denunciations over small offenses, are compared to violent revolutionaries of ages past, or even the members of a lynch mob. But there is one rather crucial difference between social justice activists on Twitter and Stalinists, Maoists, and lynch mobs: social justice activists are using words, not violence.

The Chinese Cultural Revolution was a brutal affair. In the infamous Guangxi Massacre, over one hundred thousand people were killed through "beheading, beating, live burial, stoning, drowning, boiling, group slaughters, disemboweling, digging out hearts, livers, genitals, slicing off flesh, blowing up with dynamite, and more." In certain high schools, "students killed their principals in the school courtyard and then cooked and ate the bodies to celebrate a triumph over 'counterrevolutionaries.'"[55] Those who use terms like "cultural revolutionaries" to describe the contemporary left are deliberately trying to evoke these horrors without pointing out what a vast difference there is between mass murder and mass tweeting.

I have seen one commentator refer to online leftists as "digital Robespierres" because they supposedly give the online equivalent of the guillotine to those who question their orthodoxies. But the difference between a guillotine and the "online equivalent of the guillotine" is that with the latter, your head isn't removed from your neck. When we realize that the leftists being compared to Robespierre or Stalin don't have guillotines or gulags, suddenly the comparisons don't seem nearly as forceful. Language like "authoritarianism" is used in a way to capture two very different kinds of behavior: that which *does* involve murder, torture, and imprisonment, and that which does not involve these things at all, but is *analogous* in some kind of way. (Stalin denounced those who disagreed with him. Alexandria Ocasio-Cortez denounces those who disagree with her, thus AOC is a Stalinist.)

Always be sure to examine words like "tyranny" or "authoritarianism" or "dictatorial" to see whether we are talking about something that can be *compared* with dictatorship at a certain level of abstraction but that, when examined more closely, amounts to saying, *Nazis wore boots, therefore boot-wearers are Nazis.*

How Totalitarianism Comparisons Work

Here is Jordan Peterson speaking to Cathy Newman of Britain's Channel 4 News. Newman asks Peterson to justify his comparison of transgender activists to Maoists:

NEWMAN: I mean, there's no comparison between Mao and a trans activist, is there?

PETERSON: Why not?

NEWMAN: Because trans activists aren't killing millions of people!

PETERSON: The philosophy that's guiding their utterances is the same philosophy.

NEWMAN: The consequences are—

PETERSON: Not yet!

NEWMAN: You're saying that trans activists—

PETERSON: No!

NEWMAN: —could lead to the deaths of millions of people.

PETERSON: No, I'm saying that the philosophy that drives their utterances is the same philosophy that already has driven us to the deaths of millions of people.

NEWMAN: Okay. Tell us how that philosophy is in any way comparable.

PETERSON: Sure. That's no problem. The first thing is that their philosophy presumes that group identity is paramount. That's the fundamental philosophy that drove the Soviet Union and Maoist China. And it's the fundamental philosophy of the left-wing activists. It's identity politics. It doesn't matter who you are as an individual, it matters who you are in terms of your group identity.[56]

Peterson's argument here is of the "Hitler wore pants, you wear pants, therefore . . ." variety. Maoism valued group identity, so do transgender people, therefore . . . Of course, if we took seriously the belief that "group identities" were inherently dangerous, we would conclude that anyone who described them as "an American above all" was equally similar to a Maoist.

Newman is correct to point out that a distinction between the two groups under discussion (Maoists and trans people) is that one is responsible for *the deaths of millions of people*. Peterson, knowing he cannot defend the idea that trans activists are going to begin a mass murder campaign, says that they merely share a philosophy with mass murderers. But Newman's point is that the differences between Maoists and trans activists (body count) are far more important than the similarities (thinking group categories are important). The analogy is inflammatory without being illuminating.

The Selective Omission of an Entire Other Half of the Story

Recently, studies show that thirty thousand Canadians have gone to other countries for health treatment, even though they get it free of charge in Canada and they've got to go pay for it somewhere else and they go because the quality is not the same.

—Thomas Sowell[57]

Here conservative economist Thomas Sowell cites a study showing that a large number of Canadians have gone to other countries for treatment. Sowell uses this piece of evidence to support his claim that the Canadian healthcare system, with its much larger role for government, is not all it's cracked up to be, and that the American healthcare system might not be as bad as its critics say. After all, Canadians are so dissatisfied that they leave to get treatment elsewhere!

Except, hang on: if we are serious about performing a comparison with the United States, we have to know how many *Americans* go elsewhere for treatment. We know that thirty thousand

Canadians per year do. That sounds like a large number. But is it? Well, it turns out that the number of Americans who go abroad for treatment is much, much larger. The *American Journal of Medicine* reports that in 2017, "more than 1.4 million Americans sought health care in a variety of countries around the world," mainly "because we have the most expensive health care system in the world" and "it is not difficult to find countries that offer various procedures at 30%-65% of the cost of care in the United States."[58]

Sowell didn't tell you that. Why didn't he tell you? Because he's an ideologue, so he presents only the facts that fit his story and leaves out the inconvenient ones. This can make a person's case sound very persuasive because it's full of facts that are technically true, but are picked so as to create a false impression.

Here's another example. In Glenn Beck's book *Arguing with Socialists,* Beck presents a case against raising the minimum wage to fifteen dollars an hour, as many progressives advocate for.[59] Beck cites a Congressional Budget Office report saying that raising the minimum wage this high nationwide would result in a reduction of the total number of jobs.[60] But Beck leaves out a part of the CBO report that is inconvenient for his argument: it also said that a fifteen-dollar-an-hour minimum wage would *substantially reduce poverty.* In fact, it argued that there were trade-offs to the policy: there would be some job loss, but it would also boost the wages of twenty-seven million workers and would lift 1.3 million people out of poverty![61] We can debate which of these is more important, and question whether the CBO was right (see the section on minimum wages, Argument #2). But Beck isn't interested in having a reasonable debate like this. Instead, he wants you to think that progressives are economically illiterate. Admitting that their favored policy would reduce poverty makes it hard to support his case. So he leaves out the facts.

How about this one? Here's John Stossel using communist cars to explain why the free market works better than state economic planning:

The worst car I can buy in America is much better than the best cars that governments' central planners could invent. The best the entire Soviet block produced were the Trabant and the Yugo. Remember those? They are the automotive equivalent of Obamacare: consumer goods from government "experts."[62]

Now, while the Trabant and the Yugo were indeed infamously awful cars, there were, in fact, somewhat better cars to come out of the Eastern Bloc.[63] But on the whole, Stossel is right that the Soviets did not produce great cars. He leaves out a crucial fact, though: the government wasn't trying to make good cars. If we are serious about evaluating Soviet production, we have to look at whether the government accomplished what it *was* trying to do. In fact, the Soviet Union produced highly advanced aircraft, beat the U.S. to putting the first satellite in space and the first astronaut in orbit, and the Red Army contributed more to the defeat of Hitler than any other player in World War II. As a pacifist, I'm not particularly enthralled by developments in weapons technology, but the fact that the Soviet Union invented the AK-47 and developed the largest nuclear bomb ever constructed has to be considered when evaluating whether central planning is capable of creating technological advances.

Pointing this out is no defense of Stalin, a monstrous dictator, or of the Soviet system, which nobody should want to replicate. Instead, it is merely to note that simplistic portrayals—the Soviet Union as a dismal disaster with no accomplishments to its name and the United States as gleaming capitalist paradise—are propaganda, that the real world is much more nuanced and complicated, and that we have to look at *all* of the facts instead of only the facts that favor one ideology. The Soviet Union went from being a peasant society in 1917 to winning the race to outer space by the 1950s. This was an accomplishment of central planning that has to be considered alongside the dreadful quality of many Soviet consumer goods.

Another example of "leaving out half the story": the Cato

Institute is a free-market think tank that produces academic papers. Once, out of curiosity, I selected one of these papers at random to see whether it would (as I expected it to) twist the facts to suit free-market conclusions rather than presenting them honestly. The paper in question was about paid family leave policies in other countries and included the following passage:

> Government-mandated leave has similar [negative] effects internationally. A study of 16 European countries over a period of around 20 years found that "parental leave is associated . . . with reductions in [women's] relative wages at extended durations."[64]

A good rule of thumb is that whenever you hear a right-winger cite a study, you should always look up the study because it will probably either (1) say exactly the opposite of what they say it says or (2) at least contain critical information that the right-winger left out in order to give you a false impression. I looked up the study of sixteen European countries to see if it indeed argued that parental leave reduced women's wages. Here is what the passage in question actually says:

> Rights to paid time off work raise the percentage of women employed, with a substantial effect observed for even short durations (i.e. less than 3 months) of guaranteed work absence. . . . Leave legislation increases the employment-to-population ratio of all females by around 4% and of women of childbearing age by approximately 9%. . . . Short periods of leave are found to either have no effect on or to raise female earnings. Conversely, lengthier paid entitlements are associated with substantial wage reductions, with predicted decreases in the range of 1.5% to 3% for durations of six months or more. . . . To summarize, the employment of women appears to be increased by even relatively short (less than 6 months) durations of paid leave, whereas

their relative wages may fall with more extended entitlements. This suggests that the work absences currently guaranteed in many European countries may be so lengthy as to reduce the earnings of females. Conversely, there is little indication that substantial costs would be incurred, in the U.S., if the period of parental leave were modestly extended or if payment were provided.[65]

The Cato paper is accurately quoting the study, but they are leaving out information that would influence your opinion of its meaning. The ultimate conclusion of the study is that while parental leave does cause some reductions in wages if it lasts a certain length of time, the U.S. is unlikely to see this kind of problem arise if it offers modest new amounts of parental leave. And, in fact, there are significant *positive* effects to paid parental leave, with short periods of government-mandated leave actually *raising* women's earnings. And this is just looking at the effect on *wages*: the point of government-mandated parental leave is to give new parents a chance to be with their new children during the first months of a baby's life, the value of which is almost incalculably high. But because the Cato Institute are dogmatic promoters of free markets, they must find a way to spin highly successful parental leave policies from other countries as negatives by finding *some* possible negative consequence, presenting it as the *main* consequence, and then using it to "prove" their preexisting belief that government intervention in the economy almost always does more harm than good.

We've just seen an example of how critical facts can be buried. But right-wing arguments often also work by simply caricaturing the left's position, presenting a "straw man" version that can be knocked down easily. Instead of presenting what we on the left actually think, they'll present a cartoon of what we think, and then prove that the cartoon is cartoonish. (One of my aims with this book is to show that many leftist arguments are far more reasonable and nuanced than they are commonly presented as being.)

Let us review the tendencies, then.

◊ **Speculative Fiction:** Telling a story about the horrible things that will happen when progressive policy is passed, or the wonderful things that will happen if the market is left to its own devices, before any of the evidence comes in. If the empirical studies on the topic are inconvenient for the "markets good, government bad" narrative, they can be ignored. Pass the welfare bill and everyone will become a helpless dependent, all work will stop, and the economy will shrivel.

◊ **Saying It Rather than Proving It:** China's economy is a disaster. Rioters are burning down our cities. I don't know it, but if I say it emphatically enough, who needs proof?

◊ **Universal Laws from Narrow Examples:** If a public works project was mired in graft and corruption, it shows that public works projects are inevitably mired in graft and corruption. If a campus social justice activist says something wacky, it shows that everyone on the left is wacky.

◊ **Poetic Abstractions:** Conservatism is about valuing the *spirit of the nation* and the *inheritance of the past* and the *tradition of our forefathers,* which turns out, in practice, to mean forcing trans people to use men's bathrooms.

◊ **The Rhetoric of "Facts and Logic":** Bleeding hearts let their feelings get in the way of the facts. Emotional reactions like "immigrants are human beings" are logically inferior to tough-minded conclusions like "they violated the law, so they should be deported."

◊ **Assumptions about Human Nature:** That's the way things have always been. We tried everything to change it, but we couldn't. It's inevitable.

◊ **Ludicrous Hyperbole:** Joe Biden is a Marxist.[66]

◊ **Scare Words:** BUREAUCRACY. Do you want a BUREAU-CRAT controlling your life? TERRORISTS. Do you want TER-RORISTS coming after your family? MOBS. The streets are full of MOBS.

◊ **Dismissal of Expertise:** Climate scientists are just after those lucrative research grants. Public health experts want you to wear masks and get vaccines because they want to control your life and tell you what to do.

◊ **Throwing Out Some Statistics:** Seventy-two percent of Americans who were told that Medicare for All would cause their doctor to go bankrupt responded that they would oppose Medicare for All.

◊ **Posing Questions They Think You Won't Have an Answer For:** Oh, so you want a higher tax rate? Why shouldn't the tax rate be 100 percent? You want to ban semiautomatic rifles? Why not ban carving knives? You want to have a public health department? Why not mandate everyone eat salads for lunch?

◊ **Gish Galloping:** If you speak quickly enough, nobody will have time to point out all the fallacies. The faster you go, the more you can fudge. If you go *really* fast, you can be Ben Shapiro, getting away with saying almost anything and having people assume your quick talking means sharp thinking.

◊ **Bad Analogies:** Raising taxes is like the Holocaust because it's the government taking something from large numbers of people.[67]

◊ **Omitting the Half of the Story They Don't Like:** Democrats are proposing *trillions of dollars in new spending*. (Neglects to mention that the spending will save large numbers of human lives and alleviate climate catastrophe.)

Learn how these techniques work and it will be easy to spot propaganda and sophistry when you encounter it. (It will also be easy to attain a lifetime fellowship at the American Enterprise Institute, but I presume you are not using this book to do evil.)

Tips for Arguing

Sometimes there is little point to arguing with someone who disagrees with you politically. Changing minds is hard work, and even if you "destroy" someone in intellectual combat, they are far more likely to resent and despise you than to say, "Ah, how right you are, my views are foolish, I have been bested." In fact, the better reason to get familiar with how conservative talking points work and why they are persuasive is *not* so that you can "deprogram" hardcore right-wingers, but so that you can help people who are relatively apolitical resist falling for sophistry. In other words, an uncle who watches Fox News all day might not be open to hearing another point of view (although you never know—some such people turn out to have surprisingly warm feelings about Bernie Sanders, in part because Bernie hates the Democratic establishment just as much as they themselves do). But maybe your cousin who grew up with that stuff and repeats it but doesn't feel particularly passionately about it will be more thoughtful.

If you do get in an argument with someone, though, here are some points I think you should bear in mind in order to have the maximum chance of persuading them—or, at the very least, persuading the bystanders who are watching the argument.

Do not assume they are stupid.

One of the central points of this book is that conservative arguments can be persuasive, even to intelligent and sensitive people. If you assume that the person you are speaking with is stupid, you will be overconfident in your own prowess as a debater, and you can expect to be humiliated.[1]

FAMILIARIZE YOURSELF WITH THE OTHER SIDE'S CASE.

If you live in an echo chamber, you will not necessarily know what the other side is going to say. They might surprise you. I was taken aback when I read Dinesh D'Souza's *The Big Lie* and discovered that, unlike some conservatives, he does not try to deny the hideous history of racism and genocide in the United States. In fact, in parts of his book, he almost sounds like he could be leftist historian Howard Zinn, since he admits the full horror of what was done to Black Americans and Native Americans. Instead of denying the most gruesome and embarrassing facts of American history, as some on the right do, he takes the interesting approach of saying that *liberals* were the ones responsible for these crimes. The argument doesn't work,[2] but if you don't read conservative literature, you might be unprepared for the particular points they're going to hit you with. And if you know what they're going to say before they say it, you will be less likely to be flustered and stumped in the moment. So don't just read books like this one in order to prepare yourself. Read books like Larry Schweikart's *48 Liberal Lies about American History,* Gregg Jackson's *Conservative Comebacks to Liberal Lies,* and Phil Valentine's *The Conservative's Handbook,*[3] all of which hand conservatives the talking points they will then use against you. As error-filled and exasperating as many of these books are, you should not turn down the opportunity to figure out exactly what you're going to hear them say before they say it.

ATTACK THE STRONGEST VERSION OF THE POSITION, NOT THE WEAKEST.

When someone takes the weakest possible version of an opponent's position and tears it to pieces, this is known as destroying a "straw man" argument—essentially attacking a scarecrow rather than the actual people you're supposed to be debating, and trying to convince the audience that the scarecrow is the person. Conservatives attack straw men a lot—for instance, when they say that leftists believe the "government should control everything." The opposite of the straw man is the "steel man," deliberately making your opponent's case as strong as possible, so that once you wreck it, it is wrecked for good. The reason for doing this is that, if you attack a weak version of the position, you give them the ability to point out that you are misrepresenting them, and to make a stronger case that you have failed to refute. Refute the strongest version so that there's nothing left for them to come back with.

STORIES MATTER JUST AS MUCH AS EMPIRICAL CORRECTNESS.

You have heard that there are lies, damn lies, and statistics. Well, that's a little bit too cynical. Statistics are essential for helping us understand how the world works. But it is also true that it is very easy to make up and manipulate statistics. Don't get into a competition to see who can toss out the most numbers, and lose sight of the ultimate principles at stake.

Remember that narratives can be just as compelling as numbers. The arguments for laissez-faire economics are weak and collapse under scrutiny. But the *story* told by laissez-faire economics is so compelling that it has survived. It is a tale of free people struggling against an oppressive and interfering government that cannot get anything right.

You need an alternate framework for understanding reality. You need to be able to tell a different story that provides an equally persuasive account of why things are the way they are. This is one reason why Marxism was extremely successful during the twentieth century: it gave oppressed people a clear explanation of why they were oppressed. I do not believe Marxism was correct, but its explanation fit enough of the facts of reality that it was easy to accept. It is not necessary to provide a premade, fully alternate worldview, but it *is* necessary to do more than just debunk bad statistics, and to instead give better stories to explain what is going on.

ANSWER THE RHETORICAL QUESTIONS.

We saw that a common technique is to ask a question that they think will stump you. For instance, Ben Shapiro likes to say about transgender people: "If saying I am a woman makes me a woman, does saying I am a moose make me a moose?" He believes that this question is unanswerable and exposes transgender people as silly and inconsistent. But if you've got a persuasive response to questions like this, it won't seem like the discussion-ending "gotcha" Shapiro thinks it is. So if someone lays the "if we ban guns, shouldn't we ban cars and swimming pools?" question on you, be prepared with a clear response explaining *why* those two things are distinct. (Likewise, "If America has so many problems, why do people want to live here?") Shapiro once gave his Moose Hypothetical to a college student, who replied that gender and species were different. That's true, but it wasn't enough to be persuasive. You have to be instantly ready to explain *why* the two cases are different.

BE CLEAR, CONCISE, AND NONACADEMIC.

Conservatives are often better writers than leftists and liberals, or at least far more "accessible" writers. The works of Thomas Sowell are far easier to digest than Karl Marx's *Capital*. Some of my comrades on the left might say that this problem is inherent because the right's ideas are simplistic and the left's ideas are complex. I do not agree. It's true that sometimes it can take a little while to explain, for example, why "gender" does not just boil down to chromosomes. But it's also the case that most important political and economic ideas can be readily explained in ordinary language. It's important, then, that you stay away from jargon and be prepared to explain your ideas clearly.

BE AGGRESSIVE WITH BULLIES, BE PATIENT WITH THE OPEN-MINDED.

Ben Shapiro makes clear that he has no interest in trying to find out whether leftists have a good point or two. His book *How to Debate Leftists and Destroy Them* is about how conservatives can humiliate people who disagree with them, on the assumption that conservatives are definitely right and their opponents definitely wrong. With someone like this, there is no point trying to persuade them. In fact, there is no point even *talking* to them, unless it is in front of an audience of people who *might* be open to persuasion. If someone is simply hell-bent on trying to make you look dumb, all you can do is try to prevent this by making it abundantly clear that their entire case is a failure and their worldview is monstrous. But don't assume everyone is like this. Shapiro is a uniquely horrible human being, and many people are not nearly this close-minded and arrogant. With people who hold right-wing views but might be open to hearing "the other side," be patient and empathetic. Listen to them. Bernie Sanders happens to be very good at this,[4] and one can observe the way he talked to Trump voters to see how it's possible to frame the left position in ways that can bring around people you would not expect to be sympathetic.

ASK QUESTIONS.

A reason that conservatives ask questions like "if a man can become a woman, can I become an attack helicopter?" or "if the minimum wage should be $15 an hour, why not $15,000?" is that the question is succinct and punchy but the answer might require some thought. If you don't have a snappy comeback prepared, it might look like they have caught you out. In fact, they might have *actually* caught you out, if you haven't thought before about such questions as "what should the upper limit of the minimum wage be?" or "what are the limits to how personal self-identification can define reality?"

Ask your own tough questions, then. Once, when I was publicly debating a free-market economist, I pinned him on a question that made him very uncomfortable: *Should an employer have the right to fire an employee for becoming pregnant?* As a libertarian ideologue, he believes that an employer *should* have that right. But he also knows that libertarian ideas like this are extremely unpopular because most people think workers should be protected from this kind of cruel termination of employment. So he struggled with the question, and it made him look evasive in front of the audience.

Asking the Tough Questions

Comedian and podcaster Joe Rogan, of *The Joe Rogan Experience,* is not known for being a man of the left, but he has subjected conservative guests to tougher questioning than they get elsewhere in the media. Rogan can make confident individuals sound foolish just by asking them to justify their beliefs and consistently following up when their answers are unsatisfactory. This is the same technique that Socrates deployed against the confident sophists of ancient Athens. (Be careful in trying it yourself, because in his case, it proved so irritating that they murdered him.) Instead of providing your own set of facts to disprove the person's claim, you focus on showing that they do not actually have any real knowledge of the subject they are speaking about. To see how this works in practice, let us look at Rogan's discussion with right-wing commentator Candace Owens. Owens begins by making confident claims about climate change. Rogan, through persistence, exposes her as entirely ignorant:

ROGAN: You don't think we have to care about the environment?
OWENS: [*laughs*] No, like not even a little bit.
ROGAN: Not even a little bit?
OWENS: Okay, let me clarify this. I don't throw trash on the

ground. Like, I'm not saying, like, we need to, you know, trash the environment. But do I believe in climate change? No.

ROGAN: You don't believe in climate change?

OWENS: I think the climate always changes, I guess. Do I believe that this is an issue that—? Global warming, which they've changed conveniently, got rid of the word once scientists started disproving it, now they only say climate change? No. I think that was just a way to extract dollars from Americans. They had no actual plan, it was great for Trump to get out of that deal, it was terrible.

ROGAN: Okay, but this is an incredibly complicated subject. And you would have to talk to a bunch of different scientists and see how they gather data and see what they understand about CO2 levels and what's the danger of them and what can combat it and what could not. Have you done all this?

OWENS: No.

ROGAN: Or do you take this flippant opinion based on the party line?

OWENS: This wouldn't be the hill I died on. But I've read a ton about it. But I would not be able to come to you and say, like, "This is my strong opinion." But here's the easiest way to say this: the fact that there's a disparity in the science about whether or not it's real is enough—

ROGAN: It's very little. Most scientists, the vast majority, agree that human beings are negatively affecting climate change.

OWENS: Yeah. I just don't think so.

ROGAN: So you think that the very few scientists who disagree with the consensus are the ones that are correct?

OWENS: Well, I think it's either subjective or it's objective. And there are objective truths, right? But it's subjective if you're saying that there are some—and I don't think there's very little—there are some that don't get paid to go on TV, who are not Bill Nye, who are not funded scientists. . . .

[. . .]

OWENS: Yeah, I don't believe this, like, at all, just so you know.

ROGAN: You don't believe it, "like," at all?

OWENS: I genuinely don't believe it. I know you do, but I genuinely don't believe it.

ROGAN: I believe most of time the consensus of scientists that are studying the data . . .

[. . .]

ROGAN: But this is my question: Why are you so sure? This is an extremely complicated subject.

OWENS: I said I am not so sure I would die on the hill for it. My opinion right now is that this was a means—because forget the fact of whether global warming is real, let's say it was one hundred percent real, let's say we know for a fact it's real—

ROGAN: Well, let's be clear. Global warming, global climate change is definitely real. It's happening. The question is "why is it happening?"

OWENS: But it's always happened.

ROGAN: Yes, it has always happened.

OWENS: Does the climate change? Yes, the climate changes. It was different weather yesterday than it was today. The climate is forever changing like that. That's the problem, is that people are making it seem like that's something weird.

ROGAN: No, no, no. You're misrepresenting the issue. The issue is people think that human beings are exacerbating climate change to the point where there's a tipping point, we cross over that tipping point, we're going to deal with huge problems that could be corrected if we act now and put a lot of funding into climate control. . . . [What] we have to be really careful of is letting it get too far where you can't ever stop it and pull it back. This is what scientists are warning about. This is why they want emission standards. This is why they want to figure out how to get people to be aware of the fact that this is a real issue. Now, irregardless, human beings, if they never existed, the earth has constantly gone through cycles. The question is not whether or not the earth has gone through cycles of cooling and warming. The question is: Are we exacerbating that? The vast majority of scientists say we are. Now this could negatively impact all sorts of coastal cities, this could be a gigantic problem. [. . .]

OWENS: Let's say we all agree that global warming is real. I *don't* believe it's real, so I can't sit here.

ROGAN: But here's the question: Why have a belief?

OWENS: What do you mean?

ROGAN: Why have a belief as to whether global warming is real or not real? You don't have a background in it, you don't understand the science.

OWENS: You are correct, you are correct.

ROGAN: But why have a belief in it?

OWENS: It's not a belief in it, I don't believe in it. It's not a belief.[5]

Notice that Rogan did not let up or let Owens get away with misrepresentations. He did not have to present actual studies or data in order to show that Owens was out of her depth. He just had to ask what justifications she had for her beliefs and show her that those justifications were flimsy. Philosopher of science Lee McIntyre, in his book *How to Talk to a Science Denier,* says that this form of engagement is especially effective. He calls it "technique rebuttal," showing the flaws in someone's reasons for holding a belief, as opposed to "content rebuttal," which is showing the flaws in the belief itself.[6]

Rogan also has had exchanges with Ben Shapiro (on systemic racism) and Dave Rubin (on whether the free market makes building safety codes unnecessary) that are worth watching because they show how, using very little data but

some sharp questioning and good reasoning, you can make
conservative opponents back down quickly on their most extreme positions. Watch them carefully and learn.

Do not accept faulty premises.

One of my pet peeves is when liberals use right-wing premises to
make left-wing arguments. For instance, instead of arguing that
prisons or the death penalty are *inhumane,* they will argue that
prisons and the death penalty are *costly.* In doing this, you lock
yourself into positions that you don't necessarily hold. After all, if
the problem with the death penalty is that it's costly, how will you
object if someone proposes a cheap way to execute people?

Keep your eye on the point.

Half the battle is just in keeping people focused on things that
actually matter. The way conservatives win debates about climate
change and labor rights is, generally, by trying to get people not to
talk about climate change and labor rights.

Think constantly about what actually matters. If you are trying
to convince people that a Scandinavian social democratic welfare
program is good and should be tried here, don't get yourself mired
in a debate over whether Scandinavian countries are "actually socialist" or "actually capitalist." Stick to the core points: Does the
plan work? Is it a good idea?

Have a sense of humility and humor.

Conservatives delight in mocking humorless leftists. They love
nothing more than to "trigger the libs" by trying to make you
angry and defensive. Do not be trolled into losing your temper.
Stay calm, concede where you're wrong, and be willing to laugh
at your own expense if you say something silly. Being likable is an

important part of being an effective persuader, so be thoughtful and cheerful as you enter the fray.

Know when to quit.

Some people are not going to agree with you no matter what, and when someone is convinced that they are on the side of Freedom and you are on the side of Totalitarianism, they can become frighteningly aggressive, since after all, extreme measures seem as if they would be justified to stop totalitarianism.

Convincing anyone of anything can take a very long time. Much of it depends as much on building relationships with people as on making correct and persuasive arguments. If a person doesn't trust you, they're unlikely to hear you out, and if they do trust you, they might be open to letting you challenge their worldview.

Remember that for people to change their positions, it takes time and repeated exposure to facts that challenge their assumptions. Seeing through one's own ideology is not easy. Colonists and missionaries who have seen native populations as savages in need of "civilizing" have inflicted terrible harm and suffering—all while thinking of themselves as charitable and virtuous. The right is convinced that it is on the side of freedom and liberty against the forces of totalitarianism, statism, and bureaucracy. That kind of certitude is deeply dangerous, and once you hold a position like that, you're not likely to do much self-reflection on whether the "forces of totalitarianism, statism, and bureaucracy" might make a good point or two here and there.

PART II

Brief Replies to
25 Conservative Arguments

1

Government Is the Problem, Not the Solution

The capitalist ideal is that government plays very little role in the economy—and the socialist ideal is that government plays the leading role in the economy. In that case, I say that capitalism is awesome, and socialism is terrible.

—Bryan Caplan

The nine most terrifying words in the English language are: I'm from the government, and I'm here to help.

—Ronald Reagan

The Argument

The government is wasteful and inefficient. The private market can provide most services better because the profit motive makes it responsive to people's demands. The government tends to ruin everything it meddles in, from public schools to Amtrak. We need to cut regulations, have the government do less, and let the market work.

The Response

I always find it funny that people can nod in agreement with Reagan's dictum that nobody wants to hear "I'm from the government, and I'm here to help" and yet celebrate the valiant work of firefighters, police officers, and soldiers, who are all "from the government." In fact, when you are in a burning building, your number-one desire is for someone from the government to come and help you. (The same goes if you get lost in a national park or out at sea.) There is certainly good reason to be skeptical of having a powerful, unaccountable state. But intelligent people should be able to distinguish *among* the functions of government rather than seeing "government" as a single entity. The War on Drugs is "government," but so is Medicare and the sewer system and stop signs and the Forest Service and the Hoover Dam.

Here is *National Review*'s Jim Geraghty explaining what he sees as the core of the conservative critique of government. It is not, he says, out of an ideological hostility, but rather out of empirical observations:

> A lot of progressives seem to think that conservatives distrust the government because of some esoteric philosophical theory, or because we had some weird dream involving Ayn Rand. In reality, it's because we've been told to trust the government before—and we've gotten burned, time and time again. Government doesn't louse up everything, but it sure louses up a lot of what it promises to deliver: from the Big Dig to Healthcare .gov; from letting veterans die waiting for health care to failing to prioritize the levees around New Orleans and funding other projects instead; from 9/11 to the failure to see the housing bubble that precipitated the Great Recession; from misconduct in the Secret Service to the IRS targeting conservative groups; from lavish conferences at the General Services Administration to the Solyndra grants; from the runaway costs of California's high-speed-rail project to Operation Fast and Furious; from the OPM breach to giving Hezbollah a pass on trafficking cocaine.[1]

On the surface, Geraghty might appear to have compiled quite an indictment. But it's not enough to produce a list of various things that the United States government has done wrong at various points. We have to ask questions like:

1. **Are these incidents representative or aberrational?** After all, a government with hundreds of agencies that does thousands

of things is going to screw up. The screwups, when they happen, will be more attention-grabbing than the successes. It is not a news story when a government agency buys a bunch of reasonably priced office chairs, but it *is* a news story when an agency buys a bunch of absurdly overpriced office chairs. There is going to be a natural media bias toward reporting on the *scandals* of the government, because "Sewage System Functions Successfully for Yet Another Day" cannot be a news story. To evaluate "government" in general, we cannot simply pick a series of stories of sensational government failures (as Geraghty does) but must ask questions like: Do the scandalously lavish conferences of the General Services Administration mean that government workers generally operate in conditions of excessive luxury? Are they the exception or the rule?[2]

2. **Is this what "government is like" or just what *your* government has done?** Much of the American conservative rhetoric about government can only be taken seriously because American conservatives don't know very much about the workings of more successful governments around the world. It is remarkable just how many conservative arguments about "government" are derived from anecdotes about the failures of the United States government in particular, failures that are not necessarily shared globally. For instance, many conservatives say that the failures of American public schools relative to schools in other countries occur because our schools are run by the government rather than according to a free-market, "school choice" model.[3] But this argument is irrational for a very obvious reason: many of the countries that are beating us have government-run schools that do a fantastic job. If the problem is that public schools are run by the government, then what explains the existence of excellent government-run schools elsewhere? Finland, for example, has one of the best education systems in the world and has all but abolished private

schools.[4] Or take Geraghty's example of "the runaway costs of California's high-speed-rail project." It's certainly the case that public rail projects in the United States have been infamously costly, and that Amtrak is infamously slow. But that is not an inherent feature of public rail. China, Japan, and France have highly efficient public high-speed rail services that have not been anything like the kind of boondoggle the United States is known for. The fact that *we* haven't figured out how to run our public schools well does not reflect badly on "government" in general.[5] It reflects badly on the United States.

3. **Are the examples failures that occurred *because* they were done by the government?** If these examples are going to be used to critique government in general, then they have to be problems that wouldn't have occurred in the private sector, or would have been much less likely to occur. When we go through what Geraghty has listed here, many of the examples are dubious. Take Solyndra. This was a solar panel company that received over $500 million in government loans but then went bankrupt. Conservatives pointed to Solyndra's failure, and the large amount of money it cost the Department of Energy, as proof that the government shouldn't be in the business of to "pick winners and losers" in the marketplace by extending loans. But a single failure does *not* prove that. In fact, the energy loan program ended up profitable on the whole, meaning it actually made money for the government, *and* it succeeded in its goal of helping renewable energy companies get access to necessary capital.[6] Misconduct in the Secret Service and by the IRS are indeed problems. But any large institution, public or private, will have malfeasance. The Big Dig, which Geraghty cites as an example of government failure, had a great deal of graft and fraud—by the for-profit private contractors whom the government outsourced the work to![7] The argument the right would make is that "market incentives" discipline those in the private sector in a way they do *not* discipline those in the public sector.

It's not clear at all that this is true, however. In fact, because the private sector is shielded from accountability and transparency (it is, after all, private), it can be much harder to ferret out corporate crime than government crime.[8] Government agencies have an inspector general, and inspector general reports are part of the *reason* that we know about misconduct in these agencies.

Governments around the world do a great deal of vitally important work that is rarely appreciated. For all the talk of entrepreneurs being the great innovators, it is often state institutions that drive basic research into new technologies and medicines.[9] Government failures are often visible, in part, because government handles so much that is important in our day-to-day lives, such as the collection of our garbage, the delivery of our mail, and the maintenance of our highways. Economist Rob Larson here explains the crucial role of government:

> Tax collections aren't mainly used to pay "the expenses of government," but to supply "public goods"—services that tend to be drastically underproduced by markets because they benefit the broader society more than individuals. Things like roads, streetlights, bridges, sanitation systems, and scientific research are examples. . . . Likewise, services like education or immunization against diseases benefit everyone by yielding better educated societies that can produce more sophisticated goods and services, or a lower incidence of infectious diseases that benefits everyone in society.[10]

It is a common presumption that governments always do things less efficiently than the private sector. For instance, a CNBC investigation into the appalling state of American airports relative to other countries pinned the cause on government: U.S. airports, it said, suffer because they are run by local governments rather than by private companies.[11]

But the report's reasoning was fallacious. Many of the examples it chose of the *best* airports around the world, such as the spectacular and luxurious Singapore Airport, were in fact owned and operated by governments. In fact, some of the best *airlines* in the world, such as Emirates, are state-owned. China, whose emergence from poverty is often credited to "market-friendly" policies, has over ten thousand state-run enterprises, among them some of the country's largest and most profitable companies. Sometimes governments even take over troubled private-sector enterprises and turn them around.[12] University of Cambridge economist Ha-Joon Chang shows in his book on global economic development, *Bad Samaritans*, that contrary to popular belief, *heavy* government involvement in setting industrial policy has been a critical ingredient in countries' emergence from poverty.[13]

Milton Friedman once said that "the great achievements of civilization have not come from government bureaus. Einstein didn't construct his theory under order from a bureaucrat."[14] But Friedman's attempt to downplay public-sector successes was either ignorant or dishonest. Public universities, public highways, public libraries, sewer systems, the space program, the Hoover Dam—all achievements of "government bureaus." Albert Einstein (a socialist, incidentally) was able to escape his job at the Swiss Patent Office because there were state-established universities where he could work.

Government institutions, when run well, can deliver efficient, cheap services to the public. In fact, the government can be *more* efficient than the private sector because its size means that it can reap huge "economies of scale." For example, the British National Health Service (NHS)—which we will discuss more later—manages to deliver far more comprehensive and better healthcare to the country's people than the American healthcare system, in part because having a single entity in charge of a sector rather than many overlapping institutions can streamline service delivery. This is partly why the NHS was able to deliver COVID-19 vaccines at a phenomenal pace; the government had the infrastructure in place to deliver a universal service quickly and effectively.[15]

Here is how conservative economist Thomas Sowell responds to the NHS example:

> What earthly reason is there to believe that the government, of all institutions, can make healthcare less expensive? It can refuse to pay the expenses, which is different. Other countries have gone that route. They have refused to pay the costs of maintaining the health system and so in places like Britain or Canada you don't find the same availability of healthcare that you have in the United States.[16]

In fact, there *is* an "earthly reason" to believe that the government can make healthcare less expensive. Not only does government healthcare achieve economies of scale, and avoid duplicative administrative burdens, but the absence of profit from the healthcare system eliminates an unnecessary expense.[17] The government can make healthcare cheaper for the same reason that it can make firefighting cheaper. Furthermore, the "availability" of healthcare is much *greater* in Britain than the United States, if we define "availability" as *whether people are able to get healthcare*. There may be slightly less access to high-end treatments for the superrich, but there is *no* population of uninsured people. Everyone has quality healthcare available, which is not true in this country.[18]

Likewise, critiques of regulation are generally based in fear rather than fact. You will hear "regulation" spoken of in the abstract as a bad thing, and many "small government" politicians are elected on promises to cut red tape and rein in regulation. (Donald Trump introduced a rule that for every new regulation the federal government introduced, it had to get rid of two.)[19] But while there are critiques that can be made of particular regulations (e.g., the Food and Drug Administration's sluggishness in approving new medications), there is little evidence that regulation on the whole damages the economy. A paper by economists Nathan Goldschlag and Alex Tabarrok (the latter of whom is a prominent free-market economics blogger) concluded that "regulation, lagged regulation, or changing regulation does not account for the decline in economic dynamism" in the United States.[20] Furthermore, sound regulations have produced major positive effects. Here, Daniel Greenbaum of the Health Effects Institute provides a review of the consequences of the Clean Air Act:

> [The benefits] have been dramatic. Actions to control emissions from vehicles, factories, electric power plants, and more have reduced emissions of the most prominent pollutants—particulate matter, sulfur oxides, nitrogen oxides, carbon monoxide, volatile organic compounds, and lead—by 73%, even while the U.S. gross domestic product has grown by more than 250%. The progress has been systematic and widespread. As a result of vehicle emission controls, levels of ambient carbon monoxide in the Los Angeles area have fallen from more than 40 ppm in the 1960s to less than 8 ppm today (the current National Ambient Air Quality Standard), even while vehicles and vehicle miles traveled have doubled and tripled, respectively. After detailed efforts to control acid precipitation, levels of sulfate fine air pollution (formed by emissions of sulfur oxides from coal burning) have declined by more than 70% in the Midwest and northeast United States. There is growing evidence that these reductions have translated into health improvements (e.g., a substantial improvement in lung function growth in children growing up in a recent cohort in Southern California when compared with similar cohorts who grew up there in earlier, more highly polluted air).[21]

To speak of regulation in the abstract, then, ignores the fact that there are obviously positive and necessary government regulatory actions. From the Consumer Financial Protection Bureau's efforts to keep customers from being ripped off to the Federal Aviation Administration's careful assurance of safe air travel,[22] we benefit every day from the efforts of those often derided as "meddlesome bureaucrats." It should be remembered that in years past, the "anti-regulation" crowd fought against measures such as mandatory airbags in cars, with the Reagan administration attempting to repeal the airbag requirement before being rebuked by the Supreme Court. Airbags save thousands of lives every year,[23] but automakers didn't want the extra expense, and Reagan pledged to cut the "red tape."

In fact, there are areas of life in which there ought to be *more* regulation. Opiate manufacturers, for instance, got away with marketing campaigns designed to create a generation of addicts—and keep the profits flowing.[24] In many countries, tobacco companies have to put prominent warning labels on cigarettes with disturbing illustrations of the risk of cancer. Not in the United States, where some packs of cigarettes do not even warn users that the product is carcinogenic.[25] The food industry has for years successfully lobbied to keep "Nutrition Facts" labels from being particularly informative, obscuring how harmful junk food is and making it harder for consumers to make intelligent decisions about what to put in their bodies.[26]

Government therefore performs a number of absolutely critical roles, and while we should be critical of the excessive use of police and military power, we should be expanding the role of government in a number of spheres. Other countries have shown that government health insurance programs with universal enrollment are a good way to improve the health of a population. In the face of the looming threat of catastrophic climate change, successfully transitioning to renewable energy will require substantial government action. During the COVID-19 pandemic, the American government did too little, not too much, failing to coordinate massive testing and contact tracing early on.[27] By contrast with the United States, countries like Vietnam and New Zealand developed a centralized plan for containing the spread of the virus and succeeded in avoiding anything like the kind of calamity that befell this country. (By early 2021, Vietnam had thirty-five COVID-19 deaths total in a population of one hundred million people. Cuba, another country formally under communist governance, had a total of 233 deaths.)[28]

The conservative ideal of the minimal state—with functions limited to the protection of private property rights and the provision of military and policing services—can be tempting to those who see every other government activity (schooling, regulation, healthcare) as dysfunctional. In fact, this viewpoint is based more on emotion than on fact, and governments do a great deal of work that is socially necessary but not profitable (often because the people being served have very little money).

Philosophical Opposition to Government

Leftism is defined as any political philosophy that seeks to infringe upon individual liberties in its demand for a higher moral good.

—Candace Owens, *Blackout*

To say that "society" should decide how much it values various goods and services is to say that individual decisions on these matters should be superseded by collective decisions made by political surrogates. But to say this openly would require some persuasive reasons why collective decisions are better than individual decisions and why third parties are better judges than those who are making their own trade-offs at their own expense. . . . No one would seriously entertain such an arrogant and presumptuous goal, if presented openly, plainly, and honestly.

—Thomas Sowell

Economic power is exercised by means of a positive, by offering men a reward, an incentive, a payment, a value; political power is exercised by means of a negative, by the threat
of punishment, injury, imprisonment, destruction. The businessman's tool is values; the bureaucrat's tool is fear.

—Ayn Rand

From Geraghty we heard an empirical indictment of government.
He argued that conservative opposition to government came from
an observation of its real-world activities. We have seen that this
view is inaccurate and irrational, that it comes from picking the
worst instances of government misconduct and treating them as
representative of the whole, rather than from pursuing a systematic
evaluation or looking at government performance across countries. But Geraghty had the virtue of at least attempting to ground
his critique in real-world events. Much right-wing opposition to
government is not of this character. Instead, it flows from a *philosophical* opposition to government, one that sees many government activities as inherently illegitimate and coercive intrusions
upon individual liberty.

This is the view expressed above by Owens, Sowell, and Rand.
They have a very simple view of society: the economy consists of
"free transactions" being made between millions of people—I buy
an ice cream, a hat, a surgical operation, etc., from you. This is
the private sector. Along comes Government, however, to meddle in these freely made transactions by telling my employer that
they are required to offer me paid family leave, for example, or by
insisting on inspecting the meat I buy, or by requiring an airline
to let its planes be checked before I am allowed to buy a ticket
to fly on one. For many conservatives, the *consequences* of, say,
minimum-wage laws are only part of the issue. Fundamentally, no
matter whether these laws produce benefits to workers or not, they
are illegitimate, because the state has no right to "interfere" in the
"free exchange" made between two parties. Sowell refers to anyone

who thinks the government should, for example, try to reduce income inequality, as "the anointed"—people who self-righteously believe their own values should determine which transactions are allowed to occur and under what conditions, who impose these values on others through the use of force, i.e., the state.

For those of Sowell, Rand, and Owens's persuasion, nothing I have said about the positive consequences of government action will be remotely persuasive. It does not matter if airbags save lives because it is not the government's place to interfere in "freely made" contracts between willing buyers and willing sellers. Even if the government can make everybody's lives better, it *shouldn't*, because to do so requires coercion, and coercion is almost always inherently an injustice. Nineteenth-century philosopher Herbert Spencer, who pioneered free-market, social Darwinist thought, argued that government couldn't justifiably even take public health and sanitation measures to stop disease if doing so would involve preventing free-market transactions.[29] Robert Nozick, one of the leading libertarian philosophers, argued that the only government that could be justified was "a minimal state, limited, to the narrow functions of protection against force, theft, fraud, enforcement of contracts . . . any more extensive state will violate persons' rights not to be forced to do certain things, and is unjustified . . . the minimal state is inspiring as well as right."[30]

Take, for example, the case of wealth redistribution. Jeff Bezos has $150 billion. Once you become extremely rich, each additional dollar you get means less to you. (This is called the principle of diminishing marginal utility and is central to economics. The usual illustrative example given is candy bars: one chocolate bar might make you much happier than zero, but two is not as much of an improvement over one as one was over zero.) For Bezos, the difference between having $149 billion and $150 billion is essentially negligible, even though for a lot of other people, that $1 billion difference would be *huge*. If the government decides to tax away a billion dollars from Bezos to, for example, give healthcare to people who do not have it, his own life satisfaction would hardly decrease at all, but many other people would see their "utility" drastically increase.

For a pure utilitarian, who believes in producing the greatest good for the greatest number of people, this makes a strong case for the government redistributing wealth.[31] But not to someone with a philosophical opposition to state redistribution. For such a person, it wouldn't matter how much human well-being is generated. Nor would the question of whether taxation had other negative effects (like disincentivizing Bezos from producing) be especially relevant. Taking away his money, even for a good cause, would violate his rights. It is not the role of government. End of story.

It is hard to "refute" this argument because it depends very heavily on a person's foundational moral beliefs, and foundational moral beliefs tend to be more the product of instinct than reason. If you do not think murder is wrong, it will be difficult for me to persuade you that it is. Likewise, if you think private property rights are more important than human lives, and that the government has no right to interfere with them, there is no way for me to "prove" to you that you should care more about poor people's health than about rich people's entitlement to their property.[32] I can show you the consequences of holding the "minimal government" view versus the redistributionist view. But if the consequences are irrelevant to your assessment of whether the government's conduct is legitimate, productive discussion becomes nearly impossible.

Fortunately, hardly anybody *does* think the consequences of different "rights frameworks" are irrelevant. If, hypothetically, a government could save the world from destruction by violating someone's private property rights—for example, if a rich man holds the only vaccine that can stop a deadly pandemic but refuses to sell it at any price—very few people would argue that billions should die in order that one person should have their callous invocation

of property rights respected. If someone *did* think it was necessary to let the world perish to make sure a single selfish person
didn't suffer a property rights violation, there would be little one
could say in response. But that position goes so far against ordinary human moral instincts that we will not encounter it often.[33]
And once it is conceded that *some* violations of property rights are
justified to serve *some* greater goods, we are just left arguing about
which greater goods are compelling enough to cross the threshold
where the violation of private property rights is justified. In other
words: once you admit that there are extreme situations (like the
hoarding of a vaccine) where property rights matter less than, for
instance, the right to health, what we must discuss is not whether
something "is a violation of property rights" but whether it is the
kind of violation of property rights that has a compelling argument in its favor.

A frequent conservative argument against government action
is that it's not clear *why* the government has a right to violate private property rights or *who* decides what the "greater good" is.
Ayn Rand, in her case against inheritance taxes, points out that
even though a person inheriting wealth from a parent may not
have done any work to justify earning that wealth, it is not obvious why anyone *else* (like the state) should have a greater claim to
it. Thomas Sowell and Friedrich von Hayek both emphasize that
when an argument is made that the government should do *x* or
y in order to promote the "public good," it must be shown why
the government has the right to define the public good. Sowell
says that frequently, the "public good" is effectively a euphemism
for "third parties" imposing their own conception of the good on
other individuals. In other words, the government may say it is
requiring an employer to pay its employee the minimum wage to
serve the public good, but in reality, the government is just using
its power to forcibly interfere and impose its own conception of
the good, substituting it for the "freely made contract" that would

have been made between employer and employee in the absence of the coercive state.

"Why does *government* have the *right* to decide?" can sound very compelling, and it's obvious why people are tempted by this philosophical opposition to state coercion. After all, state coercion at its worst is deeply hideous; the most brutal atrocities of all time have been carried out by governments who had no limiting principle on what they could do to individuals. But the question is not as philosophically powerful as it appears. The reason government has the right to decide is because it is the least-worst institution for making these decisions, since in theory, it is democratic and able to balance many parties' competing interests.

The answer to the question is the same as the answer to the question of why we have courts decide when two parties have a conflict they cannot resolve to punish a wrong-doer. Courts are not perfectly neutral. Their answers are not handed down from God. They can be captured by political interests. But they are an institution that is (again, in theory) separate from the parties and can thus (hopefully) adjudicate fairly between them.

For many conservatives, the market already ensures fairness, so there is no need for a third party to "meddle." But leftists look at the market and see many of its outcomes as clearly not serving everybody's interest. Nobody *wants* to be earning less than a living wage and be unable to afford rent. An employer might want to pay as little as possible, take home as much for themselves as they can, and treat workers as expendable. But there is no reason why the "market's" decision in favor of the employer needs to be respected over the employee's demand to be paid enough to live on. When there is a dispute between two parties, and one has justice on their side, it is acceptable for a third party to intervene to help somebody who needs help.

Somebody always governs. Take the decision about whether a company will dump toxic chemical waste in a river. If the government adopts a hands-off approach and leaves the decision to the company, then whether the waste is dumped will depend on whether doing so is profitable for the company's shareholders. If the government decides to take responsibility for keeping the environment clean, then the decision will depend on whether, after weighing the interests of the company in having higher profits against the interests of the people and animals who will be poisoned by the toxic waste, there is good reason to let the company do the dumping. We might say that any decision the government makes will depend on subjective valuations of whose interests matter. That is true. But better to have subjective valuations of the public good than a situation in which the *only* interests that are valued are those of the most powerful economic actors.[34]

Personally, I have anarchist sympathies.[35] I don't like the boot of the state on my neck. I detest bureaucracy. But I also believe that conservatives have a ludicrously caricatured view of government, one that unfairly treats hundreds of thousands of hardworking public employees as busybodies and bureaucrats. We should all be civil libertarians, cautious about empowering an undemocratic state to impinge too freely on basic freedoms. We should demand that the government be transparent and accountable, so that we know when people's rights have been violated and have the power to rein it in and replace poor leadership. The prison system and the military can release untold horrors and need to be kept strictly in check. But public universities, public hospitals, public housing, and public transit, for example, can be essential to guaranteeing people's basic rights. Many governments, especially ours, are dysfunctional and sluggish, in part because the democratic process is not easy. That is an argument for doing the hard work of improving the public sector. It is not an argument for, to use Grover Norquist's phrase, "shrinking government to the point where we can 'drown it in the bathtub.'"

2

Minimum Wages and Rent Control Are Economically Disastrous

One thing is certain: If government policies substantially increase the cost of entry-level labor, there will be more automation, fewer jobs and less opportunity for young people trying to get ahead.

> —Andy Puzder, former CEO, CKE Restaurants,
> "The Minimum Wage Should Be Called
> the Robot Employment Act," *Wall Street Journal*

The left's proposed solution to wage stagnation has been for government to mandate increased wages by more than doubling the minimum wage from $7.25 to $15 an hour. That causes employers to eliminate jobs and reduce hours to offset their increased costs. To increase wages without these unintended consequences, you need economic growth.

> — Andy Puzder, "Raise Wages via Growth,
> Not Mandates," *Wall Street Journal*

Minimum wage laws are about as clear a case as one can find of a measure the effects of which are precisely the opposite of those intended by the men of good will who support it.

> —Milton Friedman, *Capitalism and Freedom*

Economists of all stripes agree rent control doesn't work. A mere 2% think it has positive effects, according to a 2012 survey by the IGM Forum. In other contexts Bernie [Sanders] might cite that statistic as proof of settled science. No less definitive are the in-depth studies. An analysis last year of San Francisco's 1994 rent-control initiative found that

the landlords it affected "reduced rental housing supply by
15%, causing a 5.1% city-wide rent increase." [. . .] Sanders
says that his version of democratic socialism bears no relation to the kind practiced in Venezuela, yet his housing
policy has all the earmarks: price controls that crimp supply and cause capital to flee, then government diktats and
subsidies to counteract the damage from the controls. As in
Venezuela, the poor would suffer the most.

—*Wall Street Journal*

The Argument

The conservative argument on minimum wages is very simple:
raising the minimum wage causes the loss of jobs, because employers faced with increased labor costs will find ways to save
money by cutting hours and increasing automation. It is a simple
"supply and demand" story: once the cost of something goes up,
the amount of it demanded goes down. The minimum wage "artificially" raises wages, and thus will "distort" the market. Some
people may see their wages raised, but ultimately, many small businesses will go broke and people will lose their jobs. The costs will
outweigh the benefits.

The argument about rent control is somewhat similar. By capping the amount that landlords can raise rent, some people will pay
less in rent than they otherwise would have. But a "distortion" will
be imposed in the market, and supply and demand will get out of
whack. By controlling the price of housing, the government causes
the housing supply to be reduced, because there is less money to
be made from building and renting out housing units. Thus, rent
control "hurts the very people it's trying to help." Some people will
have their rents rise by smaller amounts than they otherwise would
have, but new housing will not be built that could have lowered
prices. If there is one thing that conservatives agree on, it is that
"rent control"—capping the amounts that landlords may charge for
housing units—is a disastrously misguided economic policy. Rent

control is often cited as the paradigmatic case of foolish magical thinking by leftists.

The Response

I am unsympathetic to the argument made by the ex-CEO of Carl's Jr., Andy Puzder, that his firm could not afford higher wages. The reason is that I have run a business myself. I started a magazine from my living room that is now successful. And we've always paid a fifteen-dollar minimum wage. My sense from my own experience is that many of those who argue that it is not *possible* to pay fifteen dollars an hour have not seriously tried.

Here's a simple test: I call it the Boss's Car Test. So long as the boss shows up to work in a nicer car than the lower-level workers have, it is factually *not* the case that the boss could not pay higher wages. They could if they were willing to drive the same car as everybody else. Now, it's true at a certain point that the company could not continue to raise wages and be viable. But it's also true that we know we haven't hit that point so long as the boss is still taking home more than everyone else. "I can't pay my employees more" often means "I really don't *want* to pay my employees more," and it is worth remembering that employers have an incentive to mislead you about how much more they could pay you. In fact, based on the Friedmanite theory that a corporation's only social responsibility is to maximize profits, a company has a *duty* to try to mislead its workers into not asking for more money. After all, if they got more money, profits would be lower. So a profit-maximizing corporation will always tell its workers that a minimum-wage increase is bad for them, even if the company knows better. This is why you should never trust anything that someone like Puzder says on this topic. Their job is to keep labor costs low, and a great way to do that is to scare workers into thinking that by asking for more money, they will jeopardize their own employment.

In fact, there is robust economic evidence that the scare stories about the minimum wage are the same old unfounded

"perversity-futility-jeopardy" speculative stories that have characterized conservative argumentation for many centuries. Economists have conducted many studies to try to determine what
actually happens when minimum wages go up. Most of the time,
there is no obvious effect on employment—it doesn't cause huge
numbers of people to suddenly be thrown out of work. Instead, it
does what it says: it raises their wages. Workers have more money,
which means they can spend more money, which means that they
stimulate new economic activity. What's more, because the *utility*
of an extra dollar in the pocket of a fast-food worker is greater
than the utility of an extra dollar in the pocket of the CEO, the
positive effects of minimum-wage raises are actually *understated*
by just looking at raw income numbers. Bumps in the minimum
wage are immensely helpful because they go to people for whom
small increases are the most meaningful.

The fifteen-dollar minimum wage has now been implemented
in many cities around the United States. The negative effects have
been minimal. In New York City, a study "found no negative employment effects of the city increasing its minimum wage to $15,"
and "restaurant workers in the city saw a pay increase of 20% to
28%, representing the largest hike 'for a big group of low-wage
workers since the 1960s.'"[1] In Seattle, "workers already employed
either saw their take-home pay go up or stay roughly the same
while working fewer hours," and *Vox*'s Matthew Zeitlin concludes
that from the available evidence, it's clear "the people advocating
for a higher minimum wage . . . were right to do so."[2] In New York,
there is no obvious pain for the restaurant industry, but workers
are far better off. Even the most negative assessments of the prospects for a nationwide fifteen-dollar minimum wage admit that
it would lift millions of people out of poverty, even if it slightly
reduced employment.

Those who continue to argue that the minimum wage kills
jobs are out of touch with the mainstream economics literature.
Economist Noah Smith, in an excellent article showing that raising

the federal minimum wage to fifteen dollars is actually a low-risk policy, explains that economists have changed their minds on the issue as several decades of empirical evidence have rolled in.[3] In 1978, 90 percent of economists surveyed by the American Economic Association believed minimum wages substantially lowered employment among low-wage workers. In a 2015 survey of economists, only 26 percent thought a fifteen-dollar minimum wage would have this effect. Smith explains that the "minimum wage can actually create jobs" under certain economic circumstances, and shows that the poverty-reducing effects of a fifteen-dollar minimum wage are substantial while the employment risks are quite low.

It's very clear that what drives scare stories about the minimum wage is ideology, not evidence. Some have a simplistic "Econ 101" understanding of the world and cannot be convinced that "price floors" on wages can be imposed without significant effects on employment.[4] Some of this may also be an instinctive defense of the rich; restaurant owners do not *want* to pay more, because that means less for them, so naturally they come up with reasons why it would be bad. They threaten to fire people if minimum wages increase, not because they actually intend to, but because they resent the increases and *wish* they could fire some people rather than accept the increased labor costs.

Whatever the reasons, the fact is that the argument fails.[5] Obviously, if the minimum wage were raised infinitely, the economic effects would be disastrous, but we are far from that point, and the United States could use a substantial boost. The Fight for $15 movement has been an unqualified success.[6] Furthermore, it is important to be clear on the actual core reason for raising minimum wages: it is so that workers can afford to keep themselves alive. Fifteen dollars an hour is more than double the existing federal minimum wage, but it is *still* not enough to afford a one-bedroom apartment in many cities. It is enough to stay out of poverty, but paying anything less than fifteen dollars an hour makes it difficult for workers to scrape by. It is extraordinary that there should even be a debate over this, and it is sad that employers do not pay a "living wage" on their own. (Republican Congresswoman Karen Handel was at least honest when she confessed, "I do not support a livable wage.")[7]

Now let's look at rent control, another supposed "distortion" of the pristine free market. In the conservative argument, we have a story about what rent control does: it reduces the housing supply. But so far, all we have is a story. Is this actually what happens?

In fact, the evidence suggests that the story isn't true. As economist J. W. Mason explains, the case against rent control, like the case against the minimum wage, was based on a simple story about supply and demand. And, as with the minimum wage, once economists actually studied the empirical reality, that simple story collapsed:

> As more state and local governments raised minimum wages, it turned out to be very hard to find any negative effect on employment. This was confirmed by more and more careful empirical studies. Today, it is clear that minimum wages do not reduce employment. . . . Rent regulation may be going through a similar evolution today. You may still see textbooks saying that as a price control, rent regulation will reduce the supply of housing. . . . [But] we are finding that the simple supply-and-demand story doesn't capture what happens in the real world.[8]

In fact, Mason says the best studies we have show that "rent regulation is effective in limiting rent increases," and "there is no evidence that rent regulations reduce the overall supply of housing." Why is that? In part, it's because housing supply is relatively inelastic, meaning the supply doesn't change very much in response to changes in price. As early as the midnineties, economists were beginning to change their minds about whether rent control was as disastrous as had earlier been predicted, with Richard Arnott writing in the *Journal of Economic Perspectives* that it was time for "revisionism" because the case against well-designed rent controls was "so weak" that economists should overcome their "knee-jerk reaction . . . to price controls."[9]

As with minimum wages, the evidence does not bear out the scare stories. In San Francisco, rent control *was* found to have reduced the supply of rental housing, but the reason was that landlords realized they could get around the law through converting rent-controlled apartments to condos and selling them off. If turning rent-controlled units into luxury condominiums had not been as easy of a maneuver legally, the rent control law could have had its intended effect. Thus, the lesson here is not to give up on rent control, but to make sure rent-controlled apartments *remain* rent-controlled apartments.

As with the minimum wage, it is worth remembering why rent controls exist and how they benefit people. Cities institute them because skyrocketing rents *hurt people*. In gentrifying areas, a small business might find their landlord hiking the rent from $4,000 per month to $40,000 per month and have no choice but to shut their doors. (This has happened in many parts of New York City and has led to the disappearance of many beloved mom-and-pop stores that have been fixtures of neighborhoods for generations, a tragedy documented in Jeremiah Moss's excellent book *Vanishing New York*.)[10] The same thing happens to residents. An elderly person might have lived in an apartment building for forty years, never getting to own their home but still dutifully paying every month, yet be kicked out onto the street because prices in the area have risen and suddenly the neighborhood is desirable. Rent control keeps families in their homes and prevents the horrible human tragedy of eviction. The right of landlords to make vast fortunes is not more compelling than the right of people to remain in their longtime homes.

Conservatives will often try to draw attention to the costs of a policy without looking at the benefits. All of the people *helped* by minimum-wage increases and rent controls will disappear from the discussion. Conservatives tend to want to portray leftist policies not as "somewhat positive, somewhat negative" but as *an unmitigated economic disaster that will end America,* which means all of the people who benefit from affordable rents and higher wages must be ignored. But these people are real even if they do not fit within the conservative story.

I am not saying here that minimum wages and rent control are ideal policies. I am a socialist, so I believe it's better to build good public housing than try to regulate greedy landlords into being virtuous.[11] The point, however, is that the scare stories are pure ideology rather than the product of honest empirical assessment. Beware anything you read about minimum wages on the op-ed page of the *Wall Street Journal.*

3

Taxation Is Theft and/or Slavery

You are walking down the street, and out from behind some bushes a mugger (Sam Slime) jumps out and threatens your life. He demands, "Your money or your life!" You give him your last $50 in your wallet or purse. . . . Sam, our local mugger, is clearly recognized as a criminal and you are his victim. . . . Now suppose that same mugger changes tactics. Sam now votes for a politician who promises to raise your taxes $50 to transfer it to the "disadvantaged" Sam Slime. . . . Once elected, the politician introduces and passes legislation raising your taxes $50 to give to his loyal supporter, voter Sam Slime. You protest by refusing to pay the new $50 in taxes. The Internal Revenue Service (IRS) declares you a criminal. . . . Now you are the criminal that goes to jail, and Sam Slime is your victim! . . . Where does the commonality between these two situations break down, or, on the other hand, is there any difference? Is stealing through the political process any less morally reprehensible than stealing done individually? Finally, does regular political expropriation of another individual's income differ from slavery?

—Thomas Rustici, final paper prompt, Economics 309,
George Mason University

Suppose someone were to stop you at gunpoint and demand that you hand over half your hard-earned income. Wouldn't you consider him a thief and consider yourself justified in resisting the robber? Now suppose that the thief is carrying a paper certifying himself as an agent of the state. In addition, he claims that the robbery is being carried out for your own good. Is his act any different now?

—Tom G. Palmer, "Against Taxes," in *Realizing Freedom*

> Slavery is when your owner takes 100% of your production.
> Democrat congresswoman Ocasio-Cortez wants 70%. . . .
> What is the word for 70% expropriation?
>
> —Grover Norquist, Twitter, Jan. 5, 2019

The Argument

It's simple: your taxes are collected by force. If you don't pay them, you go to jail. This is no different from highway robbery. In fact, it's even worse. Taxation is even comparable to slavery, because it forces people to work a certain number of hours for which they are not compensated, since part of their wages go to the government. A certain portion of your work is for Uncle Sam, not yourself. Forced uncompensated labor is slavery, whether done by the government or by a private individual.

The Response

It's hard to think that anyone who says this can *really* believe it. In this country, slavery was a condition under which people could be beaten to death if they refused to work, under which women could be raped, their children sold away from them. A slave could be told to do a task and punished for not doing it; a slave could be prohibited from marrying or forced to marry. Alexandria Ocasio-Cortez proposed that if you earn over $10 million per year, every additional dollar should be taxed highly in order to save humanity from the existential crisis of climate change. To compare these two situations seems to me to involve such a detachment from reality that I hardly even know where to begin. It trivializes the harms of slavery by comparing the condition of the slave to the condition of the present-day American super wealthy—the freest, most privileged people in human history. If you think high marginal tax rates are slavery, then I'm sure you wouldn't mind changing places with an actual slave. After all, it's *the same*. They wouldn't be losing anything, right? And if they think they would be losing something, well, that something is precisely the difference between having to pay your taxes and being a slave.

I could make you a list of about four hundred ways in which being taxed is not like slavery. If slavery involved getting to choose your government, getting to choose which labor you did and for how long, and having a *giant pile of money to do whatever you want with, plus complete freedom to move about the world as you please,* it might look more like the situation of the contemporary rich. But those things were, uh, not features of the system. Nevertheless, serious philosophers on the right have argued that taxation is a form of "forced labor." Many, responding to Prof. Rustici's economics paper prompt above (which does not necessarily reflect the professor's own position) would say that there is no meaningful difference between mugging someone and taxing them. Harvard's Robert Nozick made the argument that taxing someone means forcing them to work. Here is libertarian blogger Mark Stoval paraphrasing the argument, explaining why it follows logically from the principle that people "own themselves":

> If you do believe in self-ownership you must agree that this means that people own their time, talents and labor. Nozick argued the standard Lockean argument for private property that we produce goods by mixing our labor and talents with resources and goods in the natural world. This mixing generates the ownership of the items we have modified and made valuable. Now, if the government taxes our income it is taking away our time, talents, and goods produced by our labor. Taxation is the taking of our labor and talents by force which means that the taking means effectively that the government owns our talents and labor and so owns us. According to Nozick (and so very many others), taxation means that the government takes away our self-ownership which is called slavery.[1]

There is so much slippery sophistry in this one paragraph that I am reluctant to even begin unpacking it. First, the "standard Lockean argument for private property" is bonkers, based far more on assertion than reasoning.[2] The question it tries to answer is: How do "unowned" things come to be "owned" things in the first place? Or, since a property right is "the right to exclude others from use of a thing, by force if necessary," the question is: How come people have a "right" to exclude others by force from things that were once held in common by all? The world was once unowned, but now people have private property. Why did they get to declare things their property? Now, historically speaking, they declared things their property largely by seizing them from those who were using them. But this makes the foundations of private property rights seem very shaky, hence the argument that people obtain property by "mixing their labor" with unowned things.[3]

The "labor mixing" theory is vague and unhelpful. If I go into a public forest, and I carve a tree into a totem pole, do I now own the tree? After all, the totem pole is a fruit of my labor. What if I carve my name into it? If I open a can of soup into the ocean, spreading the soup far and wide, do I own the ocean? Who decides when I have put in adequate labor for a thing to become mine, i.e., for me to develop the right to forcibly exclude others from using it? This idea that you can claim pieces of the commons and call them "yours" is what led P. J. Proudhon to declare that "property is theft": By fencing off a park and calling it mine, I am stealing it from other people. They used to have access to it, and now they don't.

The philosophy of property rights is important, because the big holes in it make angry conservative appeals to "entitlement" somewhat nonsensical. If I live on stolen land, taken from a people who held the land as a commons, what on earth am I talking about when I say that it's my land and that I'm entitled to the fruit of the labor I put into it?

Here's Nozick elaborating:

Seizing the results from someone's labor is equivalent to seizing hours from him and directing him to carry on various activities. If people force you to do certain work, or unrewarded work, for a certain period of time, they decide what you are to do and what purposes your work is to serve apart from your decisions. This process whereby they take this decision from you makes them a part-owner of you; it gives them a property right in you.[4]

I am not sure *why* "seizing the results from someone's labor" is "equivalent" to "directing him to carry on various activities": Stealing someone's wallet means they'll have to work some more if they want to have the same amount of things as before (or they'll have to sit around and wait for some more capital income to accrue), but they won't be punished or killed for not laboring. Theft and forced labor are different, and while this is an argument that taxation is theft, it's not a good argument that it's forced labor, because the labor . . . isn't forced. We *do* have legalized forced labor in the United States, actually, thanks to the Thirteenth Amendment (which explicitly permits slavery as punishment for crimes), but it is in prisons rather than boardrooms.[5] Theft and forced labor are only "equivalent" if one ignores the aspects of forced labor that make it so repellent to us (i.e., picking what a person must do and physically punishing them if they do not do it). The pseudo-equivalence is achieved by abstracting away from the reality of what these two acts are actually like for the people who experience them.

Is taxation theft, then? Well, first, I want us to be careful: deciding whether taxation is "theft" doesn't actually tell us whether taxation is justified. The word "theft" is used to imply that taxation is illegitimate, but it could be that taxation is both a kind of theft *and* is completely acceptable. How? Because in *Les Misérables,* Jean Valjean was correct to steal that loaf of bread. It wasn't "not stealing." But it was fine. Unless you believe property rights are *absolutes,* that there is no other moral consideration that can override them, then we have to weigh the "sanctity of ownership" against other factors like "people's lives." Even the staunchest libertarians do not think property rights are absolutes—and if you press them on where to draw the line, they squirm, as you can see in a fascinating live debate between libertarian economist Bryan Caplan and socialist columnist Elizabeth Bruenig, held at 2018's LibertyCon conference.[6] Caplan says that obviously, if something he owned were necessary to save the universe, his property rights wouldn't trump everything else. But when she asks him why, he flounders and sputters, eventually saying that in that extreme case, the presumption in favor of property rights could be overcome, but declining to explain why it isn't overcome in other cases. Libertarians are uncomfortable with questions like these because once it is admitted that certain social goals are important enough that they justify overriding private property rights, it won't take much to make the case that today's socialists are justified in seeing the alleviation of widespread suffering as more important than the protection of rich people's right to the possession of endless useless luxuries.

I don't think the question of whether taxation is theft is particularly relevant, then, because I am somewhat of a utilitarian who thinks a more important question is what differing conceptions of rights produce in terms of justice. And I don't think respect for the property rights of the wealthy is morally justified.[7] A friend of mine is a teacher in the Detroit school system. She tells me that her kids are bright and gracious and wonderful, but they are poorer than you might realize. Many go to bed hungry and are hungry at school. Many are homeless and do not know where they will be spending the night. They do not have changes of clothes. They pass out in class because they couldn't get any rest. You can't ask them about what toys they like to play with, because they don't have them.

Now, Jeff Bezos has a net worth of $192,000,000,000. He could change every single one of these children's lives with the money he makes in about nine seconds.[8] I do not really give a damn whether we decide that it's "theft" for the state to seize a portion of this wealth, because whatever value we might assign to respecting property rights is outweighed a thousandfold by the needs of others. The "utility" differences are staggering: an amount of money that is literally negligible to a billionaire can be of immeasurable assistance to someone who is rationing their insulin.[9] (The justice of massive expropriation is clear regardless of where we come down on taxation being a form of "legalized robbery" or not.)

But there are still good reasons why it's not sensible to refer to taxation as a kind of theft. For one thing, taxation is foundational to a functional market economy. It's impossible to imagine a world in which everyone received their "pretax" income. The government is critical to the existence of the economy: property rights are enforced by courts, money is issued by the government, the military "protects" us. There is no world in which "pretax" income could ever meaningfully belong to its recipients, because without taxes, there is no government, and government is necessary to create the roads, sewers, streetlights, courts, etc., that make obtaining the income possible. The hand of government in creating the economy is present in myriad ways people don't notice. Consider "limited liability" and bankruptcy protection, two ways the state interferes significantly with "property rights" in ways favored by business. A corporation is *incorporated*: it makes money because it exists within a legal structure established by the state, with a set of legal protections afforded by the state.

There is a dimension of the "taxation is theft" argument that I think is worth mentioning: the interesting conception of "force" involved. The argument is quite simple: taxation is a threat—give the leviathan your money or go to jail, and if a private citizen did that, they would be a mugger. But there's another important aspect to this: not only are you not forced to earn an income or be rich, but you could always go and live somewhere else. Perhaps a floating artificial city, perhaps Bermuda, perhaps the moon.

There is an important argument that if you choose to continue living in the United States, you accept its social contract.

You could immediately object by saying that this is not a meaningful "choice": A dictator could say, "I haven't restricted free speech by banning newspapers, because they could always go and publish in some other country." Not everyone has the ability to go and live on the moon. Funnily enough, this is kind of a "left-ist" argument: "choice" is not just a matter of whether you consent, but about the pressures that cause you to feel like you have to consent. It's actually what leads us to argue that *capitalists* are the ones committing systemic theft, by forcing you to work longer hours than you would have if they hadn't used a portion of your productivity to make other people rich. People on the right say that you "consent" to your employment conditions, but for poor workers that's no different from saying that you "consent" to the restrictions on your speech imposed by a dictator by choosing not to flee the country.

We can imagine the United States as one big "company town," or a block of residences governed by a condo association. The "free market" argument is that you don't have liberties at work, or rights against private entities, because you contracted with them. If Facebook owns the city, and you live there, then you can't complain about the rules Facebook imposes. You can't say that Facebook's security officers violated the Fourth Amendment in searching you, because the Fourth Amendment doesn't apply to private entities. Corporations, as political philosopher Elizabeth Anderson has written, are kind of private dictatorships: By stepping onto their turf, you obey their rules, and you don't have any kind of democratic decision-making power (as you do with the United States government). You can't vote for your boss.[10]

Let's accept, then, that the left theory of coercion is correct: just because people enter an institution "voluntarily" doesn't mean they lack rights vis-à-vis the institution, even if the "contract" says so. Wouldn't that mean taxation is theft? Now, part of me wants to

strike a bargain: if conservatives will say that employers steal sur-
plus value from employees, I will say that taxation is theft, albeit
perfectly justified and democratically voted-for theft that is re-
turned to you in the form of countless important services. There's
another element to choice, though, which is that choice depends
on your "meaningful capacity to do otherwise." The ability of a
rich person to leave the country and go work elsewhere is greater
than the ability of a poor person to do so, because money is power.
(And rich citizens do sometimes give up their citizenship to avoid
taxes.)[11]

More importantly, though: I do not believe that billionaires
have any moral right to their wealth in the first place. They have a
legal right, but that doesn't mean very much. Legal rights are created by laws, and so if you change the laws, you change the rights.
The question is whether there is some kind of "natural" entitlement
to wealthy people having their vast wealth, and there isn't. (Property is, after all, theft to begin with, and just because you managed
to obtain something lawfully under a legal system set up by people
in your economic class doesn't mean I have to respect your natural
right to it.) This is not to say that I believe nobody deserves to have
their possessions protected: as I say, I am somewhat flexible and
pragmatic in my approach, meaning that I *do* think people without
much wealth should have their things treated as *their* things and
respected, but I don't think people *with* a lot of wealth should have
that same presumption. I think property, aka the right to use force
to exclude others, should exist to the extent necessary, and the less
you have, the more necessary it is to be able to exclude others from
using the things you have. Some socialists draw a distinction between "personal possessions" and "private property": They think
people should have their possessions, like heirlooms, clothes, a
bicycle, respected, because these things are for personal use. A
factory, on the other hand, is not for personal use, and should be
held in common by its workers. Now, don't ask me to start putting
every object on earth in one or the other of these categories. But

it's a place to start in trying to distinguish the differences between Jeff Bezos's ownership of the *Washington Post* (which enables him to tell people what to do, and fire them if he likes) and my ownership of my cravat (which entitles me only to wear it).

The "highway robber" analogue for the taxman only works if the highway robber, after taking your wallet, gave you an old-age insurance plan and saved your house from a fire, and also gave to the poor, and also you could vote him out if you didn't like it, and also he only robbed you if you had money to spare and checked what your income was and only took an amount you could clearly live without. Oh, and he didn't threaten to kill you but just to put you in jail until you followed the rules everyone else follows (because I'm a prison abolitionist, I don't like this part). Oh, and you're allowed to leave his forest if you don't like his rules. Essentially he'd be Robin Hood, but democratically accountable. Whether he's a thief or not, philosophers can argue about endlessly, I'm sure. But words like "robbery" and "slavery" simply do not apply. The aspects of those acts that make them so appalling are simply not present in a typical tax regime, and it's nauseating to hear the most pampered and freest people on earth complaining that they are being subjected to a wrong because they have to contribute some pittance to schooling for the children of the people who built the roads and bridges they drive on.

Sometimes They Just Assume You Can't Do Arithmetic

When Congresswoman Alexandria Ocasio-Cortez suggested that the top marginal tax rate in the United States should be 70 percent, Republicans instantly told the public that AOC wanted to take most of your income away. Former Wisconsin governor Scott Walker said on Twitter:

Explaining tax rates before Reagan to 5th graders: "Imagine if you did chores for your grandma and she gave you $10.

When you got home, your parents took $7 from you." The students said: "That's not fair!" Even 5th graders get it.

Of course, if Walker did explain pre-Reagan tax rates this way, he would be lying to children. Because these are marginal tax rates, if your grandma paid you ten dollars, you would pay nothing. Only people who earned millions of dollars would pay the top tax rate, and even they would only pay it on a portion of their income. AOC did an excellent job replying:

Explaining marginal taxes to a far-right former Governor: Imagine if you did chores for abuela & she gave you $10. When you got home, you got to keep it, because it's only $10. Then we taxed the billionaire in town because he's making tons of money underpaying the townspeople.

AOC was similarly sharp in replying to Congressman Steve Scalise, who tried to pull the same dirty trick by convincing people that a tax on the super wealthy was a tax on everyone:

SCALISE: Republicans: Let Americans keep more of their own hard-earned money. Democrats: Take away 70% of your income and give it to leftist fantasy programs.
AOC: You're the GOP Minority Whip. How do you not know how marginal tax rates work? Oh that's right, almost forgot: GOP works for the corporate CEOs showering themselves in multi-million dollar bonuses; not the actual working people whose wages + healthcare they're ripping off for profit.

Twitter is not known for being a place of particularly substantive discourse, but if you use it effectively (as AOC often does), it is possible to effectively expose the absurdities in the right's arguments.

4

Capitalism Rewards Innovation and Gives People What They Deserve

How much money people have earned is a rough measure of how much they gave society what it wanted.

—Ray Dalio

The disdain of profit is due to ignorance, and to an attitude that we may if we wish admire in the ascetic who has chosen to be content with a small share of the riches of this world, but which, when actualised in the form of restrictions on profits of others, is selfish to the extent that it imposes asceticism, and indeed deprivations of all sorts, on others.

—Friedrich von Hayek

On the free market, it is a happy fact that the maximization of the wealth of one person or group redounds to the benefit of all.

—Murray Rothbard

The riches of the rich are not the cause of the poverty of anybody; the process that makes some people rich is, on the contrary, the corollary of the process that improves many peoples' want satisfaction. The entrepreneurs, the capitalists and the technologists prosper as far as they succeed in best supplying the consumers.

—Ludwig von Mises, *The Anti-Capitalistic Mentality*

The objective interests of the American workingman are in living in a society in which the private sector is especially pronounced.

—William F. Buckley, *Firing Line*

Someone—in this case Trump—had the idea for that resort.
He organized it. . . . His brand attracted the clientele. He
took all the risk. The parking guy did none of this. So Trump,
not the parking guy, deserves the lion's share of the profit.
Both of them—the boss and the menial laborer—are getting
their just deserts.

—Dinesh D'Souza

The Argument

Capitalism is a miraculous economic system that has lifted billions
of people out of poverty. Under capitalism, instead of government
bureaucrats deciding what is produced, every individual is free to
vote in the marketplace. Entrepreneurs have to give people what
they want to buy in order to succeed, meaning that—as if through
the actions of an invisible hand—the stuff people want tends to
get produced. For all the talk of exploitation and misery, living
standards today are vastly better than they were hundreds of years
ago, thanks to the wondrous innovations brought about in a free-
market economic system. Under capitalism, even without people
being altruistically minded, they are able to work together for
each other's benefit. People get rewarded for satisfying others'
preferences. Capitalism makes us happier, wealthier, and more
free. To oppose it is irrational and can only lead to the misery
of bureaucratic state planning. The socialist experiments of the
twentieth century showed that there is no alternative to a free-
market system.

The Response

One of capitalism's greatest admirers was a man named Karl Marx.
Marx is better known for wanting to destroy capitalism, which he
did, but he was also in awe of its immense productive power. In
The Communist Manifesto, Marx and Engels survey the development of capitalism and invite readers to be astonished by the revolutions in production and technology it has achieved:

Modern industry has established the world market, for which the discovery of America paved the way. This market has given an immense development to commerce, to navigation, to communication by land.... The bourgeoisie, during its rule of scarce one hundred years, has created more massive and more colossal productive forces than have all preceding generations together. Subjection of Nature's forces to man, machinery, application of chemistry to industry and agriculture, steam-navigation, railways, electric telegraphs, clearing of whole continents for cultivation, canalization of rivers, whole populations conjured out of the ground—what earlier century had even a presentiment that such productive forces slumbered in the lap of social labor?

If he had gone on like this, Marx could have gotten a fellowship at the Cato Institute. But for Marx, the fact that capitalism had unleashed revolutionary productive forces did not mean that it was the best of all possible economic systems. Instead, he argued, we should look at it as a precursor that develops our ability to produce but will eventually have to be replaced.

Marx believed that capitalism would eventually need to be replaced for a very simple reason: in addition to being phenomenally productive, it was also destructive. It ruthlessly exploited people and turned them into cogs in machines. Employers tried to extract as much labor as possible from their workers for as little compensation as they could get away with. Ordinary people were not getting the leisure and fulfillment and freedom that they should get. The relentless search for new sources of profit meant that the fruits of the revolutions in production could never be fully enjoyed. Ultimately, because capitalism turns people into commodities and constantly tries to extract more labor from them, it can expand production but cannot provide the good life to all. It relies on an oppressed underclass. Therefore, while capitalism might have been necessary as a *stage* in human history, once it had expanded our productive powers, it would necessarily have to be replaced with an economic system capable of making sure those powers were actually being used to deliver the good life to people, rather than to ceaselessly increase the wealth of the rich for its own sake. To defend capitalism by pointing to its productive powers, then, is to show that you haven't read Karl Marx.

It is also worth noting that critics of capitalism are not necessarily critics of "markets," and it is important to keep the two distinct. Markets (meaning exchange relationships) predated capitalism, and there are "market socialists" who believe markets will outlast capitalism.[1] What leftists primarily object to about capitalism is the existence of a *class system*, a hierarchy whereby a few people have access to phenomenal wealth and power, and large numbers of people own very little and must sell their labor to bosses who do not especially care whether they live or die. The core of socialism, economically speaking,[2] is giving workers "ownership of the means of production," that is to say, getting rid of the boss and making sure that the proceeds of someone's labor go to them rather than to a small class of profiteers. Many defenses of capitalism miss the point, then. They are often defenses of the freedom to exchange things with each other, when what actually needs to be defended is the existence of a small class of people who own and a much larger class of people who have to sell their labor to the former.

Does Capitalism Give Just Deserts?

Does capitalism reward hard work or merit? It certainly doesn't reward the hardest workers with the most rewards. In fact, the people who work the hardest and the most difficult and unsafe jobs, such as agricultural workers, are often the least compensated and the most poorly treated. Landlords, on the other hand, often do no work whatsoever. They have "passive income" from their property. For rich people, their money makes money, meaning they do not have to do any *labor* at all.

So the myth that the people who work the hardest get rewarded accordingly can be dispelled by talking to any member of a hotel's cleaning staff. But what about other kinds of merit? What about moral virtue? Alas, moral virtue doesn't bring riches, either. There are even studies showing that rich people tend to care less about others.[3] What about innovators, people who come up with socially useful inventions? Do they get rewarded? No. Even billionaire Peter Thiel has admitted that people who invent new things and innovate important new knowledge rarely tend to be the ones to get rich from them.[4] Instead, the people who get rich are *monopolists,* those who figure out ways to make sure that they are the only ones able to provide a certain product. Ray Dalio may think that there is a correlation between the social value one produces and the money one receives. (Because he is a billionaire, I am sure this idea brings him comfort.) This is only true if we define social value and market value as the same thing.

In fact, even free-market economist Friedrich von Hayek admitted that "merit" had very little to do with who got rich under capitalism. It is an inherently unfair system, he said:

> In a free system, it is neither desirable nor practicable that material rewards should be made generally to correspond to what men recognize as merit, and . . . an individual's position should not necessarily depend on the views that his fellows hold about the merit he has acquired.[5]

Interestingly, Dinesh D'Souza, commenting on Hayek, says that if Hayek is right that rewards do not correspond to merit under capitalism, then capitalism is indefensible:

> The central question for me is whether capitalism truly distributes its rewards in proportion with what people actually deserve. If it does, it's just. If it doesn't, it isn't. . . . If it fails to give

people their due, it fails the basic test of justice . . . it must be reformed or abolished.[6]

D'Souza is, of course, a staunch defender of capitalism, and he sets about to prove that Hayek is wrong and that rewards are distributed under capitalism. D'Souza gives the example of a parking attendant at Trump Tower. It may seem unfair, he says, that Trump is paid far more than the parking attendant no matter how many hours the parking attendant works. But, if it can be shown that the attendant "is being paid commensurate with what he is producing," then "we will have shown that the rewards of the free market system are not only efficient but also fair."

Now, first, it is not clear that people who start businesses are, in fact, paid in accordance with what they "produce." It is extremely difficult to determine the productivity of an individual in an institution with many parts that all have to work together in order for it to succeed. I run a business myself, and figuring out what each employee's contribution to the sum total of revenue is would be impossible.

But there is also a leap in logic here. It *does* not necessarily follow that if a person is being commensurate with what they produce, their payment is fair. Often, the first instinct leftists have when they hear arguments like "the CEO contributed more to the profits, so the CEO deserves their share," is to show as an empirical matter that the CEO or capitalist did not, in fact, make such a contribution, that workers are the true source of value. But I think we need to emphasize that even if "productivity" determines what material rewards people get, we will not have shown the system is justified. If the parking attendant can barely afford his rent, but Trump Tower *could* pay him more and pay upper management a bit less, it should. We are used to seeing it as natural for the boss to make more money, but that's a choice, and there's no reason it *has* to be that way. In 2015, Dan Price, CEO of the payment processing company Gravity Payments, decreed that all of his employees would receive a minimum annual salary of $70,000 and cut his own pay from $1 million annually to $70,000.[7] Price had been moved by a conversation he had with an employee who said that he was being "ripped off" by Price, who was then paying him $35,000. Price had responded with the classic free-market argument: that he was paying the market rate for the employee's labor, and thereby giving him what he was worth. But the employee pointed out, correctly, that Price was making a choice to give himself far more. Nothing was forcing him to pay only the market rate. The fact that "supply and demand" only necessitated a $35,000 salary did not make it morally justified. The conversation haunted Price, who then decided on his "radical" experiment in pay equity.

Tellingly, some conservatives were enraged by what Price did. Rush Limbaugh commented that it was "pure, unadulterated socialism . . . I hope this company is a case study in MBA programs on how socialism does not work, because it's gonna fail."[8] (The company did not fail. Six years later, it is thriving.) But Price did not violate free-market principles. All he did was decide that the market rate of compensation and the moral rate of compensation are not the same. That notion alarms capitalism's defenders, because it suggests that many people may be significantly undercompensated for their work even if they are being paid the market rate for their work. A "fair" salary is a matter for moral philosophy, not economics, but the fact that many people earn significantly less than the amount needed to rent a one-bedroom apartment in their area should indicate that the American capitalist marketplace is failing to fairly compensate many workers.[9]

Does Capitalism Satisfy People's Preferences?

In a capitalist society, all human relationships are voluntary. Men are free to cooperate or not, to deal with one another or not, as their own individual judgments, convictions and interests dictate. —Ayn Rand, "What Is Capitalism?" in *Capitalism: The Unknown Ideal* (1966)

Okay, so under capitalism, the rich don't exactly *deserve* their riches, and the people who work the hardest and innovate might not get wealthy. But perhaps people's preferences are satisfied. They get the products they want to buy. But why do people want to buy the products they want to buy in the first place? We know that, at least in part, it is because companies spend huge amounts of money trying to manipulate consumers, molding their perceptions through advertising. The "father of the public relations industry," Edward Bernays, famously said that "we are governed, our minds are molded, our tastes formed, our ideas suggested, largely by men we have never heard of."[10] Advertising is designed to mold perceptions in order to create demands that did not exist before. In fact, big business uses some dirty tricks to get people to purchase things they would otherwise have had no interest in. Junk food, for instance, is carefully engineered to be as addictive as possible. (Cheetos are designed to trick the brain into thinking that a person can keep eating them indefinitely.)[11]

Are exchange relationships in a capitalist system "free"? They can look that way at first. Nobody makes you choose a particular employer. But the conditions you are in can significantly reduce the meaningfulness of your choices. Frederick Douglass went so far as to say that "the man who has it in his power to say to a man, you must work the land for me for such wages as I choose to give, has a power of slavery over him as real, if not as complete, as he who compels toil under the lash."[12] What he meant was that when the only jobs available to you are poorly compensated and exploitative, and you cannot afford to leave, your employer can have significant control over your life even though you are nominally "free."

Large corporations can have substantial control of our lives without us being able to exercise much of a "free choice" in the situation. For example, Facebook and Twitter have become crucial gatekeepers for media. As the editor of a magazine, I have found that we depend on these platforms to get our articles to reach people. That means that if Facebook or Twitter were ever displeased with our content and decided to ban our work, we might as well go out of business.[13] This gives them substantial power to dictate terms to us if they wish to. Monopolies are in extremely powerful negotiating positions because people have no alternative but to deal with them. (See the way that Amazon provides highly one-sided arrangements to the sellers who use its marketplace, which it can do because sellers depend on access to that marketplace and have few viable alternatives.) A large company can destroy smaller competitors even if they are more popular, because of the phenomenal resources it has at its disposal.[14]

Sometimes, then, what looks like "free choice" can be an illusion. Consider, for instance, the classic "company town," a place where a single company is the only employer. The company owns the stores and the land. People who work in the town are not *imprisoned* by the company, but there is no competition. The more a few giant corporations come to dominate U.S. life, the more the country resembles a giant "company town" in which you have "choice," but only such choices as the private institutions that govern the country choose to offer you.

Is Capitalism Eliminating Poverty?

Importantly, the evidence is clear that this decline in poverty has happened as countries have come to embrace market capitalism as the way forward—especially China and India. As other countries see the success of these two previously very poor countries and begin following their lead, we can expect to see poverty in the rest of the developing world significantly reduced as well.

—James Davenport, "4 Common Capitalism Myths Debunked,"
Foundation for Economic Education

A simple story is often told about poverty reduction, which is that as "free markets" spread across the world, poverty is being eliminated. But this story is wrong in several important ways. First, countries that successfully reduce poverty do *not* embrace laissez-faire capitalism. They have heavily state-led economies. Even China, which has supposedly triumphed over poverty due to "markets," has ten thousand government-run businesses and highly protectionist policies.[15] Strong public education systems, healthcare systems, and infrastructure are all vital ingredients for a country's economic success.[16]

It's also the case that many of the statistics on the supposedly miraculous reduction in poverty are rather deceptive. Often, they use an extremely low poverty line, such as two dollars a day, and then show dramatic reductions in the number of people earning this pitiful amount. But those earning five dollars a day ($1,825 per year) are still in deep poverty. Many of the achievements in poverty reduction are overstated because they treat going from "having virtually nothing" to "having slightly more than virtually nothing" as the definition of escaping poverty.[17]

It is very easy to mislead people into thinking progress has been more significant than it has been. For example, here is a well-known chart (known as the "elephant chart") showing that both people at the top and people at the bottom have seen their incomes grow over time:

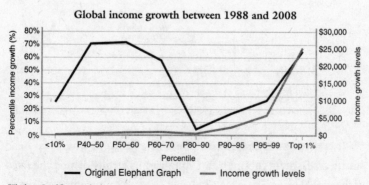

Global income growth between 1988 and 2008

— Original Elephant Graph   — Income growth levels

"Elephant Graph" versus absolute income growth levels. Source: "From Poverty to Power," Muheed Jamaldeen.

From this, you might think that some progress is being made, at least for the very poorest. But remember: a 20 percent rise in your income when you earn $1 a day is 20 cents a day, while a 20 percent income when you earn $100,000 a year is an extra $20,000 annually. If instead of looking at *percentages* we look at the *absolute* amounts that rich and poor have gained (charted on the gray line), we can see that, in fact, the *absolute* amount that the very poor have gained is almost nothing compared to what the extremely rich have made. Their status has only improved relative to their negligible previous wealth, but next to the wealth of the wealthy, it does not look like the "rising tide" is "lifting all boats."

This chart offers a look at how the global income distribution looks overall. If we were looking at an egalitarian world, we would see a flat line from one side to the other. But instead what we see is that the overwhelming majority of people in the world earn nearly nothing compared to what the richest people earn:

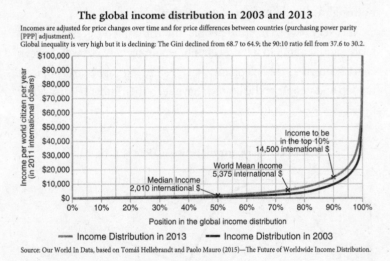

The global income distribution in 2003 and 2013

Incomes are adjusted for price changes over time and for price differences between countries (purchasing power parity [PPP] adjustment).
Global inequality is very high but it is declining: The Gini declined from 68.7 to 64.9; the 90:10 ratio fell from 37.6 to 30.2.

Source: Our World In Data, based on Tomáš Hellebrandt and Paolo Mauro (2015)—The Future of Worldwide Income Distribution.

It is these facts that need to be borne in mind when you hear sunny assessments about how capitalism has transformed the lives of the global poor. There have indeed been substantial improvements in living standards for many people around the world, often due to the diligent work of scientists and public health workers, but we still live in a world where a tiny fraction of the people enjoy extreme levels of comfort that are inaccessible to the rest.

FURTHER READING

- Ha-Joon Chang—*Bad Samaritans: The Myth of Free Trade and the Secret History of Capitalism*
- Ha-Joon Chang—*23 Things They Don't Tell You about Capitalism*
- Rob Larson—*Capitalism vs. Freedom: The Toll Road to Serfdom*
- Jason Hickel—*The Divide: A Brief Guide to Global Inequality and Its Solutions*
- Jonathan Aldred—*The Skeptical Economist: Revealing the Ethics Inside Economics*
- Samuel Bowles et al.—*Understanding Capitalism: Competition, Command, and Change*

5

The United States Is a Force for Good in the World

The United States has been a singularly generous, if not always effective, provider of assistance to other countries, including those where Americans are not popular. . . . Exceptionalism implies that the responsibility for global leadership rests on America's shoulders, not because Americans hunger for power but because there is no good alternative. . . . America is the indispensable nation. That is what makes it exceptional.

—Clifford D. May, "In Defense of American Exceptionalism," *National Review*

For those who fret about the use of American power, remember: America has always been a liberating force, not an occupying power, in the Middle East. We've never dreamed of domination.

—Mike Pompeo

If someone invades your house, you call the cops. Who do you call if someone invades your country? You dial Washington. In the unipolar world, the closest thing to a centralized authority, to an enforcer of norms, is America—American power. And ironically, American power is precisely what liberal internationalism wants to constrain. . . .

—Charles Krauthammer, *Things That Matter*

So is the wealth of America based on theft? Actually, no. The wealth of America isn't stolen, it's created. The ethic of conquest is universal. What's uniquely American is the alternative: equal rights, self-determination and wealth creation. If America did not exist, the conquest ethic would

dominate the world once again. America isn't the problem.
America is the answer.

—Dinesh D'Souza, *America: Imagine the World Without Her*

The Argument
The United States is a shining city on a hill. In a world full of repressive dictatorships, this country stands for individual freedom. Having the United States be more powerful than other countries makes the world a more free and secure place. We have not been perfect throughout our history, but in general we have been impressively committed to encouraging the spread of democracy.

The Response
Let us begin with an obvious observation: United States foreign policy is guided to a large extent by "national self-interest" rather than by the desire to spread noble values. The United States has not historically cared very much whether a country is or is not democratic. U.S. leaders have not hesitated to support brutal governments when it has benefited us to do so.

In fact, a good way to test whether the United States has a positive role in the world is to ask the people who would know best: the rest of the world. The polling shows that they have a dim view of our country, and do not think its actions are especially positive or helpful. If this country's record "global leadership" is indeed admirable, it is certainly news to the people we are supposed to be leading.[1]

We know that the United States has not hesitated to subvert democracy elsewhere. Political scientist Dov Levin shows that between 1946 and 2000, the U.S. conducted at least eighty-one efforts at electoral interference around the world.[2] In Russia, the U.S.' role in helping Boris Yeltsin ascend to power was so well known that it made the cover of *Time* magazine.[3] In 1999, President Clinton tried to swing the Israeli election, to the point of sending advisers who "[wrote] advertisements, [plotted] strategy, and [took] polls" for Ehud Barak.[4] In Iran (1953), Guatemala (1954), Congo (1960), and Chile (1973), the United States participated in the outright overthrow of governments.[5] Even in 2009, the State Department under Hillary Clinton was actively helping support the illegal government that had deposed President Manuel Zelaya in Honduras.[6]

Even during World War II, supposedly this country's proudest era, the country's leadership was not actually concerned with stopping the Nazi Holocaust from proceeding.[7] Even though the atrocities were in the paper every day, the U.S. avoided the war for as long as possible, only entering the war when Germany and Japan declared war on it. U.S. elites had, in fact, been quite sympathetic to European fascism. Franklin Roosevelt called Mussolini "that admirable Italian gentleman," and *Fortune* magazine ran a glowing special issue on the wonders that Italian fascism had produced. After the war, the United States did not see much need to intensely pursue the "denazification" of Germany. U.S. intelligence agents even helped infamous Nazi war criminal Klaus Barbie (the "Butcher of Lyon") escape European authorities because they thought he could offer useful assistance in the Cold War.[8]

The United States is able to convince itself of its virtue, in part, by failing to confront its obvious atrocities. The U.S. is the only country ever to have dropped atomic weapons, and we did it to *two* civilian populations. This was a crime against humanity. (The justifications for the bombings do not hold up under scrutiny.)[9] The U.S. gave direct support to the Indonesian government when it ordered the mass killing of communists during the mid-1960s, which resulted in the murder of up to a million people.[10] Human rights abusers from the apartheid government of South Africa to the apartheid government of Israel have found a protective friend in the United States. During the Korean War, the U.S. engaged in indiscriminate bombing of North Korea, flattening it to the point where in certain cities, there was nothing left to bomb.[11] The Vietnam War, often portrayed in U.S. media as a "tragic but well-intended mistake," was a much worse crime against Vietnam than is usually admitted. U.S. forces indiscriminately killed civilians and dropped more bombs on Southeast Asia than had been dropped in all of World War II by all parties combined.[12] The bombing of Laos, hardly ever discussed, killed countless innocent Laotian peasants and left unexploded munitions that continue to take the lives and limbs of people to this day.[13]

In 1988, after the U.S. shot down an Iranian civilian airliner, killing all 290 passengers, George H. W. Bush declared that he would "never apologize for America, I don't care what the facts are."[14] This kind of mindset is psychopathic. What if the facts are that nearly three hundred civilians are dead because the U.S. shot a missile at their plane? Bush didn't care.[15]

This kind of arrogance and self-aggrandizement is characteristic of U.S. foreign policy. We are convinced we are good, and because we know we are good, we do not listen when others tell us we are doing wrong. Instead, we insist that they must just "hate America" and not appreciate all the good we are doing.

Here is how Dinesh D'Souza defends the country's conduct, faced with the appalling record:

> Whatever you think about the Vietnam War, America wasn't stealing from the Vietnamese. And in Iraq, we spent a whole bunch of money and then we turned over the oil fields to the Iraqis. Under the conquest ethic, we would have kept it. In Afghanistan after 9/11, the US military, even while bombing terrorist targets, was delivering food rations to Afghan civilians. And far from stealing, America rebuilt Germany and Japan after World War II. Contrary to the [Howard] Zinn narrative, we're not the bad guys of the world.

We could discuss the fact that when the United States has given aid to countries it has invaded and occupied, that aid has often been given out of self-interest rather than pure benevolence. But

I am stuck on that phrase "whatever you think about the Vietnam War." This is like saying, "Whatever you think about the murder I committed, you have to admit I didn't rob the guy." The fact that the United States murdered Vietnamese peasants but did not take their rice (in many cases we burned it or poisoned it)[17] does not mitigate the conduct one iota. It's true that U.S. conduct in Vietnam was not motivated by a desire to pillage the place. It was motivated by a fanatical ideological belief, impervious to facts, that the U.S. needed to stop the spread of communism and would look weak if it admitted defeat. Lyndon B. Johnson even admitted to having dreams in which people were calling him a coward and a chicken, making him more stubbornly committed to staying in the war no matter how many Vietnamese corpses piled up.[18]

D'Souza, along with Mike Pompeo above, appear to believe that if a country does not engage in ongoing occupations of countries, it is not trying to achieve global dominance. That is not how it works. Take Iraq, for instance. D'Souza believes that because the United States government does not have ongoing possession of Iraq's oil fields, we are "not the bad guys." But here, Antonia Juhasz of CNN explains what actually happened:

> Before the 2003 invasion, Iraq's domestic oil industry was fully nationalized and closed to Western oil companies. A decade of war later, it is largely privatized and utterly dominated by foreign firms. From ExxonMobil and Chevron to BP and Shell, the West's largest oil companies have set up shop in Iraq. So have a slew of American oil service companies, including Halliburton, the Texas-based firm Dick Cheney ran before becoming George W. Bush's running mate in 2000. The war is the one and only reason for this long sought and newly acquired access.[19]

So the United States has secured its objective, which is to get *access* to Iraq's oil through our own companies, which we did not have when it was controlled by a hostile government. This is consistent with the U.S.' historic behavior toward other countries. We punish those who harm our interests. We reward those who further those interests. Should a country defy us (such as Cuba or Iran), their economies will be squeezed with sanctions.

Of course, the United States is not the only country that operates on the sociopathic logic of ruthless self-interest. But as an extremely powerful country with the world's largest military budget, which has been willing to "intervene" around the world, the United States' choices have major ramifications. This country's refusal to accept its role in causing global climate change, for instance, or to agree to equitable terms for carbon emissions reduction, has made it more difficult to secure a strong global climate framework.

Conservatives often think the American left "singles out" the United States for criticism, ignoring the crimes of other countries. Some call this "hating America." But there are good reasons for people to focus on their own government's conduct more than they focus on the conduct of other governments. America's foreign policy is conducted in the name of its people, and so those people have a duty to scrutinize their country's actions and expose its crimes, in order to stop them. Other countries' citizens have the same duty— Russian and Chinese dissidents heroically expose the authoritarian practices of their own governments. American leftists focus on the wrongdoing of our country because it is the country whose conduct we are responsible for.

Anthropologist David Vine, in his book *The United States of War*, summarizes just part of the recent toll:

> Entire neighborhoods, cities, and societies have been shattered by the U.S.-led wars. The total number of injured and traumatized extends into the tens of millions. In Afghanistan, surveys have indicated that two-thirds of the population may have mental health problems, with half suffering from anxiety and one in five from PTSD. By 2007 in Iraq, 28 percent of

young people were malnourished, half living in Baghdad had witnessed a major traumatic event, and nearly one-third had PTSD diagnoses. As of 2019, more than 10 million have likely been displaced from their homes in Afghanistan, Iraq, Yemen, and Libya alone, becoming refugees abroad or internally displaced people within their countries. . . . U.S. Americans need to reckon honestly with our history of war and with the tremendous suffering our country has caused.[20]

The United States has historically conducted too little scrutiny of its own conduct. During the COVID-19 pandemic, U.S. corporations were trying hard to make sure that developing countries didn't subvert our intellectual property laws to illegally produce proprietary vaccines for their people.[21] In other words, we were willing to let scores of foreigners die of a horrible disease to preserve the rights of U.S. corporations to make a pile of money from the pandemic. There was very little debate about this in the U.S.—it was just accepted as something normal, hardly even worth discussing. (Conservative commentators, of course, are far more interested in whatever the latest "cancel culture" flap is.) It is frightening that a country as powerful as the United States can be so convinced of its own virtue yet so oblivious to its actual actions. We do not need to hate ourselves, but we do need to learn to listen to the opinions of other nations about whether we are the force for good that we presume we are.

FURTHER READING

- William Blum—*Killing Hope: U.S. Military and C.I.A. Interventions since World War II*
- Jason Burke—*The 9/11 Wars*
- Tim Weiner—*Legacy of Ashes: The History of the CIA*

- Vincent Bevins—*The Jakarta Method: Washington's Anticommunist Crusade and the Mass Murder Program That Shaped Our World*
- Roxanne Dunbar-Ortiz—*An Indigenous Peoples' History of the United States*
- Nick Turse—*Kill Anything That Moves: The Real American War in Vietnam*
- John W. Dower—*The Violent American Century: War and Terror since World War II*
- Stephen Kinzer—*Overthrow: America's Century of Regime Change from Hawaii to Iraq*
- Dee Brown—*Bury My Heart at Wounded Knee: An Indian History of the American West*
- Noam Chomsky—*Hegemony or Survival: America's Quest for Global Dominance*
- A. G. Hopkins—*American Empire: A Global History*
- Daniel Immerwahr—*How to Hide an Empire: A History of the Greater United States*

6

There's No Such Thing as White Privilege

The idea that you can target an ethnic group with a collective crime regardless of the specific innocence or guilt of the constituent elements of that group, there is absolutely nothing that is more racist than that. It's absolutely abhorrent.

—Jordan Peterson

I suggest reading *Hillbilly Elegy* by J. D. Vance and see if these people have "privilege"?

—Letter to the editor, *Victoria News*

In recent years earnings disparities between racial groups have consistently been weaponized. . . . The median income of Asian men in America is consistently higher than any other group, including white Americans. Should there be some attempt to level this figure out by bringing Asian men down a few earning percentiles? Perhaps we could get out of this mania by treating people as individuals based on their abilities and not trying to impose equity quotas on every company and institution.

—Douglas Murray, *The Madness of Crowds*

No reasonable person can argue that white privilege applies to the great majority of whites, let alone to all whites. There are simply too many variables other than race that determine individual success in America. And if it were true, why would whites commit suicide at twice the rate of blacks (and at a higher rate than any other race in America except American Indians)? . . . There are a host of privileges that dwarf "white privilege." A huge one is Two-Parent Privilege. If you are raised by a father and mother, you enter adulthood with more privileges than anyone else in American society, irrespective of race, ethnicity, or sex. That's why the poverty rate among two-parent black families is only 7 percent. Compare that with a 22 percent poverty rate among whites in single-parent homes. Obviously the two-parent home is the decisive "privilege." Another "privilege," if one wants to use that term, that dwarfs "white privilege" is Asian privilege. Asian Americans do better than white Americans in school, on IQ tests, on credit scores, and on other positive measures. In fact, according to recent data from the Federal Reserve, Asians are about to surpass whites as the wealthiest group of Americans. Will the Left soon complain about Asian privilege?

—Dennis Prager, "The Fallacy of 'White Privilege,'"
National Review

The Argument

Despite pervasive claims by the social justice left that white people are "privileged," in fact, they are not. It is unfair to blame white people for the sins of their ancestors and to demand racial guilt. The idea of white privilege ignores the reality for many white people. Furthermore, America is less racist than it has ever been. The idea of "systemic" racism is now used to cover up the fact that there are very few actual racists left. Despite an endless effort by the left to find racism everywhere (sometimes using "critical race theory"), the fact remains that this country is relatively fair to people of all races.

The Response

First, let us dispose of the idea that the concept of white privilege is refuted by the existence of poor white people. The existence of a statistical "white privilege" does not mean that every white person lives an incredible life. We are talking about phenomena that exist in the aggregate. Statistically, a child born white is likely to inherit more wealth than a child born Black. They are likely to attend a better school. They are likely to have more access to the kinds of social networks that help people advance. This does not mean any given Black child *will* be worse off than any given white child; Barack Obama's children will grow up with many privileges that a poor white child might not. But exactly one United States president has been non-white, and it is willful ignorance to think this is a matter of pure coincidence.

There is a vast and persistent wealth gap between Black and white people. This is separate from the Black-white earnings gap, the racial difference in annual income (which is both growing wider and "cannot be fully explained by differences in age, education, job type, or location," according to economists at the Federal Reserve Bank of San Francisco).[1] The wealth gap refers to differences in total assets, and it's much, much larger than the income gap. In 2016, the median white family had a net worth about ten times higher than the median Black family.[2] A study of Boston found that in that city, the average Black family's net worth is eight dollars.[3] Not eight thousand. Eight. The average white family's wealth was in the hundreds of thousands of dollars. According to the Institute for Policy Studies, if "average Black family wealth continues to grow at the same pace it has over the past three decades, it would take Black families 228 years to amass the same amount of wealth White families have today."[4] That's assuming that white wealth won't continue to grow; in reality, absent significant change, Black wealth is never going to catch up to white wealth.

Very few Americans actually realize quite how severe this gap is. When researchers at Yale asked people how many dollars they thought each Black family had for every hundred dollars a white family had, on average people said something around eighty-five dollars. The reality is closer to five dollars.[5] Now, approximately 70 percent of white people say that the country does not need to pay more attention to race issues (about 50 percent say we already pay too much attention).[6] And yet they are oblivious to a fundamental difference between the average advantages white people have starting out versus the ones Black people have.

The wealth gap cannot be separated from slavery. Wealth is passed down intergenerationally, and slavery was very, very recent (there are people still alive today who once met former slaves).[7] The Black-white wealth gap is not something that emerged over time after both races started out with equal resources. It has existed continuously since Emancipation, when Black people were sent out into the "free" world with no compensation for their two centuries of stolen labor, their disrupted family structures, their state-enforced illiteracy, and the destruction of their cultural knowledge. A colossal wrong was done and never righted. In civil law, when one party causes harm to another, the state intervenes to try to make the person whole again, but in the case of American slavery (which was half a second ago in the lifetime of the human species), the American public is simply oblivious to the lasting effects on intergenerational wealth.[8]

For instance, I was recently reading the autobiography of Walmart founder Sam Walton. Walton presents himself as a self-made man, having built a giant retail empire from nothing. But not *exactly* nothing. At the beginning, in 1945, Sam Walton's father-in-law loaned him $20,000 to buy a store. That's equal to nearly $300,000 in today's money. Walton ran the store successfully, bought another store, and slowly built the chain that would become Walmart. His children are now some of the richest people in the world. Walton, of course, calls his a "story about entrepreneurship, risk, and hard work," the American dream fulfilled. But how likely was a Black person in 1940s Arkansas to have been able to get a giant loan from a rich in-law and sell to a white clientele? Walton won a rigged game. Walmart could not have been created by Black people no matter how hard they worked, and because "first-mover" advantage is so important, the first superstore chain was always going to be run by a white person. We can see here a very clear example of how the racial wealth gap is passed down intergenerationally. Because no

Black family had accumulated this kind of wealth in 1945, no Black person could possibly compete with Sam Walton. Today, Sam Walton's billionaire children sit on vast fortunes that were created under completely illegitimate conditions—and they think of it as an example of virtue being rewarded![9]

Generational wealth transfer affects in ways both large and small. Growing up in a family that owns their own home and doesn't have to stress about money can mean a house with less tension, where parents can devote more of their energy to raising the children well. Having parents who can pay for your college education makes it much easier to go to college. Not just much easier to *pay* for college, but much easier to actually *be in* college, because when you don't have to think about money, you're free to focus on your studies. The average Black woman "graduates college with over $10,000 more in student debt than the average white man,"[10] which means that she's going to be paying off her college education a lot longer, with all the accompanying stresses that brings.

So the wealth gap alone makes life for the average Black family very different from life for the average white family. But Black people also face widespread discrimination across a number of domains. In the housing market, there is ample evidence that landlords and Realtors discriminate against Black renters and buyers. People with Black names are discriminated against in job searches, and Black people are more likely to report being mistreated by the police.

The privileges that I get out of being white can be counteracted by other forces. Trauma, for instance, can make life much harder for anyone. But this does not change the central fact that whiteness confers a basic advantage in many situations, such as in trying to obtain housing. And over many generations, white Americans on *average* have accumulated wealth and connections that make it much easier to give their children the good life.

What about Dennis Prager's point that there are all kinds of privilege, and Asian Americans do better than white people? Well, it's largely beside the point. Indeed, having two parents with two incomes makes one better off. But that cannot possibly explain why there has been a giant interracial wealth gap for centuries that has never been addressed. Why do we discuss a "white privilege" but not an "Asian privilege" even though Asian Americans have higher incomes on average? Well, in part because that income difference was not created by a deliberate centuries-long system of "Asian supremacist" racial oppression, and in fact, Asian Americans continue to suffer from racist discrimination. In other contexts, conservatives cite Asian Americans as proof that groups who obviously *do not* have racial privileges can nevertheless succeed, so the reason "Asian privilege" is not discussed is because nobody believes it exists.

Again, it is important to emphasize that none of this diminishes the urgency of addressing poverty and "deaths of despair" among white people.[11] But it is possible to recognize simultaneously that there are significant average differences in wealth across races and that individuals may suffer injustices that do or do not have racial dimensions.

FURTHER READING

- Thomas M. Shapiro—*The Hidden Cost of Being African American: How Wealth Perpetuates Inequality*
- Jim Freeman—*Rich Thanks to Racism: How the Ultra-Wealthy Profit from Racial Injustice*
- Andrea Flynn et al.—*The Hidden Rules of Race: Barriers to an Inclusive Economy*
- Ira Katznelson—*When Affirmative Action Was White: An Untold History of Racial Inequality in Twentieth-Century America*

- Richard Rothstein—*The Color of Law: A Forgotten History of How Our Government Segregated America*
- Sheryll Cashin—*White Space, Black Hood: Opportunity Hoarding and Segregation in the Age of Inequality*
- Nikole Hannah-Jones and *The New York Times Magazine*— *The 1619 Project: A New Origin Story*
- Thomas J. Sugrue—*The Origins of the Urban Crisis: Race and Inequality in Postwar Detroit*
- Randall Robinson—*The Debt: What America Owes to Blacks*
- Keeanga-Yamahtta Taylor—*Race for Profit: How Banks and the Real Estate Industry Undermined Black Homeownership*
- A. Kirsten Mullen and William A. Darity Jr.—*From Here to Equality: Reparations for Black Americans in the Twenty-First Century*
- Matthew Desmond and Mustafa Emirbayer—*Racial Domination, Racial Progress: The Sociology of Race in America*

7

The Left Are Woke Totalitarians Trying to Destroy Free Speech in the Name of "Social Justice"

Rancorous trends such as microaggressions, safe spaces, trigger warnings and intellectual intolerance have taken hold at universities with breathtaking speed. . . . These phenomena are not just harmless fads acted out by a few petulant students and their indulgent professors in an academic cocoon. Rather, they are both a symptom and a cause of malaise and strife in society at large.

—Daniel Shuchman, "Free Thought Under Siege,"
Wall Street Journal

Nothing has done so much to destroy the juridical safeguards of individual freedom as the striving after this mirage of social justice.

—Friedrich von Hayek

Looking at stories from 1970 to 2018, several terms came out of nowhere in the past few years to reach sudden new heights of repetition and frequency. Here's a list of the most successful neologisms: non-binary, toxic masculinity, white supremacy, traumatizing, queer, transphobia, whiteness, mansplaining. And here are a few that were rising in frequency in the last decade but only took off in the last few years: triggering, hurtful, gender, stereotypes.

—Andrew Sullivan, "The Roots of Wokeness,"
The Weekly Dish

Thoughtcrimes . . . by their very nature make accusation and guilt the same thing. . . . The reach of contemporary thoughtcrime expands constantly—homophobia, Islamophobia, transphobia, bi-phobia, fat-phobia, racism, ableism, and on and on—making it difficult to know when one is treading on safe ground or about to step on a land mine.

—Rod Dreher, *Live Not by Lies:*
A Manual for Christian Dissidents (2020)

[The left]—and the country—are in a revolutionary frenzy. The San Francisco Board of Education has voted to rename more than 40 schools honoring the nation's best—Washington, Jefferson, and Lincoln—largely on racist grounds that they are dead, mostly white males. Statues continue to fall. Names change. The iconic dates, origins, and nature of America itself continue to be attacked to meet leftist demands. And still, it is not enough for the new McCarthyites. Social media are banning tens of thousands. Silicon Valley and Wall Street monopolies go after smaller upstart opponents. A wrong word destroys a lifelong career. Formerly sane pundits now call for curtailing the First Amendment.

—Victor Davis Hanson, "Will a Hard-Left Turn
Lead to Pushback?," *National Review* (2021)

In our schools, our newsrooms, even our corporate boardrooms, there is a new far-left fascism that demands absolute allegiance. If you do not speak its language, perform its rituals, recite its mantras, and follow its commandments, then you will be censored, banished, blacklisted, persecuted, and punished. . . . One of their political weapons is "Cancel Culture"—driving people from their jobs, shaming dissenters, and demanding total submission from anyone who disagrees. This is the very definition of totalitarianism, and it is completely alien to our culture and our values, and it has absolutely no place in the United States of America. This attack on our liberty, our magnificent liberty, must be stopped, and it will be stopped very quickly. We will expose

this dangerous movement, protect our nation's children,
end this radical assault, and preserve our beloved American
way of life.

—Donald Trump, Mount Rushmore speech (2020)

The Argument

The left has been captivated by a number of toxic ideas. They believe in "identity politics," where your worth as a person is reduced down to your race and gender. Whether it is called *wokeness* or *social justice* or *intersectionality*, it ultimately boils down to the same thing: trying to appear morally virtuous through creating imaginary slights like "microaggressions." Leftists practice a pernicious "cancel culture" whereby anyone who is perceived to violate their standards for what is "politically correct" is hounded and humiliated. They shut down debate on subjects they don't like. Their weapons range from getting people fired to getting speeches on campuses canceled to, in the case of Antifa, the use of outright violence. Because the left can't handle facts and evidence, they resort to thuggish tactics. They do not believe in free speech, and instead of arguing with conservatives, they simply try to silence them. They demand "trigger warnings" on content they don't like and want "safe spaces" where they are free of having to engage with ideas that hurt them. If you disagree with them, they will call you a racist and try to get you "canceled."

The Response

One of the reasons this argument is difficult to respond to is that it's a mess, with many different allegations. In fact, it's more a *narrative* than an argument, a story of what "the left" does and all the various ways that that manifests itself. Some people who are not on the right voice sympathy for this narrative; journalist Matt Taibbi, for instance, has said that the "American left has lost its mind," and "leaders of this new movement are replacing traditional liberal beliefs about tolerance, free inquiry, and even racial harmony with ideas so toxic and unattractive that they eschew debate, moving straight to shaming, threats, and intimidation."[1]

I think most of this is hugely overstated. In fact, often when you examine incidents of "leftist intolerance" closely, it turns out there is much more to the story. Conservative writer John McWhorter, for instance, begins his book *The Elect: The Threat to a Progressive America from Anti-Black Antiracists* with some anecdotes about how crazy the left has become.[2] He tells us, for instance, of Leslie Neal-Boylan, who was fired from her position as the dean of nursing at the University of Massachusetts Lowell for daring to say the phrase "everyone's life matters" in an email. McWhorter says that "because her composition included the three words 'everyone's lives [*sic*] matter,' she was reported to her superiors and quickly out of a job without even being allowed to defend herself." He is outraged by this politically correct nonsense and asks, "What kind of people did this? Why did they get away with it? And are we going to let them continue to?"

Because I have heard many of these "political correctness gone mad" stories, and have often found that crucial facts are being left out of the story, I looked into this one. An article in the local *Sun* newspaper reported that, in fact, there was "deafening silence" from the university about the reasons for Neal-Boylan's firing.[3] There had indeed been some controversy over an email that Neal-Boylan sent to the school that said "BLACK LIVES MATTER, but also, EVERYONE'S LIFE MATTERS." A student saw this as tone-deaf and posted it on Twitter. Neal-Boylan apologized. But the *Sun* says it's very unclear that Neal-Boylan's subsequent firing was because of the incident and that Neal-Boylan herself "suggest[ed] she was actually fired in retaliation for efforts to raise the profile of the nursing school." The student who had complained about the email on Twitter was disturbed to find that Neal-Boylan had been fired and that the university would not provide an explanation of why, because "firing her without any context makes it so people can flip it and make it look like BLM did this and cancel culture." The student hadn't wanted Neal-Boylan to be fired. Neal-Boylan wrote in a letter to university administrators that she had actually been fired because of a power struggle with the dean above her, and "without doubt, my firing was based solely on Dean McKinney's dislike for questioning of her authority." Neal-Boylan was frustrated that her story would be used to "fuel the conservative opposition to the BLM movement," because this "would be anathema to me."

What, then, happened here? It's shrouded in a bit of mystery, but Neal-Boylan's argument is that it looks like what probably happened is that the dean above Neal-Boylan used the email as a pretext to fire her in a conflict that was ultimately about power— someone she wanted to oust anyway. Nobody on the left had called for Neal-Boylan to be fired. No "outrage mobs" were demanding her head on a platter. One student had tweeted that the email was tone-deaf, but that student wanted Neal-Boylan to learn from it, not be fired. "The left" was only responsible for the firing in the sense that the dean cynically invoked anti-racist values in order to punish someone.

Now, you may still think what Neal-Boylan said should have been uncontroversial. But it's clear that McWhorter, in trying to tell a story of the totalitarian leftist thought police behaving outrageously, did not care to investigate the facts closely, and reported only those that fit the narrative. The truth was far less explosive. When McWhorter asks, "What kind of people did this?" he is conjuring an imaginary enemy instead of the much more complex, much less extreme people who exist in reality.

I've singled out one example, but I see this tendency over and over. Matt Taibbi cites the case of "a UCLA professor placed under investigation for reading Martin Luther King's 'Letter from a Birmingham Jail' out loud." That does sound absurd, but it's deliberately framing what happened in a way that leaves out the other side's story. In fact, the professor was asked by students not to read the N-word aloud when it came to the parts of King's text that used the word. The professor declined the request and said the word, arguing that "just that my skin is white does not prevent me from being able to say those words." The university *did* investigate in response to student complaints, and the professor apologized to the students. He continues to teach political science at the university.[4]

Now, you might think the university should not have gotten involved or investigated the incident. You might even think it was the professor's prerogative to ignore his students, although personally, I think it is a trivial request to ask white people not to say the N-word even when reading from historical documents. But the point is that *framing* this as a professor was punished for reading "Letter from Birmingham Jail" is misleading. One of the students was quoted as saying:

> None of the students were upset that the professor dedicated a lecture to the history of racial tensions in the U.S. and no one was upset that he included passages from MLK's "Letter." We were upset that a WHITE professor was so insistent on using racially charged language even after being asked not to.[5]

Over and over, reports about the excesses of Crazy Left Social Justice Culture leave out information that is relevant to assessing whether the claims of "political correctness gone mad" are actually true. Critical facts are almost always left out. You may have heard, for instance, about the Oberlin students who complained that the Asian food in their dining hall was "cultural appropriation." This story never dies; it has been cited over and over again to show What Young People Are Like These Days, and to depict them as a bunch of snowflakes who complain that everything is racism. *The Atlantic*'s Conor Friedersdorf wrote that it was possible to extrapolate broad conclusions about social justice ideology from the Oberlin dining hall incident. "Oberlin seems unable to provide dissent in anything like the quality and quantity needed to prepare these young people for the enormous complexity of life in a diverse society," he concluded.[6] But the incident was ludicrously overblown.[7] A journalism student at the school decided to do a feature for the school paper on how repulsed international students were by the school dining hall's pitiful imitations of their culture's dishes.[8] The food in question was indeed off-putting. A couple of students gave quotes to the reporter about cultural inauthenticity. Yes, the word "appropriation," was used, but the thrust was that students from Vietnam and Japan were pointing out how pathetic Oberlin's excuse for sushi and bánh mì was. From this tiny story quoting a handful of international students, national media coverage followed. The conservative *National Review* accused students of practicing "intellectual apartheid."[9] I could go through dozens of these examples. While the right are always very quick to report on instances in which a leftist is alleged to have fabricated a hate crime, they do not investigate stories of Social Justice Activists Gone Crazy, because the fictitious, caricatured version is what they want to believe in. As *Vox*'s Zack Beauchamp writes, there is a common pattern:

> Minor college campus controversies involving diversity and/or free speech get breathlessly reported by the right-wing press, laundered into the mainstream by click-hungry neutral outlets, and eventually become fodder for breathless takes from conservatives and moderate liberals about the supposed authoritarianism of Kids Today and their "woke" ideology. The cycle uses a few absurd-sounding cases to create a sense of crisis about the state of American college campuses, in complete contradiction of both the aggregate data and sometimes even the basic facts of the campus controversy in question.[10]

Sometimes it's the case that what *looks* like a demand for "ideological conformity" is actually quite reasonable criticism. For example: In 2017, *Third World Quarterly* withdrew an article it had published called "The Case for Colonialism" after a petition calling

for the article's removal. The article, by political science professor Bruce Gilley, had argued that the colonization of the Global
South by European countries had been, on balance, a good thing
for the colonized. When the article was pulled, the writer said
that a "Maoist . . . hate mob [had] tried to silence me," and in the
conservative press he was presented as a victim of the Pervasive
Liberal Bias on campus. All he had done was present an *opposing
viewpoint*, yet he was being cast as a racist.[11]

Left out from this narrative, though, was the fact that the article was appallingly bad as a piece of scholarship. Even a researcher
from the libertarian Cato Institute said it was "empirically and
historically inaccurate" and "misuses existing postcolonial scholarship."[12] The arguments it made were really, really bad.[13] Gilley
had downplayed or ignored atrocities by colonial powers, and had
failed to support his contentions with even remotely persuasive arguments. Leaving out colonial genocidal atrocities from one's cal-
culus of the "costs and benefits of colonialism," as if those atrocities
did not happen, can be morally compared with Holocaust denial.
The problem with articles that distort history this way is not that
they "differ from the ideological consensus." If a legitimate piece
of historical scholarship offers new evidence, that evidence should
be considered regardless of whether it advances a viewpoint we
"like." But when a piece of pseudo-scholarship baselessly treats
well-documented genocides as if they didn't occur, reinforcing the
myths peddled by racists, it is fair for scholars to be upset. Journals
retract articles that turn out to be egregiously wrong. Personally,
I don't know that that's what *Third World Quarterly* should have
done, because by retracting the article they allowed Gilley to create the narrative that the journal had caved to a woke mob. But
should calls to retract it be seen as "politically correct," Maoist
thought policing, or a reasonable demand for scholarship to con-
form to basic intellectual and moral standards?[14] Helen Pluckrose
and James Lindsay cite Gilley's case as an example of how "Social
Justice scholarship censors academic ideas it disapproves of."[15] But

they do not deal with the case made by the critics, which is that Gilley's work was not just politically incorrect. It was an atrocious piece of scholarship.

We often hear of universities disinviting speakers because of some outcry by students, or protesting of an event. In fact, clashes over controversial speakers happen much less than you would expect; there are only a handful of incidents each year across the U.S.' 2,600 four-year colleges and universities.[13] Furthermore, the political *left* can be the target of the suppression as well. After political pressure, Harvard revoked a fellowship it offered to heroic U.S. Army whistleblower Chelsea Manning, who was sent to prison for exposing misconduct by the military. (At the same time, Harvard gave the same fellowship to former Trump campaign manager Corey Lewandowski and former Trump press secretary Sean Spicer.) Legendary radical activist Angela Davis had a lecture at Butler University canceled over her support for the Boycott, Divestment, and Sanctions Campaign against Israel,[17] and had an award from the Birmingham Civil Rights Institute rescinded (after public pressure, it was reinstated).[18] Pro-Palestinian activists on campus can face special difficulties. Students at Fordham University have had to battle their university in court just to try to get permission to organize a chapter of Students for Justice in Palestine.[19] Zoom refused to stream a talk at San Francisco State University by Palestinian activist Leila Khaled because she had been convicted of hijacking two planes in 1969 and 1970.[20] You don't need to approve of hijacking planes in order to believe that free-speech principles mean Khaled should get to speak.[21]

Personally, I tend to believe that if a group of students wants to invite someone to campus to speak, they should get to, even if that person's views are abominable. But I also understand the argument that because speaking at a university confers a kind of prestige (people often put their invited speeches on their CVs), it is not an opportunity that should be offered to just anyone. I also see that there are extreme cases in which a speaker could pose active harm to students. Conservative provocateur Milo Yiannopoulos, in an event at the University of Wisconsin, put up pictures of one of the school's transgender students and mocked her in front of the audience.[22] That kind of speech, the bullying of a private individual, might not be *illegal,* but it doesn't contribute anything of value to campus discourse.

Now, speech questions are difficult, because the moment you start making judgments about what "contributes something of value to campus discourse," it's clear there will be sharply different views on what constitutes "valuable." There is a risk that when somebody is empowered to decide what the "valuable" speech is, they will decide that all views they disagree with are not worth hearing. This is part of why I favor a broad permissiveness about letting students host the events they like, even if the consequence is that the Young Republicans end up inviting war criminals and bigots. But we can still see why *some* controversies over who gets to speak on what platform are unavoidable. If a school's commencement speaker turned out to be a virulent anti-Semite, there would be justice to students' calls to have the speaker replaced. After all, speaking at a commencement is a great honor, one that implicitly endorses the speaker as a person of worthiness with valuable things to say to the graduating class. I would protest if George W. Bush was my commencement speaker, because I believe George W. Bush is an unconvicted war criminal[23] and that granting him such a privilege helps him whitewash his crimes.

Ultimately, I think we overestimate the amount of censorship on campus and underestimate students' openness to dealing with disagreements constructively. A few years back, Ben Shapiro was invited to the University of Connecticut by one of the campus conservative groups. There was a fuss made, but the campus Democrats decided to respond not by trying to cancel Shapiro's event. Instead, they invited me to give a "counter-speech" in a room a few doors down, where a different point of view could be heard.

My speech was called "Ben Shapiro Is Not as Smart as He Thinks He Is," and I spent it explaining both why Ben Shapiro was wrong about nearly everything *and* why I thought he should still be allowed to speak.

You might think that the "social justice"–minded leftist students in my audience would be hostile to the suggestion that muzzling Shapiro was counterproductive. In fact, none of them objected to or challenged the point, and I talked to many of them. What they were really interested in was a satisfying leftist response to Shapiro that would expose him.[24]

Is there a problem of people getting censored? Sometimes, though usually not by "woke mobs," as the right would have it. For instance, a website called CanceledPeople.com lists a number of cases in which people have been "canceled," by which the site means that they have suffered career consequences for expressing reasonable opinions. Notably, the people "canceled" have *not* all expressed right-wing views. (I myself am on the list because I was fired from *The Guardian* newspaper for a tweet criticizing U.S. military aid to Israel.)[25] But many have indeed lost work for expressing opinions that were seen as bigoted or offensive.

Take the case of Alexi McCammond. McCammond was a twenty-seven-year-old Black woman who was appointed to be the new editor in chief of *Teen Vogue*. It was soon discovered that when McCammond was a teenager, she had sent a series of racist and homophobic tweets. With discontent among the *Teen Vogue* staff, and sponsors pulling their ads, McCammond was fired. It can be argued that it was extremely unfair to fire McCammond, given that she had apologized for the tweets and they were a decade old. Roxanne Jones, writing for CNN, argued otherwise, saying that "her bigotry, whether intended or not, calls into question her ability to lead a newsroom in today's more racially conscious climate," and while Jones was "not saying McCammond shouldn't have a job or a platform ever again . . . it's hard to imagine how she can effectively take the helm at a major publication at a company where so much change is needed when it comes to institutional discrimination."[26]

Personally, I think it would have been better to establish a process whereby McCammond could make amends, rather than firing her. But one reason corporations resort quickly to firing people is that there is no *reason* for them to show people any particular loyalty or compassion. Employment in the United States is largely "at will," meaning you can be fired for any reason or no reason at all. When an employee is controversial, then, they can simply be ditched for the convenience of the company, even if those criticizing the employee aren't actually demanding the person be fired.

The problem here is often less a matter of "cancel culture" than "firing culture," which sees workers as expendable and gives them no clear right of free speech. Certainly, that was the case with my own firing. I was not "canceled" in the sense that a mob of online crusaders did not demand my head on a platter. I was reprimanded in secret by my boss, who did not like my tweet. It had nothing to do with "social justice" and everything to do with the fact that bosses can exercise a lot of control over what those that work for them tweet.

Thus, the big problem here is at-will employment. It happens to people on the left as well, such as the Black Lives Matter supporter fired from Deloitte over a TikTok video,[27] or Marc Lamont Hill, fired from CNN for endorsing a pro-Palestinian slogan.[28] If there's even a slight controversy around you, no matter how small it is, your boss may well just can you to avoid the headache. This means that even if it's a misunderstanding and the person accusing you deletes their accusation, you will still be let go. The solution to this is for workers to have labor unions.

In fact, the "outrage mobs" that "come for" people are often relatively powerless. Although white supremacist pseudo-scholar Charles Murray controversially had an event disrupted at Middlebury College, around the same time he successfully gave speeches at Harvard and Yale.[29] As Osita Nwanevu documents in an excellent *New Republic* essay on the myths around "cancel culture," generally speaking, the main thing the "social justice mobs" can do to people is yell at them on Twitter, and that what is called "cancellation" is usually "ordinary public disfavor voiced by ordinary people across new platforms."[30] And while nobody likes getting yelled at on Twitter, invoking the specter of "lynch mobs," "Robespierre," and "Maoism" is an insult to the millions of historical victims of actual violent repression by actual powerful oppressors. Nwanevu shows that generally, the "problematic" people who are "canceled" end up doing just fine. They suffer reputational consequences sometimes, meaning part of the public doesn't like them. But such is the price of having controversial opinions in public. (I get a lot of hate mail myself!)

The actual people who end up being "silenced" tend not to be those who say "politically incorrect" things. In fact, we should find it curious that so many of those who talk about silencing and censorship are so very widely heard. The voices that vanish from discussions, on the other hand, are immigrants in detention facilities, or incarcerated men and women in COVID-ridden prisons.[31] The nationalistic biases of the American media, for instance, are far more Orwellian than anything the left does.[32] Conservatives do not want us to talk about the actual "manufacturing of consent" in this country, so they spin a tale about a topsy-turvy world in which college students and Black and transgender people hold all the power, and rich white men are persecuted and sent to the gulag.

None of this is to say that "political correctness" is never annoying or unreasonable, or that social justice activists never do or say anything absurd. I believe we should have a forgiving and empathetic culture on the left that does not write people off for their transgressions. But I also think that many of the right's attacks on "social justice warriors" are unfair and misunderstand the arguments. They tend to involve stringing together the most extreme examples they can find (often college students) rather than trying to fair-mindedly examine the serious work of academics, activists, and journalists on racial and gender inequality.

Let me just finally discuss a few of the terms that people on the right love to hate, the kinds of "buzzwords" that are associated with the social justice left.

◊ **Microaggressions**—The "microaggression" concept, referring to actions and statements that are discriminatory in a subtle way, often annoys conservatives, because it appears to say that unintentional small offenses can be "aggressive." But whether we think the term is precise or not, the underlying phenomenon it's trying to point to is a very real one. Oftentimes, people *do* say things that are based on prejudiced underlying assumptions. And being subjected to lots of those small comments on a day-to-day basis can be a wearying and oppressive experience. The microaggression concept is meant to capture the fact that a lot of the bigotry that marginalized people experience is on the "micro" level, that it is in day-to-day encounters, and it is often subtle to the point where people are left wondering whether it was really there. (A Black person might wonder, for instance, whether what *looked* like a flicker of surprise when they said they were the manager was, in fact, surprise, or if they were just imagining it.) It is fair to say that it can be hard to prove the existence or intent of microaggressions, and personally, I am not wild about the *term*, but zeroing in on the way that prejudice subtly operates in ordinary encounters is critically important.[33]

◊ **Critical race theory**—The Trump administration's Office of Management and Budget adopted a measure designed to purge "critical race theory" (CRT) from federal agencies. Tom Cotton introduced a bill banning CRT from use in military training, saying, "Critical Race Theory teaches that race is a person's most important characteristic, and that America is an evil, oppressive place."[34] But is this true? I do not have space here to go into a full-length discussion of critical race theory,[35] but let me just give an anecdote: In college, I was assigned one of the seminal CRT texts, Derrick Bell's *Faces at the Bottom of the Well.* A professor at Harvard Law School, Bell staged a protest over the university's failure to hire any African American women as faculty. The book was not what I expected from a law professor. It contains a chilling science fiction story called "The Space Traders," in which extraterrestrials offer the United States a chance to pay off all its debts and receive incredible new energy-efficient technologies in exchange for sending the country's Black population to another planet to work as slaves. When I first read the story, I thought it was absurd, and that Bell was too cynical in thinking white people would make such an outrageous moral compromise. But as I continued to learn about the world, I came to realize that Bell's story made a profoundly important point: terrible trade-offs like this are already made all the time. The use of fossil fuels creates prosperity for some but terrible climate consequences for the Global South. White Americans who move to the suburbs and put their children in private schools, thereby starving Black schools in cities of their tax money, are showing this very kind of indifference. I was disturbed by Bell's story, but it challenged me profoundly, and I began to see that it was truer than I initially wanted to admit. Much of critical race theory is more conventionally "scholarly," but the academics who have developed it have challenged received wisdom in important ways. Everyone would benefit from engaging their ideas.

◊ **Safe spaces**—What is a "safe space"? It's a space for people to have conversations that are difficult to have in an ordinary public setting. Perhaps they are discussing a traumatizing experience. Perhaps they are worried people will judge them. Perhaps they believe they will be harassed. A safe space might be a particular place, or an event, but the point is to create an environment where people feel open to discussing something without suffering certain kinds of consequences. Alcoholics Anonymous, for instance, is a safe space for people who struggle with alcoholism to be honest and not have to fear judgment. Having safe spaces does not mean that people are being "coddled."[36]

◊ **Trigger warnings**—Much of the discourse about university students being "coddled" focuses on "trigger warnings," which are warnings placed on content that might be disturbing. The "trigger" term refers to content that might trigger a response from someone who has post-traumatic stress disorder (PTSD). The criticism points out that sometimes, content is given a warning in contexts that do not seem likely to trigger PTSD. Personally, I think the use of the "trigger" term is a little unfortunate, and that instead we should talk about "content warnings." It does not seem to me to be objectionable or infantilizing to place warnings on content that includes violence, sexual assault, racial slurs, etc. People's experiences vary and some people might need to prepare themselves to encounter things that are particularly disturbing. There's no "censorship" here, just a courtesy warning to people of what they are about to encounter. We place content warnings on *Current Affairs* articles so that people are not taken back when they encounter graphic content. It is simple politeness, and the conservative panic is strange.

◊ **Intersectionality**—It's a bit of a clunky term, but the basic premise of "intersectionality" is quite simple and reasonable, which is that people are part of many different groups, and they experience the world differently as a result of the way those groups diverge and overlap. A Black man, for instance, may be discriminated against for being Black, but will not experience the sexism that a white woman will receive. A Black woman will experience both sexism and racism. It is bizarre that a useful analytical tool for understanding the way that people can simultaneously be *in* an oppressed group and *not* in an oppressed group is treated by the right as some sort of esoteric theorizing.

◊ **Social justice**—Jonah Goldberg argues that "social justice" is an "abracadabra phrase" used to stand for "good things no one needs to argue for and no one dare be against." But that's not just true of "social" justice, it's true of justice generally. In fact, it's true of words like "progress" and "the good." These are terms that are vague, and people have many different ideas about what "justice" requires or what "progress" means. But that doesn't make the terms useless. "Social justice" is helpful because it draws our attention to the ways that justice is not just a matter of how each individual treats each other, but how the collective results of aggregate individual decisions can be just or unjust. For instance, you might be decent and kind to every individual person in your life, and give them their due, but you might also live in a country whose government is failing to meet people's basic needs. We will always disagree about what a "just society" looks like, just as we'll differ on what "democracy" looks like. But the fact that "democracy," too, is an abstract and contested term doesn't mean it is meaningless or unworthy of discussion.[37]

◊ **Identity politics**—Here is Jordan Peterson discussing "identity politics": "I think the whole group identity thing is seriously pathological. . . . Where we're making your group identity the most important thing about you. I think that is reprehensible. It is devastating. It is genocidal in its ultimate expression."[38] Genocidal! But Peterson here is only expressing an extreme version of a common argument, which even some leftists make, which says that "identity politics" is pernicious because it emphasizes group membership over individuality. I think part of this is a straw man, or at least goes after the least-defensible articulation of a position, because most people do not say that "the most important" thing about a person is their

group membership. What they do say is that your membership in certain groups affects your life in very important ways
whether you like it or not. It may be that transgender people
do not want being transgender to be a significant part of who
they are and simply want to live as the person they are, but
unfortunately, there are those like Peterson who are constantly
throwing doubt on their claims. In a non-oppressive world,
group identity wouldn't necessarily mean as much—the women's
movement only had to be a *women*'s movement because women
were subject to injustices that men were not subject to. Martin
Luther King Jr.—despite the attempts to misrepresent him as a
promoter of "color-blind" rhetoric—spoke constantly of broad
differences between Black Americans and white Americans
and the needs and interests of Black people. ("It is an unhappy
truth that racism is a way of life for the vast majority of white
Americans, spoken and unspoken, acknowledged and denied,
subtle and sometimes not so subtle—the disease of racism per-
meates and poisons a whole body politic.")[39] He did so because
Black people were being viciously oppressed by white people.
Identity politics has a purpose. I think this is often overlooked
by conservatives. Jonah Goldberg, for instance, says that identity politics means "my tribe deserves more than your tribe."[40]
But generally, the demands of identity groups are for equality,
not superiority. Black Lives Matter is not asking for Black lives
to matter the most, but for Black lives to stop being devalued.

◊ Much of the criticism of "identity politics" is also inconsistent;
many who oppose it are fine with proud group identities in
other contexts. They do not object to a proud Canadian or
proud New Yorker, but object to LGBT pride as something
perniciously anti-individualistic. Of course, it is absolutely
true that if particular groups lose interest in broader issues of
justice, and care only about their particular group interests, it
is more difficult to achieve justice. But this is precisely what
"intersectional" leftists are trying to overcome by showing that

while many of us suffer from different injustices in different ways, with overlap and divergence, we can all be part of a collective project together to build a more just world for all.

FURTHER READING

- Renni Eddo-Lodge—*Why I'm No Longer Talking to White People about Race*
- Emmanuel Acho—*Uncomfortable Conversations with a Black Man*
- Angela Y. Davis—*Women, Race & Class*
- Heather McGhee—*The Sum of Us: What Racism Costs Everyone and How We Can Prosper Together*

8

Socialized Medicine Will Kill Your Grandmother

[Medicare for All] would transform our entire health-care system into an iron-fisted centralized technocracy, with government bureaucrats and bioethicists controlling virtually every aspect of American health care from the delivery of medical treatment, to the payment of doctors, to even, perhaps, the building of hospitals. It would obliterate the health-insurance industry and legalize government seizure of pharmaceutical manufacturers' patents if they refuse to yield to government drug-price controls.

—Wesley J. Smith, "Medicare-for-All's Bitter Pill," *National Review*

Because of the massive support for M4A, the time is now to educate Americans on why such a system is the wrong prescription for our health care system. . . . We will have: new higher and new taxes, long waiting times, rationed care, and doctor shortages. . . . If America adopts single payer in the next few years, this country will be on the "Road to Serfdom."

—Sally Pipes, *False Premise, False Promise*

The Democrats' plan means that after a life of hard work and sacrifice, seniors would no longer be able to depend on the benefits they were promised. By eliminating Medicare as a program for seniors, and outlawing the ability of Americans to enroll in private and employer-based plans, the Democratic plan would inevitably lead to the massive rationing of health care. Doctors and hospitals would be put out of business. Seniors would lose access to their favorite doctors. There would be long wait lines for appointments

and procedures. Previously covered care would effectively
be denied. . . . In practice, the Democratic Party's so-called
Medicare for All would really be Medicare for None. Under
the Democrats' plan, today's Medicare would be forced to
die.

—Donald Trump, "Donald Trump: Democrats 'Medicare for All'
Plan Will Demolish Promises to Seniors,"
USA Today, Oct. 10, 2018

The Argument

Leftists advocate a government takeover of the healthcare system
in the form of the "Medicare for All" plan proposed by Senator
Bernie Sanders and Congresswoman Pramila Jayapal. Under this
single-payer plan, people would lose their health insurance by the
millions and their taxes would massively increase. The quality of
the healthcare they receive would go down, and there would be
massive rationing of services. People would not be able to pick
insurance plans that suited them, and government bureaucrats
would determine whether you live or die. Medicare for All is an
attempt to take away choice and impose centralized control.

The Response

The United States' healthcare system has very serious systemic
problems. You are probably familiar with them—multi-hundred-
thousand-dollar surprise bills, the search for "in-network" providers, protracted negotiations with insurance companies, sudden
losses of coverage, the endless confusing bureaucracy.[1] Tragically,
among sick Americans under sixty-five, approximately half had
trouble affording healthcare, and more than a third of people with
serious illnesses spend all or most of their savings on their care.[2]
People lose their entire retirement savings because of an unex-
pected medical problem. In plenty of other countries, this could
simply never happen. It's an entirely avoidable disaster.

The inefficiency of the current system is astounding. Health

scholars Abdul El-Sayed and Micah Johnson cite research showing that "one-sixth of a physician's work burden is attributable to
administrative overhead," and in one studied hospital, "staff spent
73 minutes preparing bills for an average patient," with "the emergency department [spending] more than 25 percent of its professional revenue simply processing bills."[3]

The core problem is that U.S. healthcare costs people far too
much money, and what you get for that money isn't actually very
good unless you're wealthy. As doctor and healthcare reporter
Elisabeth Rosenthal puts it in *An American Sickness: How Healthcare Became Big Business and How You Can Take It Back,* "The
American medical system has stopped focusing on health or even
science. Instead it attends more or less single-mindedly to its own
profits."[4] We are paying too much and we aren't getting enough
in return. The U.S. still has millions of people uninsured and un-
derinsured, and even people *with* insurance often find themselves
unable to afford the care they need.

But in other developed countries, this affordability problem has
largely been solved. In the U.K., for instance, the government simply runs hospitals that offer healthcare free at point of use.[5] The system is wildly popular and frees people of the burden of having to
think about money in relation to their medical care. In Canada, the
nationwide Medicare system pays for most health services for every
citizen and permanent resident.[6] Around the world, countries with
universal government health plans consistently outperform the
United States on a wide number of performance metrics. Their
healthcare systems are easier to use, cheaper, and deliver better
care. When you look at actual studies, instead of anecdotes about
a bad thing that happened in a British hospital, it's obvious that we
have problems that other countries do not. Here's the verdict of a
Commonwealth Fund report:

> The U.S. ranked last on performance overall, and ranked last
> or near last on the Access, Administrative Efficiency, Equity,

and Health Care Outcomes domains. The top-ranked countries overall were the U.K., Australia, and the Netherlands. Based on a broad range of indicators, the U.S. health system is an outlier, spending far more but falling short of the performance achieved by other high-income countries. The results suggest the U.S. health care system should look at other countries' approaches if it wants to achieve an affordable high-performing health care system that serves all Americans.[7]

The proposal known as "Medicare for All" simply gives the United States what these countries already have: a financing system that is proven to work. At the moment, health financing is a mess—a mixture of Medicare, Medicaid, employer-based private insurance plans, and plans purchased on the public exchanges. M4A would simplify the system, funding the whole system through progressive taxation rather than a mixture of taxes plus insurance premiums, co-pays, and deductibles. At the moment, Americans pay a fortune for healthcare, but a large amount of that money is wasted, siphoned off by the shareholders of private insurance companies or gobbled up by administrative costs. Medicare for All would just make all basic health coverage operate the same way Medicare already does for seniors, by having the federal government reimburse providers for their care.

This truly isn't a radical idea. It's no more of a "Big Government" idea than it is to have a public fire department.[8] We can easily see why it makes sense to have the government handle the provision of firefighting services rather than having a series of private fire departments (and private firefighting insurance companies). It's more efficient and it means people don't have to worry about whether they can afford to have a fire put out, because everyone knows they'll be covered. Yet even though the public service provision model obviously works for two 911 emergency services (fire and police), we hear stories about how scary and impossible it would be to apply it to the third (medical).[9]

One of the reasons these scare stories are effective is that a lot of skilled PR operatives work hard to make them sound plausible. Wendell Potter, a former top executive at Cigna who is now a pro–Medicare for All activist, told me in an interview that insurance companies like the one he worked for spend considerable resources figuring out how to mislead the public. This is because they know that insurance industry profits are dependent on the maintenance of our current dysfunctional system. Potter said that the efforts to mislead us are very sophisticated:

> I was pretty good at spreading misinformation and obscuring important truths about the health insurance business and the health care system in this country. I became a really pretty good propagandist, so I know how it's done. I know how much money is spent to hire PR firms to work with linguists, to work with a lot of different people to come up with just the right words and phrases to manipulate public opinion and to come up with campaigns that are designed to scare people away from any kinds of proposals to create a system that's not like ours. . . . Over many years, we were successful in getting people to believe things that just simply are not true about the Canadian healthcare system. . . . The work that my colleagues and I did was to really make the term "single-payer," for example, very toxic so that Democrats in Congress would shy away from it.[10]

And shy away from it they did! Democrats like Joe Biden and Pete Buttigieg have refused to endorse a Medicare for All system, sometimes echoing insurance industry talking points in the process.[11]

But if we try to escape the mental influence of carefully crafted insurance industry talking points, and think about healthcare rationally, it becomes obvious why a "single payer," Medicare for All system makes sense. Having a single government plan would create a formidable new mechanism for reining in the spiraling costs of healthcare, because Medicare would have the power to set rates unilaterally. This is a good thing, because it would keep for-profit drug companies and hospitals from being able to extort sick people. M4A would also be far more efficient than private insurance, and make life easier for both doctors and patients by drastically simplifying the financing process. By funding healthcare through taxation, the government could ensure that costs were borne fairly according to people's ability to pay. Finally, because the people have some democratic control over the government, unlike with private insurance companies, their health dollars are actually being spent by an institution they have a say in the running of, and which exists to serve their interests rather than the interests of profiteers.

Unfortunately, it is difficult to have an intelligent conversation about Medicare for All because there is a great deal of confusion around what exactly it would consist of and what exactly it would do. That confusion is, in part, deliberate, as Potter notes, because of the decades that for-profit insurance companies have spent spreading misleading information about single-payer plans in an effort to sway American public opinion. So we need to cut through the thicket of bad talking points and understand precisely what M4A would mean for them and for the healthcare system. There isn't space to deal with all of these here—though between them, the "Further Reading" selections respond to just about everything that could possibly be said against the idea. But here are some ways the talking points are misleading.

◊ **Medicare for All will raise your taxes.** You should be insulted by this talking point, because it assumes that you are stupid. The point of Medicare for All is to *save* people money, because instead of you paying premiums, co-pays, and deductibles, healthcare payments will be made by the government and funded with taxes. People who point to the taxes are only looking at one side of the equation: the money you pay in taxes will be more than made up for by the money you save from not having to pay your insurance company or healthcare provider directly.[12] Only the wealthiest would pay more in taxes than they had saved. It's almost certain to be a good deal for you financially.[13]

◊ **Medicare for All will take away your insurance.** Medicare for All is very popular in polls, but opponents often cite polling showing that when you tell people it takes away their insurance, they are much less supportive. But telling people M4A "takes away their insurance" is very misleading because it implies that it is leaving them uninsured and that they won't have coverage. In fact, M4A *supersedes* their insurance and leaves nobody uncovered. Instead of misleadingly implying that people will be left without coverage, it's important to tell them the truth, which is that their coverage would immediately improve without any gaps.

◊ **Medicare for All will take away choices.** In fact, the private health insurance industry already reduces choices, by only paying for care for providers within your "network." When people talk about "reduced choice," what they mean is that there are fewer choices of *insurance plans* under a single-payer system. But this is like saying that the switch from private firefighting companies to public fire departments "took away people's choice of firefighting insurance plans." It's technically true, but what people want from a fire service is not "choice." They want their house to be protected! Likewise, in medicine, they want access to care, and that's what M4A maximizes.

◊ **Medicare for All will create a rationing bureaucracy that determines what healthcare you can receive.** You already live with a rationing bureaucracy. It's called your insurance company, and the difference between it and the federal government is that your insurance company is financially incentivized to deny you care because every dollar it doesn't spend on you is a dollar it can keep in profits. No healthcare system will have limitless funding and resources available, but the choice is not between "bureaucracy" and "no bureaucracy," but between a private, for-profit bureaucracy and a public, democratically overseen, not-for-profit bureaucracy.

FURTHER READING

- Abdul El-Sayed and Micah Johnson—*Medicare for All: A Citizen's Guide*
- Gerald Friedman—*The Case for Medicare for All*
- Wendell Potter—*Deadly Spin: An Insurance Company Insider Speaks Out on How Corporate PR Is Killing Health Care and Deceiving Americans*
- Elisabeth Rosenthal—*An American Sickness: How Health-care Became Big Business and How You Can Take It Back*
- James F. Burdick—*Talking about Single Payer: Health Care Equality for America*

9

Scandinavian Social Democracy Won't Work in the United States

I'm not denying the existence of Nordic socialism. Nor do I deny that this type of socialism works to a point. What I deny is that it can be imported here. We cannot have Scandinavian socialism because we don't have the conditions for it. Our type of society doesn't permit it.

—Dinesh D'Souza, *United States of Socialism*

Finland is as big as two Missouris, but with just 5.2 million residents, it's ethnically and religiously homogeneous. A strong Lutheran work ethic, combined with a powerful sense of probity, dominates the society. Homogeneity has led to consensus: Every significant Finnish political party supports the welfare state and, broadly speaking, the high taxation that makes it possible.

—Robert G. Kaiser, an associate editor of the *Washington Post*, after a three-week trip to Finland in 2005

It's easier to get people to buy into a collectivist idea when everyone has a lot in common.

—Jim Geraghty, "Ten Reasons We Can't, and Shouldn't, Be Nordic," *National Review*

The Argument

Many progressives point to the generous welfare states of European countries as a model the United States should follow. But these countries' models simply will not work here because the United States is very different.

The Response

Some conservatives acknowledge that the Nordic countries work well despite generous social safety nets. But they argue that this model could not possibly work in the United States because those countries are small and ethnically homogeneous, whereas the United States is large and multiethnic. They argue that Scandinavian social democracy is built on a cultural solidarity that is absent from the American context. I refer to this argument as the "fjords argument," because to me, the logic of it makes me think of an argument like:

> Norway has generous paid family leave policies. But Norway also has fjords. The United States does not have fjords. A policy that works in a country with fjords will not necessarily work in a country without fjords.

In other words, the argument depends on identifying differences between Scandinavian countries and the United States, but only weakly tries to actually explain why those differences are relevant to the discussion. Here's Fox News's Pete Hegseth in *American Crusade*:

> Besides a handful of small, homogeneous, isolated, and irrelevant countries, can you name one country in which socialism has ever worked? . . . Socialism apologists always cite countries such as Norway, Sweden, Finland, and Denmark. Their argument is so foolish. First, the combined population of these countries is roughly 26.5 million people, less than 10 percent of the United States' population. . . . Second, when was the last time that Norway, Sweden, Finland, or Denmark mattered in the international context?[1]

There is a missing link in the argument here, of course, which is *why* the population difference is relevant, or why it matters for the viability of social welfare programs that Norway doesn't "matter in the international context." But as bad as Hegseth is, D'Souza is somehow even worse, writing that Scandinavian socialist policies were "developed for people named Sven." Because the United States does not have many Svens, and "no American socialist wants America's racial landscape to resemble that of Denmark, Norway, Sweden, or Finland," we cannot have these socialist policies.

But why would the U.S.' greater racial diversity make it impossible to have, for example, more guaranteed family leave? Why would Svens-per-capita make a difference? Usually, people making this argument point to high levels of social trust in Scandinavian countries. But the question is what about the *policies* makes them incapable of functioning in the U.S. There is no reason to think that the United States *is* "collectivist" enough for Medicare and Social Security to be popular, but *not* collectivist enough for a truly universal healthcare program or paid parental leave. The idea is that here in the U.S., we distrust and despise one another and follow an Individualist Ethic that prevents us from pulling together. But while many of us may be tempted to believe that cynical story about the country, the question is whether it's *true,* and public support for social democratic policies suggests that the real problem is politicians who repeat that the U.S. simply cannot have these programs.

For instance, take family support. The socialist think tank People's Policy Project notes that "relative to its European peers, the United States spends virtually nothing on benefits for families with children," which "denies many people the ability to have the families that they want and inflicts financial ruin on many of those who go through with parenthood despite the lack of social support."[2] To rectify this, the PPP proposes that the United States introduce policies similar to those found in many European countries. Specifically, the PPP advocates a suite of five new benefits it calls the "Family Fun Pack":

1. Expectant parents will "receive a baby box that contains essential baby items like clothes, diapers, and wipes."
2. "Around the time of the birth of a child, parents will be eligible to take a total of 36 weeks of job-protected leave from work and receive an income benefit from the Social Security Administration while they are on leave."
3. "Parents with children between the ages of six months and three years will be provided a free spot in a public child care center."
4. "Children between the ages of three and five will be eligible to attend free public pre-K."
5. "All children in public child care, public pre-K, and public K–12 schools will be eligible to receive a free lunch during the day."

The PPP notes that many of these policies exist in countries around the world (Finland and Scotland offer baby boxes), and some even exist in U.S. states (for instance, Oklahoma offers free, high-quality public pre-K).[3] There is no reason why these pro-family policies can't be introduced nationwide, and conservative attempts to prove that they are impossible often smack of desperation. For instance, Kevin D. Williamson, in *The Politically Incorrect Guide to Socialism,* says that "effective public institutions are characteristic of societies with high levels of social trust, and Sweden is just such a society. The bad news for the rest of the world—but especially for highly complex societies such as the United States, India, and China—is that the social conditions that produce the high levels of trust are not generally transmutable."[4] But this is pure baloney: China, for instance, has produced some *extremely* effective public institutions,[5] reluctant as those in the U.S. might be to admit it.

Americans who believe their country is the best in the world sometimes don't like to accept that other countries have it better in many respects. It's possible to have good public schools and good public transit, but we don't. If Americans take a look around the world, they might be frustrated, even enraged, that in the richest country in the world, we don't have certain things that plenty of other less-rich countries have managed to provide to their people. A convenient way to rationalize this is to say that these countries are simply *different*, and to point to features they possess that allow them to do things that we can't. So, for instance, these countries have ethno-religious homogeneity. The U.S. doesn't. So take your eyes off Scandinavia. But this is cheap trickery. Public childcare centers can be built in the U.S., and the only question is whether we can muster the political willpower to build them.[6]

FURTHER READING

- Mary Hilson—*The Nordic Model: Scandinavia since 1945*
- George Lakey—*Viking Economics: How the Scandinavians Got It Right—and How We Can, Too*
- Nik Brandal et al.—*The Nordic Model of Social Democracy*
- Anu Partanen—*The Nordic Theory of Everything: In Search of a Better Life*

10

The Welfare State Will Lead Us Down the "Road to Serfdom"

The increasing veneration for the state, the admiration of power, and of bigness for bigness' sake, the enthusiasm for "organization" of everything (we now call it "planning") and that "inability to leave anything to the simple power of organic growth" . . . are all scarcely less marked in England now than they were in Germany.

—Friedrich von Hayek, *The Road to Serfdom*

The Argument

In 1944, free-market economist Friedrich von Hayek published a book called *The Road to Serfdom,* which argued that the government direction of economic activity was dangerous. Centralized planning, he argued, was not only inefficient and bureaucratic, but inherently took us toward authoritarianism. Hayek worried that Western democracies, though they might defeat Nazi Germany at war, were themselves on the "road to serfdom" because they had embraced a collectivist ideology. "What our generation has forgotten is that the system of private property is the most important guarantee of freedom, not only for those who own property, but scarcely less for those who do not," Hayek wrote. Hayek's book made an unabashed *slippery slope* argument, suggesting that today's "idealists" would be tomorrow's "fanatics," unless Western countries took a sharp U-turn from their present course.

The Response

Hayek's book became one of the most influential staples of conservative literature and experienced a significant revival during the Tea Party years. But it's strange that it should have become a classic, when its core argument was almost immediately refuted. Britain, in 1944, did not listen to Hayek's critique that it had become "scarcely less" state-worshiping than Hitler's Germany. Instead, after the war ended in 1945, the British public immediately voted out Winston Churchill and his Conservative government, putting the openly socialist Labour Party into power instead. Under Prime Minister Clement Attlee, Labour drastically *expanded* the use of government power, nationalizing public utilities and major industries and introducing a new national old-age insurance system as well as new unemployment benefits, widow's benefits, sick leave, and orphans' allowances. They increased subsidies for public housing and created a system of national parks and a nationalized town-planning system. Most notably, Attlee's government—under militant socialist health minister Aneurin Bevan—introduced the National Health Service, a fully socialized healthcare system that offered all Britons a full range of medical services free at point of use at government-run hospitals.

The Attlee government's policies were Hayek's nightmare fulfilled, a massive escalation of state "planning." And what happened? The National Health Service became the most respected institution in Britain, by some accounts even more cherished than the monarchy.[1] Contrary to anecdotal accounts of poor care, the NHS ranks highly on international comparisons of healthcare delivery systems. Clement Attlee is consistently ranked by historians as one of the greatest, if not the greatest, prime ministers in British history for his successful rebuilding of the country after World War II and establishment of the modern welfare state.

Conservatives will undoubtedly point out that by the 1970s, some of Britain's nationalized industries had developed a reputation for poor performance. But the question of the relative economic performance of public versus private industry is separate from the question of whether Hayek was right about planning being the route to *totalitarian government*. Passenger cars produced by the partly nationalized British Leyland Motor Corporation in the late seventies may not have been known for their reliability or speed, but at no point did the United Kingdom become anything that a rational person could conceivably call a "totalitarian society." In fact, "free at point of use" health services were a boon for people's personal freedom.[2]

Even conservative political philosopher Francis Fukuyama argues that Hayek's basic thesis that "the smallest move toward the expansion of government would lead to a cascade of bad consequences that would result in full-blown authoritarian socialism" was "the slipperiest of slippery slope arguments,"[3] and that the subsequent five decades of history refuted the idea decisively. The British experience was repeated elsewhere. In the 1960s, Canada introduced its single-payer Medicare system. Today in Canada, there is "overwhelming support—86.2 percent—for strengthening public health care rather than expanding for-profit services,"[4] and Tommy Douglas, the socialist minister credited with bringing about the program, is nationally beloved, having been voted the "greatest Canadian" in a 2004 poll.[5]

Hayek's extreme formulation, then, was simply silly. Whether a state-run enterprise succeeds or fails, there is nothing inherent about having the government produce and distribute goods and services that makes it likely violent authoritarianism will result. We can understand why, looking at the horrors of both Nazi Germany and Stalin's USSR, Hayek might have feared that a similarly oppressive and all-powerful state could appear in Britain. Indeed, perhaps it could have. But that was not an inevitable result of nationalizing industry, which can be conducted in more democratic or less democratic fashions. The experience of countries that defied Hayek's recommendations shows that he was decisively refuted.

FURTHER READING

- John Bew—*Citizen Clem: A Biography of Attlee*
- Nicholas Timmins—*The Five Giants: A Biography of the Welfare State*

11

The Nazis Were Socialists

With Hitler . . . we see a dedicated socialist who, shortly after assuming the leadership of the German Workers' Party, changed its name to the National Socialist German Workers' Party (NSDAP). . . . If you read the Nazi platform without knowing its source, you could easily be forgiven for thinking you were reading the 2016 platform of the Democratic Party.

—Dinesh D'Souza, *The Big Lie*

The Argument
It should be obvious that a group calling itself the "National *Socialists*" were socialists, but the left has persisted in portraying Nazi fascism as a right-wing phenomenon. In fact, the Nazis were Big Government collectivists who believed that the individual will should be subordinated to the glory of the group, just like today's leftists. In their desire for complete state control over economic and cultural life, the Nazis did not resemble any political tendency of the right—which believes in small government and individual liberty. Rather, Nazism was just a variation on the same collectivist tendencies that animated Stalinist socialism.

The Response
It should be perfectly easy to see why Adolf Hitler's "National Socialists" had nothing to do with socialism, just as it should be easy to see why Kim Jong-un's "Democratic People's Republic of Korea" has nothing to do with democracy or republicanism. After all, what do socialists stand for? Well, a few core principles are:

◊ *A classless society*—socialists believe that there shouldn't be a small caste of people who own and control everything, and a large majority of people who must sell their labor to the powerful.

◊ *Anti-racism and women's liberation*—socialists believe that "workers of the world must unite," and see ethnocentrism as a way of dividing people so that they do not recognize what they have in common. And because socialists deplore hierarchy and exploitation, the domination of women by men has historically been an important socialist concern.

◊ *Anti-militarism*—socialists have historically deplored war and conquest, in which working people are forced to murder their counterparts in other countries. From Eugene Debs's imprisonment for opposing World War I, to the Vietnam protest movement, to the Iraq War, socialists have been the ones saying no to aggressive and futile wars and envisioning a world of peace.

Socialists follow the principle of solidarity. You can hear this in Debs's famous quote: "While there is a lower class, I am in it . . . and while there is a soul in prison, I am not free." There are echoes of it in Bernie Sanders's exhortation to "fight for someone even if they are not like you and you do not share their problems." If you ask socialists what they believe, they will talk about elevating the weak and downtrodden and guaranteeing the basic rights of all to a decent standard of living.

We can therefore ask: How many of these beliefs did the Nazis share? And the answer is: absolutely none of them. Nazis did not believe in the elimination of social class, but in a rigid caste system. They were not feminists and anti-racists; they practiced racist genocide. They were not against militarism and prisons and the death penalty; they were history's worst murderers.

Did they believe, like Debs, that their own freedom depended on the elimination of prisons, that "while there is a soul in prison,

I am not free"? No, they built giant death camps! Did they believe in the principle of "from each according to their ability, to each according to their need"? No, they massacred and enslaved the weak and disabled. Did they believe in worker ownership? Did they think, as socialists do, that racism is an illusion used to divide workers and keep them from recognizing the common interests of the working class? Everything socialists stand for was opposed by the Nazis, which is why they killed countless communists and members of the socialist German Social Democratic Party.

So the most obvious reason for thinking that Nazism wasn't socialism is that the things Nazis believed are rejected entirely by socialists, and the things socialists believe were rejected entirely by Nazis. All that is left is the name "National Socialism," but Hitler himself said that "our adopted term 'Socialist' has nothing to do with Marxian Socialism."[1] Instead, it was a piece of branding, like all the dictatorships that call themselves the Extremely Democratic Totally Non-Dictatorial People's Democracy.

How—given that Bernie Sanders is Jewish and advocating free-at-point-of-use healthcare and workplace democracy, while Adolf Hitler was advocating the extermination of all Jews and the elimination of democracy—can anyone even making the argument that "the Nazis were socialist" do so with a straight face? Well, usually they do it by offering an incorrect definition of socialism that renders the case much easier to make.

The incorrect definition is: socialism means "government control of the economy." Many critics of socialism use this definition. Senator Rand Paul uses it in *The Case against Socialism,* which includes a part about how the Nazis were socialists.[2] Jamie Dimon appeared to use it when he said that young socialists don't understand that "most state-owned enterprises don't do a good job."[3] And George Reisman uses it in his Mises Institute article "Why Nazism Was Socialism and Why Socialism Is Totalitarian."[4] Reisman says the actual substance of ownership of the means of production resided in the German government. Reisman says that "socialism, understood as an economic system based on government ownership of the means of production, positively requires a totalitarian dictatorship," and he sets out to prove that in Hitler's Germany, it was "the German government and not the nominal private owners that exercised all of the substantive powers of ownership." Reisman says that it is strange that so few people think of Hitler as a socialist, given that he called himself one and that the Third Reich satisfied the criteria for a socialist economy.

One thing I find funny about socialism's critics is that they have a tendency to say things like "young people today don't understand what socialism means," even as they themselves offer an obviously wrong definition of the term. I say "obviously wrong" because when we think about the implications of "socialism" being synonymous with "government control of production," we realize instantly that this can't be right. It would mean that any government that was sufficiently powerful would automatically be "socialist" no matter who ruled it. The worst dictatorships would all be socialism *by definition,* because socialism is *defined* as government control. A monarchy could be "socialist" if the king was powerful enough. A feudal aristocracy could be "socialist" if those who "governed" also "controlled production." This would be ludicrous, though, because it would mean that an economy in which a giant caste of wage laborers served a tiny wealthy aristocracy would be "socialist," so that a society violating every single principle socialists endorse would be said to satisfy their principles.

The reason this definition goes so badly off the rails is that it fails to consider basic socialist concepts like class, democracy, equality, and exploitation. Government control of production gets you nothing if your society is still stratified by class, undemocratic, highly unequal, and filled with exploitation. Everything depends on the kind of government you have. When socialists talk about their economic ideal, they speak of worker ownership, which is not the same as "government ownership." The government, after all, could be feudalism, in which case government ownership would give the workers nothing. Socialists want to see a world in which the people who *do the labor* have control over their workplaces. This is also why "communist" countries that are authoritarian dictatorships should not be called "socialist" even if they claim the label for themselves. To know whether an economy is socialist, you have to look at how equal it is, how much power workers have, whether people are exploited, and who is in charge of what. (When you do this, you find that the more socialistic a country is, the better off people are.)[5]

Now, socialism may *involve* some government ownership of production, because democratic government is the institution through which people are able to act collectively. But it also might not involve government at all; many socialists historically have been anarchists. Government ownership is a means for achieving socialistic ends, it is not *inherently* or automatically socialistic. For example, I believe in publicly owned airports[6] and fret about the possibility of private corporations replacing public services,[7] but if we lived under a dictatorship, I'd favor less government ownership and more cooperative "private" ownership. The public sector is good to the extent that it's democratic, just like the private sector is bad to the extent that it's undemocratic.[8]

All right, so socialism does not mean "government control of production." Therefore, proving that the Nazis controlled production does not prove they were socialists. But it is worth noting here that *even if* socialism was "government control of production," the argument that "the Nazis were socialists" would still be incredibly misleading. When people say "the Nazis were socialists," what they want you to *hear* is "socialism and Nazism are synonymous." They want you to believe that if they can prove Nazi Germany had a socialist economy, it shows that socialist economies are totalitarianism. But the reasoning is fallacious for the same reason that "Hitler was a vegetarian, therefore vegetarianism and Nazism are synonymous" is fallacious. Let us stipulate, for the sake of argument, that (1) socialism means "state-controlled production" and

(2) Nazis had state-controlled production. This is *only* for the sake of argument, since (1), as I have pointed out, is false, and (2) can be the subject of historical critique over the extent of public versus private control in the Third Reich.

But for now, let's say they're true: What have we proven? Very little. The features that horrify us about Nazi Germany generally relate to their racist militarism: they were homicidal maniacs who tried to conquer the world. My problem with Nazis is not that the state was too involved in the economy, but that they tortured and murdered millions upon millions of people. If they had had "government control of production" *without* the racist, genocidal, militaristic, antihuman elements, then they would lack the elements that horrify us. People who say, "The Nazis were socialists because the state controlled production," are trying to get you to associate one aspect of Nazi Germany (power of the state sector in the economy) with the other (the racist genocide). Like "vegetarian Hitler," the attempt is to show that because two things occurred together in an instance, they are related. The reason you know it's silly is that the moment we look at other cases, we see that it is *not* true that state direction of economic activities means a Nazi-like government. You can say, "The Nazis had a state-run healthcare system."[9] But Britain has a state-run healthcare system and does not have a Nazi government.

George Reisman, in his Mises Institute article, attempts to prove that government intervention in the economy *requires* totalitarianism of the Nazi kind by necessity. He says, for example, of price controls:

> The requirements merely of enforcing price-control regulations is the adoption of essential features of a totalitarian state, namely, the establishment of the category of "economic crimes," in which the peaceful pursuit of material self-interest is treated as a criminal offense, and the establishment of a totalitarian police apparatus replete with spies and informers and the power of

arbitrary arrest and imprisonment. Clearly, the enforcement of price controls requires a government similar to that of Hitler's Germany or Stalin's Russia, in which practically anyone might turn out to be a police spy and in which a secret police exists and has the power to arrest and imprison people. If the government is unwilling to go to such lengths, then, to that extent, its price controls prove unenforceable and simply break down. . . . In order to obtain convictions, the government must place the decision about innocence or guilt in the case of black-market transactions in the hands of an administrative tribunal or its police agents on the spot. It cannot rely on jury trials, because it is unlikely that many juries can be found willing to bring in guilty verdicts in cases in which a man might have to go to jail for several years for the crime of selling a few pounds of meat or a pair of shoes above the ceiling price.

Here you see an example of free-market rhetoric as speculative fiction. Instead of examining the world as it *is*, Reisman tells a story about a world as it could be, if a certain set of assumptions were true, and how things would operate in that world. In fact, we have minimum wages and we have rent control and laws against price gouging, and neither has required a "government similar to that of Hitler's Germany or Stalin's Russia." Now, libertarians argue that these are bad policies (they say that minimum wages cause unemployment and rent control limits the housing supply, neither of which appears to be true, see Argument #2), but to say that the enforcement of these laws has been Nazi-like requires an abuse of language that insults the victims of the Holocaust and Stalin's gulags.[10]

In conclusion, then:

1. You can only argue that "Nazis were socialists" if you adopt a definition of socialism that conflicts with the values held by socialists and ignores the entire point of the doctrine, which is not to increase the power of the state but to eliminate class

hierarchy. In order to understand what socialism is, you should listen to the people who call themselves socialists rather than saying that *they* don't understand their own political ideology, while you (with an unworkable and clearly false definition) do understand it.

2. Even if Nazis had complete control of production, and control of production was synonymous with socialism, that still wouldn't tell us that socialism was bad or that socialism is Nazism, because the actual thing that is bad about Nazism is its crimes against humanity and not its industrial policy. The fact that a Nazi did something is not proof that it is bad (vegetarian Hitler argument), and if the Nazis *had* been economic socialists, then the "socialism" part would not have been the crime.

3. Hitler himself said that the thing he was calling "socialism" had nothing to do with leftist socialism. The Nazis deplored Marxism and wiped out social democrats by the score.

It's rather ironic that the Mises Institute tries to connect socialism and fascism, given that Ludwig von Mises himself, the great free-market libertarian, infamously said that "it cannot be denied that Fascism and similar movements aimed at the establishment of dictatorships are full of the best intentions and that their intervention has for the moment saved European civilization."[11] But the important point is this: Wherever this argument comes up, we must laugh it out of the room. It makes no sense. It has never made sense. The only people who deploy it are people who are unwilling to look seriously at history or to try to understand what socialism has historically meant to those who have believed in it.

Further Reading

For this argument, it may help to read some books explaining what socialism *actually* is, so that you can show the *complete lack of overlap* with Nazi racist nationalism.

- Nathan J. Robinson—*Why You Should Be a Socialist*
- Danny Katch—*Socialism . . . Seriously: A Brief Guide to Human Liberation*
- Hadas Thier—*A People's Guide to Capitalism: An Introduction to Marxist Economics*
- Bernie Sanders—*Our Revolution: A Future to Believe In*
- Bhaskar Sunkara—*The Socialist Manifesto: The Case for Radical Politics in an Era of Extreme Inequality*

12

Feminism Hurts Both Men and Women

Their cry is they want to abolish the patriarchy, and anything that hurts men is something that pleases the feminists. . . . There is a war on men, and [feminists] are very open about it. . . . They don't conceal it; they brag about it. . . . They said that husbands are not necessary in a marriage, they're not necessary in raising children.

—Phyllis Schlafly, quoted in *WorldNetDaily*

#MeToo is perceived as a feminist crusade, but the truth is more complicated. Feminists were early adopters of the sexual revolution, perceiving it as a key tenet of their liberation agenda. By rejecting modesty, courtship, and chivalry, feminists of the 1960s and 1970s rejected the safe harbor of marriage and family and invited the social chaos that has left so many women struggling to raise children by themselves and feeling exhausted, insecure, and cynical. It has also left many men aimless, addicted, angry, and alone.

—Mona Charen, "The Price of Feminism," *National Review*

[It's] the feminists, celebrities and politicians spreading this wage gap myth who have the math problem. Here's why: The 77-cents-on-the-dollar statistic is calculated by dividing the median earnings of all women working full-time by the median earnings of all men working full-time. In other words, if the average income of all men is, say, 40,000 dollars a year, and the average annual income of all women is, say, 30,800 dollars, that would mean that women earn 77 cents for every dollar a man earns. 30,800 divided by 40,000 equals .77. But these calculations don't reveal a gender wage injustice because it doesn't take into account occupation, position, education or hours worked per week. Even a study by the American Association of University Women, a feminist organization, shows that the actual wage gap shrinks to only 6.6 cents when you factor in different choices men and women make. And the key word here is "choice." The small wage gap that does exist has nothing to do with paying women less, let alone with sexism; it has to do with differences in individual career choices that men and women make.

—Christina Hoff Sommers,
"There Is No Gender Wage Gap," PragerU

The Argument

Feminists are militants who despise men and refuse to accept biological facts about male-female differences. They peddle phony, easily debunked statistics purporting to show the existence of a "rape culture" or "patriarchy." Feminists attribute differences in men's and women's roles and jobs to gender discrimination when, in fact, they are the result of freely made choices. They have contempt for women who accept traditional gender roles, even though feminism does not actually empower women. Feminism overlooks the unique harms that are visited on boys and men, and ultimately hurts both men and women. Furthermore, the #MeToo movement, while well-intentioned, erodes due process and encourages false accusations.

The Response

Let's first deal with the question of whether the gender wage gap exists. First, note that while Sommers says she is arguing that there "is no" gender wage gap, she is not in fact arguing this. She is arguing that the gender wage gap exists, but is *justified*. This is important to notice. The people who say the gender pay gap "doesn't exist" actually admit there is a pay gap, because women working full-time earn, on average, much less than what men do. What they, in fact, are arguing is that this gap is acceptable because it is the result of women's own choices rather than the result of discrimination. Women's jobs might pay worse, but that is because they chose to have worse-paying jobs rather than better-paying jobs. Notice that while Sommers says she is going to prove that there is no gender wage gap, she quickly slips into arguing something very different, which is that there is no gender wage "injustice."

The question, then, is whether we think the fact that women working full-time jobs tend to earn less than men working full-time jobs is an injustice. Those, like Sommers, who think it isn't an injustice, argue that when you take into account things like "position" and "education," the gap disappears. So, if at a company there are five male managers and one female manager, the female manager probably does not earn a substantially different salary to the male managers. Any "gender pay gap" at the company exists because women are in lower-ranked, lower-paid positions in the company. Or, if we take the fields of teaching and engineering, it is probably the case that a similarly experienced male teacher and female teacher at the same school earn similar salaries. Same with a similarly experienced male engineer and female engineer at the same company. But in the group as a whole, there is a gender pay disparity because teaching is a lower-paid profession than engineering, and teaching tends to have more women than men, while engineering has more men than women.

For libertarians like Sommers, this eliminates the injustice. This is because they adopt (1) a free-market conception of social value, where people get paid in accordance with what they produce and (2) a notion of choice that sees people's occupations as functions of their desires and decisions rather than unjust social and economic pressures. If you think engineers get paid a lot because they create more value for others than teachers, and you think people are perfectly free to choose whatever profession they like, then the gender pay gap becomes a nonissue. Clearly women are making the rational choice to earn less because they like teaching more, which is okay. Accepting that there is no gender wage injustice, then, means accepting the moral premises of laissez-faire libertarianism. As leftist policy writer Matt Bruenig writes, "Unequal pay for identical work is not the only way that a labor market can be sexist. A labor market that sorts men into higher-paying jobs and women into lower-paying jobs is still sexist, just in a different way."[1]

Next, let's look at "patriarchy" and the #MeToo movement. It is indisputable that, until 1920 (meaning during the lifetimes of some people who are still alive), the United States was explicitly a patriarchy, because women were not even allowed to exercise any control over the government. This, it should be remembered, means that many laws that are still on the books (including the U.S. Constitution itself) were made through a process that 50 percent of the population was not allowed any input into.

But we live in 2022, not 1920. Is there still a "patriarchy"? *The Guardian* notes that "many people would question the existence of something called 'patriarchy' to begin with—pointing to the strides made in gender equality over the past century, and insisting that instances of sexism are individual and isolated, destined to fade further over time, rather than evidence of a persistent structure of inequality."[2] Indeed, the vice presidency of Kamala Harris was inconceivable in 1920. And yet: it is not only still the case that there has never been a female president, but women make up just over one-fourth of Congress, and *none* of the country's top-twenty highest-paid executives are women.[3] The gender pay gap is actually huge—the median woman between ages 25 and 54 earns $25,000 while the median man earns $41,000, meaning that a woman will tend to earn an astonishing 39 percent less than a man.[4]

Now, those numbers include the population of people who do not work full-time jobs, meaning that one reason a woman might be earning much less than a man is that she is a full-time home-maker rather than holding formal employment. Christina Hoff Sommers would find the statistic outrageously deceptive: these women are *choosing* not to work. But raising children can be a full-time job, and it is one that people are not paid to do. No matter what the *reasons* for the gap are, the fact remains that women are accumulating far less wealth than men. And because wealth con-fers freedom and power, this means that women are far less free and far less powerful, and not just because there are fewer women in high-ranking positions of decision-making power. Now, you can blame this on "choice" if you like, but much of it clearly isn't choice in any meaningful sense—women clearly don't *want* to hold more student debt than men, but they do. If women start with less wealth, and thus must take on more debt for their educa-tions, they are choosing to go to school, but they are not choosing for it to be more of a financial burden on them than it is on men. That's a situation they have inherited.

Economic wealth and power are only one dimension of gender inequality. The #MeToo movement has arisen to expose the ways that powerful men are able to get away with sexual harassment and assault, often for many years, because women (especially in the workplace or at school) have a limited ability to hold them to account. The movement brought forward a cascade of accounts that had been kept secret for years, often because the perpetrator was someone in a position of power, like the boss with control over promotions or the professor with control over grades.

Critics of #MeToo have suggested that men have been un-fairly targeted and do not receive "due process"—journalist Glenn Greenwald has said the "whole Me Too movement was about de-stroying people based on accusations that are unproven."[5] But it's often *impossible* to prove incidents of abuse and harassment, in part because abusers and harassers carefully select situations in which there are no witnesses and the incident will be "he said, she said." This is part of why even serial rapists like Harvey Weinstein or Bill Cosby are able to get away with crimes for decades. It is certainly the case that #MeToo, being a social movement and not a judicial process, is not an optimal way of ensuring accountability for wrongdoing, and many accusers would prefer that there was a means of redress other than having their assault splashed all over the press. But those who think it has "gone too far" need to answer serious questions about how harassment and abuse can be prevented and dealt with.

Common to criticism of feminism is a lack of interest in the very serious problems that feminism has arisen in response to. We see this in the way that Hoff Sommers dismisses the pay gap; it exists, she admits, but she just doesn't care about it because she chalks it up to choice. Likewise, those who lament the fates of men accused should show similar interest in the pain of women whose lives are wrecked by predators.

Phyllis Schlafly said that feminists wage a "war on men" in part because they don't think "husbands are necessary." Well, husbands *aren't* necessary. If people want husbands, they can have them, but Schlafly assumes that what she enjoys is what ought to be enjoyed by everyone. There is no "war on men," there is a war on the *dominance* of men. It is a war on the idea that men's prejudices are rational while women's are emotional, and on the endless subtle ways in which men tend to have life easier. (I've found in my own life that many things I do that are taken as signs of eccentric genius would be treated as symptoms of insanity if I were female.) Hyperbolic nonsense about feminism—which has been repeated ad nauseam since the feminist movement first arose—has made it impossible to have a sensible discussion about the central claims, namely that there are specific gender-based social injustices that need to be addressed.

FURTHER READING

- Cordelia Fine—*Delusions of Gender: How Our Minds, Society, and Neurosexism Create Difference*
- Kate Manne—*Down Girl: The Logic of Misogyny*
- Laura Bates—*Everyday Sexism: The Project That Inspired a Worldwide Movement*
- Chimamanda Ngozi Adichie—*We Should All Be Feminists*
- Caroline Criado Perez—*Invisible Women: Data Bias in a World Designed for Men*
- Mikki Kendall—*Hood Feminism: Notes from the Women That a Movement Forgot*
- Elinor Cleghorn—*Unwell Women: Misdiagnosis and Myth in a Man-Made World*
- Mary Beard—*Women & Power: A Manifesto*
- bell hooks—*Feminism Is for Everybody*

13

Price Gouging, Child Labor, and Sweatshops Are Good

Price Gouging

The next time you see a high price, instead of grumbling as I did, think of the bigger picture: that entrepreneur is reserving a scarce good for the person who values it the most. In fact, it's the *duty* of a responsible business to raise prices when necessary.

—Steve Patterson, "Thank Goodness for Price Gougers,"
Foundation for Economic Education

The impulse to denounce the greed reflected in such prices is human. But price hikes are a response to scarcity, and signals that reveal the true severity of scarcity are critical during storms and other crises.

—Donald J. Boudreaux, "'Price Gouging' after a Disaster
Is Good for the Public," *Wall Street Journal*

My own version of dealing with price gougers would be to thank them for the good work they're doing.

—Tim Worstall, "Hurricane Harvey Is When We
Need Price Gouging, Not Laws Against It,"
Forbes (column deleted after public outcry)

I honestly feel like it's a public service. I'm being paid for my public service.

—A man who bought up seventeen thousand bottles
of hand sanitizer in the COVID-19 pandemic so that he
could resell them at a profit, quoted in the *New York Times*
("He has 17,700 bottles of hand sanitizer and nowhere
to sell them," March 14, 2020)

Child Labor

As any historian could tell you, no society has ever pulled itself out of poverty without putting its children to work. Back
in the early 19th century, when Americans were as poor as
Bangladeshis are now, we were sending out children to work
at about the same rate as the Bangladeshis are today. Having
had the good fortune to get rich first, Americans can afford
to give Bangladeshis a helping hand, and there are plenty
of good ways for us to do that. Denying Third Worlders the
very opportunities our ancestors embraced, whether through
full-fledged boycotts or by insisting on health and safety
standards they can't afford to meet, is not one of those ways.

—Steven E. Landsburg, from his blog, *The Big Questions*

The *Washington Post* ran a beautiful photo montage of children at work from 100 years ago. I get it. It's not supposed
to be beautiful. It's supposed to be horrifying. I'm looking at
these kids. They are scruffy, dirty, and tired. No question.

But I also think about their inner lives. They are working
in the adult world, surrounded by cool bustling things and
new technology. They are on the streets, in the factories, in
the mines, with adults and with peers, learning and doing.
They are being valued for what they do, which is to say being
valued as people. They are earning money.

Whatever else you want to say about this, it's an exciting
life. You can talk about the dangers of coal mining or selling
newspapers on the street. But let's not pretend that danger
is something that every young teen wants to avoid. If you
doubt it, head over [to] the stadium for the middle school
football game in your local community, or have a look at the
wrestling or gymnastic team's antics at the gym.

And I compare it to any scene you can observe today at
the local public school, with 30 kids sitting in desks bored
out of their minds, creativity and imagination beaten out of
their brains, forbidden from earning money and providing

value to others, learning no skills, and knowing full well that
they are supposed to do this until they are 22 years old if
they have the slightest chance of being a success in life:
desk after desk, class after class, lecture after lecture, test
after test, a confined world without end.

> —Jeffrey A. Tucker, "Let the Kids Work,"
> Foundation for Economic Education

It is important to end prohibitions of employment of children for the sake of their peaceful and voluntaristic transition into adulthood. . . . Can a labor contract with a mere
"child" be truly voluntary, given his tender years, lack of
experience, etc.? The answer is yes. . . . In a free market society, the employer will *not* be able to take advantage of the
misery of the young worker if by this is meant that he will
not be able to pay him less than his marginal product. . . .
However destitute and helpless the youngster who is looking
for work may be, it is not the fault of the potential employer.

> —Walter Block, *Defending the Undefendable*[1]

Sweatshops

Well-meaning American university students regularly campaign against sweatshops. But instead, anyone who cares
about fighting poverty should campaign in favor of sweatshops, demanding that companies set up factories in Africa.
If Africa could establish a clothing export industry, that
would fight poverty far more effectively than any foreign aid
program. American students should stop trying to ban sweatshops, and instead campaign to bring them to the most desperately poor countries.

> —Nicholas Kristof, "In Praise of the Maligned Sweatshop,"
> *New York Times*[2]

It is easy to understand why nice people in rich countries
are aghast at the working conditions in Central American

factories. It is true that thousands of children work nights, that
workers are locked in until production quotas are fulfilled, that
wages are obscenely low, and that, in extreme cases, women
and children are beaten up by their supervisors. But it is also
true that there are no slaves in Central America. People
choose to work in the maquila shops of their own free will,
because those are the best jobs available to them. Given
that unemployment compensation is unheard of in Central
America, a lousy job is always better than no job at all. . . .
If major U.S. retailers stop doing business with countries
where exploitation is a fact of life, maquila production will
decline further in Central America, and thousands of workers, children and adults, will join the ranks of the unemployed. The ensuing regressive climate is sure to encourage
far more exploitation of those who will have even less means
of defending themselves.

—Lucy Martinez-Mont, "Sweatshops Are Better
Than No Shops," *Wall Street Journal*

The Argument

I place these three arguments together because they have important similarities. Each concerns a phenomenon that violates many
people's convictions about what is morally right. Each says that
when examined closely, using the principles of economics, this
phenomenon that looks appalling will, in fact, turn out to be good.
Each suggests that liberals and leftists, who think with their emotions rather than reason, are incapable of a hardheaded look at
the facts, and thus end up hurting the very people whose interests
they say they value.

Here is the argument on price gouging: When, after some
horrific catastrophe, limited amounts of emergency supplies are
available, sellers who possess the remaining supplies will often
be tempted to jack up the prices as high as possible. This is because they know that people will pay much higher prices when

they desperately need the supplies and there are few to go around. This looks like a bad thing, because it seems obscene to charge one hundred dollars for a bottle of water just because you happen to have the last one and others need it. But it is not a bad thing. It means that the water goes to the person who is willing to pay the most, and thus wants it the most, rather than just the person who just shows up first. As Michael Munger of the American Institute for Economic Research writes, "If the price is kept artificially low, there is no reason for the person with mild needs to leave some for those still waiting in line."[3] Steve Patterson of the Foundation for Economic Education writes that price gouging helps "allocate" a good to "those willing to give up the most for it."[4]

Furthermore, high prices will cause opportunists to rush in with new supplies hoping to make a killing. If, for example, it looks like there is a great deal of money to be made by being the first person to rush a shipment of new water bottles to the disaster zone, the entrepreneurially minded will flood in. John Stossel writes that "pursuing profit is simply the best mechanism for bringing people supplies we need" because "without rising prices indicating which materials are most sought-after, suppliers don't know whether to rush in food, or bandages, or chainsaws."[5] He cites real-world examples like a Kentucky man who bought nineteen generators and drove south to sell the generators to Hurricane Katrina victims for twice what he paid for them. The man was arrested under anti-gouging laws, but Stossel argues that this was emotion trumping reason: the man was increasing the supply of much-needed generators.

What about child labor and sweatshops? Here again, the argument is that while what is happening might *look* immoral and exploitative, in fact, it is helping the world. Children might prefer work to school, but child labor laws get in the way. Family businesses are prohibited from having the kids help out. With regard to sweatshops, they look bad (sometimes they collapse and kill hundreds of workers, sometimes people get limbs lopped off, or they work long hours in oppressive heat), but people who take these jobs clearly think they are better than the available alternatives. Thus, we should be thankful for sweatshops, and the anti-sweatshop movement is hurting the very people it is trying to help. You may look at price gouging and see unfairness. You may look at a sweatshop and see the kind of brutal and exploitative work environment that nobody should have to experience. But they are not as bad as you think.

The Response

In February of 2021, a freak cold front blasted through the United States. The state of Texas was particularly affected, with millions losing power. Those whose lights stayed on thought themselves the lucky ones—at first. Then they got their electric bills. The *New York Times* reported that where "electricity prices are not fixed and are instead tied to the fluctuating wholesale price, the spikes have been astronomical." One sixty-three-year-old Army veteran, who lives on Social Security in a Dallas suburb, received a bill for $16,752.[6] The bill ate up his entire savings, and across Texas, people found themselves facing bankruptcy over their surprise sky-high electric bills. The power companies received a windfall, with one gas company CFO telling investors they had "hit the jackpot."[7]

Texas senator Ted Cruz pronounced himself outraged at the situation, tweeting:

> This is WRONG. No power company should get a windfall because of a natural disaster, and Texans shouldn't get hammered by ridiculous rate increases for last week's energy debacle. State and local regulators should act swiftly to prevent this injustice.[8]

But Cruz's demand for regulation of the utility companies was a remarkable shift in tone from previous public comments. Cruz had described himself as someone who had "spent my whole life fighting for free-market principles"[9] and said that the "success of Texas energy" was built "on principles of free enterprise and low regulation."[10] He had said "regulated public utilities" were not "bold" or "innovative."

There was, in fact, a clear link between "free-market principles" and the $16,752 bill received by the Army veteran after the winter storm. Texas had deregulated power companies and declined to control the fluctuating price of power services. Those high bills were the result of the market at work. And when a committed capitalist like Cruz saw what this meant in practice, he didn't like it at all. It seemed wrong that poor people should face bankruptcy just for trying to keep themselves alive during a storm.

When we are talking about "gouging" people, it is important to be clear on what this actually is: using the opportunity of a disaster to make as much money as you can convince desperate people to fork over. If you are drowning, and I offer to throw you a life preserver on the condition that you give me your life savings or agree to work for me for ten years after, I am taking advantage of the fact that you are in dire need of something in order to enrich myself. Most people find this kind of action immoral and unfair because it seems coercive, even if you "voluntarily" agree to exchange your life savings for the life preserver.[11]

Notice that in the defenses of price gouging, goods are described as being allocated to those "willing to pay" the most. This is sometimes used to suggest that in a free market, the people who want something the most will be the ones who get it, because they will be willing to pay the most. But of course, the existence of vast wealth inequality means that isn't necessarily the case. A poor parent may *want* the last bottle of water in the store for their thirsty child. They may want it more than a rich parent. But the rich parent will be able to "outbid" the poor parent even if they want or need the item much less. If I am rich, I can buy as much as I like even if I don't need it at all.

Price gouging does not, therefore, allocate goods to the people who most *want* them, but to those who can *pay* the most,[12] which may well be those for whom money means the least. A fairer system of allocation when emergency supplies are scarce is to distribute them based on need. And instead of price fluctuations causing people to limit the quantity they buy, merchants can simply impose per-customer limits on the number of purchases. (This is often called "rationing" because the word conjures images of bread lines, but "one per customer" policies are perfectly humane and sensible.)

So, unless we believe that the rich are more entitled to emergency supplies than the poor, price gouging makes it more likely that there will be an unjust distribution of supplies, and that poor people will have their remaining wealth extracted just to secure basic necessities. But what of the argument that it helps replenish supplies? Well, we can furnish anecdotes, like the one about the man with the generators, in which that is what happens. But there are also plenty of cases in which it doesn't happen. Take the man who bought up all the hand sanitizer when the COVID-19 pandemic began.[13] The increased demand for hand sanitizer was already present, and sanitizer manufacturers were rushing to make more. All the profiteer did was try to seize control of the remaining supplies so that before the new supply arrived, everyone would have to go through him if they wanted sanitizer. An equivalent situation would be something like this: There are two roads leading out of a town. A sinkhole swallows up one road, forcing everybody to temporarily use the other. A clever businessman realizes that while the damaged road is being repaired, if he can buy the land on which the backup road sits, people will have no choice but to pay him to use it. He will *not* be doing anything to increase the number of roads people can choose. He will simply be taking advantage of an opportunity to temporarily monopolize something people need.

There are situations in which the profit motive can incentivize the increase in supply. But there are situations in which the replenishing of supplies will occur at the same rate regardless of whether the remaining stockpile is distributed in accordance with need or in accordance with the ability to pay the highest price. This does not necessarily justify *arresting* people for price gouging—as a skeptic of the criminal punishment system, I think that many immoral and socially harmful practices should not necessarily be dealt with through the use of criminal law—but it does mean that the theory of price gouging as "a good thing" doesn't work. There is no reason to, as Tim Worstall of *Forbes* suggested, "thank" the gougers just for putting their prices up. In fact, as Texas discovered after its storm, it can just create windfall profits for a small group of people. The *Wall Street Journal* quoted an energy economist who says that the Texas crisis would be "an incredible transfer of billions of dollars from Texas consumers to generators" with some "spectacular winners and losers," the biggest loser being "the state of Texas," with municipalities having to take on debt to pay off the hundreds of millions of dollars in electric bills they now owe to power companies.[14]

The story told about "good" price gouging, then, may make it sound harmless, but as even arch-capitalist Ted Cruz discovered, when you actually see it in practice, it looks deeply unfair. Cruz went from a staunch free marketeer to calling for new regulations because he saw a deregulated market in action.

What about child labor and sweatshops? Child labor is, fortunately, something that few conservatives openly defend nowadays, but there are a few who will say openly that rather than sending children to public school it would be better to have them get jobs. Libertarian economist Bryan Caplan, in his *The Case against Education*, writes:

> When children languish in school, adults rush to rationalize. Making kids sit at desks doing boring busywork may seem cruel, but their pain trains them for the future. Why then is child labor so reviled? Toil may not be fun, but it too trains

kids for their future. Child labor has a dark side. Then again, so does book learning. When my mom was a schoolgirl, the nuns in charge freely hit kids with sticks. Judging either activity by long-gone creepy abuses is folly. In modern times, is there any decent reason to discourage kids from getting jobs and learning job skills?[15]

The argument for child labor uses a technique that is common in right-wing arguments: treating "better" as synonymous with "good." If public schools are so bad that even work would be better, then child labor is good. The same goes for the sweatshop argument. If sweatshops are the best-existing alternative for desperate people, offering the highest wages of any available job in the area, then they are "good" and we should defend them. This line of reasoning is why conservative think tanks like the Cato Institute are constantly pumping out articles with headlines like "Why You Shouldn't Knock 'Sweatshops' If You Care about Women's Empowerment."[16] Because working a sixteen-hour day in unsafe conditions beats starving to death, and therefore poor women may line up in droves to work at a local garment factory, then the factory therefore "empowers women" by putting money in their pockets.[17]

The reason this line of argumentation needs to be rejected is that it can lead to the embrace of hideously unjust things. The sharecropping system in the South following the Civil War was a "better" situation for free Black people than slavery had been. But the sharecropping system was still exploitative and racist, enriching white landowners with the fruits of Black labor.[18] It is not a justification of sweatshops to say they are an improvement. It is morally wrong to overwork people and keep them in unsafe conditions. It's a practice that has to be eliminated and is especially abhorrent in a world overflowing with abundant wealth. It might be the case that simply *banning* sweatshops is a crude and ineffective solution that will make people worse off. But that is not an argument for not trying to end sweatshop practices. It is an argument for doing so more effectively, with international labor standards treaties adopted and enforced in ways that do not stifle the ability of developing countries to grow and prosper.

"Better than some other horrible alternative" and "actually good" are mixed up all the time.[19] If an employer is told their wages are too low, they may reply that they pay "well above the market rate for the area." But that tells us very little. If the market rate isn't nearly enough to pay one's rent and raise a family, then it's no defense to say one pays "more than almost nothing." The question is not how it compares to everything else, the question is whether it conforms to a set of basic principles. In a world full of injustice and misery, relative progress might not tell us much about how we're doing. What matters most is not whether we're doing better than before, but whether we're doing as well as we can and should.

Caplan asks whether there is any decent reason to discourage kids from getting jobs, and suggests that those who oppose child labor conjure up images of abuses that have long since disappeared. In fact, the world of child labor is still horrific. For instance, in the United States, child labor is permitted in the agricultural sector, and the result is, predictably, that kids who should be having fun and getting to be curious and learn spend their days doing back-breaking labor in fields.[20] If there is one thing that sucks more than being in school, it is being at work,[21] and you only need to think for a moment about what mass child labor in the twenty-first century would look like (think Amazon warehouses) to realize what a dystopia Caplan is calling for.

Both Caplan and Jeffrey Tucker (of "Let the Kids Work" quoted above) argue that jobs are actually less rotten for kids than being bored in school all day. It is indeed true that many kids languish in school, and that adults come up with spurious rationalizations of how their pain is good for them. But instead of sending kids out into the workforce, we should take this as a cue to *make school better*. If it's the case that literal child labor would actually be better than public school as it is now, that's not a case for child labor; it's a case that we need to drastically overhaul the public school system to make it engaging and fun and improve student morale.[22]

FURTHER READING

The best way to learn to see through simplistic "Econ 101" arguments is to go beyond "101" and study the more sophisticated critiques of free-market assumptions. A number of useful books are available that decimate Friedmanite reasoning.

- Rod Hill and Tony Myatt—*The Economics Anti-Textbook: A Critical Thinker's Guide to Microeconomics*
- James Kwak—*Economism: Bad Economics and the Rise of Inequality*
- Jonathan Aldred—*Licence to Be Bad: How Economics Corrupted Us*
- Moshe Adler—*Economics for the Rest of Us: Debunking the Science That Makes Life Dismal*
- Stephen A. Marglin—*The Dismal Science: How Thinking Like an Economist Undermines Community*

14

We Don't Need a Green New Deal

The solution to climate change is not this unserious resolution, but the serious business of human flourishing . . . fall in love, get married, and have some kids.

—Senator Mike Lee, Twitter, March 26, 2019

The only thing certain about CO2 is that it's necessary for life on Earth. It's plant food. NASA satellite images have charted the greening of the Earth since the early 1980s. The notion that climate change is necessarily bad is an assumption, and possibly an unfounded one.

—Steve Milloy, "The Case for a Green 'No Deal,'"
Wall Street Journal

The concept of global warming was created by and for the Chinese in order to make U.S. manufacturing noncompetitive.

—Donald Trump, Twitter, November 6, 2012

With all of the hysteria, all of the fear, all of the phony science, could it be that man-made global warming is the greatest hoax ever perpetrated on the American people?

—Jim Inhofe (Senate speech, July 28, 2003)

The alleged "climate emergency" is merely a premise for achieving the political goals that the left has sought for decades. The Green New Deal will mean a complete takeover of a massive swath of the U.S. economy, disrupting and destroying lives as formerly free decisions are turned over to the bureaucratic state. The Green New Deal would bestow upon the bureaucratic state a massive increase in power to manage the economy and redistribute wealth, taking choices out of the hands of individual consumers and businesses and putting them into the hands of those who are allegedly more enlightened. The GND will also lead to another massive round of government "investment" in solar and wind power, picking winners and losers with taxpayer money. . . . The Green New Deal is about much more than the climate or the environment. It is about transforming modern America into a centrally planned and managed society and imposing an ideology that will reign [sic] in the freedoms of individual Americans. The premise of the Green New Deal is very simple: if you pay more taxes, regulate industry, drive up the cost of energy, micromanage every aspect of your life—we can then control the climate in order to avoid a climate emergency. Left out of the equation is when we will finish paying and doing our World War II-style sacrifice of our freedoms (already severely depleted under COVID lockdowns) so the government can allegedly control the climate. What criteria will the overlords of the Green New Deal use to say "Okay, that's enough taxes, spending, and regulations; the climate has been fixed"? Or is this just an endless parade of money, regulations, bureaucracy, loss of freedom, redistribution of wealth, and enforced mandates on people? At what point do we say we've achieved the Green New Deal's goals? . . . Fossil fuels—coal, oil, and natural gas—have been one of the greatest liberators of mankind in the history of our planet. Is it greedy to want heat, air conditioning, lower infant mortality, and longer life expectancy?

—Marc Morano, *Green Fraud*

The Argument

Progressives love to prophesize doom about the environment. They tell us that global warming will be apocalyptic. But their predictions have always been wrong. To the extent that there is global warming, and to the extent that it is caused by humans, its consequences will not be so serious as to justify all the panic. Humans can adapt to changing climates. We certainly do not need the "Green New Deal," an incredibly costly proposal that will destroy the economy. The Green New Deal is not about stopping climate change, it is about forcing socialism on America by manufacturing a phony crisis. The policy has many components that have nothing to do with climate change and are just pet issues of the left. The climate scare is just a way for leftists to sneak their policies through by making people afraid and trying to get them to blame capitalism.

The Response

There are a number of different conservative claims made on climate. Some downplay the extent of it or try to absolve humans from responsibility. Others admit the facts of climate change but suggest that leftist proposals for dealing with it are unnecessary and counterproductive.

At the very extreme end, there are those, like Donald Trump, who simply insist that human-caused climate change is not happening.

Few people fall into this category anymore. In fact, toward the end of his term, even Trump seemed to shy away from repeating his allegation that climate change was a "hoax" peddled by the Chinese. Instead, he simply didn't mention it. This is far more common on the right these days: just not bringing up climate change at all, spending far more time talking about whatever the latest "cancel culture" flap is instead. It's understandable that conservatives don't really want a major public debate about what to do about climate change, because so few people with any expertise on the subject sympathize with the right-wing approach.

Some are perfectly willing to admit that human-caused climate change is happening, but downplay its potential risk. We can find this kind of approach in books like Michael Shellenberger's *Apocalypse Never* and Bjorn Lomborg's *False Alarm*.[1] These books are insidious because they appear credible and insist they accept the consensus among climate scientists. But a closer look reveals that in order to support their claim, they have to twist the facts in ways that can easily fool nonexperts.

Let us look at an example. When the horrific 2019 wildfires occurred in California, many on the left mentioned climate change as a contributing factor. But the right pushed back. Donald Trump said the fires had everything to do with "bad forest management." Tucker Carlson ran a segment claiming that anyone who blamed climate change was doing so for "political" reasons and exploiting a tragedy. "It took no time at all for the usual vultures and parasites to swoop in and try to make a political advantage," Carlson said. Showing clips of Barack Obama and Gavin Newsom saying that climate change was responsible, and an MSNBC anchor calling the fires the "direct result of climate change," Carlson said that these people were "lying on television" and that there's "no evidence" climate change is responsible.

Carlson then brought on Michael Shellenberger to provide support for the claim. Shellenberger said the fires on the West Coast happened because there are "more people and more electrical wires that they've failed to maintain because we've focused on other things like building renewables" and we've been "so focused on renewables, so focused on climate change." He further tweeted that "it is gross misinformation to blame climate change for our fires."[2] (Elsewhere Shellenberger chastises those who show "pyrophobia"—fear of fires—like, I suppose, the residents of Paradise, California, which burned to the ground in the 2018 wildfire.)

Carlson and Shellenberger were just lying. From a paper by six climate scientists:

> Since the early 1970s, California's annual wildfire extent increased fivefold, punctuated by extremely large and destructive wildfires in 2017 and 2018. This trend was mainly due to an eightfold increase in summertime forest-fire area and was very

likely driven by drying of fuels promoted by human-induced warming.[3]

A recent paper from seven climate scientists was called "Climate Change Is Increasing the Likelihood of Extreme Autumn Wildfire Conditions across California."[4] UCLA's Daniel Swain says there's been a "really big increase [in high fire-risk days] over a relatively short period of time that can be attributed directly to the changes in climate."[5] Friederike Otto, then director of the University of Oxford's Environmental Change Institute, says: "There is absolutely no doubt that the extremely high temperatures are higher than they would have been without human-induced climate change. A huge body of attribution literature demonstrates now that climate change is an absolute game-changer when it comes to heat waves, and California won't be the exception."[6] Then here's Jennifer Balch, director of the Earth Lab at the University of Colorado Boulder, on the connection between that heat and the fires: "As a fire scientist, I can say fires are really responsive to warming. With just a little bit of warming, we're seeing a lot more burning. We have twice as much burning now as we were seeing in the early 1980s."[7]

Sometimes, then, conservatives just pretend that expert opinion says something other than what it actually says. But sometimes the distortions are a little more clever: someone trying to convince you that we spend too much on renewable energy might tell you a large sum of money that the government has paid in renewable energy subsidies, but *not* note the even larger sum of money that has been spent on fossil fuel subsidies.[8] This is what's known as "paltering." It is essentially "lying with facts," saying things that are all *true* but giving a wholly misleading picture of reality. It is important to learn how to spot this, because at first it can be hard to even accept that "lying with facts" is possible—if everything you've said is true, how can what you're saying be false? But by cherry-picking only small pieces of reality, one can make it seem as if things are the opposite of what they really are. Dinesh D'Souza, for instance, gleefully tweeted a CNN news story about a glacier that had unexpectedly grown rather than shrunk.[9] For D'Souza, this was evidence that the "melting glacier" problem is a myth. But the actual CNN article pointed out that the trend was still the same. Only presenting outlier events or choosing an unusually hot year in the past to show that there has been "no warming since that year" has long been common among climate change deniers.

But I don't feel the need to spend *too* much time here debunking right-wing dishonesty on the fundamentals of climate change,[10] because there is such an overwhelming consensus at this point about the problem's urgency.[11] (This does not prevent shameless pundits like Mark Levin from writing things like "suffice to say, there is simply no consensus.")[12] Donald Trump may see it as a "Chinese hoax,"[13] but thirteen of Trump's own administrative agencies put out a major report during his presidency discussing the urgency of climate action. The report "details how climate-fueled disasters and other types of worrisome changes are becoming more commonplace throughout the country and how much worse they could become in the absence of efforts to combat global warming," and shows that we are "more certain than ever that climate change poses a severe threat to Americans' health and pocketbooks, as well as to the country's infrastructure and natural resources."[14] Even fossil fuel companies Shell and BP have now switched to accepting the reality of climate change and promising (dubiously) to become net-zero emissions companies.[15]

Always Check Their Sources

Ben Shapiro, in a passage displaying his signature combination of extreme ignorance and extreme confidence, explains climate change as follows:

> The evidence that man's production of greenhouse gases causes climate change is questionable at best. . . . Lest we forget, the

climate change protagonists were global warming protagonists originally; when the earth got cooler, they simply changed their man-
tra to "climate change" so that they wouldn't have to be pegged
down to predictions of hotter temperatures. Now, as the ultimate
scare tactic, environmentalists peg wild weather events like tor-
nados and hurricanes to climate change. Thus, your Range Rover
or F-150 is responsible for Katrina. Are you happy yet, you racist
pig? So, how do the environmentalist bullies prove all of this?
They don't. The truth is that the planet hasn't warmed for fifteen
years. According to new estimates, we might even be looking at
an ice age rather than a warming period. Who admitted this? The
University of East Anglia Climate Research Unit, one of the world's
leading anthropogenic global warming proponents. . . . As Henrik
Svensmark, director of the center for Sun-Climate Research at
Denmark's National Space Institute—and a guy we should listen
to because he sounds European—said, "World temperatures may
end up a lot cooler than now for 50 years or more."[16]

This is one of those examples of a paragraph where so
much that is wrong is said so quickly that setting it all straight
can take an agonizingly long time:

- The first sentence is a classic example of "saying things
  rather than proving things"—there are no citations to support the claim that the evidence linking greenhouse gases to
  climate change is "questionable."
- The stuff about "climate change" replacing "global warming" as a way to cover scientists' asses for getting their
  predictions wrong is a common conservative talking point,
  and also nonsense. It was done to be more precise, though
  personally I think we should use the term "global warming"
  more because it is terrifying.
- Environmentalists *do* prove the connection between hurricane intensity and climate change, as Shapiro would know if
  he so much as looked up a scientific paper on the subject.[17]

- To support the claim that the University of East Anglia predicts an ice age and the world has stopped warming, Shapiro cites an article in the *Daily Mail*. In fact, it turns out the *Mail* completely misrepresented the research. According to environmental scientist Dana Nuccintelli in an analysis for *The Skeptical Scientist,* its claims were "entirely fabricated," and "virtually every point made in the article was factually incorrect."[18]

- Henrik Svensmark may indeed "sound European" and be affiliated with an institute, but he is a fringe scholar who Shapiro only quoted because he is desperate to find an expert who can help him avoid concluding his Range Rover might be bad for the planet.[19]

We then get to the position of those who accept the reality of climate change, but do not believe that a "Green New Deal" is needed in order to deal with it. Take the American Enterprise Institute's report on the Green New Deal, which warns of the following:

> *The GND at its core is the substitution of central planning in place of market forces for resource allocation, in the US energy and transportation sectors narrowly and in the broad industrial, business, and housing sectors writ large. . . . While the effect of the inexorable increase in government authoritarianism resulting from the GND will be difficult to measure, its costs will be very real. Given the tragic record of central planning outcomes worldwide over the last century, the GND should be rejected.*[20]

Here we see a classic case of the conservative "speculative story" about negative unintended consequences. We have a few tropes here, such as the invocation of *planning* as inherently scary, and intimations that Stalinist tyranny will result from too much state investment in renewable energy.

What *is* the Green New Deal? It is a large-scale plan to address climate change and social injustice that has been proposed by progressives as a sensible way to tackle some of the most crucial challenges currently facing the country and the world. Its clearest articulation currently exists in the form of a Congressional resolution whose primary sponsors are Rep. Alexandria Ocasio-Cortez and Sen. Ed Markey. That resolution lays out a very general argument: First, it details the catastrophic potential consequences of climate change, including mass migration by refugees, increasing wildfires, deadly heat waves, colossal damage to the economy, and the destruction of the world's coral reefs. Then it proposes that the United States commit itself to achieving net-zero carbon emissions by 2050. The resolution then discusses the fact that as we face the climate crisis, we face several related crises, including stagnant wages, low economic mobility, an inadequately resourced public sector, and colossal income inequality. The Green New Deal proposes to make sure that our climate solutions are designed so that they will simultaneously address these other social problems. It calls this a "fair and just transition," meaning that the transition to renewable energy will need to be orchestrated in a way that ensures it is fair to the least well-off.

This is an important aspect of the Green New Deal, because it would be very easy for solutions to climate change to be economically unfair. For instance, if we simply impose a high gasoline tax, in the recognition that driving a car has a cost to the climate that we wish to discourage, we may well reduce emissions, but we will do so in a way that hurts low-wage workers who have to drive to work. This is deeply unfair, especially because we know that oil and gas companies have reaped immense windfall profits from the sale of a destructive product. They manipulated public understanding by casting doubt on the science of climate change in order to continue to make vast sums of money. If the costs of trying to undo this damage are borne by the least wealthy, then repairing an environmental problem is creating a new kind of economic injustice that will make people angry. It will also make them less supportive of efforts to mitigate climate change, as we saw in the case of the "yellow vests" protests in France, which objected in part to rising fuel costs.[21] This is important to understand: the GND framework is often derided as a "left-wing wish list" because it includes ideas, like a federal job guarantee, that do not *look* climate-related. But an important part of the theory behind the Green New Deal is that addressing people's economic needs has to happen at the same time as addressing climate policy; otherwise, they are unlikely to get on board with climate policy. For instance, if there is new federal funding for retrofitting a school building to be environmentally sustainable, but kids are still coming to school hungry, both parents and teachers might find climate policy to be an absurd and infuriating priority.

So what does the Green New Deal propose? It aims to give people "clean air and water, climate and community resiliency, healthy food, access to nature, and a sustainable environment" while "creat[ing] millions of good, high-wage jobs and ensure prosperity and economic security for all people of the United States." It will do so through new government spending on: investments in "zero-emission vehicle infrastructure and manufacturing, clean, affordable, and accessible public transit, and high-speed rail," "land preservation and afforestation," "cleaning up existing hazardous waste and abandoned sites, ensuring economic development and sustainability on those sites," "meeting 100 percent of the power demand in the United States through clean, renewable, and zero-emission energy sources, including by dramatically expanding and upgrading renewable power sources, and by deploying new capacity," and "spurring massive growth in clean manufacturing in the United States and removing pollution and greenhouse gas emissions from manufacturing and industry as much as is technologically feasible." It would involve funding renewable manufacturing and power production, retrofitting America's buildings to be sustainable, building the "smart grid," overhauling transportation and agriculture, planting trees, and restoring the ecosystem.

The economic justice components of the Green New Deal are achieved, in part, by making sure that the jobs created through these initiatives will be high-quality, well-paying union jobs. The GND is meant, in part, to address the fairness problem facing those who currently work in the fossil fuel industry and who face the prospect of losing their livelihoods. Realizing that coal miners do not deserve to suffer through the transition, the Green New Deal emphasizes the importance of treating the energy transition as a jobs program. This aspect of the Green New Deal has been derided by Bill Gates as communistic,[22] but it means that people will see a real material benefit from climate policy, and thus will be more likely to get on board with something that they otherwise might feel would only affect future generations.[23]

Green New Deal proposals are easy to caricature, in part because they are deliberately sketchy. When I talked to Green New Deal policy architect Rhiana Gunn-Wright, she told me that the specific programs that would be funded by the plan are intentionally left slightly vague because the Green New Deal needs to be developed through a democratic process:

> I love a detail. I have not found a detail yet that I do not love. I talk about service delivery and public goods way more than anyone should. . . . But I'm actually glad, right now, that we aren't talking about prescriptive policy details, because right now we have to get consensus around these goals, and we have to actually listen. This is going to be such a big transformation, and the Green New Deal, even in resolution form—it's an economy-wide transition, so everyone is going to be affected, so we actually have to take the time to talk to people, to listen to different groups, to hear the debates, to try to build consensus, and then move forward to try to figure out prescriptive policy details from then. . . . I think it actually shows that we're being more

judicious than less judicious, because racing to have details right now, that's about nothing but impressing the press. . . . So why not just take the time, talk to people, try to get folks on board, and have a truly participatory policy design process?[24]

This means that climate policy should *not* be put forth in a completed form by elite policy wonks who have gotten together and decided what is best for the country and asked us to give it an up or down vote. Instead, it should be a statement of what the goals we are trying to achieve are, and then there should be an inclusive process to decide how exactly they are best achieved. What we need right now is a consensus around the values and targets. A city, for instance, should not be told how it is going to achieve zero-emissions public transit; it should come up with a plan and the federal government should support it. This democratic aspect of the Green New Deal's development means it is quite the opposite of the conservative caricature, which treats it as a plan by centralized bureaucrats to seek power. In fact, the whole reason that the plan has yet to be fully fleshed out is that its designers do not want centralized bureaucrats to have too much control and want to emphasize the importance of local participation in the plan.

The Green New Deal is not opaque or arcane or a sinister attempt to seize power. It is grounded in a simple recognition that we face, as a country, a series of major problems, many of which are linked together and can be addressed together. It asks us to make a commitment to a series of goals. It is interesting that Marc Morano in *Green Fraud* asks "what criteria" will be used to decide when enough is enough. The criteria are actually laid out quite explicitly: We are trying to power the U.S. with 100 percent renewable energy and make sure that everyone in the country is paid a living wage and has a high standard of living. When the country is powered by renewables and its people are taken care of, the need for the Green New Deal ceases. What we are committing to is: (1) a recognition of the problems; (2) a shared set of goals; (3) the government action necessary to reach the goals and solve the problems. This should be uncontroversial. Debates over what to do should take place *within* the context of broad agreement that a Green New Deal should and will happen.

Further Reading

- Noam Chomsky and Robert Pollin—*Climate Crisis and the Global Green New Deal: The Political Economy of Saving the Planet*
- Naomi Klein—*On Fire: The (Burning) Case for a Green New Deal*
- Ann Pettifor—*The Case for the Green New Deal*
- Kate Aronoff et al.—*A Planet to Win: Why We Need a Green New Deal*
- Kate Aronoff—*Overheated: How Capitalism Broke the Planet—And How We Fight Back*
- Varshini Prakash and Guido Girgenti (eds.)—*Winning the Green New Deal: Why We Must, How We Can*
- Jeremy Rifkin—*The Green New Deal: Why the Fossil Fuel Civilization Will Collapse by 2028, and the Bold Economic Plan to Save Life on Earth*
- Aviva Chomsky—*Is Science Enough: Forty Critical Questions About Climate Justice*
- Henry Shue—*The Pivotal Generation: Why We Have a Moral Responsibility to Slow Climate Change Right Now*
- George Monbiot—*Heat: How to Stop the Planet From Burning*
- Bill McKibben—*Fight Global Warming Now: The Handbook for Taking Action in Your Community*

15

Academia Is a Radical Indoctrination Factory

We have ceded education to the radical Left. . . . Every college has federal funding for deans of diversity, courses on gender studies, on so-called "Critical Studies" which is really the criticism of all that is Western and good. They've created generations obsessed with environmentalism, which is the god of the atheist left. We have arrived at the point where you can major in English at otherwise serious universities without ever having studied Shakespeare. That is what the conservative surrendering of education has wrought in America.

—Sebastian Gorka, *The War for America's Soul*

Many professors are Marxists or other varieties of radicals who hate America.

—Phyllis Schlafly, "Feminist Mischief on College Campuses," *Phyllis Schlafly Report*

The professors are the enemy.

—J. D. Vance, quoting Richard Nixon

The Argument

A distrust and dislike of academia runs through a great deal of conservative thought. In his 1951 book *God and Man at Yale*, William F. Buckley painted a picture of a Yale faculty that had abandoned its commitment to educating good Christians and been overtaken by secularism and progressivism. Subsequent books like Allan Bloom's *The Closing of the American Mind*,

Dinesh D'Souza's *Illiberal Education,* and Roger Kimball's *Tenured Radicals* developed the argument that academics were poisoning the minds of the young. Conservatives argue that there are too few conservative faculty members, and that young people are taught (perhaps even brainwashed into thinking) that liberalism and leftism are correct. Often, this accusation includes the charge that "postmodernism" and "relativism" have taken hold on campus. In the book *Cynical Theories,* Helen Pluckrose and James Lindsay take aim at critical theory, and fields like gender studies and disability studies, arguing that Enlightenment values are disappearing from the university.

The Response

Having spent a great deal of time in American universities myself, I have always found the conservative pictures of them to be rather amusing and disconnected from reality. When I was a political science major at Brandeis University, which explicitly prides itself on its social justice tradition and which graduated radicals Abbie Hoffman and Angela Davis, I was frustrated with how *apolitical* the education generally was. I had to become a leftist on my own time, because the political education was very much in the classical tradition. "Theory" meant Hobbes, Locke, and Rousseau.

The truth is that the departments frequently derided by conservatives (gender studies, Black studies, queer studies) are a marginal presence at colleges and universities. At Brandeis—one of the more left-wing universities—as an undergraduate, we actually had to organize students and faculty to try to keep the African American studies department from being dismantled.[1] The fact is that business, accounting, marketing, economics, and finance majors are, together, far larger than any single other part of the contemporary university. Gender studies does not even make the list of the top twenty.[2]

The university is actually, in general, a fairly conservative place. Not *conservative* in the sense that it is dominated by Republicans—it isn't. But conservative in the sense that very little of what happens on campus is a challenge to the economic or social status quo. It's very easy to paint a distorted picture of what an average university looks like by cherry-picking examples. But anecdotes are not data, and the fact is that while professors are stereotyped as "Marxists," statistically almost no professors actually *are* Marxists. About 3 percent identify with the label, which rises to about 5 percent in the humanities. Even in the departments where the influence of Karl Marx is at its strongest, such as sociology, it's only around 25 percent.[3] Having spent time in a sociology PhD program, however, I can confirm that even ostensibly Marxist sociologists are rarely activists, let alone revolutionaries. Usually, they are more likely to use a term like "Marxian," meaning that rather than subscribing to Karl Marx's political program, they simply have a form of social analysis somewhat influenced by his theories (not terribly surprising, since Marx's analytic powers as a sociologist and economist have been recognized even by pro-capitalist scholars like Joseph Schumpeter).[4]

In fact, it would be helpful to the left if a few more professors were committed to the class struggle. During my time at Harvard, the university's dining hall workers went on strike, demanding higher wages. The "tenured radicals" of the Harvard faculty did not rise up with one voice to support the workers—only a small minority of professors signed a petition supporting the workers' demands.[5]

The truth is that academics are actively discouraged from becoming too *political* because it is seen as compromising the neutrality and trustworthiness of their scholarship. Very few professors are activists. Most have joined academia in part because they desire a life of contemplation and study. In fact, my own experience of the university is that graduate students who drift too far in an "activist" direction will be gently encouraged to focus on research instead. The picture of the political university is easy to paint from afar, but up close, the campus tends to be a quiet place. Most students are being ushered into the workforce, and most professors and graduate students are studying something arcane with limited practical applications. (I do not mean that as an insult. I actually think it is very important to study things that are not "practical" but merely interesting for their own sake.) A more accurate (but still unfair) stereotype of an academic would be someone who has vague liberal politics but shies away from participating in political demonstrations, preferring the library to the picket line.

What of the disciplines profiled by Pluckrose and Lindsay in *Cynical Theories*, though? They argue that a virus called "postmodernism" has spread through the university:

> Postmodernism was developed in relatively obscure corners of academia as an intellectual and cultural reaction to [the decline of communism and the collapses of white supremacy and colonialism] and since the 1960s it has spread to other parts of the academy, into activism, throughout bureaucracies, and to the heart of primary, secondary, and post-secondary education.[6]

Pluckrose and Lindsay say that postmodernism holds a "radical skepticism about whether objective knowledge or truth is obtainable and a commitment to cultural constructivism," and believes "society is formed of systems of power and hierarchies." The idea, which they say is "most evident in postcolonial and queer Theories," is essentially that there is no truth, and that knowledge is the product of power struggles between oppressor and oppressed identity groups.

Now, I happen to believe that Pluckrose and Lindsay fundamentally don't understand the theories they're critiquing, which frequently are less about denying the existence of *truth itself* (as in, the existence of reality) than about the way that shared understandings of what truth is come about. They, like many critics of the left, suggest that there is some crazy left denial of "Enlightenment rationality," as if we are at war with the rational. In fact, the more typical criticism is of the way that Enlightenment "rationality" is *not actually rational*, and what passes for "science" or "common sense" incorporates highly contestable value judgments and assumptions. Psychologist Steven Pinker enjoys pointing out that those who critique "reason" do so *using reason*, which he thinks shows that they are silly and ignorant. In fact, what it shows is that the critique is being misunderstood. They assume we are attacking facts, reason, and science, when we are in fact attacking what *passes* for "facts," "reason," and "science" by those who do not examine their own prejudices.[7]

But separate from the question of whether they are right about the theories, it is also not true that "postmodernism" is now at the heart of the education system. To see how distorted and delusional this picture is, just look at the classes being offered in Fall 2020 at my own alma mater, Brandeis, in the Department of Politics:

◊ Introduction to Political Theory
◊ Introduction to International Relations
◊ Quantitative Methods for Policy Analysis
◊ Polling the American Public
◊ Elections in America
◊ Red States, Blue States: Understanding Contemporary American Voters and Parties
◊ Politics of Russia and the Post-Communist World
◊ Elections and Electoral Systems in Comparative Perspective
◊ Latin American Politics
◊ Dynamics of Dictatorship: Authoritarian Politics in the 20th and 21st Centuries
◊ European Culture & Politics
◊ The War on Global Terrorism
◊ The United Nations and the United States

◊ National Security Strategy: The Case of Israel
◊ Gender in American Politics

Of all the departments to contain Political Ideology, of course, the Department of Politics should be high on the list. But as we can see, the undergraduates in politics at Brandeis are learning about diplomacy, elections, dictatorships, and the theory of the state. The "postmodernism" that is supposedly at the core of a contemporary education is simply irrelevant to most of what an undergraduate in politics will study. It's a bit of a giveaway that Pluckrose and Lindsay say the ideas they critique are "most evident" in postcolonial and queer theory, because there is so *little* postcolonial and queer theory in most political science, economics, and philosophy departments. Even in sociology, there's little evident "postmodernism" in the Pluckrose and Lindsay sense. A glance at the November 2020 issue of the *American Journal of Sociology* (an issue I selected at random) reveals that the main articles were about: (1) how legal change affects social change, specifically looking at how those who entered into same-sex marriage attained social as well as legal legitimacy for their marriages; (2) why young people bully, specifically looking at young people who are cruel to their friends; (3) why grain yields were exaggerated during the Chinese Great Leap Forward; (4) how to study people's movement between occupations using networks.

Is some of this work informed by an underlying belief in social justice? Surely. But it is empirical and it is rigorous, despite sociology being a discipline one would expect to be severely infected with the "postmodernism" that has supposedly penetrated all corners of the academy. This is not to deny the *existence* of postmodernist thinkers, nor to defend their work (though I think the critics often misunderstand and misrepresent it, which we will have to discuss another day). Instead, it is to deny that postmodernist thought plays more than a small role in the current education system.

FURTHER READING

To understand how poor conservatives' grasp of university curriculums is, the best course of action is to actually study the material yourself. Pick up works of sociology, anthropology, history, political science, philosophy, gender studies, and (yes) critical race theory.

16

There Is a War on Cops When We Need to Be Tougher on Crime

The biggest myth about the criminal justice system is . . . that the disproportionate number of blacks in prison reflects bias by police, prosecutors, and judges. . . . It is not marijuana smoking that lands a skewed number of black men in prison; it is their disproportionate rates of violent and property crime. . . . Sentences got longer until, in conjunction with a policing revolution that began in New York City, that finally put a lid on crime, ushering in the biggest national crime drop in recorded history. . . . America does not have an incarceration problem, it has a crime problem. And the only answer to that crime problem is to rebuild the family—above all, the black family. . . . The demonization of the police and the criminal justice system must end. . . . Liberal elites have successfully kept attention focused exclusively on phantom police and criminal-justice racism while squelching even the most tentative discussion of the crime-breeding chaos of inner-city underclass culture.

—Heather Mac Donald, *The War on Cops*

We have a major under-incarceration problem in America. and it's only getting worse.

—Senator Tom Cotton (R-AK), Twitter, April 6, 2021

This year has seen the lowest crime numbers in our Country's recorded history, and now the Radical Left Democrats want to Defund and Abandon our Police. Sorry, I want LAW & ORDER!

—Donald Trump, Twitter, June 8, 2020

The Argument

The left wants to abolish the police and let lawlessness and rioting reign in our cities. They say cops are racist, when they are not, and use examples of "bad apple" police officers who are unrepresentative of the majority. By trying to roll back police protection, the left will increase crime. The Black Lives Matter movement is demonizing the police unfairly, and its criticisms of law enforcement ignore the reality that we need tough law enforcement to keep people safe.

The Response

To understand criticisms of police, it is first important to understand that the United States criminal punishment system has long been completely dysfunctional and cruel. The U.S. keeps 2.3 million people—the equivalent of the entire population of a small country—in prisons and jails.[1] It is, with the possible exception of China, the world's biggest jailer. Prisons, as we know, are environments of extreme deprivation. Solitary confinement, which is widely used, is accurately described as a form of torture.[2] Keeping people in cages for years at a time may be one way to "get criminals off the streets," but if we care about the intrinsic worth of all people, it is like treating a cold by cutting off your head. Prisons should be a last resort, but instead, the U.S. for decades pursued a "tough on crime" approach that followed the principle "when people commit a crime, throw them away for as long as possible," the idea being that if we were brutal enough to wrongdoers, many would be deterred from wrongdoing, and the ones who weren't would be out of our hair.

The consequences of this approach should outrage anyone. Under "three strikes" and "habitual offender" laws, people guilty of trivial offenses have been sent to prison for decades.[3] Prosecutors have immense power to coerce guilty pleas out of people, to the point where the threat of a prison sentence can make even an innocent person plead guilty in order to avoid the catastrophic risk of losing one's freedom for decades at a time.[4] If people cannot afford a good lawyer, the representation they receive is often woefully substandard, and poor people are systematically deprived of a meaningful right to counsel.[5]

The police are the frontline enforcers of this cruel system. Even good people who enter the police force must face the fact that their job is defined as *law enforcement,* meaning the application of force to those who disobey rules. To begin to understand why the left is so harshly critical of police, we must understand what police *represent,* which is the policy of solving social problems through the application of violence. The police are not mediators or social workers. They are not good at dealing with the mentally ill, and in some cases even shoot people who are clearly just in need of medical care.[6] While critics of police behavior believe that murders and sex crimes should be solved, we understand that in many communities, police harass and intimidate regular people going about their business. Anyone who has dealt with an aggressive police officer knows how terrifying it can be; they can seem totally impervious to reasoned arguments, devoted completely to ensuring the maintenance of their own authority in a situation even if this means roughing someone up.

To understand the anger at police, you must first understand that many people have been eyewitnesses to police doing outrageous things and not suffering any consequences. We talk about deadly police *shootings* a lot, but the shootings are only the most extreme events. For example, have a look at the Department of Justice (DOJ)'s 2017 investigative report on the Chicago Police Department (CPD),[7] which documents meticulously that the CPD constantly violates people's rights. The DOJ "found that CPD officers engage in a pattern or practice of using force, including deadly force, that is unreasonable":

> We found that officers engage in tactically unsound and unnecessary foot pursuits, and that these foot pursuits too often end with officers unreasonably shooting someone—including unarmed individuals. We found that officers shoot at vehicles

without justification and in contradiction to CPD policy. We found further that officers exhibit poor discipline when discharging their weapons and engage in tactics that endanger themselves and public safety. . . .

These include "incidents in which CPD officers shot at suspects who presented no immediate threat," and the use of "force against people in mental health crisis where force might have been avoided." Some of the most egregious instances involved the use of force on children. In one incident, "Officers hit a 16-year-old girl with a baton and then Tasered her after she was asked to leave the school for having a cell phone in violation of school rules." According to the DOJ, "This was not an isolated incident," and in other cases "officers unnecessarily drive-stunned students to break up fights, including one use of a Taser in drive-stun mode against a 14-year-old girl." The DOJ could not find any justification for this use of force. The DOJ documented an instance in which a police officer, irritated by having to stop for a minor in a crosswalk, got out and pushed them into a newspaper stand, and another in which an officer discovered some boys playing basketball on his property and "pointed his gun at them, used profanity, and threatened to put their heads through a wall and to blow up their homes," then "forced them to kneel and lie face-down, handcuffed together, leaving visible injuries on their knees and wrists." Sometimes, if a youth suspected of gang activity would not give desired information to the police, they would "take [the] young person to a rival gang neighborhood, and either leave the person there, or display the youth to rival gang members, immediately putting the life of that young person in jeopardy."

The DOJ found that the CPD allowed misconduct to go unpunished, and that out of thirty thousand complaints of police misconduct over a five-year period, only 2 percent were sustained. Officers were rarely severely disciplined even for serious wrongdoing, and even cases that the city was required by law to investigate went uninvestigated. When the DOJ checked video evidence against officers' own testimonies about their use of force, they found that officers routinely lied about what had happened and covered up abuses. Because the DOJ did not always have evidence against which officers' accounts could be checked, and many of the facts it documented had to come from CPD's own records of its behavior, the report notes that the problems are probably worse than what the DOJ is able to definitively substantiate.

Unsurprisingly, the "unreasonable force and systemic deficiencies fall heaviest on the predominantly black and Latino neighborhoods on the South and West Sides of Chicago," and "CPD uses force almost ten times more often against blacks than against whites." The CPD also "tolerated racially discriminatory conduct that not only undermines police legitimacy, but also contributes to the pattern of unreasonable force."

The DOJ report documents all of its assertions meticulously, and it shows why the problems of policing are *not* problems of "bad apple" officers. It shows how, from the police academy onward, officers are trained poorly, and the system *creates* misconduct because it lacks any means of ensuring fair policing.

If you think this is only Chicago, I can go through other investigations into police misconduct. For instance, when the DOJ investigated the Ferguson, Missouri police department,[8] it found that the city was essentially using poor Black residents as a piggy bank, "increas[ing] municipal fines and fees each year" and then getting police to enforce municipal ordinances as aggressively as possible in order to raise revenue for the city. This led to constant violations of people's rights, in which officers would go up to normal law-abiding citizens, accuse them of crimes, and try to find something they were guilty of. Take the following instance:

> For example, in the summer of 2012, a 32-year-old African-American man sat in his car cooling off after playing basketball in a Ferguson public park. An officer pulled up behind the

man's car, blocking him in, and demanded the man's Social Security number and identification. Without any cause, the officer accused the man of being a pedophile, referring to the presence of children in the park, and ordered the man out of his car for a pat-down, although the officer had no reason to believe the man was armed. The officer also asked to search the man's car. The man objected, citing his constitutional rights. In response, the officer arrested the man, reportedly at gunpoint, charging him with eight violations of Ferguson's municipal code. One charge, Making a False Declaration, was for initially providing the short form of his first name (e.g., "Mike" instead of "Michael"), and an address which, although legitimate, was different from the one on his driver's license. Another charge was for not wearing a seat belt, even though he was seated in a parked car. . . . The man told us that, because of these charges, he lost his job as a contractor with the federal government that he had held for years.

This sort of stuff occurs all around the country every day,[9] and it is not because individual officers are especially heinous people. It is, in part, as the DOJ report on Ferguson lays out, because officers can have little training, little accountability, biases, and perverse incentives. The reports show that for many people, the local police department is not a source of comfort but instead terrorizes them. Black people, especially, report in overwhelming numbers that they have experienced police misconduct, including nearly half who felt their life was in danger after encounters with the police,[10] and over 40 percent of encounters Black people have with police are not positive.[11]

The Black Lives Matter movement has arisen as a response to the racially unfair consequences of the existing system. BLM is not *exclusively* about police and prisons—in fact, the Movement for Black Lives agenda offers a comprehensive set of proposals for improving the lives of Black people.[12] But it tends to focus on police and prisons, in part because these are some of the most obviously tangible and harsh forms of injustice, and because they are perpetrated by the state. There is very clear evidence that the criminal punishment system is racist—that police brutalize Black people more often and that Black people receive longer sentences for the same crime.[13] "Stop and frisk" searches subject people of color to an invasive surveillance regime that makes ordinary life miserable for young Black men, who must constantly fear being stopped and harassed by police.[14] The horrifying killings of Eric Garner, George Floyd, Breonna Taylor, and many others are only *part* of the problems in the criminal punishment system.

Conservatives tend to argue, in response to Black Lives Matter, that police are not racist, and that the left ignores the evidence. Here is Coleman Hughes, writing in *City Journal,* that Black Lives Matter is based on an empirical falsehood:

> The basic premise of Black Lives Matter—that racist cops are killing unarmed black people—is false. . . . I no longer believe that the cops disproportionately kill unarmed black Americans. . . . To demonstrate the existence of a racial bias . . . you must do what all good social scientists do: control for confounding variables to isolate the effect that one variable has upon another (in this case, the effect of a suspect's race on a cop's decision to pull the trigger). At least four careful studies have done this—one by Harvard economist Roland Fryer, one by a group of public-health researchers, one by economist Sendhil Mullainathan, and one by David Johnson, et al. None of these studies has found a racial bias in deadly shootings. Of course, that hardly settles the issue for all time; as always, more research is needed. But given the studies already done, it seems unlikely that future work will uncover anything close to the amount of racial bias that BLM protesters in America and around the world believe exists. . . . The core premise of the movement is false. And if not for the dissemination of this falsehood, social relations between blacks and whites would be less tense, trust in police would be higher,

and businesses all across America might have been spared the looting and destruction that we have seen in recent weeks.[15]

As we know, when people cite a pile of studies, it is best to go and look at what they have cited to see what the research actually says. One of the four studies Hughes cites has been completely retracted for drawing erroneous conclusions.[16] But the other three do indeed conclude that there is no racial bias in police shootings. But the question is: How did they find out and what does that mean? We need to dwell on this, because Hughes has cited these studies to discredit the Black Lives Matter movement. If the finding is correct, he says, the whole "premise" of the movement is false. BLM, he says, has disseminated a falsehood and harmed society with it.

Before we think about *how* it is possible to figure out whether police shootings are racially biased, let's think about what we're asking. The question, as Hughes frames it, is whether police officers are more likely to shoot a person dead if that person is Black than if a person is white. If they are, then BLM is founded on a sound "premise." If they are not, then BLM's premise is discredited.

But is this right? If individual police officers aren't biased in who they shoot, does that mean race is irrelevant? It might seem like it does, but let us imagine a hypothetical: A city has police officers that tend to be aggressive and quick to use excessive force. They are, essentially, trained to be machines: rough up the suspect, whoever they are. They don't care what your race or gender is. Now, the city is also deeply racially segregated, and controlled politically by members of Race A. Members of Race A fear members of Race B and enact laws that send more squads of police to neighborhoods where members of Race B tend to live. Members of Race B have always been poorer than members of Race A,[17] and poverty is highly correlated with crime. As a result, five times as many members of Race B are roughed up by police as members of Race A.

Notice something here: the *individual* officers were not exhibiting bias in who they did their violence to. They were, essentially, soldiers carrying out a program. But would it therefore make sense to say that police violence in this city was not racist? No. It's deeply racist, because policies made out of racial fear and animus are sending violent police to disproportionately harm people of one race over another.

This is important, because it means Hughes is making a logical error when he says that if police officers are not individually racially biased in who they shoot, BLM's story of racist violence by police is false. That cannot be concluded from the findings of the studies. The racism may just be elsewhere in the system than in the decision over whether to shoot or not shoot a given suspect. It may be that a Black person is more likely to be *confronted* by an armed police officer, *not* that out of all the people who will be confronted, Black people are more likely than white people to actually be shot.[18]

So even if the studies are correct, they do not, in and of themselves, undermine BLM's central claim. But are they correct? The most publicized of the studies was conducted by Roland Fryer of Harvard. Now, importantly, the study *did* find that in similar situations, if a suspect was Black rather than white, police were more likely to (1) push the suspect into a wall, (2) use handcuffs, (3) draw their weapons, (4) push the suspect to the ground, (5) point their weapon, and (6) use pepper spray or a baton. So it found that police officers *were* racially biased in their use of force, in many different respects. It just did not find that in a given confrontation, they were more likely to *shoot* the suspect for being Black.[19] Fryer, in fact, concluded that the roughing up of young Black people by cops was an important factor in making those young people disillusioned with police and other institutions. He reported that in his interviews with Black youths, "almost every single one of them mentions lower-level uses of force as the reason why they believe the world is corrupt." This is critically important, so let me emphasize it over again: *even the study cited to show that BLM is wrong about police being racist, actually shows that they are right about police being racist.* It shows that cops are explicitly racist in their application of many types of force and only contests the idea that *shootings* specifically are racist.

But even given the study's finding on shootings, we still can't reach Hughes's conclusion that shootings aren't racially biased. First, we need to recognize that we're dealing with evidence that is likely to yield conclusions more favorable to police than the actual facts. Fryer's paper was criticized by social scientists because the evidence he had access to does not allow him to confidently make the inference he made.[20] In fact, as libertarian journalist Radley Balko explained in the *Washington Post,* a huge problem with any study of this kind is that it relies on *officers' own reports* in determining the reality of the situations they faced.[21] So we might look at police reports and determine that in situations where officers perceived a threat to their lives, they were just as likely to fire their weapons if the suspect was Black or white. But how do we know whether the perception of a threat to their life was influenced by racial bias?

It's important to remember that even according to the Fryer study, as a matter of raw numbers "black people were over 5 times as likely to be shot relative to whites." So Black people *did* get shot a lot more than white people. All Hughes and Fryer are saying is that perhaps officers shot more Black people because they were *threatened* by more Black people, and fired their weapons in circumstances where they were threatened, regardless of the race of the person threatening them. Now, it's true that this is possible, but it's also true that police have a strong interest in writing reports that present every shooting as justified, so looking at police reports cannot resolve the issue. We might be able to tell from the report that every time a police officer shot a Black person, they felt threatened, and every time they shot a white person, they felt threatened, and thereby conclude that "feeling threatened" was what caused an officer to shoot *rather* than the race of an offender.

But how do we know that their threat perceptions are not influenced by the race of the person they're considering shooting?

Unfortunately, determining whether there is racial bias in police shootings turns out to be incredibly difficult. There is no easy way to check. Social scientists are doing their best to figure out ways to investigate the question, but there is absolutely no way to come to Hughes's strong conclusion that racial bias in shootings has been disproven.[22]

We know that Black experiences with police tend to be negative. Over *half* of Black Americans report that either they or a member of their family has been stopped or treated unfairly by police because of their race, and Black people often feel *less* rather than more safe around police.[23] Even Black conservative Jason L. Riley, in *Please Stop Helping Us*, recounts having had numerous unpleasant encounters with police that were clearly racially motivated. Even though "my closet was full of khakis, button-downs, and crew-neck sweaters," he was "stopped regularly" as he drove through a white suburb while in college, and when he was an intern at *USA Today* had a "terrifying" encounter in which he was pushed facedown on the pavement by police and searched because he "fit the description" of a suspect. Riley says he was "almost certainly" regularly racially profiled and discriminated against. Riley is a sharp critic of the left and actually defends the police by suggesting that discrimination was, in part, a rational response to crime rates.[24] But surely we should take seriously his testimony about what tends to happen. (Similar testimony comes from another Black conservative, South Carolina senator Tim Scott, who writes that "even today, while I have the privilege of serving as a United States senator, I am not immune to being stopped while driving at home in South Carolina or even while walking onto the grounds of the Capitol. Each time, I hold my breath and each time, I have been able to exhale and go about my business.")[25]

There are other ways in which shootings are rationalized. Sometimes conservatives point to the many white people who are also shot by police as being counterevidence. This ignores, first, the fact that Black people are shot far more relative to their percentage of the population. But more importantly, it does not diminish the indictment of policing, it just suggests that there are problems that go *beyond* the racial ones. Cops shoot poor and disabled people of all races, and it's a serious, horrible problem.[26] We should be angry about the racial injustices *and* other injustices. Another talking point that only succeeds until you think about it is "crime rates": supposedly disparities in shootings can be explained by disparities in crime rates. But this only justifies shootings if we believe that the extrajudicial administration of the death penalty is justified. *You should not get shot even if you commit a crime.* Eric Garner had committed a crime—he sold untaxed cigarettes.[27] Daunte Wright, the Minnesota man shot by a police officer who supposedly thought she was using her taser, had an illegal air freshener dangling from his rearview mirror.[28] This is indeed criminalized in some states, and perhaps it is true that Black people are more likely to commit this "crime" than white people. But murder is murder regardless of whether the person being murdered violated a law beforehand.

But is there a "war on cops"? It's true that some on the left have called for "defunding" or even "abolishing" police.[29] Some have seized on this to suggest that activists want a world of lawless anarchy where criminals can do as they please. Critics of the left point to studies showing that reductions in policing lead to increases in crime as evidence that any kind of rollback of police power risks compromising public safety.[30]

It's important to pay close attention to what activists are actually advocating, though. They are not calling for defunding police and putting that money in a safe or setting it on fire. They are calling for *redirecting* money that currently goes to police to institutions that are better at building safe communities without using brutal punitive methods. Many activists have emphasized the need for services currently performed by police to be performed by unarmed mental health professionals—some of the saddest cases of killings by police occur when people suffering from severe mental illness encounter police officers who are totally ill-equipped to handle the situation. Personally, I wish fire departments would handle more emergencies—firefighters tend to save lives rather than take them, and sociologist Roscoe Scarborough suggests that police reform should begin with a recognition that fire departments clearly get aspects of institutional culture correct that police get wrong.[31]

Studies showing that increasing a police presence in a neighborhood reduces crime miss the point. There are more possibilities for bettering the world than simply adding or reducing the number of police officers. The correct questions are: What happens if you reduce the number of police *while* increasing the number of unarmed aid workers? What happens if firefighters and EMTs constitute a greater percentage of emergency responses?[32] What if armed officers were only used in situations where there was reason to believe armed officers were required? What happens if, instead of sending cops to bust up homeless encampments, we build quality public housing? What if we don't criminalize selling untaxed cigarettes or having an air freshener in your car? It is not just that we need less policing. We also need better schools, public daycare centers, free mental health services, free public housing, and a supportive society that reduces the problems to which policing is a "brute force" solution. The left is not just trying to imagine a "world without police." We're trying to imagine ways of making policing less necessary. It's not *easy*. You can mock us for our failures, for our sloganeering. But we start from the position that having the government kill a thousand people a year without arrest or trial is a social failure, and so is putting millions of people in cages. We are trying our best to figure out how to fix this failure. And what is aggravating to me about the right is that instead of helping us come up with answers to that, they spend their time rationalizing the existing state of affairs, thus proposing a bleak future in which we simply accept these atrocities as a normal feature of everyday life. This we must refuse to do.

FURTHER READING

- Bryan Stevenson—*Just Mercy: A Story of Justice and Redemption*
- Alec Karakatsanis—*Usual Cruelty: The Complicity of Lawyers in the Criminal Injustice System*
- Jed S. Rakoff—*Why the Innocent Plead Guilty and the Guilty Go Free: And Other Paradoxes of Our Broken Legal System*
- Larry Krasner—*For the People: A Story of Justice and Power*
- Paul Butler—*Chokehold: Policing Black Men*
- Radley Balko—*Rise of the Warrior Cop: The Militarization of America's Police Forces*
- Khalil Gibran Muhammad—*The Condemnation of Blackness: Race, Crime, and the Making of Modern Urban America*
- Derecka Purnell—*Becoming Abolitionists: Police, Protests, and the Pursuit of Freedom*
- Angela Y. Davis—*Are Prisons Obsolete?*
- John F. Pfaff—*Locked In: The True Causes of Mass Incarceration—and How to Achieve Real Reform*
- Mariame Kaba—*We Do This 'Til We Free Us: Abolitionist Organizing and Transforming Justice*
- Kristen Henning—*The Rage of Innocence: How America Criminalizes Black Youth*
- Zach Norris—*Defund Fear: Safety without Policing, Prisons, and Punishment*
- David Cole—*No Equal Justice: Race and Class in the American Criminal Justice System*
- Devah Pager—*Marked: Race, Crime, and Finding Work in an Era of Mass Incarceration*

- Michelle Alexander—*The New Jim Crow: Mass Incarceration in the Age of Colorblindness*
- James Forman, Jr.—*Locking Up Our Own: Crime and Punishment in Black America*

17

Labor Unions Hurt Workers

The decline of union power is good news, not bad. That conclusion is driven not by some insidious effort to stifle the welfare of workers, but by the simple and profound point that the greatest protection for workers lies in a competitive economy that opens up more doors than it closes. The only way to achieve that result is by slashing the various restrictions that prevent job formation. . . . Unions are monopoly institutions that raise wages through collective bargaining, not productivity improvements. The ensuing higher labor costs, higher costs of negotiating collective bargaining agreements, and higher labor market uncertainty all undercut the gains to union workers just as they magnify losses to nonunion employers, as well as to the shareholders, suppliers, and customers of these unionized firms. They also increase the risk of market disruption from strikes, lockouts, or firm bankruptcies whenever unions or employers overplay their hands in negotiation. These net losses in capital values reduce the pension fund values of unionized and nonunionized workers alike. Employers are right to oppose unionization by any means within the law, because any gains for union workers come at the expense of everyone else.

—Joseph Epstein, "The Decline of Unions Is Good News,"
Hoover Institution

The fact that Americans have dumped unions at an astonishing rate since 1950 is due to the fact that the vast majority of employees aren't all that interested [in] them, despite Democratic Party and media wishcasting.

—Ben Shapiro

The Argument

The American labor movement is not what it was. Just over 10 percent of American workers are in unions today, down from nearly one-third at midcentury. But for some conservatives, like Joseph Epstein, this is a good thing. Unions, it is argued, are bad for the economy. They increase unemployment and create inefficiency. When the workers at a company are considering forming a union, companies often tell them that this would ultimately hurt the workers, reminding them that unions collect dues from their members and suggesting that the firm's financial success would suffer. Unions are frequently portrayed as selfish, corrupt, parasitic institutions that hurt rather than help workers. Their leaders are interested in power, not improving the lives of workers.

The Response

Notice something interesting about Epstein's case against unions: the phrase "any gains for union workers." He's arguing that unions are, *in the aggregate,* bad for the working class. But for *individual* workers, being in a union may well bring significant benefits. In fact, while critics of unions decline to mention it (and you won't hear about it in your employer-sponsored video presentation on Why This Company Is Just Fine Without A Union), any given employee is likely to be much better off if they join a union. A 2017 review of the economic literature found that "men in the private sector at unionized workplaces make about 15 to 25 percent more than those at non-unionized ones."[1] Another found that the "union premium has been remarkably consistent over the decades," and that both less-educated and higher-educated workers receive benefits from union membership.[2] A unionized worker typically has higher pay and better job security. A "union job" is a good job. American workers at multinational corporations often do not realize that workers at the *same company* in other countries have much better contracts than they do—because those workers are in unions.

A 2003 report from the Economic Policy Institute concluded that the union advantage goes beyond raw pay and job security:

> The most sweeping advantage for unionized workers is in fringe benefits. Unionized workers are more likely than their nonunionized counterparts to receive paid leave, are approximately 18% to 28% more likely to have employer-provided health insurance, and are 23% to 54% more likely to be in employer-provided pension plans. Unionized workers receive more generous health benefits than nonunionized workers. They also pay 18% lower health care deductibles and a smaller share of the costs for family coverage. In retirement, unionized workers are 24% more likely to be covered by health insurance paid for by their employer. Unionized workers receive better pension plans. Not only are they more likely to have a guaranteed benefit in retirement, their employers contribute 28% more toward pensions. Unionized workers receive 26% more vacation time and 14% more total paid leave (vacations and holidays).[3]

It is, in other words, a very good deal for union workers.

There's an old labor song called "There Is Power in a Union." And there sure is. In France, for instance, unions representing Amazon workers were able to force the company to put in hundreds of coronavirus safety precautions. American workers had no such power to extract concessions from the company, and as a result many had to work in unsafe conditions no matter how much they objected.

White-collar workers need unions, too. Consider what happened at the *New Republic*, a storied political magazine that announced in 2021 that its offices would be moving from New York to D.C. The magazine's management had not told the staff that they would be suddenly expected to uproot their lives, and many were furious. But the *New Republic* is unionized. The union immediately began negotiating with management and secured an agreement that the existing New York staff did not have to relocate and would not be punished for not doing so. Nobody had to suddenly pack up their lives, because the union had power.[4]

Without a union, on the other hand, workers do not have good ways of fighting back against objectionable decisions by management. Amazon delivery drivers, for instance, regularly have to urinate in bottles while they are on their rounds because their intensive delivery quotas mean there is no time to stop and find a bathroom.[5] The situation is especially bad for women. One female driver told *Business Insider* that the inability to use a bathroom made menstruation a "nightmare."[6] *The Atlantic* interviewed female Amazon warehouse workers who had gotten multiple urinary tract infections because the workload made it impossible to regularly empty their bladders.[7] *The Atlantic* also reported that at Amazon warehouses they studied, "the rate of serious injuries for those facilities was more than double the national average for the warehousing industry," concluding that "ruthless quotas are maiming employees."

Amazon workers have no obvious remedies. If they need their jobs, it's hard to quit. If they protest, they are likely to be fired. A union, however, gives them a powerful way to push back against unsafe working conditions and excessive quotas. A union has the power to negotiate rights like bathroom breaks and safe conditions. Because these could cost Amazon money, it's no wonder the company has fought hard against unionization efforts. With a union, you can fight back.

Of course, there are more and less democratic unions, and it's certainly true that many unions have "sold out" their members and failed to fight hard. But that means we need democratic unions, *not* that we need employees to be unable to bargain collectively. The existence of unions that let down their workers does not mean we need fewer unions, but that we need more militant unions that actually go the distance for their members.

The fact is that for most of us, our employers wield significant power over us. "At-will employment" means we can be fired for any reason, or no reason at all. This means that for people who need their paychecks (and because the United States has an employer-based health insurance system, their health insurance), there are strong incentives to comply even with unreasonable or abusive practices by employers. Amazon warehouse workers who resist its unforgiving, physically taxing quotas, or who want longer bathroom breaks, will lose their jobs immediately. There is no right of appeal. If they don't like you, you're out.

Workers form unions to address this imbalance of power. When workers negotiate with employers as a unit, rather than individually, they can get a better deal. Because a union can threaten to strike, and therefore cost the company a significant amount of money, it can extract concessions from employers that they would have no incentive to offer to workers who were not organized into a bargaining unit.

I can offer a personal example about how this works: for several years I was a columnist for a major newspaper, *The Guardian*. In February of 2021, I was fired when the editor in chief objected to a tweet I had posted criticizing U.S. military aid to Israel. Columnists at *The Guardian* were contractors rather than full employees, which meant that the editor in chief's decision, even if arbitrary and unfair, could not be protested or appealed. Other employees at the paper, however, were members of the NewsGuild union. If the editor in chief wanted to fire one of the unionized employees, it would be much more difficult, because the union-negotiated contract spells out the conditions under which a union employee can be fired, and there is an entire adjudication process that must be followed. This does not mean that an incompetent union employee cannot be fired. Instead, it means that the employee has some rights to "due process" that must be followed before they are fired. There is an analogy here to "due process" under criminal law. At-will employment is like a system where a judge can declare somebody guilty and sentence them without having to consider any evidence or apply any legal standard. A union contract provides something akin to a set of constitutional rights. The employee has to have a chance to contest the charges against them. "Due process" does not mean that nobody can ever be found guilty; it means they can't be found guilty arbitrarily, which helps protect people from unjust punishment.

Without unions, employer power can be terrifyingly extreme. A 2019 *Wall Street Journal* investigation called "The New Ways Your Boss Is Spying on You" painted a picture of a terrifying twenty-first-century workplace in which the boss is a kind of privatized Big Brother:

> Your employer may know a lot more about you than you think. The tone of your voice in a meeting. How often you're away from your desk. How quickly you respond to emails. Where you roam in the office. What's on your computer screen. To be an employee of a large company in the U.S. now often means becoming a workforce data generator—from the first email sent from bed in the morning to the Wi-Fi hotspot used during lunch to the new business contact added before going home. Employers are parsing those interactions to learn who is influential, which teams are most productive and who is a flight risk. Companies, which have wide legal latitude in the U.S. to monitor workers, don't always tell them what they are tracking.[8]

If you don't *want* your employer installing software relaying what is on your computer screen to your supervisor, or monitoring your bodily functions, you can threaten to quit. But assuming you are replaceable—and most of us are, as I found out quickly at my newspaper job—quitting is your only option. An employer can tell you what to say on social media, can ask for a drug test, can even tell you what you are and aren't allowed to do in your spare time, and thanks to the "freedom of contract," your only choices are: take it or leave it.[9] Give up your income or accept the restrictions. It doesn't matter that there is a First Amendment guaranteeing that the *government* will not tell you what you can and can't say. Employers, which serve as "private governments,"[10] effectively have coercive power over workers. To counter that coercion, you need a union.

Amusingly enough, a good place to find some personal pro-union testimony is in the Facebook comments section on a Ben Shapiro video purporting to "debunk" unions. Some of the commenters didn't buy Shapiro's anti-union arguments, mainly because they had their own experiences being in unions, and they pointed out that Shapiro's views did not comport with the realities they had witnessed in their own working lives:

◊ "Nothing is perfect, but since joining the IBEW in 2015 after 8 or so years working non-union in the electric utility industry (lineman), my income has doubled, some years tripled, my family gets employer paid health insurance vs. nearly $1000 a month premiums for trash coverage, I have over $150k in employer paid annuity in just 5 years (last statement), and us, the workers, get a say so on jobs, and quite often what we ask for if it's reasonable. The safety standards and training on this side of the fence are light years ahead of non-union, and we don't have many problems culling shitty hands. I'm sure there's some dirty deeds at the top, but down low we take care of each other, and get compensated well, or we'll pack our tools and drag. A union is only going to be as strong as its members make it. Remember, the union works for YOU."

◊ "Yeahhh my family has probably only prospered as well as it has because of teamsters union. I'm not really down with anti-union propaganda; someone needs to stand up for the working class against the abusive corporations."

◊ "I can't complain about my union, they've treated me pretty fairly so far. Do I think there could be changes? Yes, I do. But all in all, I have job security amongst other key benefits."

◊ "... I know as a member of a trade union many non-union guys in my area with more experience than me average making $10 less than I do now as an apprentice, with little to no benefits or retirement plan and often have to work 10–12 hour days with no overtime pay and no guaranteed breaks. ..."

The simple fact is that the presence of a union in your workplace is likely to give you more money in your pocket at the end of the day. This is a fact that does not appear in Ben Shapiro's video, and that employers work hard to obfuscate—e.g., by pointing to union dues but not to the increased pay that results from those dues—but it is a basic economic reality.[11]

But even if you *personally* should join a union, it could still be that unions in the aggregate have negative effects on the economy. Unions might help their members at the expense of everyone else, meaning that it makes sense to unionize but it also makes sense for a country to reduce its union density. This is the core of Epstein's argument, that regardless of the fact that unions are good for the average worker who is in them, they have an overall negative economic effect.

But there's no good evidence that this is true. Economies with high union density function perfectly well. Norway, for instance, has more than half of its workers in unions and has a highly competitive economy with lower unemployment.[12] The libertarian Library of Economics and Liberty says that "some of the gains to union members come at the expense of those who must shift to lower-paying or less desirable jobs or go unemployed,"[13] while the Heritage Foundation says that according to economic theory, unions "raise the wages of their members at the cost of lower profits and fewer jobs, that lower profits cause businesses to invest less."[14] Once again, note the concession that being in a union is probably good for you. But *do* gains to union members come at the expense of other workers? In fact, there is some evidence that the opposite is the case, that even *non*unionized workers in unionized industries receive "spillover" benefits from the presence of unions. Furthermore, it is not at all clear that unions cause companies to become more sluggish and less productive. A 2020 study published in the *Economic Journal* took a close look at how "increasing union density at the firm level leads to a substantial increase in both productivity and wages."[15] Unions are definitely bad for two groups of people, shareholders and CEOs, because they limit the amount of the "pie" that those groups can take for themselves. But unionized workers have an incentive to keep the company productive and innovative, because they will reap greater rewards from that productivity than at a company where they have less of a stake in success.

Some people who start off anti-union, because they believe their employer's talking points, shift their perspective once they see labor organizing in action at their workplace. For example, German Lopez, a writer at *Vox*, once opposed the idea of his colleagues forming a union and believed strongly that unions were unnecessary. But in a mea culpa several years later, Lopez explained that he had swallowed faulty talking points, and failed to actually look at the evidence:

> As I dug deeper and deeper into the research, and as I engaged in the actual organizing and bargaining processes, I was repeatedly proven wrong, in large part because I initially focused way too much on the bad examples of unions instead of the good ones. When you stack up all the research and look at the broader picture, though, the net effect of unions—bad examples included—is good for the typical worker. I hope more Americans go through the transformation that I did. We'd all be better for it.[16]

Lopez realized that the union was a crucial ally of the work-force, and that the reason management so strongly opposed it was *not* that management simply cared about workers' interests, but that management knew that a unionized workplace is one where managers have less power to dictate to workers. Martin Luther King Jr. understood the same thing. He was an opponent of "right-to-work"[17] laws and a champion of unions (at the time he died, he was in Memphis to support a labor strike), and said: "The labor movement did not diminish the strength of the nation but en-larged it. Those who today attack labor forget these simple truths, but history remembers them."[18]

Companies fight hard against unions not out of benevolence, but because they know that unions make for a more democratic workplace that has to share more with its lower-level workers. The CEO who makes two hundred times what the average employee of the company makes is rightly terrified of a labor union, which could significantly reduce the status and power of executives.

FURTHER READING

- Michael D. Yates—*Why Unions Matter*
- Jane McAlevey—*No Shortcuts: Organizing for Power in the New Gilded Age*
- Jane McAlevey—*A Collective Bargain: Unions, Organizing, and the Fight for Democracy*
- Kim Kelly—*Fight Like Hell: The Untold History of American Labor*
- Erik Loomis—*A History of America in Ten Strikes*
- Steven Greenhouse—*Beaten Down, Worked Up: The Past, Present, and Future of American Labor*
- Philip Dray—*There Is Power in a Union: The Epic Story of Labor in America*

- Alice and Staughton Lynd—*Rank and File: Personal Histories by Working Class Organizers*
- "How to Unionize Your Workplace" YouTube video: https://www.youtube.com/watch?v=JvrldZIUwe0
- *Labor Notes*, *Jacobin*, and *In These Times* are periodicals that regularly report on labor news.
- *Daisy Pitkin—On the Line: A Story of Class, Solidarity, and Two Women's Epic Fight to Build a Union*

18

Transgender People Are Delusional and a Threat

Why should feeling like a man—whatever that means—make someone a man? Why do our feelings determine reality on the question of sex, but on little else? Our feelings don't determine our age or our height. And few people buy into Rachel Dolezal's claim to identify as a Black woman, since she is clearly not. What about people who identify as animals, or able-bodied people who identify as disabled? Do all of these self-professed identities determine reality? If not, why not? And should these people receive medical treatment to transform their bodies to accord with their minds? Why accept transgender "reality," but not trans-racial, trans-species, and trans-abled reality? The challenge for activists is to explain why a person's "real" sex is determined by an inner "gender identity," but age and height and race and species are not determined by an inner sense of identity. Of course, a transgender activist could reply that an "identity" is, by definition, just an inner sense of self. But if that's the case, gender identity is merely a disclosure of how one feels. Saying that someone is transgender, then, says only that the person has feelings that he or she is the opposite sex. Gender identity, so understood, has no bearing at all on the meaning of "sex" or anything else. But transgender activists claim that a person's self-professed "gender identity" is that person's "sex." The challenge for activists is to explain why the mere feeling of being male or female (or both or neither) makes someone male or female (or both or neither).

—Ryan T. Anderson, "Transgender Ideology Is Riddled
with Contradictions. Here Are the Big Ones,"
Heritage Foundation

> The left would love to frame [the issues of trans women in sports and medical care for trans youth] as if they pitted reason and science against superstition. But on all of these issues social conservatives are on the side of the biological facts. The Democratic Party and the left are the science deniers. . . . The scientific point of view confirms the biblical teaching that humans are created male and female. It requires no faith to know that a boy who "identifies" as a girl isn't one and shouldn't be allowed into private female spaces.
>
> —Ryan T. Anderson, "Religious Liberty Isn't Enough,"
> *Wall Street Journal*, Jan. 31, 2021

> I'm not denying your humanity if you are a transgender person; I am saying that you are not the sex which you claim to be . . . if you're going to dictate to me that I'm supposed to pretend that men are women and women are men, no.
>
> —Ben Shapiro

The Argument

The core argument is that to be transgender is to deny the basic facts of biology. Humanity is divided into men and women, and these are fixed biological categories. One can pretend the categories do not exist, but saying you are something does not make it so. Shapiro says that for a "man" to claim to be a "woman" is as if he, Shapiro, claimed to be a moose. Even if society recognized him as such, it would still be false.

Books like Ryan T. Anderson's *When Harry Became Sally: Responding to the Transgender Movement* and Abigail Shrier's *Irreversible Damage: The Transgender Craze Seducing Our Daughters* go further and argue that not only does the concept of being transgender not make sense, but the "transgender movement," or "craze," is causing active social harm. Sometimes this takes the form of a worry that transgender women will commit sex crimes in women's bathrooms. Some worry about a phenomenon they call "rapid onset gender dysphoria," by which young people allegedly turn transgender with unusual rapidity. Sometimes the argument is made that people regret transitioning from one gender to another and are having their "delusion" indulged with damaging effects.

The Response

Let us deal first with the question of whether transgender people are delusional about their gender. They are not. It is striking that commentators like Shapiro and Anderson seem to have spent very little time listening to transgender thinkers and writers. If they had, they would know precisely why the "I can't become a moose by saying I'm a moose" talking point doesn't hold up.

Let us first hear from several such trans writers, discussing their experiences. First up is a woman who we actually met earlier, Deirdre McCloskey. McCloskey is a free-market libertarian, but she is also transgender, and she wrote a memoir called *Crossing* about her experience. She describes it like this:

> It's strange to have been a man and now to be a woman. But it's no stranger perhaps than having been a West African and now being an American, or once a priest and now a businessman. Free people keep deciding to make strange crossings, from storekeeper to monk or from civilian to soldier or from man to woman. . . . I visited womanhood and stayed. It was not for the pleasures, though I discovered many I had not imagined, and many pains too. But calculating pleasures and pains was not the point. The point was who I am. . . . I did not change gender because I liked colorful clothing (Donald did not) or womanly grace (Donald viewed it as sentimentality). The "decision" was not utilitarian. In our culture the rhetoric of the very word decision entails cost and benefit. My gender crossing was motivated by identity, not by a balance sheet of utility. Of course you can ask what psychological reasons explain my desire to cross. . . . But a demand for an answer to why carries with it

in our medicalized culture an agenda of treatment. If a gender crosser is "just" a guy who gets pleasure from it, that's one thing (laugh at him, jail him, murder him). If it's brain chemistry, that's another (commit him to a madhouse and try to "cure" him).

I say in response to your question of Why? "Can't I just be?" You, dear reader, are. No one gets indignant if you have no answer to why you are an optimist or why you like peach ice cream. . . .

You become a woman by being treated as one of the tribe. Nothing else is essential. Being Dutch is being treated as Dutch. You can be a masculine woman, as by some stereotypes many women are, yet still be treated as one of the tribe. No piece of conventionally feminine behavior is essential if the overall effect makes you accepted in the tribe. Biology is not decisive. Big hips, small frame, high voice, hairless face, sexual interest in men, more-than-male amounts of sympathy and readiness to cry: We all know women almost anywhere who vary on these dimensions, in this direction or that, but who are still part of the tribe. . . . Why, then, did Deirdre join the women's tribe? The question does not make sense, because it asks for a prudential answer when the matter is identity. Asking why a person changes gender is like asking why a person is a Midwesterner or thoughtful or great-souled: She just is.[1]

Next up, here is a quote from transgender writer Julia Serano. Serano has a PhD in biology, which in and of itself should make us wonder a little about the argument that transgender people simply "do not understand biology." Serano says:

From my own experience in having transitioned from one sex to the other, I have found that women and men are not separated by an insurmountable chasm, as many people seem to believe. Actually, most of us are only a hormone prescription away from being perceived as the "opposite" sex. Personally, I welcome this idea as a testament to just how little difference there really is between women and men. To believe that a woman is a woman because of her sex chromosomes, reproductive organs, or socialization denies the reality that every single day, we classify each person we see as either female or male based on a small number of visual clues and a ton of assumptions. The one thing that women share is that we are all perceived as women and treated accordingly.[2]

McCloskey and Serano challenge the simplistic view that there simply "are" two groups, men and women, and that nobody can ever pass from one to the other. In fact, they say, it's more complicated than that, and being a woman has more to do with being *treated* as a woman than with anything about your biology.

Transgender YouTuber Natalie Wynn, in an excellent video debunking Ben Shapiro's central talking point,[3] explains this in a helpful way. She says it is not the case that transgender people are misunderstanding biology. They understand every aspect of their biological makeup and think about it far more than cisgender people do. Rather, it is that those who think fixed aspects of biology determine who is a "man" and a "woman" are failing to understand *language* and the way the words we use to describe someone are a choice we make based on our values.

This can be a little tricky to grasp at first, because it requires you to think. Ben Shapiro is good at winning debates in part because debates are often rapid-fire affairs in which the most compelling *speaker* wins. (Compelling thinkers are not always compelling speakers.) Hence, it's easy to get away with a talking point that is revealed to be nonsense only after you think about it for a few seconds.

Wynn, to illustrate her point that Shapiro misunderstands how language works, asks us to think about *parents*. Who are your parents? They might be the people who contributed your genetic material. But you might have adoptive parents. The fact that they did not contribute your genetic material does not mean they are any less *your parents,* if that's what you consider them. The word "parents" can refer to biological parents *or* adoptive parents.

A Ben Shapiro type might say, "No. Adoptive parents are not parents. To be a parent is a function of biology. If you're not the biological parent, you're not a parent."

But why? Who says? Who says the word "parent" needs to refer to biology? Language is socially created; nature does not prescribe which words we have to use for what. If it makes sense to use the word "parent" to describe both biological parents and adoptive parents, we can do so.

How does this relate to gender? Well, we *could* use the words "men" and "women" to refer solely to those who have certain chromosomal makeups. But nothing forces us to. It's not "science." We could also choose to use the words "men" and "women" to refer to those who are perceived as men and women by others. Serano and McCloskey are right that in society, *perception* is what tends to get people placed in one category or another, not chromosomes. When Serano and McCloskey meet strangers, those strangers treat them as women. If they are prejudiced against women, Serano and McCloskey will be on the receiving end of those prejudices. If they are asked who they just talked to, they will use the pronoun "she."

The anti-trans perspective is that this "perception" is different from the *reality,* that while people might go through their entire lives being treated as women, they are not "actually" women, and thus the label is an error. But it's only an error if you have *decided* that the words "men" and "women" refer to chromosomes, just as it's only an error to call adoptive parents "parents" if you have made the (bizarre) linguistic prescription that only biological parents are real parents.

Let me ask another question: Who is a "real" American? Do you have to be born here to be an American? If you came here as a baby and were never given citizenship, but grew up like any other average American kid, are you "American"? If you were born here, and thus are a U.S. citizen, but moved away as a child, have never been back since, do not speak English, and do not know anything about the U.S., are you "American"? The answer to these questions is that there *is* no definitive answer to these questions, because it all depends on what we *decide* to put in the category of "American."

Essayist Scott Alexander, in a critique of the anti-trans argument called "The Categories Were Made for Man, Not Man for the Categories," says that we must distinguish between labels that are true or false and labels that are created to serve social purposes.[4] He points out that whether we think the West Bank "is" Israel or Palestine depends on what, to quote a U.S. president, the meaning of "is" is. National borders are decided upon politically. They are not facts of the universe. Likewise, gender categories are choices, not dictates handed down by biology.

Transgender people are not denying a single fact of biological reality. They do not dispute that chromosomes and hormones and reproductive organs exist. They are not "delusional" about any aspect of their anatomy. Instead, they point out that defining gender categories by biology leads to an absurdity.

To see why, let's look at pictures of men and women. Here are two women:

And here are two men:

Both of the women are transgender women, and both of the men are transgender men. Each is treated in their day-to-day life as the gender they identify with and present as, *not* as the gender Ben Shapiro would call them. But this should tell us that the Shapiro definition is missing something critical. Gender is more than a matter of chromosomes (which, after all, were only discovered in the 1880s,[5] long after the linguistic categories of male and female had already been formed).

Even Ben Shapiro cannot actually put his silly position into practice. In discussing transgender actress Laverne Cox, Shapiro accidentally called her "she," before remembering that in his framework, Cox is a "he." The slipup is natural; it is very hard to think of Cox as a "man" because beyond her chromosomes (which we cannot see), she does not have any "male" traits. She appears to us as a woman. So why not call her a woman? Why try to apply a category that doesn't seem to fit? Insisting on calling her a man, even though it feels like the completely wrong label for her, is both pointless and cruel.

Critics of transgender people often argue that if we do not use chromosomal sex to determine how we will publicly identify someone's gender, gender becomes confusing. Is gender just a feeling? Is it a collection of stereotypical "masculine" and "feminine" traits? Serano and McCloskey tell us that to be a woman is to be seen as a woman, but some transgender women who do not yet "pass" socially nevertheless identify as women. Abandoning chromosomes makes definitions much more complicated. Gender is defined subjectively, but *what is it*? Serano points out that "nearly every single word that refers to some aspect of transgender identities, bodies, or life experiences exists in a perpetual state of debate or dispute, with individual trans people espousing differing word preferences and alternative definitions." In other words, *things get complicated*. But there's nothing wrong with that.[6]

Now that we have accepted the legitimacy of being transgender (did it really need to be that hard?), we face the other conservative talking point: that the transgender "movement" is causing harm, through trying to admit "men" into women's bathrooms, or through trying to turn children transgender who will later regret it. One writer critical of the transgender movement, Katie Herzog, even claims that the increasing presence of trans people is causing lesbians and lesbian culture to disappear,[7] as young women who in a previous generation might have identified themselves as lesbians are instead becoming trans men. (In fact, the data show that the number of self-identified lesbians continues to increase generation to generation, and Herzog admits her "sense that the lesbian is endangered is purely anecdotal.")

The bathroom complaint is particularly silly. There is no evidence that transgender women will use the ability to enter women's bathrooms to assault cissexual women.[8] The theory underlying the scare story doesn't even make sense. If someone wants to commit assault in a bathroom, there is no physical force field in the universe stopping them from entering a bathroom of the opposite sex and carrying out assault. Bathrooms do not check your genitalia at the door; there are no bouncers. In practice, how exactly would punishing trans women for entering the ladies' room prevent assault?

It's not going to prevent assault, because the whole fear about trans women assaulting people is based on bigoted and cruel stereotypes that suggest trans women are predatory. What it *will* do, however, is make it even more difficult to be transgender. Every trans woman will face a difficult choice: Does she use the women's room, where she will be seen as just another woman using the bathroom, *unless* she is discovered to be trans, in which case the police could be called? Or does she use the men's room, where men will wonder why there is a woman in the bathroom, and where *she* risks harassment or assault? Proponents of measures like the North Carolina "bathroom bill" never appear to consider the effects that these types of punitive sanctions will have on trans people in terms of creating stigma and fear. The effects of these kinds of measures do not help cis women—many of whom have already been in bathrooms with trans women without noticing—but they *do* create an invasive new policing regime that makes it much harder to live a normal life as a trans person.

What about the claim that children are being turned trans? It's true that the youngest generation has a higher percentage of open transgender people than any previous generation.[9] Many of them are nonbinary—they reject both male and female categories. There's nothing to worry about here, though. It may well be something to celebrate; perhaps the phenomenon shows that where people in previous generations would have had to suppress their nonconforming gender identity, young people today are in a less socially oppressive environment. But even if there *are* more people feeling like their assigned gender category doesn't fit them, so what? For some, binary gender categories seem basically irrelevant or inapplicable, and they feel neither like a "man" nor a "woman." Others feel more comfortable living as the opposite gender to that traditionally associated with their chromosomal sex. It's fine. Abigail Shrier's *Irreversible Damage* is full of stories of troubled parents who are alarmed that their children are transgender,[10] but she doesn't talk to the kids, who may have a very different story to tell, one in which being openly trans is a positive.[11]

Sometimes conservatives point to the stories of people who have "detransitioned," who have changed their gender and regretted it, and suggest that children are being encouraged to pursue irreversible transition procedures that they may come to regret. It's important, of course, that young people be given the medical assistance they *want,* rather than being pressured. But the fact is that a far bigger problem facing transgender children is a *lack* of support for their transition. Being trans still carries an enormous stigma, and threats of violence. The rate of suicide attempts is very high. It is very difficult to get needed medical care. This is not a friendly society to trans people. Why focus on the small number of people who regret transitioning and ignore the testimonies of the majority of people, like Serano and McCloskey, for whom it was a life-changing positive step?[12]

The problem in the contemporary United States is not transgender people. It is people like Shapiro who treat them as delusional and ignore the hostility and bigotry that make trans people's lives difficult. Such people do not seem to have read writings by trans people, and so they make arguments they think are clever but have been responded to hundreds of times.

FURTHER READING

- Julia Serano—*Whipping Girl: A Transsexual Woman on Sexism and the Scapegoating of Femininity*
- Nicholas M. Teich—*Transgender 101: A Simple Guide to a Complex Issue*
- Deirdre McCloskey—*Crossing: A Memoir*
- Jan Morris—*Conundrum*
- Lou Sullivan; Ellis Martin and Zach Ozma, eds.—*We Both Laughed in Pleasure: The Selected Diaries of Lou Sullivan*
- Brynn Tannehill—*Everything You Ever Wanted to Know about Trans (But Were Afraid to Ask)*

- Shon Faye—*The Transgender Issue*
- Susan Stryker—*Transgender History: The Roots of Today's Revolution*
- Kate Bornstein—*Gender Outlaw: On Men, Women, and the Rest of Us*

19

Abortion Is Murder

A first-trimester fetus has moral value because whether you consider it a potential human life or a full-on human life, it has more value than just a cluster of cells. If left to its natural processes, it will grow into a baby. So the real question is, where do you draw the line? So, you're going to draw the line at the heartbeat—because it's very hard to draw the line at the heartbeat? There are people who are adults who are alive because of a pacemaker, they need some sort of outside force generating their heartbeat. Are you going to do it based on brain function? Okay, well, what about people who are in a coma? Should we just kill them?

—Ben Shapiro

No matter how safe or clean a business might appear to be, every abortion ends with an empty womb and the death of an unborn child. That is the simple, horrible fact that supporters of legal abortion are desperate to avoid. It's far easier to defend the right to abortion when it is covered up with phrases such as "women's health care" or "the right to choose." Acknowledging that every abortion ends the life of a distinct human being and defending it on those terms is far more difficult and far less popular.

—Alexandra Desanctis, "What the Media Won't Tell Us about Abortion," *National Review*

It is a matter of biological fact. . . . In view of the established facts of embryogenesis and early intrauterine development, the real question is not whether human beings in the embryonic and fetal state are human beings. Plainly they are. The question is whether we will honor or abandon our civilizational and national commitment to the equal

worth and dignity of all human beings—even the smallest,
youngest, weakest, and most vulnerable.

—Robert P. George, *Conscience and Its Enemies*

At the end of every political speech, most of us say, God
bless America. But how can He do that when we continue
to slaughter 4,000 babies a day? And I want to be the president that treats every person, including the unborn, as a
person.

—Mike Huckabee, 2016 campaign debate

I believe abortion should be treated like any other premed-
itated homicide.

—Kevin D. Williamson[1]

The question is whether that baby is a human life or is not a
human life. If it's a human life, well, if you are raped, then
you don't get to kill the person sitting next to you.

—Ben Shapiro

The Argument

An unborn child is a human being. To take the life of an embryo
or fetus is tantamount to murder. Abortion is morally wrong and
must be criminalized. So-called pro-choice activists think abortion should be a matter of individual rights, left to the mother. But
if the mother does not get to kill their child after it is born, there is
no reason they should be allowed to before it is born. Once a life
is created through the process of conception, there is no right to
choose to take it away, regardless of how inconvenient it may be.

The Response

I was once walking across the campus of my university when I
came across a pro-life demonstrator who had a large foam presentation board. The board showed about ten different phases of the
development of an embryo into a fetus and then into a newborn

child. At the top was the heading "WHERE DO YOU DRAW THE LINE?" The demonstrator had a pointer and as people were passing by, he would challenge them to say at which of the stages they thought that "killing" became unacceptable.

The demonstrator's presentation was effective because it highlighted the fact that for people who are pro-choice (that is, they believe in the legal right to abort a pregnancy), there is no easy answer to the question of where a human being becomes a "person." For the person who believes life begins at conception, the question is an easy one. Every one of the phases depicts a "person," whom it would be wrong to "kill." But if you believe life begins later than that, the question of "when exactly" can catch people out.

The demonstrator did not pick on me to answer the question. But if he had, the answer I would have given to the question "Where do you draw the line?" is: you don't draw a "line." It's tempting to want a clear and obvious distinction, with nothing on one side and a fully formed, morally independent human being on the other. But that's not how lives come about. Personhood develops slowly. You're clearly a person when you come out of the womb, crying your eyes out. You're clearly *not* a "person" when you are virtually microscopic, because other than genetic material, you have none of the qualities that make you yourself (and it is unclear why genetic material should be the deciding factor). Conception is convenient because it provides a "line." But sometimes we just have to accept that precise line drawing is doomed. When someone grows a beard, for instance, there comes a certain point at which they go from being "merely unshaven" to "having a beard." But to identify the precise moment at which they have transitioned from the one phase to the other is impossible. There are cases that fall clearly on one side or the other, but if someone put up a "phases of beard growth" chart like the one of fetal development, there might be similar disagreements over where exactly a hairy man became a bearded man. That disagreement wouldn't mean the answers were fallacious or stupid. It would mean that the dividing line is difficult to draw.

This is important, because a large part of the case for "life begin-ning at conception" rests on the fact that it is complicated to "draw a line" anywhere else. If you *do* draw a strict line at conception, then an embryo is a full human being and to destroy one an act of murder tantamount to killing a human adult. This way of think-ing helps give a definitive answer to otherwise tricky philosophical questions about what life and personhood are. You don't need to think very hard about them, because you already know: Life and personhood begin when a sperm fertilizes an egg. The end. But in finding a way to avoid difficult line drawing, the "pro-life" individ-ual also leads themselves to conclusions that are hard to accept.

I say "hard to accept" because I do not think many people *se-riously* believe that there is no moral difference between the pre-meditated murder of a fully grown adult human being and the destruction of a brand new human embryo. While opponents of abortion often use words like "genocide" or "baby killing," if they felt on an emotional level the same way about abortion the way one would feel about an actual genocide, we would expect more of them to be taking up arms in order to stop the practice. There are occa-sional acts of anti-abortion terrorism in this country by people who truly do seem to feel that abortion is an act of mass murder. But if abortion was indeed a genocide, we would expect right-wing poli-ticians to talk about nothing but abortion. Why would the deficit matter next to the colossal act of mass murder occurring every day?

Even opponents of abortion, then, despite their rhetoric, seem to give embryos and fetuses something less than *full* human sta-tus. And that makes sense: one reason the morality of abortion is a tricky business is that an unborn child is in the process of becoming a human being, but isn't *quite* one yet. We sense it is not quite a person but also that it is not nothing, and people's varying instincts on exactly what it *is* make the abortion debate one of the most intractable in all of politics.

One point should be clear, though: at the core of the question of whether abortion should be legal is one's view on the moral

status of the unborn at various phases of development. That
sounds obvious, but it has implications that sometimes go unno-
ticed. For example, pro-choice activists sometimes use slogans like
"my body, my choice" or "if you don't like abortion, don't have
one." But these slogans will never be persuasive to conservatives,
because *if* the fetus should have the moral status of a fully grown
human, claiming the "right" to take its life sounds like claiming
the right to kill one's toddler. Note, however, that strong arguments are also made that even if the embryo or fetus did qualify as
a human being, the right to bodily autonomy would still mean that
the mother had a right to terminate her pregnancy. Likewise, one
cannot require someone to donate an organ even if it would save
a life. Deciding the moral status of the fetus doesn't automatically
resolve the question of whether abortion should be legal. The right
for a woman to "do what she wants with her body" is inviolable
as long as the thing she "wants" is not "murdering someone." But
differing instincts on what the legal status of abortion should be
do tend to depend in part on what one thinks the fetus is.

This means that your instincts on what the legality of abortion
should be come down, in part, to what you think a fetus is. The
dispute over "rights" can't be resolved without first resolving the
philosophical dispute about whether the growing entity in a womb
is a "person" or not. If you *do* think it's a "person," outright bans on
abortion seem quite reasonable, and if you don't, then they seem
like needless infringements on basic bodily autonomy. Here, Karen
Swallow Prior of Southeastern Baptist Theological Seminary defends Texas's strict prohibitions on abortion, arguing that they are
reasonable given certain assumptions:

> Because most abortion procedures in Texas take place after six
> weeks, the new law, as one of the nation's most restrictive, will cer-
> tainly reduce abortions in Texas drastically. It will also continue
> to be challenged in the courts. But if we start from the biological
> and ontological reality that each human life begins at conception,

the law is hardly "extreme," as President Biden has called it. A law preserving the life of a human being at any stage can be considered "extreme" only within a distorted social context.[2]

Indeed, it is correct that *if* we start from the premise that "life begins at conception," and by "life" we mean "a life morally equivalent to that of a human adult," rather than something living but not quite yet morally equivalent to a human adult, then extreme restrictions on abortion no longer seem extreme. But this assumes we have already resolved the core philosophical question in the way that conservatives want us to.

In this passage, conservative jurist Robert Bork agrees that the question of when a "human being" comes into existence is the core question:

> It cannot be too strongly emphasized that whether or not an unborn child is a human being is the critical question in this debate, and the question was definitively answered decades ago. Whatever might be said for an earlier time, today there can be no scientific disagreement as to the biological beginning of human life. Embryology, fetology, and medical science all attest to the basic facts of human growth and development, and medical textbooks have declared that distinct and individual human life begins at conception.[3]

Bork is wrong that "science" can resolve this question. Science can tell us "the basic facts of human growth and development," but the question "Is an embryo a 'person'?" cannot be answered by citing embryology because it is a philosophical rather than scientific question. This is a matter more of instinct than of reason. It is hard for a pro-choice person to argue with a pro-life person, because a pro-life individual will insist they know that the unborn fetus is a person, the pro-choice individual will insist it isn't, and nobody can *prove* the answer either way. "Science" can't answer it—science can answer when the fetus is viable outside the womb, and how much it has developed physically, but it can't tell us what a "person" is or what "killing" is, because these are philosophical questions.

Disappointingly, perhaps, I do not have a way to respond to right-wing claims that a fetus deserves the moral status of a human being. Personally, I see "life" as something that grows slowly and achieves the status of "a human being" as it gets closer and closer to being born. If someone wishes to insist that a zygote is a human being, however, I cannot *disprove* their assertion. All I can do is to note the fact that they do not act as if they believe this to be the case. Hardly any pro-life activists advocate the death penalty as punishment for abortion.[4]

There is a certain way to reach a compromise between pro- and anti-abortion views, however. Personally, I am uncompromisingly pro-choice, in that I believe in the full protection of the legal right to an abortion. But I also believe it is possible to have a world with very few abortions in it. It is also desirable, because women do not want to be in the position where they need to have abortions. An abortion is the termination of an *undesired* pregnancy, meaning that it would be better for that pregnancy never to have occurred in the first place. If birth control were more accessible, or if men were more willing to do their part in using it, the number of abortions would plummet. (Indeed, as contraceptives have gotten better and more ubiquitous, that is exactly what has happened.)[5] Many abortions also occur because in the United States, there is little social support for raising children. We make raising a child extremely difficult—this country has *no* mandatory paid parental leave[6]—and then are surprised when economic pressures lead many women to have abortions. Free universal daycare and pre-K, generous cash allowances to parents, and generous paid leave will all make it more likely that a pregnant person sees the prospect of having a child as more joyful than terrifying. (It will always be somewhat terrifying, but we can adjust the balance through family-friendly policy.)

What is so despicable about the conservative attitude toward abortion is not that it gives some moral status to the unborn. It is, rather, that it tries to force women to have children that they obviously do not feel they are in the position to have, while offering no support whatsoever for the raising of those children. It uses the coercive instrument of law and tries to *criminalize* abortion, instead of trying to improve birth control methods and access to prevent unwanted pregnancies from arising in the first place. When was the last time you heard a conservative demand free condoms in schools? They never do, because they think this would encourage or condone promiscuity. But surely, for someone horrified by abortion, a bit more (safe) promiscuity would be a small price to pay for reducing the number of pregnancies terminated.

The fact is, no matter what we think about the morality of abortion, nobody should want to criminalize it, because criminalizing it has horrific consequences.[7] The rich will still get abortions—as they do in countries where it has been criminalized—but the poor will resort to unsafe procedures. Criminal laws have to be enforced to mean anything, and in this case, enforcement means putting women and their doctors in jails and prisons. The criminalization of abortion will create a brutal legal regime that will make lives worse, not better. Far better would be to accept that some abortions will always occur and to not attach any moral stigma to them. Make them easily accessible and cheap. But give women a real choice by making sure that having a child is *also* as easy as possible.

When I was younger, I spent a summer working at the reception desk at a Planned Parenthood clinic. Part of my job was scheduling abortion appointments, and I had to administer a questionnaire to women who were seeking financial aid. They often ended up telling me the life circumstances that led them to have abortions. They frequently wanted children, but could not afford it because they had lost a job, or their boyfriend had left, or (in one case) their house had burned down. If conservatives cared at all about the moral status of the unborn fetus, they should have offered to help these women who were reluctantly giving up their pregnancies. Instead of wanting to punish, criminalize, and stigmatize them, the right should have recognized that the woman seeking abortion generally has good reasons and understands her own life and needs better than they do. But nobody did. That summer of work made me forever resent pro-life activists, who afterwards seemed purely sanctimonious, interested in preaching about the immorality of abortion without wanting to actually make themselves useful in solving a "problem" they supposedly care about.

Many women, of course, do *not* get abortions reluctantly. I am not saying that it is always a "tragic choice." In fact, it is a choice that's not for third parties to judge. Because I do not accept the validity of the pro-life argument on the moral status of the unborn, I do not consider there to be a moral issue about abortion at all. But since many people disagree on this, let us note that *even* if we consider the fetus a life-form, the pro-life solution should converge with the pro-choice position: universal free birth control, universal free childcare. On no moral view of the fetus does *criminalizing* abortion make sense.[8]

FURTHER READING

- Katha Pollitt—*Pro: Reclaiming Abortion Rights*
- Meera Shah—*You're the Only One I've Told: The Stories behind Abortion*
- Michelle Oberman—*Her Body, Our Laws: On the Front Lines of the Abortion War, from El Salvador to Oklahoma*
- David S. Cohen and Carole Joffe—*Obstacle Course: The Everyday Struggle to Get an Abortion in America*
- Diana Greene Foster—*The Turnaway Study: Ten Years, a Thousand Women, and the Consequences of Having—or Being Denied—an Abortion*
- David Boonin—*A Defense of Abortion*
- L. W. Sumner—*Abortion and Moral Theory*
- Leslie J. Reagan—*When Abortion Was a Crime*

20

There Is a War on Christianity

I think what we're seeing from the left now is they have put aside that sort of really qualified tolerance they had before where they said, "Well, you can be Christian in church or in your school. Just not out in public. Don't throw it in our face." Now they're saying, "Well, if you're Christian, even in your private school, that's going to be a problem, too. Because we can't have any of that as well." . . . I think that's the next phase. They're saying no, even in your private areas, Christianity is no longer acceptable.

—Matt Walsh, on *Fox & Friends*

How did a nation as "churched" as America and as steeped in traditional Christianity . . . permit itself to be de-Christianized, almost without a fight? . . . People now seek happiness in alcohol, drugs, pornography, and recreational sex. . . . But what is another man's septic tank is another's hot tub. . . . To our cultural elite, divorces, abortions, and the junking of obsolete Christian concepts like sacramental marriage may be seen as milestones of freedom.

—Patrick J. Buchanan, *The Death of the West*

Religion is primary. Unless a culture is aspiring toward the good, the true, and the beautiful, and wants the good and the true, really worships God, it readily worships Satan. If we turn away from God, our culture becomes dominated by "Real Crime Stories" and rap music and other spew.

—George Gilder

If Christianity goes, the whole of our culture goes.

—T. S. Eliot

The Argument

To some Christians, the United States today is a moral morass. Only 65 percent of American adults now self-identify as Christians, down 12 percent from ten years ago. In that same ten-year period, the number of people identifying as "atheist, agnostic, or nothing in particular" has increased from 17 percent in 2009 to 26 percent today. Many Christians believe they are losing the culture wars. Birth control, abortion, pornography, divorce, and sex work are commonplace in the United States. Public education is almost completely secular. The next generation is even less Christian than the population at large, with nearly as many millennials as likely to be nonreligious as Christian. There is good evidence that their abandonment of faith is permanent.[1]

Some on the right speak of the decline of Christian faith as a deliberate assault on their religion by secularists and a sign of general moral decline. As examples of people being intolerant or hostile toward Christianity, they would cite examples like the effort to force Christian bakers to make cakes for LGBT people's weddings and the Obama administration's effort to require Christian employers to cover their employees' birth control.

The Response

This is an instance where I certainly see the conservative point of view. *If* my moral worldview was a socially conservative Christianity, I would be deeply troubled by the erosion of Christian faith, because it would inherently mean the erosion of morality itself. It is also understandable why people who see a "war" on Christianity feel attacked. They do not believe their religion is irrational, unpersuasive, or irrelevant, so they would be unsatisfied with an explanation for the trend like "millennials are becoming less Christian because they are less persuaded by irrational dogmas like creationism and miracles." The decline of Christianity cannot, for the believer, be occurring naturally because the faith is irrational and is being exposed as such.

Because I am not a Christian believer, however, I do believe that the faith is eroding more for natural reasons than because of any coordinated "war" by secularists. For many millennials, the central tenets of Christianity are unpersuasive.[2] These younger people do not view pornography, abortion, divorce, etc., as bad and immoral, and see no reason to accept the teachings of religious authorities. I confess to being among them, and I concede: to the extent that rejection of socially conservative Christian beliefs constitutes a "war" on Christianity, I suppose we are engaged in one. It is, however, a very passive war. We do not do much evangelizing. Many of us simply do not see any compelling reasons why we should accept religious teachings. We are in many cases agnostic, deistic, or vaguely spiritual, but to the extent that Christian morality is relevant for our lives, we are inspired more by the compassionate aspects than the judgmental ones.

It is true that, if by Christian morality, one means traditionalist approaches to homosexuality and divorce, the United States is losing its Christian morality and losing it badly. Same-sex marriage has gone from being a fringe aspiration to being the law of the land across the entire country. There is no serious effort to roll back no-fault divorce or the availability of birth control (though on abortion, pro-life activists have been very effective at rolling back the constitutional right to an abortion as much as possible, and they may yet succeed in eliminating it).[3] A Christian who sees porn and gambling as a sign of civilizational collapse is not likely to see America change its ways and save its soul. The "battle" is being lost.

To those of us who are godless, it is difficult to care about this. For us, no-fault divorce helps free people from being stuck in marriages they don't want to be in, which is a good thing. Birth control prevents people from having unwanted pregnancies, which is a good thing. Pat Buchanan is right to say that what looks like a "septic tank" in his worldview is a "hot tub" to those who do not share it. He is horrified by social phenomena that, to us, look like freedom and empowerment.

This is one of those areas where it is difficult to have a discussion because it is not obvious how one side would ever persuade the other. Until I am shown that fundamentalist Christianity is rational, I will not be able to believe in it, and thus I will not be able to care that its moral teachings are being ignored. Until the fundamentalist Christian loses their faith, they will see creeping secularism as the erosion of virtue. Unless there are mass conversions among millennials, or faith evaporates entirely, there will continue to be a clash that is very difficult to resolve. Some Christians will continue to see this as a battle for the survival of morality. But unless they can persuade those of us who do not share their morality to do so, it will never look the same way to us.

A Christian defending the idea that there is a "war" on Christianity might point to the "same-sex wedding cake" case and the "mandatory birth control" case as examples of *force* being used to try to combat Christian beliefs. It is fine for secular people to win a battle of public opinion. But these are instances of trying to use the power of the government to require Christians to act against their own morality. That goes well beyond a peaceful trend toward religious apathy. It is an active attempt to prevent Christians from acting in accordance with their beliefs.

This can sound superficially compelling. Take the instance of the "gay wedding cake." There have been several instances in which Christian bakers have declined to bake cakes for same-sex couples' weddings, citing their disapproval of same-sex marriage. And there have been attempts to use the law to *require* these bakers to serve the same-sex couples. Defenders of the bakers insist that this is an infringement on religious liberty. One of these controversies made it to the Supreme Court in 2018, which issued a narrow ruling in favor of the baker.[4]

But there is a strong argument in favor of requiring bakers by law to make cakes for same-sex weddings. When a seller of a product enters a marketplace, they are generally prohibited from engaging in discrimination on the basis of race and sex. A person cannot refuse to sell a house to a Black person because they are Black. Those who believe in LGBT rights see the situation as analogous. Declining to serve someone for being gay is no different from declining to serve them for being Black. There is no religious exemption to the Civil Rights Act; one cannot say that because one has a white supremacist religion, it is a violation of "religious freedom" to enforce nondiscrimination. Thus, refusing to serve a same-sex couple is no different from refusing to serve an interracial couple, which is already illegal.

Defenders of the bakers have certain arguments here. They claim that they are not discriminating against the couple for being of the same sex, because they would sell them, for instance, a birthday cake. What they oppose is endorsing a practice, the *wedding*, that goes against their religious teaching. But again, this argument wouldn't work in the context of other categories of discrimination. Imagine how it would sound to say: "I am not refusing to sell a wedding cake to this interracial couple because they are interracial. I am refusing to sell it to them because I do not endorse the practice of interracial weddings." It doesn't work, because it's still the case that if the couple's races were the same, the baker would be willing to bake the cake; thus, the discrimination is based on race.

It may well be the case that Christian bakers are being made to violate their religious beliefs by being required to produce same-sex wedding cakes. But we already require people to violate their religious beliefs if those beliefs require racial discrimination. The "gay wedding cake" case is not uniquely coercive; all it is doing is applying the same antidiscrimination protections that already exist for other categories of people to LGBT people. That might violate someone's faith, but the fact that one has a religious belief that discrimination is good is not a compelling reason for exemption from the law—just like a religious belief that murder, rape, or robbery are good would not entitle one to be found innocent of these charges in a court of law.

This may sound quite coercive. But it is also worth noting that it is *conditional* on a person's choices. No Christian will ever be forced to bake a cake for a same-sex wedding. A Christian will only have to do this *if* they want to open a bakery to the public, and thus be subject to antidiscrimination laws. This does matter, because the government is not forcing random people to make cakes at gunpoint. Instead, they are setting conditions on access to a market: If you want to have a business doing this, you must agree to treat everybody equally. If you don't want to treat everybody equally, that's fine, but you need to make your cakes in private rather than opening a shop to the public. Once you are "public facing," conditions apply, and the government is entitled to create those conditions because the government makes the market function (by offering limited liability, building infrastructure, creating currency, enforcing property rights, etc.).

What about the birth control case? Should Christian employers be "forced" to provide healthcare that includes coverage for birth control? Here it is worth realizing that there are two parties whose rights are at issue. The employer wants to be able to deny birth control coverage to the employee. But the employee wants to get birth control and not to have their healthcare benefits determined by the religious beliefs of their employer. Your moral values will determine which you think matters more: the right of employees to comprehensive health coverage or the right of employers to regulate their employees' sexuality.

Personally, I am more sympathetic to the employee than the employer, and do not find the employer's claim of a "right" compelling. If you enter a labor market and agree to employ people, you should provide a comprehensive package of healthcare benefits, and you should not get to personally decide what that consists of. I do not believe, for instance, that if an employer decided they were religiously opposed to blood transfusions, and so wouldn't pay for their employees to get them, the employer would have a compelling "religious liberty" argument. This is because a workers' right to healthcare is far more important to me than the right of an employer to pick and choose what care they want to pay for, and I do not think a boss should be able to impose their eccentric and cruel personal beliefs about healthcare.

But note that I say "personally." Christian conservatives will not find what I am saying persuasive because their instincts are the opposite: an employee has no entitlement to whatever health benefits they want. For them, the right to "freedom of contract" means the employer can offer whatever bargain they like and the employee who doesn't like it shouldn't take it. Views of rights differ, and they are difficult to argue about because like philosophical questions about "personhood," there is no easy way to adjudicate the dispute by showing the "right" answer. This is one of those cases, as discussed in the first part of this book, where differing instincts about the good simply clash.

This leaves us without the ability to offer a "snappy" response. What I think we have to do instead is encourage Christian conservatives to justify their position, to show *why* they oppose birth control or believe in anti-LGBT discrimination. Because religious arguments are ultimately grounded in religious text and teaching, they will be deeply unpersuasive to anyone who cannot be persuaded to accept the authority of that text. In other words, once we get away from simplistic rhetoric about Liberty of Conscience, and start asking why discrimination is an important moral value, the social conservative will have to try to justify the correctness of their underlying faith, something it is infamously difficult to do.

21

We Must Respect the Constitution and the Founding Fathers

The genius of the founding generation's work was that it established a series of political doctrines that, like a shining beacon in the night, lit the way for the outcast and the downtrodden and gave vital ammunition to the weak.

—Charles C. W. Cooke, *The Conservatarian Manifesto*

At heart, American conservatives like myself are believers in the Constitution. We believe that the principles embodied in the Constitution are enduring, and that to whatever extent we deviate from them we put our liberties at risk. Our views are consistent because we believe in absolute truths and the essential soundness, even righteousness, of the Founders' vision of government.

—Sean Hannity, *Let Freedom Ring*

LARRY SCHWEICKART, author of *Seven Events That Made America America*: In each one of these chapters I tried to find "What would the Founders have thought about this event?" . . . Would they have approved? Would they have said, "Yes, that's the way we expected Americans to respond?" Or would they have said, "Did they ever get this one wrong!"

GLENN BECK: They wouldn't have recognized America anymore. They would have said, "When did you stop living the Constitution?" Do you think?

LARRY SCHWEICKART: Exactly. I mean, when we talk about the war on meat. It's inconceivable that Washington would ever allow anyone to tell him what to eat.

—*Glenn Beck*, Fox News, June 16, 2010

The Argument

The left tries to tarnish the Founding Fathers as racists and shows little respect for the Constitution. But this country was built on the values of its framers as embodied in this original document. Those values are timeless, and rather than trying to update or replace the Constitution, we should respect the achievement of the Founding Fathers in designing a system that could last. We should interpret the Constitution in accordance with their original meanings. They prescribed a limited government based on a system of checks and balances that would keep majorities from oppressing minorities, and we should strive to maintain that vision.

The Response

Right-wing defenses of the Founding Fathers tend to treat their ownership of slaves, extermination of Native Americans, and total exclusion of women from participation in power as minor failings. How we view the Founding Fathers, and whether we believe we should defer to their moral judgments or care about what they would have thought, depends in large part on whether we see their belief in a white supremacist patriarchy as being of major or minor concern. For instance, when we read of George Washington "extirpating" recalcitrant Indians, do we see a patriot or a genocidaire?[1] When we discover that Washington, in addition to his military heroics and legendary honesty, was a tough slave owner who "aggressively pursued runaways, took steps to prevent his enslaved people from being freed accidentally while visiting free states," and once ordered an enslaved man to be "whipped for walking on the law,"[2] do we treat this as a footnote in an otherwise laudable career, or do we see it as evil? Personally, I am opposed enough to slavery to call it evil and to believe that successfully overthrowing British rule is not enough to morally outweigh it.

We are, in these discussions, not so much disputing the facts as how much they should matter in our assessment. Whether the

Founding Fathers *were* racist and hypocritical is not a matter of dispute. Thomas Jefferson, for instance, had a low opinion of Black intelligence, saying that Blacks "are inferior to the whites in the endowment both of body and mind" and that "never yet could I find that a black had uttered a thought above the level of plain narration; never see even an elementary trait, of painting or sculpture." Jefferson did not even consider the possibility that because painting and sculpture require access to equipment and training, the people he kept in chains at Monticello were unlikely to spontaneously indulge in it.

It is tempting to rationalize such sentiments as being "of a different era." But there were contemporary thinkers "calling out" Jefferson's racism. Benjamin Banneker, a formerly enslaved Black man who became a land surveyor and astronomer, wrote a letter to Jefferson begging him to "readily embrace every opportunity to eradicate that train of absurd and false ideas and opinions which so generally prevails with respect to us" and castigated him for writing movingly of liberty while simultaneously "detaining by fraud and violence so numerous a part of my brethren under groaning captivity and cruel oppression."[3] Jefferson gave a brief, polite reply that did not give any indication he understood or cared about Banneker's point.

Abigail Adams had no more luck when she tried to educate John Adams about his sexism. In a 1776 letter, she made a simple and polite request: "In the new Code of Laws which I suppose it will be necessary for you to make I desire you would Remember the Ladies, and be more generous and favourable to them than your ancestors." She said that patriarchy was an obvious problem ("That your Sex are Naturally Tyrannical is a Truth so thoroughly established as to admit of no dispute") and pointed out that intelligent people rejected it ("Men of Sense in all Ages abhor those customs which treat us only as the vassals of your Sex.") She suggested that her husband remember the Golden Rule, to treat women as he would wish to be treated, and that men "give up the harsh title of Master for the more tender and endearing one of Friend."[4]

John Adams was unmoved by his wife's plea on behalf of her sex. "As to your extraordinary Code of Laws, I cannot but laugh," he said. "We know better than to repeal our Masculine systems." Adams told his wife that male superiority did not exist in practice, suggesting that it was actually *women* who treated men as their subjects, and that if men abandoned their claim to be in charge, they would soon be subject to "the Despotism of the Peticoat."[5] History does not record Abigail Adams's sigh as she read this reply, but we can surmise that it was long and deep.

The Founding Fathers viewed the majority of human beings as inferior, and believed in their right as white men to rule over them. Not a single woman, Indian, or Black person was permitted to contribute to the framing of the United States Constitution. The majority of the population, therefore, was deliberately excluded from participating in the creation of its own laws. The Constitution was, therefore, not an exercise in self-government. It is in no way democratic to make rules for other people without asking for their input or consent.

We might think, then, that the Constitution is a sound document. I, for one, am a particular fan of its First Amendment, which I regularly make use of to say controversial things. But regardless of whether we are impressed by the Constitution, the fact remains that it was never a *legitimate* document because it made the basic law of the land without the "consent of the governed."

Abigail Adams understood better than her husband that in order for a set of laws to be worthy of deference and obedience, the people need to have a hand in making them. In her letter on women's rights, she warned:

> If perticuliar care and attention is not paid to the Laidies we are determined to foment a Rebelion, and will not hold ourselves bound by any Laws in which we have no voice, or Representation.[6]

The idea that you are not bound by laws that you have no voice in making is the elementary principle of democracy. The commands of a dictator do not carry moral force, and might does not make right. If men make the laws for women, they cannot expect women to feel obligated to obey merely because men have the power to enforce their commands.

That has grave implications for the degree to which we should feel bound to respect the Constitution. The Constitution was never approved through a democratic process; thus, its moral authority is limited. We should respect the ideas in it that are good, but we have no obligation to respect the ones that aren't. The Founding Fathers designed institutions that preserved their preferred hierarchy. They were very concerned about the "tyranny of the majority," but by this they did *not* mean the tyranny of a white majority over people of color. This was, in the words of James Madison, a "minority of the opulent."[7] Madison worried that if elections "were open to all classes of people, the property of landed proprietors would be insecure." John Jay firmly believed that "the people who own the country ought to govern it." The Constitution's "counter-majoritarian" institutions were designed to keep women, Indians, Blacks, and the poor from "tyrannizing" over their social superiors by participating in the lawmaking process.

As a result, the institutions designed by the Founding Fathers were deeply flawed. Not only did they originally permit the wholesale disenfranchisement of the majority of the population, but even now that there is "universal" suffrage,[8] the structural flaws of the political system still create injustice. The power of the presidency is ill-defined, which has allowed presidents to accumulate an almost unbelievable amount of unitary power.[9] The Supreme Court is an absurd institution, the existence of which means that the whims of a handful of unelected judges, selected for political reasons and installed at arbitrary and irregular intervals, can determine whether a democratically passed piece of legislation will stand or be stricken.

(I have previously suggested that the United States should more properly be called a "Neilocracy" than a democracy, because the absolute power to decide whether a law is constitutionally kosher often depends on how Neil Gorsuch feels about it.)[10]

The system of choosing representation is grossly unfair. The United States Senate, for instance, because it gives equal representation to both heavily populated and lightly populated states, gives massively more input to the average citizen of Wyoming or Vermont than the average citizen of California or Florida. The existence of the "Electoral College" means that the person who gets the most votes can easily still lose the presidential election, thanks to the way states are weighed.[11] Residents of non-state U.S. territories like Puerto Rico and Washington, D.C., are governed by Congress and the president, yet do not get to choose who represents them. This is the same kind of "taxation without representation" that led to the original American secession from Great Britain.

The Founding Fathers' moral deficiencies were not just minor flaws. Their antidemocratic instincts and contempt for large swaths of the human population affected the government they designed. We can't be bound by their vision. Their rhetorical emphasis on freedom and egalitarianism was powerful—that is why from Frederick Douglass to Martin Luther King Jr., those who fought against the oppressive system these men created have been able to use their own words as ammunition. The emphasis on liberty of conscience and thought is something we have to preserve, and the rejection of monarchy in favor of republicanism freed this country from the tyranny of hereditary rule.[12] But there is nothing illegitimate about proposing big structural reforms to the Constitution to make our government work better. If the Founders had been less oblivious to their own serious biases, they might have devised better institutions in the first place.

Founder-worship is taken to extreme lengths on the right. In Gregory Jackson's *Conservative Comebacks to Liberal Lies: Issue by Issue Responses to the Most Common Claims of the Left from A to Z* (which is essentially the right-wing equivalent of this book, except poorly written and unpersuasive), a number of the conservative "comebacks" simply consist of repeating what the Founders believed. In response to the claim "landlords are acting selfishly when they demand higher rents of tenants," Jackson writes: "RESPONSE: An individual private property owner has the right under the U.S. Constitution not to be deprived of life, liberty or property without due process of law, nor shall private property be taken without just compensation." In response to the claim that there is a right to affordable housing, Jackson writes: "RESPONSE: The U.S. Constitution outlines Americans' rights and nowhere is there any stipulation of an individual's 'right to affordable housing.'" But the claims being made are moral ones, and replying that "the Constitution does not agree" only serves to indict the Constitution, not contradict the claim.

The attitude of an intelligent person is not to ask, "What did the Founders think?" and then do it ("It's inconceivable that Washington would ever allow anyone to tell him what to eat.") but to reason independently. We can find wisdom in the words of past lawmakers, but the fact that they believed something does not, in and of itself, provide reason to give it any credence, since we know they believed some awful things. We are entitled to build the society we deem just, rather than the one our ancestors would have wanted.

Does "Originalism" Make Sense?

This simple idea—that the law is not only binding but that it should continue to mean what it meant when it was adopted—is a wholly uncontroversial idea in the United States, except, for some reason, when it relates to the Constitution. Then, we are told that the law must "grow" and "evolve"; that hard-and-fast rule must "adapt" to "changing times"; that the application of established standards is to be contingent upon circumstance and upon who is involved in the dispute; that words are malleable and sentiments fluid; and that the amendment process, which was put in place to accommodate and to codify evolving standards, is too complex to be respected. . . . If our judges are not making their decisions by closely examining the original intent of the law and applying it to the cases before them, then what are they doing?

—Charles C. W. Cooke, *The Conservatarian Manifesto*

If the Constitution is law, then presumably its meaning, like that of all other law, is the meaning the lawmakers were understood to have intended.

—Robert Bork, *The Tempting of America*

I'll stipulate that you can reach some results you like with the other system, but that's not the test. The test is, over the long run, does it require society to adhere to those principles contained in the Constitution or does it lead to a society that is essentially governed by nine justices' version of what equal protection ought to mean, what cruel and unusual punishment ought to mean, whether it ought to be eighteen or sixteen before you can execute [someone]. . . . There are no answers once you abandon the original understanding of the text.

—Antonin Scalia[13]

"Originalism," the belief that legal texts should be interpreted in accordance with the original meaning they carried at the time they were enacted, is often considered a conservative legal philosophy. But proponents of originalism insist it is nothing of the kind. In fact, it is just applied common sense. How could you *not* interpret legal texts in accordance with their original meanings? The alternative is "judge-made law," in which jurists impose their own values about what the law *ought* to say, rather than telling us what the law *does* say.

Like many simple ideas, originalism can sound extremely persuasive until we think a little. It is easy to say that laws ought to mean what they meant when they were enacted. It is harder to figure out what that means in practice. Take 1954's *Brown v. Board of Education*. The Fourteenth Amendment to the United States Constitution guarantees the "equal protection" of the law to all Americans. When this was passed in 1868, no lawmaker thought it prohibited the existence of public institutions that separated people by race. For many years, "equal protection" meant that "separate but equal" facilities could be provided. But in *Brown*, the Court ruled unanimously that "equal protection" prohibited racially segregated schools, which were inherently unequal. What "equality" meant in the nineteenth century was different to what it meant in the twentieth century.

Originalists do not necessarily think *Brown* was wrongly decided. But it does show that interpreting laws is not just a matter of looking at what the people who wrote them said they meant. In fact, judges are constantly called upon to resolve questions that simply *cannot* be answered by looking at the "original meaning." What does the Second Amendment mean for semiautomatic weapons, which the Founders could not conceive of? What does the Fourth Amendment's protection against unreasonable searches say about the police's power to look through your internet search history? Given that the first prisons in the United States were not even built until after the Bill of Rights was enacted, do long prison terms for children violate the "cruel and unusual punishment" clause? What does the First Amendment say about whether the government can require membership in a labor union as a condition of public sector employment?

You might have your answers to these questions. But they are not found in the Constitution. Judges bring their subjective interpretations to the meaning of words like "unreasonable" in the phrase "unreasonable search." It is impossible not to do this. Judges who think they are not doing it are delusional. What is called "originalism" is often just an elaborate way of portraying one's own value judgments as settled historical fact. Judges like to portray themselves as mere "umpires," who have no politics and just "look at the text" of a law, without bringing "politics" into it. But politics is already in it. Judging is a political task.

Originalism does tend to be conservative because as we have seen, the framing laws of this country, the ones that establish the process through which all other laws are made, were written by men who had a very strong interest in preserving a certain kind of social hierarchy. To accept their interpretations of words like "equality" and "reasonable" is to incorporate their own biases, and to allow the dead to rule over the living. Instead, judging should be a pragmatic endeavor. Where a rule's original meaning makes sense, it should be used. Where it doesn't, or it conflicts with our contemporary notions of justice, there is little reason to respect it. Of course, this opens up the possibility for exercising all kinds of "value judgments." But value judgments are good and necessary. Without the exercise of value judgments, judges can end up enforcing monstrously unfair laws that have no democratic legitimacy.[14]

FURTHER READING

- Eric J. Segall—*Originalism as Faith*
- Sanford Levinson—*Our Undemocratic Constitution: Where the Constitution Goes Wrong (and How We the People Can Correct It)*
- Erwin Chemerinsky—*The Case against the Supreme Court*
- Fred Rodell—*Woe Unto You, Lawyers!*

22

People Should "Pull Themselves Up by Their Bootstraps" and Not Need "Handouts"

Here are the three rules that you need to fulfill as a person before you can start complaining about your life failures being the result of somebody else's actions. Number one: you need to finish high school. Number two: you need to get married before you have babies. Number three: you need to get a job. That's it. You do those things you will not be permanently poor in the United States of America. According to the Brookings Institute, 2 percent of Americans who followed these rules are in poverty.

—Ben Shapiro

The results of the Great Society experiments started coming in and began showing that, for all its good intentions, the War on Poverty was causing irreparable damage to the very communities it was trying to help.

—Charles Krauthammer, *Things That Matter*

Indeed, this is one of the great evils of Welfarism—that it transforms the individual from a dignified, industrious, self-reliant spiritual being into a dependent animal creature without his knowing it. There is no avoiding this damage to character under the Welfare State.

—Barry Goldwater, *The Conscience of a Conservative*

The Argument

People should stop complaining about poverty. Only through "personal responsibility" can people achieve prosperity and success. Efforts to address injustices through federal programs like the War on Poverty and affirmative action are doomed to fail.

The Response

Ben Shapiro says that people wouldn't be poor if they graduated high school, got married, and got jobs, implying that in the United States, poverty is the fault of the poor, who have made bad life choices and who just need to work harder to get ahead.

If Shapiro is correct, it certainly sounds like a strong argument against the left. After all, those three things don't sound very demanding. If a few simple steps by the poor are all it would take to end poverty, then it's easy to see why you wouldn't be too concerned about it. Our first instinct here might be to wonder whether Shapiro has pulled this number out of his ass. But while he sometimes does,[1] in this case he hasn't. The Brookings Institution, a liberal-leaning think tank, said what he says it said. And they have even said that "work and marriage are the way to end poverty and welfare."[2] This finding has been used by columnists at the *Washington Post* and *Wall Street Journal* to hector millennials and tell them to stop being whiners, get jobs, and get married.[3]

But if the number is correct, then don't they have a point? If people who are married with full-time jobs and high school degrees are rarely poor, then can't following "the success sequence" eliminate poverty? Something should strike us as strange about this number, though. Let's isolate the "full-time job" part. The federal minimum wage is $7.25 an hour. If you work full-time, that means a minimum-wage worker has an annual income of $15,000. The poverty line for a single individual is $12,500. So forget marriage and high school: as long as you have a full-time minimum-wage job, you won't be "poor."

What is happening, then? Are the poor just the portion of the population who refuse to get jobs? Before we agree with Shapiro, maybe we should actually look closer at *who* the poor are. Here's a helpful chart from, of all places, the Brookings Institution:

Characteristics of individuals living in poverty, 2016

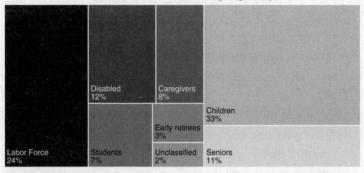

Source: Brookings Institution.

What you should notice right away is that the largest percentage of poor people are children. Fully one-third of those below the poverty line are kids. According to the Children's Defense Fund, "1.4 million children enrolled in public schools experienced homelessness during the 2016–2017 school year," and "5.9 million children live in families with 'worst-case housing needs' meaning they are extremely rent burdened, have low income and receive no housing assistance from the government."[4] Already, Shapiro's argument has become absurd when applied to one-third of poor people. Graduate high school? Get married? Get a job? This is what you're going to tell a nine-year-old? Are child labor and child marriage the solutions to poverty?

Another 11 percent of the poor are seniors, and another 12 percent are disabled. How useful is it to point out that old people and disabled people wouldn't be poor if they were working forty-hour weeks? Seven percent are students, who would have a very hard time doing forty-hour weeks. Eight percent are caregivers, people who are doing unpaid labor taking care of other people who can't take care of themselves. Perhaps that's just their fault: if they didn't want to be poor, they should have neglected the care of others and gone into the labor force.

Less than 30 percent of poor people are working-age adults who could be in the labor force. Put simply, the main reason poverty occurs is because there are large parts of the population who can't be full-time workers, and under capitalism, your survival is dependent on the market value of your labor. It's also the case that the poverty line in the United States is set absurdly low—try paying your rent, food, transportation, and healthcare costs on $12,500 a year. Yes, if you're lucky enough to be an able-bodied adult, you can nudge yourself above that line through hard and poorly compensated work. But this is far from the Great American Success Story that Shapiro describes.

There are a number of other reasons why, once we actually start thinking, Shapiro isn't making a very good point. Getting married to a person with a full-time job is indeed a way to have more money, but the conservative argument here is strange because it implies that people should get married even if they haven't found anybody that they love or even like enough to marry. And that *is* the conservative argument: George Will criticizes the "soulmate model of marriage" that sees marriage as something you do for "fulfillment" rather than to "form a family."[5] It suggests that, to escape poverty, a single mother should find a stepdad for her children as soon as possible, even if that stepdad has no value other than as an income stream. The leftist position is different: We think that you should be able to survive even if you'd prefer not to be married. We think you should be able to raise a child without having to leave them at home alone to go and work a full-time job and that parenting itself should be compensated.

Here we see how a reasonable-sounding statistic, given context, can turn out to be absurd. Poverty is concentrated among children, old people, sick people, caregivers, and parents, the populations that find it hardest to do full-time work. "If you have a full-time minimum-wage job, you won't be below the poverty line" is true, but what does it tell us about getting most of the poor out of poverty?

I will add, however, that because I am something of a radical, I personally do not accept Shapiro's moral hectoring even when it is applied to able-bodied adults who could be married and in the workforce but choose not to be. First, I find the idea that people "ought" to get married if they don't want to be poor repulsive—what if you never find someone you want to marry, or no one wants to marry you? Marriage should not be mandatory in order to not be poor; there is no reason we should demand or expect people to get married. Second, I believe in a basic income, even for the laziest person alive. It is our job as human beings to take care of each other, and you deserve care because you are a person, not because you produce goods and services. People ought to be well-compensated for their labor, but the *basics* shouldn't depend on your labor. They should be something we give each other because we care. So yes, I believe you shouldn't be poor even if you don't work. Shapiro differs from me on this, but he and I have fundamentally different moral orientations toward our fellow creatures. He thinks it's fine if people suffer, so long as their suffering is the result of their own choices. I do not think it is fine if they suffer, no matter what choices they have made.

Finally, let us note that the War on Poverty did not, in fact, fail. In fact, there is some good evidence that it was hugely successful.[6] But the empirical success or failure of existing federal programs is a separate question from the basic matter of what our obligations to each other are. I think housing, food, and healthcare are basic rights, and this is a fundamental point of difference between leftists and conservatives. The question of whether "personal responsibility" *could* get people out of poverty becomes irrelevant if you are the sort of person who believes that all people, regardless of their moral virtue or industriousness, deserve the basics of food, shelter, healthcare, and education. The argument is not the causes of social trends, then, but about whether someone believes in allowing preventable deprivation to persist.

FURTHER READING

- Jason DeParle—*American Dream: Three Women, Ten Kids, and a Nation's Drive to End Welfare*
- David K. Shipler—*The Working Poor: Invisible in America*
- Chris Arnade—*Dignity: Seeking Respect in Back Row America*
- Jonathan Kozol—*Savage Inequalities: Children in America's Schools*
- Jill Quadagno—*The Color of Welfare: How Racism Undermined the War on Poverty*
- Martin Gilens—*Why Americans Hate Welfare: Race, Media, and the Politics of Antipoverty Policy*
- Walter I. Trattner—*From Poor Law to Welfare State: A History of Social Welfare in America*
- Joanne Samuel Goldblum and Colleen Shaddox—*Broke in America: Seeing, Understanding, and Ending U.S. Poverty*

23

Immigration Is Harmful

The American piñata has been getting pummeled for decades and now it has finally come apart. Our national wealth is up for grabs by whomever gets here first, and they are coming.

—Tucker Carlson

Illegal immigration [is] a national crisis that you're apparently not supposed to notice. . . . Americans are begging Congress, mayors, governors—anyone who will listen—to simply enforce our laws. But they're not listening. . . .

—Glenn Beck, *Arguing with Idiots*

We need to build a big, beautiful wall along our border because the Left has used every mechanism at its disposal to ensure that illegal immigrants can come to our county [*sic*] and steal—yes, steal—the benefits paid for by taxpayers: health care, schooling, and food stamps. Establishment politicians refuse to fix immigration or our bloated welfare system because the Left doesn't care about productive citizens; it cares only about political power. . . . Illegality and dependency are their calling cards, undercutting the American dream from those who play by the rules.

—Pete Hegseth, *American Crusade*

As a rule, the conservative position is that nations are not nations unless they have borders; that culture matters enormously; that a country cannot absorb an infinite number of newcomers and expect automatically to preserve its way of life . . . that in an age of international terrorism, some form of screening of travelers is imperative; and that the United

States should thus have strict and tailored immigration laws
that are enforced to the letter.

—Charles C. W. Cooke, *The Conservatarian Manifesto*[1]

Our Southern Border is under siege. Congress must act now
to change our weak and ineffective immigration laws. Must
build a Wall. Mexico, which has a massive crime problem,
is doing little to help!

—Donald Trump

The Argument

The argument against immigration is not always that *all* immigration is undesirable, but that present levels of immigration, usually from certain countries or regions, are harmful. This can be for one of several reasons. Immigrants are said to lower the wages of native-born workers by competing for jobs. Or they take social welfare benefits. Or they damage the country's cultural cohesion. Or they are associated with crime, even perhaps terrorism. The argument usually suggests that we need new controls, perhaps a more meritocratic system in which "good" (rich, educated) immigrants are admitted. Sometimes the argument takes the form of a plea to merely "enforce existing law"—regardless of whether immigration is good or not, many people are here *illegally,* which means they are being allowed to violate the law. These laws, regardless of whether they are just, should be enforced in order to be fair to everyone.

The Response

The first thing that should make us suspicious of anti-immigrant arguments is the fact that similar arguments have been made about all groups of new immigrants for centuries. Every group that is perceived as different (whether Chinese, Jewish, Italian, German, or Irish) from those already in the country has been the subject of vicious and unfair stereotypes about criminality, sneakiness, and sloth. For the most part, immigrants have always come for the same reasons: to find work, to take care of their families, to offer the next generation better prospects. Yet newcomers who speak different languages or have different skin tones are always met with hostility.

The way immigrants are demonized is always the same. Anecdotes are chosen selectively and then treated as representative and used to inflame people. So, for example, the story of *one* unauthorized alien committing a crime will be used to show that unauthorized aliens are, as a group, a risk. Bill O'Reilly breathlessly covered the case of Kate Steinle,[2] a white woman killed by an unauthorized immigrant from Mexico, in an effort to show the dangerous consequences of having "sanctuary cities" (cities that do not enforce federal immigration laws).

It is easy to inflame people emotionally with a simple chain of reasoning: Person X was killed or assaulted by an unauthorized immigrant. If they had not been here, the crime would not have happened. *Thus,* the enforcement of the immigration laws would have saved a life. As a strictly logical matter, this is not necessarily true. If an immigrant prone to violence had been deported, it does not mean they would not have hurt anybody; it means they would have hurt someone in a different country, possibly one where the criminal punishment system is actually less likely to catch them.[3] But when people see photographs on the news of a smiling teenager and the gruff-looking drifter who took the teen's life, logical thinking falls by the wayside.

The stereotypes about immigrants can be debunked. They do not, in fact, tend toward criminality and laziness. Immigrants tend to be, unsurprisingly, just like other people, except they tend to be poorer. To the extent that they consume any of the meager government benefits offered in this country, it is because they do not have very much money. As to the theory that immigrants hurt the ability of Americans to get jobs, it is simply not supported by existing economic scholarship, as economist Noah Smith explains in an article called "Why Immigration Doesn't Reduce Wages."[4] The reason for this, Smith explains, is that the effect of immigrants on the economy is the same as the effect of people having babies: they are new people who compete with existing people for jobs, but they spend their salaries on goods and services, which expands the demand for goods and services, which creates jobs. Reviewing the empirical literature, Smith concludes that "immigration can occasionally have some small negative impacts on labor markets," but on the whole has "little or no impact on native-born wages." The positive effects of immigration are more difficult to notice (someone can see the job they lose to an immigrant, but they can't see the jobs created as immigration grows the economy).

Many myths about immigrants do not hold up under scrutiny. Here, for instance, is Donald Trump Jr. making the case that immigrants are costing taxpayers a lot of money:

> According to a recent report by Fairness and Accuracy in Reporting (FAIR), a supposed media watchdog that is actually fair only to the left, taxpayers "shell out approximately $134.9 billion to cover the costs incurred by the presence of more than 12.5 million illegal aliens, and about 4.2 million citizen children of illegal aliens." The real number might be $250 billion. Forget about a wall; with that kind of money we could build a dome! The bottom line is that the cost of illegal immigration is unsustainable.[5]

Trump Jr., being a nincompoop, has confused Fairness and Accuracy in Reporting, which *is* a left-wing media watchdog, with the Federation for American Immigration Reform, an anti-immigrant lobbying group founded by a eugenics-promoting white nationalist.[6] The statistic manufactured by the anti-immigrant FAIR is entirely bogus. Libertarian Cato Institute scholar Alex Nowrasteh has showed at length how FAIR reached the number through "vastly overstating the costs of illegal immigration, undercounting the tax revenue they generate, inflating the number of illegal immigrants, counting millions of U.S. citizens as illegal immigrants, and by concocting a method of estimating the fiscal costs that is rejected by all economists who work on this subject."[7]

Take another myth: the fear that immigrants do not "assimilate." In fact, the opposite is the case: immigrants assimilate to American culture so quickly that the second and third generations of immigrant families tend to abandon the customs, language, and religion of their people.[8] It is not nonimmigrant Americans who should be worried; it is *immigrant* Americans who take a risk, moving to this country, that their children and grandchildren will "forget where they came from." The English language, and American culture, continue to take over the world, and if there is one country that need have no fear of its waning cultural influence, it is the United States.

It is easy to prove that immigrants do not in fact do *harm* to native-born Americans, or at least no harms that could not be addressed through good economic policy. But too much discussion about the effects of immigration revolves around its consequences for the people who are already here rather than for immigrants themselves. Instead of asking, "Do immigrants benefit us?" we should develop greater empathy and ask why we shouldn't share the abundance of this "land of milk and honey" with people from other places seeking better lives. We have a moral duty to let as many people in as we can, in part because it is not clear where the "right to exclude" comes from in the first place. I did not build this country and neither did you. It was created by the labors of many who came here freely (as well as many who came here against their will). One reason we should be willing to share is that the land is not "ours" to begin with, and as long as our own basic material needs are taken care of, there is no reason to disallow others from satisfying their own.

What about the argument that we must "enforce the law" and get tough on unauthorized immigrants, even if the consequences of their presence for nonimmigrants range from the negligible to the beneficial? Well, first we must understand what we are talking about when we talk about "enforcing the law." If we are talking about the mass deportation of every unauthorized immigrant, then we are talking about something that is monstrously cruel. We are talking about dragging perfectly ordinary and innocent people out of their homes and sending them to countries that they may have almost no remaining connections to. At its worst, doing this is effectively sentencing someone to death. In 2019, the Trump administration deported an unauthorized immigrant, Jimmy Aldaoud, to Baghdad from Detroit. Aldaoud was diabetic and mentally ill, and did not speak the language, having grown up in the United States with no memory of his family origins in Iraq. Aldaoud wandered the streets of Baghdad for a time, homeless, before dying after being unable to secure medical treatment. Escalating deportations will result in countless more cases like this.[9]

Deportation is an extreme measure to deal with the violation of immigration law. If someone is truly concerned about those who "jump the line," the offense can be dealt with easily through a small fine. Destroying someone's life to preserve the "rule of law" is a case of getting one's values backwards: the law is not an end in itself, but exists to secure people's pursuit of happiness. If there is no limit to the human happiness we are willing to destroy in order to uphold the law, we have got a legal system that is in bad need of reform.

The fact is that unauthorized immigration is far less of a problem than the cruelty of the immigration laws themselves. The reason people "jump the line" is that the United States *can* accommodate plenty more immigrants than it presently lets in, but we have pointlessly sharp restrictions on who can come in, and there is a cumbersome and unfair bureaucratic system determining who can move here. Any commitment to enforcing the law should be matched or exceeded by our commitment to making the existing system fairer. At the moment, there are people who have been waiting dutifully in the line for *decades* without being given authorization to move here.

For people fleeing violence and persecution, the United States has always been a beacon of hope. For centuries, this country barely imposed any restrictions at all on who could come here. In the early twentieth century, if you wanted to go from the United States to Mexico, or vice versa, in many border towns all you had to do was cross the street. Now border crossings are fully militarized, and people wait in long lines for permission to travel the few feet from one country to the other.

The fact is, for all the talk of "open borders" as something to fear, the world once had much more open borders, and it was a much freer place because of them. You sometimes hear it said that we "don't have a country" if we don't decide who comes across the border,[10] the idea being that policing entrance is a fundamental part of a nation-state's purpose. But the United States survived until the 1900s without policing its borders, and somehow managed to remain a country.

The idea of sharply restricting who can and cannot cross a particular imaginary geographic line is a fairly new one. When certain changes happen, it's easy to accept them as natural and forget that there was a time when they did not exist. (Immigration and Customs Enforcement [ICE], which seems such an entrenched part of the federal bureaucracy, has only existed since 2003.) A more open-borders world, in which people could move around freely, would be a "small government" world in which people's individual choices, rather than the controlling decisions of states, determined where everybody lived.[11]

Immigrants to the United States actually face a terribly unjust set of rules and procedures. Children, who have done nothing wrong, are kept in isolating "detention facilities"[12] (essentially prisons) while their immigration cases are pending. Refugees fleeing violence are often detained and deported, sometimes to their deaths. People living in this country without authorization often work long hours and pay taxes, yet must live in constant fear that they could be rounded up and deported. Their employers are able to underpay them and threaten to report them to the government if they do not unquestioningly obey orders. Families are constantly torn apart, living on other sides of the border. I know an immigrant who has been unable to hug his mother for nearly ten years because he has a job in the United States but came here unauthorized when he was a child, and she was deported. A moral person should care far more about the lives of immigrants than about preserving the unjust bureaucracy we have built to keep them out.

Fortunately, American public opinion is not nearly as anti-immigrant as Donald Trump's presidency might lead one to believe. In places like New York City and Los Angeles, which have high concentrations of immigrants, multiculturalism is an accepted part of everyday existence—it is places that do not have much experience with immigrants that fear them as a bogeyman.[13] The plurality of Americans believe that current levels of immigration are either perfectly fine or even not *high enough,* while under a third believe that the numbers of immigrants should be reduced. Look at the polls! A cross-country comparison from Pew last year showed that the U.S. is one of the least anti-immigrant countries.[14] It's remarkable, actually: even with all the attempts by Trump and Fox News to turn public hatred toward immigrants (instead of billionaires), most people aren't having it. The statistics are staggering: according to Gallup polling, in 1995, 65 percent of people thought immigration levels should be decreased. In 2021, only 31 percent did![15] In the same time, the number of people who thought immigration should be increased went from 7 percent to over 33 percent. True, the public often ranks "immigration" as a high-priority issue come election time,[16] but that includes both people who fear immigrants and people (like me) for whom immigration is an important voting issue because we think borders are a crime.

Sometimes conservatives try to relate terrifying anecdotes from "on the ground" to demonstrate the real-world harms caused by mass immigration. Tucker Carlson has warned his viewers of "gypsies" pooping in public in a Pennsylvania town.[17] Fox's Pete Hegseth reports on the terrors of Islamic Minnesota, a "near-perfect reflection of Europe: blindly open, fully apologetic, willfully ignorant and stupidly tolerant." Hegseth says he "walked the streets of 'Little Mogadishu' in Minneapolis for hours" and found that many people did not speak English. He even "asked a Somali teen what his school taught about the Constitution and he said he didn't know."[18] (A teenager who doesn't know much. Horrors!) Victor Davis Hanson of the Hoover Institution related anecdotes about the undocumented Mexican Americans in his California town. One of them once ran a stop sign and hit Hanson's truck. ("We were bruised but not hurt; the truck dented but drivable.") Once, Hanson found two migrants digging for truffles around his cypress trees. ("I politely asked that they not periodically dig up my tree [sic] cypress-tree roots but could sell their already collected *hongos* in their bags at the local swap meet as they said they had intended. We left amicably enough.") And if that weren't bad enough, "Our local town has erected a sort of clannish statue of the Aztec goddess Coatlicue, the mother snake goddess to whom thousands were sacrificed."[19]

Funniest of all was a 2018 report in the *Wall Street Journal* from Andy Ngo, who explored the ruin that an influx of Muslims had brought to Britain. Entitled "A Visit to Islamic England," the travelogue did its best to portray a population of perfectly normal people going about their days as a spooky Other. Ngo describes a terrifying world of "failed multiculturalism" in which "nobody made eye contact":

Within minutes, we walked by three other mosques, which were vibrant and filled with young men coming and going. We passed a church, which was closed and decrepit, with a window

that had been vandalized with eggs. We squeezed by hundreds
of residents busy preparing for the Eid al-Adha holiday. Girls
in hijabs gathered around tables to paint henna designs on their
hands. All the businesses had a religious flair: The eateries were
halal, the fitness center was sex-segregated, and the boutiques
displayed "modest" outfits on mannequins. Pakistani flags flew
high and proud. I never saw a Union Jack. . . . [20]

Painting henna designs on their hands! Eating the foods of
their culture! Going to mosques instead of the church! Celebrating
their holidays! *Dressing modestly!* What has happened to the England of yore? Ironically enough, the American writer attributes
qualities to "Muslim" Britain that are actually just universal British
qualities, like standoffishness and "not flying the Union Jack." He
even wrote that in the Muslim neighborhoods, he saw signs that
said "alcohol-restricted zone," implying a creeping sharia regime.
This necessitated a correction from the paper when it turned out
such signs "[prohibit] public drinking and appear in many English
neighborhoods, irrespective of Muslim population." More importantly than any of this, though, Ngo doesn't seem to have had a
single substantive conversation with anyone in the neighborhood.
(He did ask an imam for some leaflets.) So often, conservatives
suggest that cultural differences make it impossible to understand
one another, without putting the slightest bit of effort into understanding other people's perspectives.

It is, unfortunately, very easy for politicians to use immigrants
as scapegoats—often to distract from their own failures. Because
it can be difficult to communicate and empathize across language
barriers, people can quickly come to fear the mysterious "other"
moving into their neighborhood. But xenophobic attitudes need
to be fought, because they are irrational and immoral. This country should allow in as many immigrants as it possibly can, and a
world of open borders with complete "freedom of movement" is a
worthy goal to aspire to.

How to Lie with Statistics

Tucker Carlson is one of the most aggressive critics of U.S. immigration, as well as the most popular host on Fox News. He is sometimes explicitly bigoted (having called Iraqis "semiliterate primitive monkeys")[21] and laments that the United States, a place that was "overwhelmingly European, Christian, and English-speaking fifty years ago," has "become a place with no ethnic majority, immense religious pluralism, and no universally shared culture or language."[22] Segments like "Gypsies: Coming to America" should have gotten him pulled from the air, but he is lucrative for his network.[23]

Carlson not only relies on dubious anecdotes about Roma people supposedly coming to small-town America and defecating in public, but uses classic examples of *lying with statistics*. Consider, for example, a monologue he gave in 2018, in which he claimed that unauthorized immigrants commit more crimes than U.S. citizens:

> This evening we've got brand-new numbers, striking numbers that have never been seen before, and they may reshape how you think about illegal immigration. . . . So you've heard the same line a million times, it's repeated like a mantra by the left during every debate on the subject: all immigrants are hard-working and law-abiding. In fact . . . undocumented immigrants actually commit fewer crimes on average than native-born Americans. Stop complaining. They're your superiors. Are people who are in this country precisely because they were willing to break our immigration laws really less likely to break other kinds of laws? It doesn't make a lot of sense.[24] . . . Yet until today, strangely enough, no one could say for sure whether it was true. . . . Somehow, the government went for years without honestly trying to track the volume of crime committed by illegal immigrants in this country. Maybe they were too incompetent

to do it. More likely they didn't want you to know the answer. According to statistics from the U.S. Sentencing Commission, noncitizens are actually far more likely to commit serious crimes than Americans are. Noncitizens account for 22 percent, more than a fifth, of all federal murder convictions. So that is a massively disproportionate amount of crime. Not even close. No, immigrants are not more law-abiding and less dangerous than Americans. That's totally untrue. Indeed, it's the opposite of the truth.[25]

In fact, the numbers weren't new or previously undisclosed. They were published by the Sentencing Commission every year, meaning that this allegation of a government conspiracy to make immigrants look better is completely baseless. But more importantly, the statistic itself is nonsense. There's a reason Carlson picked *federal* offenses; criminal cases in the United States are overwhelmingly prosecuted in *state* court, not federal court. Even serious crimes like murder tend to be prosecuted at the state level. In the 2015 data Carlson cited, the "22 percent of federal murder convictions" were out of a total of 84 murders prosecuted federally that year. There were 15,696 murders in the country as a whole that year. So all we know from the data he cites is that 19 out of the 15,696 were committed by noncitizens. In other words, *we know absolutely nothing from this about the rates at which unauthorized immigrants commit crimes compared to citizens.*

Furthermore, federal prisoners are inside for *federal* offenses, which are often cases that touch on other countries, such as trafficking. Immigration offenses are also prosecuted in federal court, which means that a large number of the people in federal prison are there for immigration crimes. Yet Carlson asks things on air like: "Forty-four percent of all federal inmates are noncitizens, that's a huge number, why wouldn't we be upset by that?" Well, one reason we wouldn't be upset by it is that it is the equivalent of saying, "The majority of immigration crimes are committed by immigrants." In other words, it's a very stupid thing to say, and a very stupid thing to be upset about.

The state-level data is what we would need to make a serious conclusion about relative rates of offending, but it's somewhat patchy because not all states check people's immigration status. Still, the evidence we do have is "so one-sided" in favor of the conclusion that immigrants commit fewer crimes that even Mark Krikorian, who runs the anti-immigration Center for Immigration Studies, has said that "a lot of data does suggest immigrants are less likely to be involved in crime."[26] We *certainly* cannot conclude, like Carlson, that secret data shows immigrants are involved in more crimes. This is pure propaganda. We do, however, have a useful lesson here in how to take a statistic that is technically numerically accurate and use it to mislead people.

24

Inequality Is Fine

To fret about political, social, or economic inequality in a free society is to fret about the problem of freedom itself, for in the presence of freedom there will always be inequality of some kind. . . . There is nothing inherently bad about an elite.

—Jonah Goldberg, *Suicide of the West*

The egalitarian conception of justice amounts to a perverse inversion. Instead of rewarding people for their achievements, it rewards people for *not* achieving anything. Instead of teaching us to celebrate success, it teaches us to condemn the successful for making society more unequal. . . . It teaches us that the only way to show compassion toward others is to grind everyone down to the lowest common denominator.

—Don Watkins and Yaron Brook, *Equal Is Unfair*

Inequality is, after all, a purely formal characteristic; and from this formal characteristic of the relationship between two items, nothing whatever follows as to the desirability or value of either, or of the relationship between them. Surely what is of genuine moral concern is not *formal* but *substantive.* It is whether people have good lives, and not how their lives compare with the lives of others.

—Harry G. Frankfurt, *On Inequality*

[Equality of opportunity] means that no person should ever be denied an opportunity for progress in a productive direction for reasons that are unrelated to their competence or, to put it another way, that movement forward towards production

of individual and social utility should never be interfered
with by arbitrary prejudice (which is discrimination that has
nothing to do with the task at hand). This is also a fundamental principle of Western culture, to the degree that
it manages to be meritocratic—which it tends strongly towards, driven by the desire for profitably productivity. . . .
Equity is a whole different ballgame. It is predicated on the
idea that the only certain measure of "equality" is outcome,
educational, social, and occupational. The equity-pushers
assume axiomatically that if all positions at every level of
hierarchy in ever [sic] organization are not occupied by a
proportion of the population that is precisely equivalent
to that proportion in the general population that systemic
prejudice (racism, sexism, homophobia, etc.) is definitely at
play, and that there are perpetrators who should be limited
or punished that have or are currently producing that prejudice. There is simply no excuse for this doctrine.

—Jordan B. Peterson, "Equity: When the Left Goes Too Far"

The Argument

People are naturally unequal, and attempts to make them equal by
force are forever doomed to end in disaster. Some people are more
endowed with intelligence and virtue than others. Some people
will produce more than others. This is okay. Instead of trying to
force equality on nature, we should accept natural hierarchies.
Besides, there is nothing inherently valuable about equality. We
should care about poverty, but inequality itself is irrelevant. To the
extent it does matter, we should focus on creating "equality of opportunity" rather than "equality of outcome."

The Response

The philosopher Harry G. Frankfurt, in his short book *On Equality*,
makes the case that for all the talk of "inequality" as a social problem, inequality does not actually matter and we should not care
about it. This is because inequality is just a ratio: if my income is

$10,000 and yours is $100,000, what matters is not that yours is 10 times mine but that mine is too low to live comfortably on. Say we were offered a change in which your income would be multiplied by 100, and became 10 million, and mine would be multiplied by 10, to become 100,000. This would make me better off, and thus would be an improvement, even though the *ratio* between our incomes has only gotten worse. We are less equal, but I am less poor. By contrast, if we reduced your initial $100,000 income to match my $10,000 dollar income, we would become more equal, but I would be no less poor.

This argument is very tempting, and Frankfurt is far from the only one who makes it. The implication of it is that it doesn't matter how rich the rich are. It is often used as part of a defense of capitalism: yes, it may be true that the wealthy are obscenely wealthy, but if the incomes of the poor are growing, too—and, after all, poor people today have smartphones and refrigerators—we should not resent the rich for their success.

There are two key flaws in the argument. First, though those who make the argument deny that this is true, wealth is ultimately "zero-sum" in some important ways. In *Equal Is Unfair*, Watkins and Brook argue that criticisms of wealth inequality are based on a "fixed pie fallacy." This means that people view the sum total of wealth in society as being like a pie divided into slices, so that if I have more, you necessarily have less. In fact, economies are not like pies, because their sizes change. The pie grows, so that I could have a larger "slice" tomorrow without you having any less of a slice. Steven Pinker uses this reasoning to argue that "the poor are not poor because the rich are rich."

But in important ways, wealth *is* zero-sum, in that every dollar you have is a dollar I don't have. A millionaire *could* give their wealth away but chooses not to. In theory, the pie could grow over time, and usually does, slowly. But the actually existing economic deprivation at any given point could easily be alleviated through the redistribution of wealth from those who have vastly more than they need to those who have almost nothing.[1] In other words, while the economic "pie" may grow over time, in the short term, it has a certain size and is distributed in a certain way.[2] The noblemen that Robin Hood stole from to give to the poor *could* have argued that "over time, there is no reason why the poor cannot have their welfare improved without my sacrificing this purse of gold." But Robin Hood would point out, quite rightly, that at the moment, there is one purse of gold in front of us, and a decision to be made over who gets it, and if the rich man has it, the poor man doesn't.[3]

The second problem with the "inequality doesn't matter" argument is that it overlooks the ways in which wealth confers power, and power inequalities are unjustified. Let us imagine an election in which ninety-nine people got one vote each, and one person got one hundred votes. The person with one hundred votes would get their way even if *everyone else disagreed with them*. In a political context, we can see why this would be unfair. But markets can work a lot like elections. If a historic building is for sale, and ninety-nine people want to buy it and turn it into a community center, but a billionaire wants to buy it and turn it into a private garage for his collection of supercars, if the ninety-nine together have less to spend than the billionaire, they will be outbid. This is a direct function of inequality, the relationship between the relative amount of money held by each side.

Consider also a feudal system, in which a lord owns all the land, and the peasants work it but must remit a portion of what they earn to the lord. In such a system, the lord could point to statistics showing that life for the peasants is getting better all the time, and that there is no necessary reason why he should have to be less wealthy in order for them to become more prosperous (perhaps through technological improvements). But the unequal relationship is an *inherent* problem: there is no just reason why they ought to work the land and he ought to own it. The problem with feudal relations is not just that peasants are poor, it is that they are peasants.

So wealth inequality matters, in part, because it means an inequality of *power* that makes democracy impossible. This also helps us to understand why another conservative talking point on inequality, the difference between "political equality" and "economic equality," is less persuasive than it initially seems. The basic argument here is that while each person is equal *before the law*, in that they have the same formal rights under the Constitution (they get a vote, due process of law, free speech, etc.), social and economic inequalities (such as workplace hierarchies and wealth differences) are legitimate and do not need to be addressed by the government. You have equal rights, but there still may be huge differences of wealth and status.

The first reason that this doesn't work is that it's impossible to have real political equality while there is economic inequality. Every person may be "equal before the law," but if one can afford to hire an army of lawyers and the other can't, then courtroom disputes will never be fair. If I own a news network or social-media website and can use them to push my political views, while you work twelve hours a day and don't even have time to stand holding a picket sign, our equal status as voters with First Amendment rights doesn't mean much in practice. If billionaires can self-fund their political campaigns, everyone who isn't a billionaire is at a serious disadvantage. If corporations can pay for armies of lobbyists, while you and I can't, then "political equality" is purely a formal abstraction rather than a real description of how the government operates.

Huge disparities of wealth create de facto oligarchies, in which important political decisions are made by the superrich. Many poor cities, for instance, are essentially held hostage by rich companies, who promise to come to town in exchange for tax breaks and other perks. Amazon infamously launched a contest among U.S. cities to bid for the company's new second headquarters. Many desperate mayors produced revoltingly obsequious pleas to Amazon, and promised the company as many generous handouts as they could. Atlanta offered to give Amazon executives their own lounge at Hartsfield-Jackson International Airport (with free parking) alongside $1.7 billion in tax incentives, Boston offered zero-interest loans for Amazon employees to put down payments on homes, Chicago offered to spend $400 million on improving infrastructure like roads and sewers to better serve Amazon (and had William Shatner narrate its bid video, since Jeff Bezos is a *Star Trek* fan), Columbus offered to form a task force to bring down its murder rate (not clear why it took the prospect of an Amazon headquarters for them to propose this), Dallas offered to create a new university called Amazon U, Maryland offered an astonishing $6.5 billion in tax incentives through a special piece of legislation called the PRIME Act, and Pittsburgh offered to pay a portion of the wages of Amazon workers so the company didn't have to.[4] (Some cities kept their bids secret.) But while it may seem ridiculous to have struggling cities paying the expenses of one of the richest companies in the world, we can understand precisely why it happened. City governments were tantalized by the prospect of the fifty thousand jobs that Amazon said would be created in the winning municipality. Amazon is so powerful that it was essentially able to dictate its terms. Bezos, despite being unelected, has decisions about the economic future of whole cities in his hands. Because wealth is an entitlement to decide how resources are used, it is a form of political power, and so wealth inequality *is* political inequality. We're not going to have democracy until we have less private economic power concentrated in the hands of a small number of people.

The importance of "equality" to the left does not come simply because we resent and despise the rich.[5] It's also because wealth confers relative power in bidding contests for social outcomes. If you have more wealth than me, you have more power than me, and if you have more power than me, we do not have a democratic society. In a democratic society, people get to participate (to the extent reasonably possible) in decisions that will affect their lives. If power accrues disproportionately to one person or group of people, those left out are going to be subjected to the whims of others rather than being given autonomy.

Equal "Opportunity" and Equal "Outcome"

> The liberal will therefore distinguish sharply between equality of rights and equality of opportunity, on the one hand, and material equality or equality of outcome on the other.
>
> —Milton Friedman, *Capitalism and Freedom*

Sometimes, in response to concerns about inequality, conservatives draw a distinction between two different kinds of equality: equality of "opportunity" and equality of "outcome." The people who draw this distinction often say that they believe in the former but not the latter. Equality of "opportunity" is desirable, but equality of "outcome" is not. As they frame it, one of these is fairly basic while the other is radical and frightening. If we were to try to ensure equal "outcomes," we would have to create a colossal social transformation. It would resemble the dystopia of Kurt Vonnegut's famous short story "Harrison Bergeron," in which able-bodied people are saddled with weights so that they cannot dance better than disabled people, and everyone is forcibly made "equal." The people who distinguish *opportunity* and *outcome* often do so in order to discourage us from trying to redistribute wealth from rich to poor—what matters is not whether people end up highly unequal, but whether they have the same opportunities at the start. If life is a race, it's okay if there are "winners" and "losers" so long as the race is played fairly. So "equality of opportunity" describes the conditions under which the results of the race should be accepted: everyone went in with the same ability to succeed, but some people came out ahead of others, which is okay.

It's very tempting to accept this framework because it allows for a clean distinction between "capitalist" and "communist" equality. Capitalists believe that everyone should be equally able to pursue the good life, whereas the communists make the error of believing that everyone is equally entitled to the good life, and introduce all kinds of distortions and horrors in their efforts to force equality upon a highly unequal world. The sensible egalitarian simply makes sure the "rules of the game" are set up fairly and doesn't try to meddle with the outcome, even if that outcome is highly inegalitarian.

But there are severe problems with this way of looking at things. Frankly, it only makes sense until you think about what it means. It sounds nice, but when you start examining it closely, the boundaries between "opportunity" and "outcome" become very unclear. One generation's outcomes structure the next generation's opportunities. Let's say we start with a fair economic "race," but then a few people become much richer than others. Those people can send their children to private schools; they can pass on all of their connections and knowledge and wealth to their children. Even if Generation A has equal opportunities, Generation A's unequal outcomes mean that Generation B will have dramatic variations in opportunities. If you want to create equal opportunities, you'll have to constantly be meddling with outcomes.

In fact, when we actually imagine real "equal opportunity," we can see just how radical a notion it is. Providing anything close to equal opportunity would require exactly the kind of transformation that "equality of outcome" is criticized for pursuing. Consider what it would mean for schools. I recently gave a talk at Phillips Academy Andover, one of the oldest and most expensive private schools in the country.[6] It's a remarkable place, with a five-to-one student-to-teacher ratio and a gorgeous leafy campus. Meanwhile, a friend of mine who teaches in the Detroit public school system has approximately thirty children in her elementary school class.

Because several are severely autistic and require a great deal of personal attention, it can be difficult to teach any of the others. Yet look at these descriptions of some of the best elementary schools in the country:

> On a 26-acre campus with an amphitheater, certified wildlife habitat, trails, and outdoor classrooms, children in nursery school through eighth grade enjoy a varied STEAM (science, technology, engineering, arts, and math) curriculum. Students in grades one through eight each have computer access. In nursery and preschool, the young students have a dedicated indoor gym, and physical education begins at age three. There are four playgrounds and four school buildings. The New School has over 350 students, 52 part-time teachers, and 63-full time teachers.[7]

If we believed in equal opportunity, every school would have to be like this. You wouldn't have a $23 billion funding gap between predominantly white and predominantly nonwhite school districts.[8] You probably wouldn't even have private schools at all, because allowing private schools means allowing rich parents to buy their children more opportunity than other children have. If we're in favor of 'equal opportunity rather than equal outcome,' and children need to 'compete in a level playing field,' then rich parents' wealth can't be used to put their children ahead of others. That means no private tutoring, no test prep courses, nothing for the children of Georgetown that the children of Baltimore don't get.

Even "equality under law" would require radical transformations. For instance, we would all need to have the same quality of legal representation. There would be no difference between the outcome you would get with the Alabama public defender's office or Harvey Weinstein's legal defense team. If we had equality before the law, nobody would mind being given a public defender, or even being randomly assigned a lawyer.

Real equality of opportunity is inconceivable. It would mean that nobody had any genetic disadvantages, everybody had equally good parents, schools, communities. And that's just within a country. When we start thinking about the world, equality of opportunity becomes a laughable concept. How can you have equality of opportunity in a world where militarized borders between countries exist? If a child born on one side of a geographic line lives in an area with lower crime rates, lower poverty, better schools, etc., than a child born on the other side of that line, and the second child is prohibited from crossing the line, in what sense is there anything resembling equal opportunity? The United States bestows distinctly unequal opportunities on its own children, keeping the rest of the world locked outside its fortress gates.

Think about what it would take for everyone to have an equal "chance" in life, for the only variations in individual outcomes to be the product of individual effort and hard work rather than the accident of birth. It would be a radically different world from the one we live in. We would have to have a far more equal distribution of wealth, because as we've discussed, wealth is power, and power buys opportunity. We'd have to ensure that people never got jobs because of who their parents knew, that their parents barely affected their lives at all! Personally, I believe that meritocracy is impossible precisely because these differences can never be corrected, which is why I think "opportunity" rhetoric needs to be discarded entirely. Equality of outcome is actually a far easier goal!

It's very easy to say that equality should be of opportunity rather than outcomes, that if we start the race in the same place, then it doesn't matter if people finish differently. But what does it mean to "start the race in the same place"? If there has been a Black-white wealth gap since the time of slavery, then surely we'd need reparations. Differences in child mortality across races and countries certainly create differences in opportunity. There should be no poor parents and no rich parents, if we think that the amount of money your family has might affect your opportunities.

The Inevitability of Some Inequality
Does Not Undermine the Case for Equality

If equality of opportunity is just as radical as equality of "outcome," then how can we aspire to equality at all? Jonah Goldberg, in criticizing Bernie Sanders's belief that the top 1 percent have too much wealth and power, suggests only extremely destructive methods could achieve social equality:

> A Bernie Sanders of a Stalinist bent could, in theory, liquidate the ranks of the top one percent and, in that very act, create an entirely new top one percent. Remove the top floor of a building and the next floor down becomes the top floor. The only way to ensure there is no top is to tear down the whole structure to the foundation.[9]

Now, Goldberg is deliberately obscuring the issue here. It's certainly true that as long as there is a range of incomes, there will always be a top 1 percent, but what Sanders is concerned with is making sure the top 1 percent isn't absurdly more wealthy than the remaining 99. We are not "ensuring there is no top," but rather ensuring that the top is not unreasonably far from the bottom.

Of course, complete equality is not achievable, and there are plenty of values other than equality that need to be balanced against it. But the principle that one person, or group of people, should not be *too* much more powerful than any other is a core part of democracy. As we shall see, however, parts of the right aren't wild about democracy, either. . . .

25

Democracy Is Overrated

We're not a democracy. . . . Democracy isn't the objective: liberty, peace, and prospefity [*sic*] are. We want the human condition to flourish. Rank democracy can thwart that.

—Senator Mike Lee (R-UT)

Liberty and democracy are eternal enemies, and every one knows it who has ever given any sober reflection to the matter.

—H. L. Mencken

Why should we assume there's a right to participate in democratic process? . . . A right to participate in politics seems fundamentally different because it involves imposing your will upon other people. So I'm not sure that any of us should have that kind of right, at least not without any responsibilities.

—Jason Brennan, author of *Against Democracy*

A pure democracy, by which I mean a society consisting of a small number of citizens, who assemble and administer the government in person, can admit of no cure for the mischiefs of faction. . . . Such democracies have ever been spectacles of turbulence and contention; have ever been found incompatible with personal security or the rights of property; and have in general been as short in their lives as they have been violent in their deaths. Theoretic politicians, who have patronized this species of government, have erroneously supposed that by reducing mankind to a perfect equality in their political rights, they would, at the same time, be perfectly equalized and assimilated in their possessions, their opinions, and their passions. A republic, by which I mean a government in which the scheme of representation takes place, opens a different prospect, and promises the cure for which we are seeking.

—James Madison, *Federalist,* no. 10

Why shouldn't we believe the opposite? That the republic would be better served by having fewer—but better—voters? . . . There would be more voters if we made it easier to vote, and there would be more doctors if we didn't require a license to practice medicine. The fact that we believe unqualified doctors to be a public menace but act as though unqualified voters were just stars in the splendid constellation of democracy indicates how little real esteem we actually have for the vote, in spite of our public pieties. . . . One argument for encouraging bigger turnout is that if more eligible voters go to the polls then the outcome will more closely reflect what the average American voter wants. That sounds like a wonderful thing . . . if you haven't met the average American voter. Voters—individually and in majorities—are as apt to be wrong about things as right about them, often vote from low motives such as bigotry and spite, and very often are contentedly ignorant. That is one of the reasons why the original constitutional architecture of this country gave voters a narrowly limited say in most things and took some things—freedom of speech, freedom of religion, etc.—off the voters' table entirely.

—Kevin D. Williamson, "Why Not Fewer Voters?,"
National Review

The Argument

Democracy, the equal participation in governance, is not necessarily a good thing. Many voters are neither intelligent nor rational. There is nothing admirable about letting policy be made by a foolish majority that does not know its own desires or interests.

Government should be conducted by the knowledgeable and wise, and majorities must be restrained from becoming tyrannical.

The Response

The response to this argument has never been put better than in that classic quip from Winston Churchill: "Democracy is the worst form of Government except for all the others."[1] It is very easy to point out ways in which voters are ill-informed and make bad choices. Finding flaws in democracy is a cinch because it just involves finding flaws in *people,* and people are indeed very flawed. These antidemocratic arguments are thus tempting, because it is easy to become a cynic about people after seeing them at their worst.

But cynics do not solve social problems, and the antidemocrats have a lot of complaints but few solutions. Jason Brennan, in *Against Democracy,* argues that society ought to be run by "epistocrats," people with knowledge and judgment rather than the unwashed masses. Indeed, many of us wouldn't mind if enlightened philosopher-kings just took care of our problems, as it would eliminate the burden of having to think about and participate in politics ourselves. Unfortunately, enlightened philosopher-kings are hard to come by, and most of the people who think they ought to hold the position are the ones you'd least want to have it. The immediate question for the antidemocrat is: How would a nondemocratic system keep from becoming corrupt and oppressive? The meritocrats get to design the tests of merit, and will surely believe that the people who agree with them the most are the most "intelligent." I am sure Brennan, as an ardent libertarian, probably thinks socialists (like myself) are too ignorant on economic matters to have a say in them. Of course, personally, I am inclined to think the opposite is true and that the libertarians are the uninformed ones. In a democratic system, I have to try to convince people I am right and he has to try to convince them he is right. In an *undemocratic* system, the question of which of us gets to decide is resolved behind closed doors through private power struggles. As Ryan Cooper of *The*

Week writes, "Once one side starts disqualifying voters, political competition will tend to become less about winning more votes and more about rigging the electoral system."[2]

One reason people on the right don't like democracy, though, is that it produces outcomes that they personally dislike. The overwhelming majority of people believe in economically progressive policies such as minimum-wage raises, increased corporate taxes, government-provided healthcare, and a federal job guarantee. If the people had their say, right-wing economic proposals would never be adopted.[3]

It is partly because conservatives believe their economic ideas are synonymous with "liberty" that you hear complaints that democracy and liberty are enemies. It's true that democracy is the enemy of the liberty to, say, pay your workers one dollar an hour. If the workers get to vote on that question, they'll vote for a living wage. Those who value the "liberty" of the owner to pay whatever they please will indeed find minimum wages an outrageous injustice and might curse democracy. But if we have a different conception of liberty—one that emphasizes the freedom that comes with having a basic guaranteed income—then democracy is the best way of *ensuring* liberty.

Examine the arguments against democracy closely, then, to see which liberties it supposedly infringes on, and which decisions made by the "people" are considered so dastardly and inept. Often, it turns out that those skeptical of democracy see it as a threat to the private property of the rich. Remember James Madison's assertion that the government's job was to "protect the minority of the opulent against the majority." If you are less sympathetic to the rights of the "opulent," you might be less fearful of the "tyranny of the majority." In fact, it would be nice for the majority to have its say more often. We might finally get universal healthcare that way.

This is not to say that majorities are automatically wise, or that they cannot be tyrannical. I oppose the death penalty while the majority of Americans support it.[4] America is 61 percent white, and with such emphasis given to majorities, there are only such antidiscrimination protections as white people can be persuaded to support.[5] It's easy to selectively invoke popular opinion when you like what it says and condemn the "tyranny of the majority" when you don't. But democracy is more than just "majority rule," which is often treated as synonymous with it. Democracy is supposed to be a participatory and inclusive process in which everyone is heard and their interests are respected, not just a tally of which opinion is held by the most people. A democracy that does not incorporate minority rights is not actually a democracy, because a portion of the people are being disenfranchised.

To understand this a little better, think about racial distributions in congressional districts. Let's say we have five districts, each 70 percent white and 30 percent Black, and that people vote along racial lines. This means that even with a substantial Black population, 100 percent of the congressional representatives will be white. This is "majority rule," but it isn't democracy, because a hugely important constituency is not being represented in the legislature. Figuring out what democracy requires is not necessarily *easy* given the many different issues on which there are minorities deserving representation, so how do we draw districts fairly?[6]

The same problem occurs in direct democracies. In a democratic workplace, for instance, what happens in the case of a 55–45 split on some decision? Are the 45 simply overridden every time? Is this fair? Or should there be some way of achieving a compromise that satisfies a greater majority of people? There are no obvious or "correct" answers to questions like these, and we have yet to design perfectly functional democratic institutions that make everyone happy.[7]

Nobody has ever said that democracy is easy or simple. But taking away the franchise from people, eliminating it as a basic right, is the true "road to serfdom." For all the abstract talk about how democracy is bad, in the real world, women and people of color have had to wage a long fight to secure voting as a universal right,[8] and rolling back that right would undermine that colossal collective achievement. We should always be moving in the direction of greater, not lesser, enfranchisement. Monarchies and aristocracies have a dismal record of serving the people well, and many of the problems in our own society are because it is insufficiently, rather than excessively, democratic. Instead of rolling back democracy in the political sphere, we should be expanding it in other sectors by making corporations, universities, and nonprofits more internally democratic. If there is one thing I disagree most with the right on, it is their distrust of ordinary people and contempt for the democratic process.

Conclusion

In this book, I have first attempted to go through some of the common tendencies in conservative arguments to show why they are so effective at persuading people and explain some of the best tactics for dealing with them. The right is constantly spitting out new talking points, so I have been unable to exhaustively cover every argument you will ever hear made. But I've addressed some of the most common. In the endnotes to this book, you will find references to some other articles by me and others that go into more depth on different arguments or address different and related ones. (I've also left out some major issues, the most prominent of which is probably gun control. If you want refutations of pro-gun talking points, see Nathan J. Robinson, "The GOP's Indifference to Mass Shootings is Depraved and Sickening," *Current Affairs* (June 2, 2022). David Hemenway's *Private Guns, Public Health* (Ann Arbor, MI: University of Michigan Press, 2006) carefully dismantles the conservative talking point that more gun ownership reduces crime and makes people safer.)

Somewhat ironically, considering the low regard in which I hold conservative politics, one of the central messages of this book is: take conservative arguments seriously. They are usually completely wrong, but they are insidious because they can be very persuasive. Oftentimes, they are built on "simple questions" that are designed to stump you ("Why should immigrants be allowed to break the law?" "Why should a man get to decide they are a woman?"). You might have a good response, but on a complicated issue, it often will be difficult to know where to start. The simple questions often have rhetorical force not because they're impossible to answer, but because they're impossible to answer in quick sound bites.

In reading conservative books and articles, I have often noticed that conservatives tend to be better writers than liberals and leftists. Not better *thinkers*. But better at using clear and vivid prose, at structuring their arguments in simple and easy-to-understand ways, at getting their points across forcefully. The quality of conservative ideas is very poor, but the quality of conservative rhetoric is very high. It can be tempting to assume that bad ideas are obviously bad, and can be combated easily. But this is not necessarily so.

I would recommend arming yourself with answers, then.

Is There Anything Good about Conservatism?

After I have gone through so meticulously and thrashed the conservative position on so many issues, you might wonder whether I have anything *good* to say about the right. Is there some kernel of insight lying within the rotten husk of conservative thought?

A small one, perhaps. I think there are a few positions I give some credence to:

◊ **Many authoritarian "socialist" governments of the twentieth century were horrific and oppressive.** My own assessment of the Stalin-era Soviet Union or Mao's China overlaps fairly closely with that of the Heritage Foundation. But you don't have to be a conservative to oppose Stalinism. George Orwell was both a committed opponent of communist totalitarianism and a committed believer in democratic socialism.[1] It is a right-wing myth that socialists all support oppressive dictatorial regimes. The "libertarian socialist" tradition has always been sharply critical of concentrated power.[2] So while I agree with the conservative factual assessment here, I still reject conservative conclusions about what the facts mean.

◊ **Some leftists are toxic, unpleasant, and self-righteous.** I don't deny that "political correctness" can be very annoying and can go too far sometimes. There are instances in which people have been quickly fired for saying offensive things, when my personal belief is that in general we should try to offer second chances and the opportunity to make amends. On the whole, though, this is just as much a problem of "at will" employment as of politically correct culture. When workers do not have union contracts and can be fired for any reason (or no reason), employers are able to terminate them over even trivial infractions. I think much of the focus on "cancel culture" should actually be focused on the lack of rights people have in the workplace.

◊ **"Limousine liberalism" is hypocritical, and the Democratic Party is pretty worthless.** Many politicians loathed by conservatives—Charles Schumer, Nancy Pelosi, Pete Buttigieg, Joe Biden—are people I have no interest whatsoever in defending. The right often conflates liberals and leftists, when the truth is that democratic socialists like Bernie Sanders are constantly at war with the Democratic establishment, who are unfortunately beholden to corporate donors. I'm no fan of those who speak concernedly about inequality and then go and stuff their pockets with money from Wall Street. Half the time when I see Fox News criticizing some absurd hypocrisy by a Democrat, I completely agree with the critique.

◊ **Conserving things is good.** I love traditional architecture, traditional cultures, and the preservation of the environment. To the extent that conservatism is about making sure that precious institutions and practices that have been built over centuries are not wrecked, I am a conservative. Unfortunately, conservationism and conservatism tend to be worlds apart in practice. You would think a conservative, for instance, would be deeply interested in preserving the Amazon rain forest against its destruction by logging and agricultural interests. But far-right Brazilian president Jair Bolsonaro has given the green light for more destructive incursion into the rain forest than ever before.

One of my problems with conservatism, then, is that even when I agree with its *rhetoric,* I do not agree with what is *meant* by that rhetoric. Environmentalism should be seen as conservative in the sense that it is trying to keep the planet from being transformed in ways that damage our precious inheritance. But here is Ann Coulter talking about conservation:

The ethic of conservation is the explicit abnegation of man's dominion over the Earth. The lower species are here for our use. God said so: Go forth, be fruitful, multiply, and rape the planet—it's yours. That's our job: drilling, mining and stripping. Sweaters are the anti-Biblical view. Big gas-guzzling cars with phones and CD players and wet bars—that's the Biblical view.

—Ann Coulter, "Oil Good; Democrats Bad,"
Townhall, October 12, 2000

That is definitely not my view. That sounds mindlessly destructive. No thank you. Coulter doesn't care whether climate change produces millions of refugees. She doesn't care if the rain forests disappear. Conserve *what*? Well, if we are to judge by her book *Adios, America,* the main thing she's interested in conserving is the majority-white demographic composition of the United States.[3] My own interest is in preserving things that the free market threatens to destroy. We are nothing alike except in the narrow abstract sense that we believe in changing some features of society and keeping others. If we examine the actual substance of what each side wants to change, getting past pleasant abstractions about freedom and seriously considering what the right's agenda would mean for human lives, the right's vision is shown to be something that is, in my view, utterly dystopian.

Have a look, for example, at the official 2021 policy platform of the Texas GOP.[4] It contains 337 different proposals, many of which would totally reshape the social and legal landscape. Let me list a few of the more significant ones, to aid you in imagining what a world governed by the American right might be like: opposing any effort to classify carbon emissions as a pollutant; abolishing the EPA; repealing the Endangered Species Act; prohibiting teaching "sex education, sexual health or sexual choice or identity in any public school"; recognizing pornography as a "public health crisis"; abolishing Child Protective Services; abolishing the Department of Education; teaching American history courses "heavily weighted toward the study of original founding documents"; opposing the use of any national or international education standards; requiring mandatory daily pledges of allegiance to both the United States and Texas; banning critical race theory from schools; banning any lockdowns, contact tracing, or mask mandates as public health measures; newly limiting the time disabled people can receive SSDI benefits; eliminating the minimum wage; banning cities from passing paid sick leave ordinances, rent control, or plastic bag bans; abolishing school-based mental health care providers; "oppos[ing] all efforts to validate transgender identity"; repealing all limits on campaign contributions to politicians; repealing all estate taxes; eliminating same-sex marriage; eliminating no-fault divorce and supporting covenant marriage; entirely eliminating abortion; introducing a right to use cryptocurrency to the Texas Bill of Rights; requiring employers to verify citizenship status through E-Verify; abolishing all federal welfare programs; drug testing state welfare recipients; adding "the right to refuse vaccination" to the Texas Bill of Rights; stopping fluoridation of the water supply; disallowing prescription drugs manufactured outside the U.S.; limiting Medicaid; banning Drag Queen Story Hour from libraries; allowing people to bring guns into schools; a prohibition on using gas or vehicle taxes for public transit or bike lanes; opposing a path to citizenship for unauthorized immigrants and using mass deportation instead; abolishing the refugee resettlement program; eliminating birthright citizenship; new criminal penalties for desecrating the American or Texas flag; revoking the tax-exempt status of any organization that "knowingly aid[s] and abet[s] illegal immigrants"; ending the H-1B foreign worker visa program; ending daylight saving time; "support[ing] an aggressive war on terrorism"; requiring cities that cut police budgets to cut property taxes by the same percentage; eliminating all public funding for public broadcasting; repealing the "motor voter" law that allows voter registration at state DMVs; withdrawing from the United Nations; and "unequivocally oppos[ing]" the ratification of the UN Convention on the Rights of the Child.[5]

So government services would be starved of funding, climate change would continue to spiral out of control, the (privatized) schools would be patriotic reeducation camps, endangered species would all be exterminated to make way for new strip malls, all effective public health measures during a pandemic would be banned (leading to mass unnecessary deaths), children would be taught nothing about safe sex but it would be a criminal offense to abort a pregnancy, unauthorized immigrants would live in constant fear, the disabled would be sent to work, and international institutions designed to prevent a world war would be dismantled. Not a country I want to live in. The Republican Party of Texas is, of course, on the extreme end of right-wing politics, having pushed through some of the strongest restrictions on voting and abortion (two things the right wants as few people as possible to do), and all but eliminated any regulation of gun ownership. But Republicans elsewhere may well follow Texas's lead (some are treating its abortion law as a model, for instance).

So while I can agree with the right that, for example, freedom is important and bureaucracy is bad, I still see the world much differently. Freedom, to me, includes the freedom not to be preyed upon by private corporations trying to suck every penny from your bank account. Bureaucracy does not just mean the DMV; it also means private for-profit insurance companies that force you to jump through endless hoops and file reams of paperwork in order to get a claim processed. Conservatism takes us into a topsy-turvy land where white people are actually the oppressed, sweatshops are good, selfishness is virtue, Ebenezer Scrooge is the hero,[6] the people who mow lawns and wash dishes for a living are a threat to the civilized order, and the people who have studied subjects the most are actually ignorant of them.[7] I do not go so far as John Stuart Mill did when he said that "stupidity has a tendency to Conservatism."[8] But I do think that at its core, conservatism has almost everything backwards.

I do not believe that political disagreements are illusory or that, underneath it all, "we all believe the same things."[9] In fact, there are very different competing visions of what a good society looks like. We must find overlap. But sometimes we must just win the argument, then defeat the other side in a political fight.

The Limits of Argument

In practice, sometimes it is not worth arguing. Sometimes you get to the point where you just have different underlying values from someone, and there is no way to persuade people to alter those values. Consider the following passage about the death penalty:

Nor is capital punishment unjust. Indeed, justice is the most powerful argument in favor of capital punishment. When a man wantonly kills two boys, as did [California death row inmate Robert Alton] Harris, it is hard to think of any penalty short of death that would restore the moral order that has been so brutally violated.

—Charles Krauthammer, *Things That Matter*

I don't know how I would persuade Krauthammer or how he would persuade me. We have different conceptions of what the moral order requires. He thinks killing a killer restores it. I think it does nothing of the kind. A conversation between us would be completely unproductive. One is either instinctually revolted by executions or one is not. He is not. I am.

Certain issues are just like that. Abortion, as we have seen, is one of them. If two people look at a fetus at a certain stage, and one sees a human being and the other sees an entity that is not yet a human, how can they persuade each other? Our instincts often clash in irreconcilable ways, and the only thing we can do is try to understand the other person's position as best we can, then try to show them our position as best we can. We might achieve compromise, or "agree to disagree." But not every dispute can be resolved.

I am a believer in the power of discourse. I am not one of those who thinks it is "not worth debating" people who have monstrous beliefs. I believe we can debate them and make them look silly. I think we should confront them directly. But have no illusions: knowing how to respond as effectively as possible will not guarantee that anybody will listen.

In fact, one of the things I tell people who ask how to respond to the right is that relationships are just as important as arguments. If you're having a public debate with someone, or writing a response to some article they've written, you'll need arguments (and maybe some flashy rhetorical tricks). But if we're talking about people in your *life*, if you want to persuade them, getting them to trust, respect, and like you enough to take you seriously is just as important as being right. Being patient, empathetic, and making people feel listened to can be more effective than just having the best point. Furthermore, the work of building strong political movements involves far more than words. Don't let the intellectual and theoretical aspects of politics distract too far from the practical realities of movement building. We will respond to the right with good arguments, but we will also respond with organized political action.

Acknowledgments

My colleagues at *Current Affairs* have been wonderfully supportive of me and are the reason I was able to finish a book while keeping the magazine running. Thanks especially to Lily Sánchez for all her many, many hours of tireless work on *Current Affairs*. But we also couldn't have made it without Yasmin Nair, Jessica Elliott, Paul Waters-Smith, Tim Gray, Rob Larson, Briahna Gray, Sarah Grathwohl, Ann Hubbard, and Anne Summer. My mother, Rosemary Robinson, has also volunteered a staggering amount of her time to help keep our little independent magazine alive. My dad, Peter Robinson, always keeps my spirits up. Special friends and family who deserve recognition here are Samuel Miller McDonald, Lauren Lueder, Sherry Waters, Daniel Ohrenstein, Ben Burgis, Vicky Matthews, and Audrey Matthews. My agent, Mark Gottlieb, and my editor, Kevin Reilly, are two of the best people in the publishing industry and I'm so glad to have found them.

Notes

Introduction

1. I say "supposedly" because frequently, when you examine the actual arguments, erudite conservatives like Buckley are pushing the same prejudices with fancier language. For a discussion of Buckley in particular, see Nathan J. Robinson, "How to Be a Respectable Public Intellectual," *Current Affairs*, Sept. 10, 2020, https://www.currentaffairs.org/2020/09/how-to-be-a-respectable-public-intellectual.

2. Polls vary on this, actually, with Lincoln coming out on top sometimes. In 2011, however, Gallup polling indicated that "Americans are most likely to say Ronald Reagan was the nation's greatest president—slightly ahead of Abraham Lincoln and Bill Clinton." Frank Newport, "Americans Say Reagan Is the Greatest U.S. President," *Gallup*, Feb. 18, 2011, https://news.gallup.com/poll/146183/americans-say-reagan-greatest-president.aspx.

3. For a discussion of the way Obama did this, see Nathan J. Robinson, "Obama's Words," *Current Affairs*, Oct. 9, 2020, https://www.currentaffairs.org/2020/10/obamas-words. For an exhaustive investigation of Clinton, see my book *Superpredator: Bill Clinton's Use and Abuse of Black America* (W. Somerville, MA: Current Affairs Press, 2016).

4. For responses to D'Souza's books in particular, see Nathan J. Robinson, "Is Socialism Evil?," *Current Affairs*, Aug. 11, 2020, https://www.currentaffairs.org/2020/08/is-socialism-evil; Nathan J. Robinson, "Who Are the Real Nazis?," *Current Affairs*, Dec. 1, 2017, https://www.currentaffairs.org/2017/12/who-are-the-real-nazis; and Nathan J. Robinson, "Why Review Bad Books?," *Current Affairs*, Oct. 9, 2018, https://www.currentaffairs.org/2018/10/why-review-bad-books.

5. This is not a paranoid concern. A chilling *Wall Street Journal* investigation reports that companies are developing sophisticated new tools for monitoring employees' activities, even off the clock. Sarah Krouse, "The New Ways Your Boss Is Spying on You," *Wall Street Journal*, July 19, 2019, https://www.wsj.com/articles/the-new-ways-your-boss-is-spying-on-you-11563528604.

6. Deirdre McCloskey, "Free Market Liberalism Is Humane," Hayek Lecture Series, 2018, https://www.youtube.com/watch?v=T7w1GcV6BVo.

7. Specifically, McCloskey was the Inaugural Michael Polanyi Visiting Scholar of Ideas and Innovation at the Charles Koch Institute in 2017.

8. Milo Yiannopoulos's fifteen minutes of fame have long since elapsed, but for a brief period several years ago he was a "bad boy" figure on the American right. He lost much of his conservative audience after appearing to rationalize pederasty. He most recently tried to attract attention by claiming that since he "stopped" being gay, dogs no longer bark at him. Josh Milton, "'Ex-Gay' Milo Yiannopoulos Says Dogs No Longer Bark at Him—and He Sees It as a Sign from God," *PinkNews*, June 6, 2021, https://www.pinknews.co.uk/2021/06/06/ex-gay-milo-yiannopoulos-dogs-no-longer-bark-trunews/. If you should, for some reason, desire an introduction to his brief career as a public speaker, see Nathan J. Robinson, "What We'll Tolerate, and What We Won't," *Current Affairs*, Feb. 21, 2017, https://www.currentaffairs.org/2017/02/what-well-tolerate-and-what-we-wont.

9. Rachel Sheffield and Robert Rector, "Air Conditioning, Cable TV, and an Xbox: What Is Poverty in the United States Today?," Heritage Foundation, July 19, 2011, https://www.heritage.org/poverty-and-inequality/report/air-conditioning-cable-tv-and-xbox-what-poverty-the-united-states.

10. George Gilder, "Freedom from Welfare Dependency," *Religion and Liberty* 4, no. 2 (July 20, 2010), https://www.acton.org/pub/religion-liberty/volume-4-number-2/freedom-welfare -dependency. "Religion is primary. Unless a culture is aspiring toward the good, the true, and the beautiful, and wants the good and the true, really worships God, it readily worships Satan. If we turn away from God, our culture becomes dominated by 'Real Crime Stories' and rap music and other spew."

11. Note: These two positions are not mutually exclusive. Marx and Engels, in *The Communist Manifesto*, showed awe for capitalism's accomplishments while deploring the inhuman misery created by relentless profit-seeking.

12. Rand Paul, "Advocating for Sanctity of Life," https://www.paul.senate.gov/issues /advocating-sanctity-life.

13. Buckley later famously came around on drug use, horrifying some fellow conservatives by calling for the legalization of narcotics. "Legalizing drugs is a terrible idea that would only raise the white flag of surrender," said then–Republican senator Bob Dole. Christopher S. Wren, "Leading Conservative Voice Endorses Legalizing Narcotics," *New York Times,* Jan. 22, 1996, https://www.nytimes.com/1996/01/22/us/leading-conservative-voice-endorses -legalizing-narcotics.html.

14. For a review of Cooke's book, along with David Boaz's *The Libertarian Mind: A Manifesto for Freedom,* see Nathan J. Robinson, "Oh God, Please Not Libertarianism . . . ," *Current Affairs,* April 13, 2016, https://www.currentaffairs.org/2016/04/oh-god-please-not -libertarianism.

15. Whittaker Chambers, "Big Sister Is Watching You," *National Review,* Dec. 28, 1957, https: //www.nationalreview.com/2005/01/big-sister-watching-you-whittaker-chambers/.

Conservatism versus Rationality

1. You may think I am referring to the conservatism of centuries gone by when I speak of the opposition to universal suffrage. Sadly, no. As we will see in Argument #25, opposition to democracy is quite common on the right to this day.

2. Michael Oakeshott, "On Being Conservative," in *Rationalism in Politics and Other Essays,* 2nd ed. (Indianapolis, IN: Liberty Fund, 1991).

3. Quoted in Albert O. Hirschman, *The Rhetoric of Reaction: Perversity, Futility, Jeopardy* (Cambridge, MA: Belknap Press of Harvard University Press, 1991), p. 21.

4. William F. Buckley, "Why the South Must Prevail," *National Review,* Aug. 24, 1957.

5. Although, of course, in practice, Republicans are still indeed trying to curtail this right. See Nathan J. Robinson, "The Escalating War between the Republican Party and Democracy," *Current Affairs,* Nov. 30, 2020, https://www.currentaffairs.org/2020/11/the-escalating-war -between-the-republican-party-and-democracy.

6. You might well argue that left ideology *also* sounds similar from generation to generation. Hirschman did identify progressive fallacies as well as conservative ones, showing that the rhetoric of progress also had an element of faith to it. I am not here to defend the rhetoric of progress, though, or any kind of leftist ideology that is unresponsive to facts. I subscribe to a leftism that believes in self-scrutiny, and I try not to be dogmatic.

7. Corey Robin, *The Reactionary Mind: Conservatism from Edmund Burke to Donald Trump,* 2nd ed. (New York: Oxford University Press, 2018).

8. I reviewed Langone's book, along with a number of other memoirs by billionaires, in Nathan J. Robinson, "How Billionaires See Themselves," *Current Affairs,* Jan. 5, 2021, https://www .currentaffairs.org/2021/01/how-billionaires-see-themselves. In this article, you will find an in-depth discussion of why billionaires should not be seen as entitled to their riches, and examples of the ways they try to find moral justifications for their obscene wealth.

9. However, I do think something profound was expressed by Karl Marx and Friedrich Engels in *The German Ideology,* when they wrote that "each new class which puts itself in the place of one ruling before it, is compelled, merely in order to carry through its aim, to represent its interest as the common interest of all the members of society, that is, expressed in ideal form: it has to give its ideas the form of universality, and represent them as the only rational, universally valid ones." In other words, the wealthy and powerful, in

order to make sure they remain wealthy and powerful, present it as being in the interests of *everyone* to keep them in their current positions, and come up with rationalizations showing that their privileges are not arbitrary but are socially beneficial. We would expect a king to think monarchy was good for his subjects, and we would expect a rich capitalist to argue that capitalism serves the workers as well as the boss, regardless of whether this was in fact true.

The Terror of Having to Think

1. Jonathan Haidt, *The Righteous Mind: Why Good People Are Divided by Politics and Religion* (New York: Vintage, 2012).

2. "Umpires don't make the rules, they apply them," Roberts said during his confirmation hearings. See "Chief Justice Roberts Statement—Nomination Process," United States Courts, https://www.uscourts.gov/educational-resources/educational-activities/chief-justice -roberts-statement-nomination-process.

3. Milton Friedman, "A Friedman Doctrine: The Social Responsibility of Business Is to Increase Its Profits," *New York Times*, Sept. 13, 1970, https://www.nytimes.com/1970/09/13 /archives/a-friedman-doctrine-the-social-responsibility-of-business-is-to.html.

4. See Art Van Zee, "The Promotion and Marketing of OxyContin: Commercial Triumph, Public Health Tragedy," *American Journal of Public Health* 99, no. 2 (February 2009), pp. 221–227, https://www.ncbi.nlm.nih.gov/pmc/articles/PMC2622774/. The opioid crisis is a tragic example of what happens when businesses take seriously Friedman's reassurance that the pursuit of private gain will ultimately work out for the best and that companies do not need to take other considerations into account.

5. Shannon Hall, "Exxon Knew about Climate Change Almost 40 Years Ago," *Scientific American*, Oct. 26, 2015, https://www.scientificamerican.com/article/exxon-knew-about -climate-change-almost-40-years-ago/.

6. See Nathan J. Robinson, "What We Did," *Current Affairs*, July 8, 2018, https://www .currentaffairs.org/2018/07/what-we-did. In this article, I provide an introduction to the facts of the Vietnam War that often go undiscussed in the United States. For testimony on what the U.S. did in Laos, see Fred Branfman, ed., *Voices from the Plain of Jars: Life under An Air War*, 2nd ed. (Madison, WI: University of Wisconsin Press, 2013).

7. The best biography of Bush, which covers all this comprehensively, is Jean Edward Smith, *Bush* (New York: Simon & Schuster, 2016).

Common Tendencies in Conservative Arguments

1. Jason L. Riley, *Please Stop Helping Us: How Liberals Make It Harder for Blacks to Succeed* (New York: Encounter Books, 2015).

2. Maria Sacchetti and Emily Guskin, "In Rural America, Fewer Immigrants and Less Tolerance," *Washington Post*, June 17, 2017, https://www.washingtonpost.com/local/in-rural -america-fewer-immigrants-and-less-tolerance/2017/06/16/7b448454-4d1d-11e7-bc1b -fddbd8359dee_story.html.

3. Bryan Caplan, "Open Borders: A Long-Read Q&A with Bryan Caplan," interview by James Pethokoukis, *Political Economy Podcast*, American Enterprise Institute, Nov. 29, 2019, https://www.aei.org/society-and-culture/immigration/open-borders-a-long-read -qa-with-bryan-caplan/.

4. Commonwealth Fund, "U.S. Ranks Last among Seven Countries on Health System Performance Measures." See also Ajay Tandon et al., "Measuring Overall Health System Performance for 191 Countries," World Health Organization, GPE Discussion Paper Series: No. 30, https://www.who.int/healthinfo/paper30.pdf?ua=1.

5. This argument was made by Milton Friedman in *Capitalism and Freedom*. Friedman's argument was that "any firm that discriminates on the basis of race, gender, ideology, or any other attribute unrelated to worker performance imposes a cost upon itself, and thus the owners would eventually be driven out of business by firms that do not discriminate." This is a paraphrase by the *Berkeley Economic Review*, not a direct quote. It is from an article that shows why Friedman's theory does not hold up to empirical scrutiny. In fact, when

members of a dominant racial group devalue members of another group, the incentives can actually run the *other* way. For instance, a landlord whose white tenants would prefer not to live with Black neighbors would be incentivized to discriminate against Black prospective renters. See Matthew Forbes, "Does the Free Market Protect against Discrimination?," *Berkeley Economic Review,* April 20, 2018, https://econreview.berkeley.edu/does-the-free-market-protect-against-discrimination/.

6. "Updating Social Security for the 21st Century: 12 Proposals You Should Know About," AARP, updated Oct. 2015, https://www.aarp.org/work/social-security/info-05-2012/future-of-social-security-proposals.html.

7. Editorial Board, "Doctors Join the Climate Lobby," *Wall Street Journal,* Sept. 7, 2021, https://www.wsj.com/articles/doctors-join-the-climate-lobby-medical-journal-editorial-bmj-11631048529.

8. See Roger Harrabin, "World's Wealthiest 'at Heart of Climate Problem,'" *BBC News,* April 13, 2021, https://www.bbc.com/news/science-environment-56723560. The article cites research from the Cambridge Sustainability Commission on Scaling Behaviour Change showing that "the world's wealthiest 1% produce double the combined carbon emissions of the poorest 50%," and the "wealthiest 5% alone—the so-called 'polluter elite'—contributed 37% of emissions growth between 1990 and 2015." Critics of left-wing proposals for "degrowth" (i.e., reducing the size of carbon-intensive global economic activity) frequently suggest that the left wants to take basic necessities away from the global poor, when the climate crisis is very much caused by the rich—including both rich countries like the United States *and* the rich in developing countries like China and India.

9. See Tim McDonnell, "Can Farmland Fix Solar Power's Real Estate Problem?," *Quartz,* Oct. 8, 2020, https://qz.com/1913868/why-agricultural-land-is-better-than-rooftops-for-solar-panels/. Adding solar panels to a farm can help farmers make extra money and is especially useful for farmers who do not want to see their land turned into strip malls. The *Wall Street Journal* professes to care about preserving farmland, but since it does not care about other kinds of development that reduce farmland, it's quite clear that all it really cares about is bashing renewable energy and defending existing patterns of fossil fuel use.

10. Stephen Colbert's satirical phrase "truthiness" captures this well. Colbert's parody of a right-wing pundit argued that his *feeling* that something was true was far more important than whether it was, in fact, true. Right-wing arguments are usually like this: they are persuasive because they have a certain *truthiness,* i.e., they *feel* kind of true. They just happen not to be true.

11. Lucy Martinez-Mont, "Sweatshops Are Better than No Shops," *Wall Street Journal,* June 25, 1996, https://www.wsj.com/articles/SB83565161836713000.

12. "Ben Shapiro Speaks at UC Berkeley," YouTube, Sept. 14, 2017, https://www.youtube.com/watch?v=w9eWuqir9J0.

13. *Suicide Attempts among Transgender and Gender Non-Conforming Adults: Findings of the National Transgender Discrimination Survey,* UCLA School of Law Williams Institute (2014). I say "must have been" because I could not find a study from the Anderson School.

14. Greta R. Bauer et al., "Intervenable Factors Associated with Suicide Risk in Transgender Persons: A Respondent Driven Sampling Study in Ontario, Canada," *BMC Public Health* 15, no. 525 (2015), https://doi.org/10.1186/s12889-015-1867-2.

15. For a fascinating look at the question of whether and when central planning works, see Leigh Phillips and Michal Rozworski, *The People's Republic of Walmart: How the World's Biggest Corporations Are Laying the Foundations for Socialism* (Brooklyn, NY: Verso, 2019).

16. Howard Husock, "We Don't Need Subsidized Housing," *City Journal,* winter 1997, https://www.city-journal.org/html/we-don%E2%80%99t-need-subsidized-housing-11954.html. Husock, in attempting to prove that the free market adequately provides housing, goes so far as to defend 1900s tenement slums.

17. Meagan Day, "We Can Have Beautiful Public Housing," *Jacobin,* Nov. 13, 2018, https://jacobinmag.com/2018/11/beautiful-public-housing-red-vienna-social-housing.

18. Ally Schweitzer, "How European-Style Public Housing Could Help Solve the Affordability

Crisis," *NPR*, Feb. 25, 2020, https://www.npr.org/local/305/2020/02/25/809315455/how-european-style-public-housing-could-help-solve-the-affordability-crisis.

19. Andrew Sullivan, *The Conservative Soul: Fundamentalism, Freedom, and the Future of the Right* (New York: HarperCollins Publishers, 2006), p. 280.

20. Scruton, who had written articles praising smoking, was revealed in 2002 to be on the payroll of a Japanese tobacco company. In a leaked email, he asked the company to bump his monthly pay from 4,500 pounds to 5,500 pounds, for which he would use his position as a public intellectual to place articles downplaying the health effects of smoking in prominent newspapers and magazines. Kevin Maguire and Julian Borger, "Scruton in Media Plot to Push the Sale of Cigarettes," *The Guardian*, Jan. 24, 2002, https://www.theguardian.com/media/2002/jan/24/advertising.tobaccoadvertising. It is noteworthy that *even* in the case of one of the most refined, erudite conservative scholars, the intellectual output was in the service of economic interests rather than the result of a dispassionate inquiry into truth. Scruton died of lung cancer in 2020.

21. Roger Scruton, *How to Be a Conservative* (London: Bloomsbury, 2014), pp. viii–ix.

22. Quoted in David Edgar, "The Scruton Affair: Picking on a Harmless Old Fogey?," Institute of Race Relations, May 23, 2019, https://irr.org.uk/article/the-scruton-affair-picking-on-a-harmless-old-fogey/.

23. Paul Waldman, "Campaign in Poetry, Govern in Prose," *American Prospect*, Nov. 8, 2010, https://prospect.org/article/campaign-poetry-govern-prose/.

24. I have written many essays exposing the way "reason" is used by the right as a piece of rhetoric rather than a description of a process of serious inquiry. See Nathan J. Robinson, "Everything Ben Shapiro Says Is Still Worthless," *Current Affairs*, June 30, 2021, https://www.currentaffairs.org/2021/06/everything-ben-shapiro-says-is-still-worthless. For a thoroughly excellent article on the tendency of certain men to use the word "logical" to describe themselves without actually thinking logically, see Aisling McCrea, "The Magical Thinking of Guys Who Love Logic," *The Outline*, Feb. 15, 2019, https://theoutline.com/post/7083/the-magical-thinking-of-guys-who-love-logic.

25. Quoted in Hirschman, *The Rhetoric of Reaction*, p. 13.

26. For a short, illustrated history of labor in the United States, see Priscilla Murolo, *From the Folks Who Brought You the Weekend: A Short, Illustrated History of Labor in the United States* (New York: The New Press, 2001).

27. See Samuel Bowles and Herbert Gintis, *A Cooperative Species: Human Reciprocity and Its Evolution* (Princeton, NJ: Princeton University Press, 2011). For a superb refutation of the right's determinist arguments about nature, see Richard C. Lewontin et al., *Not in Our Genes: Biology, Ideology, and Human Nature* (New York: Pantheon Books, 1984).

28. Charles Murray, *Human Diversity: The Biology of Gender, Race, and Class* (New York: Twelve, 2020), 300–19.

29. Nathan J. Robinson, "Why Is Charles Murray Odious?," *Current Affairs*, July 17, 2017, https://www.currentaffairs.org/2017/07/why-is-charles-murray-odious.

30. For instance, "If you say [the racial scholarly achievement gap] is environmental and so therefore we can reduce the gap, I come back to you and I say . . . tell me what we're going to do that we haven't been doing for the last thirty years that has had no effect whatsoever that we can measure."

31. I have written a *very* long article diving much further into the way that spurious arguments about human nature are drawn from thin evidence, and showing why it is usually not possible to reach conclusions about the limits of human capacities: Nathan J. Robinson, "We Don't Know Our Potential," *Current Affairs*, Sept. 20, 2020, https://www.currentaffairs.org/2020/09/we-dont-know-our-potential.

32. Jordan Peterson, "Lessons from Lobsters," posted by WordToTheWise, July 2, 2020, YouTube video, https://www.youtube.com/watch?v=5ZOkxuNbsXU.

33. "Jordan Peterson debate on the gender pay gap, campus protests and postmodernism," Channel 4 News, YouTube (Jan. 16, 2018). https://www.youtube.com/watch?v=aMcjxSThD54.

34. Ants, for instance, have many socialist qualities: Benjamin D. Blanchard, "The Socialist

Ant," *Current Affairs*, Dec. 2, 2020, https://www.currentaffairs.org/2020/12/the-socialist -ant. Anarchist naturalist Peter Kropotkin also wrote about the many impressive examples of cooperation in the animal kingdom in his classic *Mutual Aid: A Factor of Evolution* (New York: Phillips & Co., 1902). But for a caution against drawing too many lessons from animals about human potential, see Logan W. Cole, "Why Biology Can't Tell Us How to Organize Society," *Current Affairs*, July 29, 2021, https://www.currentaffairs.org/2021/07 /why-biology-cant-tell-us-how-to-organize-society.

35. See David Graeber and David Wengrow, *The Dawn of Everything: A New History of Humanity* (New York: Farrar, Straus and Giroux, 2021).

36. Kate Nocera, "Paul: 'Right to Health Care' Is Slavery," *Politico*, May 11, 2011, https://www .politico.com/story/2011/05/paul-right-to-health-care-is-slavery-054769.

37. Thomas Sowell (@ThomasSowell), "Many of the great disasters of our time have been committed by experts," Twitter, Nov. 15, 2020, 10:57 p.m., https://twitter.com/thomassowell /status/1328185468018683907.

38. See NASA, "Scientific Consensus: Earth's Climate Is Warming," *NASA.gov*, https://climate .nasa.gov/scientific-consensus/.

39. When the American Medical Association discussed systemic racism in healthcare at one of its policy meetings, for instance, the *Wall Street Journal* put out an editorial claiming that the AMA "seems to be evolving into another arm of progressive politics, like the teachers unions." No need to listen to a word it says, then. Editorial Board, "Doctors for Progressive Conformity," *Wall Street Journal*, June 18, 2021, https://www.wsj.com/articles/doctors-for -progressive-conformity-11624055333.

40. Florida Republican lawmaker described those who push mask mandates as "mask nazis," which got him in trouble with the Anti-Defamation League. A. G. Gancarski, "Florida Lawmaker Mocks Anti-Defamation League in 'Mask Nazi' Dispute," *Florida Politics*, June 30, 2020, https://floridapolitics.com/archives/345320-sabatini-mask-nazi-adl/.

41. Sally C. Pipes, *False Premise, False Promise: The Disastrous Reality of Medicare for All* (New York: Encounter Books, 2020).

42. The whole book consists of cherry-picked numbers like this, as well as anecdotes about bad things that happen in Canadian and British hospitals.

43. For a more thorough explanation of why this statistic is complete horseshit, see Nathan J. Robinson, "How Conservatives Use Made-Up and/or Misleading Nonsense to Justify Police Killings," *Current Affairs*, June 26, 2018, https://www.currentaffairs.org/2018/06/how -conservatives-use-made-up-nonsense-to-justify-police-killings/.

44. Nathan J. Robinson, "A Guide for High School Students on How to Avoid Propaganda," *Current Affairs*, Nov. 23, 2020, https://www.currentaffairs.org/2020/11/a-guide-for-high-school-students-on-how-to-avoid-propaganda. The video itself is: "Free the Freelancers," PragerU, YouTube, Oct. 19, 2020, https://www.youtube.com/watch?v =JiJzHn3aA-s.

45. Dara Kerr, "Uber and Lyft Paid $400K to Firm Conducting 'Independent Studies' on Proposition 22," *CNet*, Oct. 31, 2020, https://www.cnet.com/tech/mobile/uber-and-lyft-paid -400k-to-firm-conducting-independent-studies-on-proposition-22/.

46. Interestingly, he did say that by "drivers" he meant "anyone who did a ride for a rideshare app in a given year," meaning that many of the drivers who would "lose their jobs" might have barely ever used the platforms.

47. I have elaborated on the point at greater length here: Nathan J. Robinson, "If You Really Want to Know Why Diversity Is Good . . ." *Current Affairs*, Sept. 10, 2018, https://www .currentaffairs.org/2018/09/if-you-really-want-to-know-why-diversity-is-good. That said, I believe we are better off making arguments for ethnic pluralism on the basis of human rights than because it makes our food and music better. I do not like "diversity is our strength" as a slogan even if I celebrate the richness of human variety.

48. On what day of facial hair growth does a man cease to be "merely unshaven" and start to have a beard?

49. Laura Hollis, "What's behind Multiculturalism?," *Daily Progress*, July 28, 2017, https:

//dailyprogress.com/whats-behind-multiculturalism/article_406a4ce6-3cec-54aa-9497
-4b1577e5a16c.html.

50. Samuel P. Huntington, *Who Are We?* (London: Free Press, 2004), p. 226.

51. It is worth noting, however, that since much U.S. territory was illegitimately seized from Mexico, it is not entirely clear that the American resisters would be in the right in the situation described by Huntington.

52. Francesc Ortega and Amy Hsin, "What Explains the Wages of Undocumented Workers?," *EconoFact,* July 24, 2019, https://econofact.org/what-explains-the-wages-of-undocumented -workers.

53. American College of Obstetricians and Gynecologists, "Health Care for Unauthorized Immigrants," Committee Opinion, no. 627 (March 2015), https://www.acog.org/clinical/clinical -guidance/committee-opinion/articles/2015/03/health-care-for-unauthorized-immigrants.

54. Doug Bandow, "The Chinese Cultural Revolution: Lessons for America's Cancel Culture," *American Spectator,* Sept. 14, 2020, https://spectator.org/the-chinese-cultural-revolution -lessons-for-americas-cancel-culture/.

55. Nicholas D. Kristof, "A Tale of Red Guards and Cannibals," *New York Times,* Jan. 6, 1993, https://www.nytimes.com/1993/01/06/world/a-tale-of-red-guards-and-cannibals.html.

56. Jordan Peterson, "Jordan Peterson Debate on the Gender Pay Gap, Campus Protests and Postmodernism," interview by Cathy Newman, Channel 4 News, YouTube video, Jan. 16, 2018, https://www.youtube.com/watch?v=aMcjxSThD54.

57. Thomas Sowell, interview by Peter M. Robinson, *Uncommon Knowledge,* Hoover Institution, July 2, 2009, YouTube video, https://www.youtube.com/watch?v=5GoAGuTIbVY.

58. James E. Dalen and Joseph S. Alpert, "Medical Tourists: Incoming and Outgoing," *American Journal of Medicine* 132, no. 1 (July 15, 2018), https://doi.org/10.1016/j.amjmed.2018.06.022.

59. For a full response to Beck's *Arguing with Socialists,* see Ben Burgis and Nathan J. Robinson, "Arguing with Glenn Beck," *Current Affairs,* Nov. 7, 2020, https://www.currentaffairs .org/2020/11/arguing-with-glenn-beck. In this review, we debunk many of Beck's antisocialist arguments using both devastating logic and cheerful mockery.

60. Congressional Budget Office, *The Effects on Employment and Family Income of Increasing the Federal Minimum Wage,* July 2019, https://www.cbo.gov/system/files/2019-07/CBO -55410-MinimumWage2019.pdf.

61. The Economic Policy Institute wrote that the CBO finding is that raising the minimum wage "would increase the wages of millions of low-wage workers, increase the average incomes of low- and lower-middle-income families, reduce poverty, shift money from corporate profits to the wages of low-wage workers, and reduce inequality." Heidi Shierholz, "CBO Report Shows Broad Benefits from Higher Minimum Wage," Economic Policy Institute, July 8, 2019, https://www.epi.org/press/cbo-report-shows-broad-benefits-from -higher-minimum-wage/.

62. John Stossel, *No, They Can't: Why Government Fails—But Individuals Succeed* (New York: Threshold Editions, 2012), p. 120.

63. For an interesting look at Soviet autos, see automotive YouTube channel Carfection's video "Retro or Rubbish? Cool Communist Cars of the Soviet Union," July 20, 2019, https:// www.youtube.com/watch?v=6Xiy2NUdMGE.

64. Vanessa Brown Calder, "Parental Leave: Is There a Case for Government Action?," Cato Institute, Oct. 2, 2018, https://www.cato.org/policy-analysis/parental-leave-there-case -government-action.

65. Christopher J. Ruhm, "The Economic Consequences of Parental Leave Mandates: Lessons from Europe," National Bureau of Economic Research, Working Paper #5688 (July 1996).

66. I hadn't actually heard anyone say this, but I assumed *someone* on the right probably had, so I looked it up and sure enough: Bill Glauber, "[U.S. Senator] Ron Johnson Called Joe Biden 'a Liberal, Progressive, Socialist, Marxist.' Can Someone Be All Those Things?," *Milwaukee Journal Sentinel,* June 11, 2021, https://www.jsonline.com/story/news/politics/2021/06/11 /ron-johnson-joe-biden-a-liberal-progressive-socialist-marxist/7655294002/.

67. "It's like when Hitler invaded Poland in 1939," billionaire Stephen Schwarzman said of

Barack Obama's desire to tax private equity firms. Jonathan Alter, "Schwarzman: 'It's a War' between Obama, Wall St.," *Newsweek*, Aug. 15, 2010, https://www.newsweek.com /schwarzman-its-war-between-obama-wall-st-71317.

Tips for Arguing

1. To see an example of an overconfident debater, look up the debate between atheist Christopher Hitchens and theologian William Lane Craig on YouTube. Hitchens clearly underestimated his opponent's abilities, in part because he thought Christianity primitive and irrational. Craig got the better of him.

2. I showed exactly why the argument fails in my review of the book: Nathan J. Robinson, "Who Are the Real Nazis?," *Current Affairs*, Dec. 1, 2017, https://www.currentaffairs.org /2017/12/who-are-the-real-nazis.

3. Valentine was a right-wing radio host who strongly opposed mask mandates and was skeptical of vaccination efforts during the COVID-19 pandemic. In July 2021, he contracted COVID-19. Despite taking ivermectin, Valentine died of the virus in August 2021. Martin Pengelly, "Tennessee Radio Host Who Criticised Vaccine Efforts Dies of Covid-19," *The Guardian*, Aug. 21, 2021, https://www.theguardian.com/us-news/2021/aug/21/tennessee -radio-host-phil-valentine-vaccine-vaccination-dies-covid-19. Valentine's family now encourages the public to get vaccinated!

4. Watch Bernie's interactions with Trump supporters: "Bernie Sanders Transforms Trump Supporters Into Liberals," YouTube, Dec. 13, 2016, https://www.youtube.com/watch?v= dvNkdakBexU. See also Bernie's Fox News town hall: "Town Hall With Bernie Sanders," Fox News, YouTube, April 14, 2019, https://www.youtube.com/watch?v=p4ozAACcc8I. Bernie's interview on *The Joe Rogan Experience* was also a master class in how to explain your ideas to someone who isn't in your political camp.

5. Candace Owens, "#1125—Candace Owens," interview by Joe Rogan, *The Joe Rogan Experience* (podcast), May 30, 2018, https://open.spotify.com/episode/4yV5O4PBIq56MczfSGmQfn.

6. For an interview with McIntyre in which he expands on effective techniques of engaging with obstinate people, see Nathan J. Robinson, "How Can You Talk Effectively to Anti-Vaxxers, Flat Earthers, and Climate Deniers?," *Current Affairs*, Oct. 15, 2021, https://www .currentaffairs.org/2021/10/how-can-you-talk-effectively-to-anti-vaxxers-flat-earthers -and-climate-deniers.

Chapter 1: Government Is the Problem, Not the Solution

1. Jim Geraghty, "Ten Reasons We Can't, and Shouldn't, Be Nordic," *National Review*, March 12, 2018, https://www.nationalreview.com/2018/03/ten-reasons-we-cant-and-shouldnt -be-nordic/.

2. When news broke in 2012 that the GSA had spent $800,000 on a conference in Las Vegas, it became a national scandal and led to the imposition of strict new rules limiting what government agencies could spend money on at conferences. These rules ensured that public servants no longer get to experience the kind of frivolous joy that their counterparts in the private sector might enjoy at conferences, but it's not clear that the problem was as large as it seemed, and the changed rules may have been an overreaction. Personally, I am of the view that government workers deserve the best, even if that means the bureaucrats get an occasional taxpayer-funded weekend in Vegas. See Eric Katz, "Looking Back at the GSA Scandal: Did the Administration Overreact?," *Government Executive*, Jan. 26, 2015, https://www.govexec.com/management/2015/01/looking-back-gsa-scandal-did -administration-overreact/103764/.

3. Kevin D. Williamson, for instance, argues that public schools are dysfunctional *because* they are public. He says that the reason that food stamps work, but "government schools" do not, is that food stamps are "a straightforward subsidy that relies on a market system for the delivery of goods" while schools "do not rely on a market system for the delivery of goods." Williamson describes public schools as a monopoly and teachers' unions as a "cartel" and argues that market competition is necessary to fix the schools. Kevin D. Williamson, "Inequality in Education," *National Review*, Aug. 8, 2014, https://www.nationalreview.

com/2014/08/inequality-education-kevin-d-williamson/. See also the chapter on public schooling in Williamson, *The Politically Incorrect Guide to Socialism* (Regnery, 2010).

4. See Melissa Benn, "The Only Way to End the Class Divide: The Case for Abolishing Private Schools," *The Guardian*, Aug. 24, 2018, https://www.theguardian.com/news/2018/aug /24/the-only-way-to-end-the-class-divide-the-case-for-abolishing-private-schools.

5. It is also worth noting that American public schools are not as bad as the right makes them out to be. I went to a superb public school in Florida, which always made me question why the right thought public schools *couldn't* be run well. I had evidence in front of my eyes that that wasn't true and that it was perfectly possible for a school to be both public and high quality. There is nothing *inherent* about a school being government-run that dooms it to inadequacy.

6. Justin Doom, "Solyndra Program Vilified by Republicans Turns a Profit," *Bloomberg News*, Nov. 13, 2014, https://www.bloomberg.com/news/articles/2014-11-13/solyndra-program -vilified-by-republicans-turns-a-profit. This does not mean, of course, that investing in Solyndra was a wise bet, but any loan program like this will inevitably fund a few duds, which is why instead of fixating on the bad choices, we also need to look at what the program has done *overall* in order to evaluate it.

7. Gregory W. Sullivan, *A Big Dig Cost Recovery Referral: Poor Contract Oversight by Bechtel/ Parsons Brinckerhoff May Have Led to Cost Increases*, Massachusetts Office of the Inspector General, Feb. 2004, https://www.mass.gov/doc/big-dig-cost-recovery-referral-poor -contract-oversight-by-bechtelparsons-brinckerhoff-may-have/download.

8. Free-market libertarians would respond, of course, by arguing that the reason for-profit government contractors bilk taxpayers is that government itself does not have an incentive to keep costs low, thus finding a way to blame the government for what looks like straightforward private-sector malfeasance. But first, note that the argument involves conceding that for-profit corporations are indeed trying to grab as much money as they can and deliver as little in return as possible. Second, we know that corporate crime occurs whenever corporations are able to get away with it, which is not limited to circumstances in which they have a government contract. Wage theft is an obvious example: when employers can get away with not paying workers what they were owed, they frequently engage in blatant theft. See David Cooper and Teresa Kroeger, *Employers Steal Billions from Workers' Paychecks Each Year*, Economic Policy Institute, May 10, 2017, https://www.epi .org/publication/employers-steal-billions-from-workers-paychecks-each-year/.

9. See Mariana Mazzucato, *The Entrepreneurial State: Debunking Public vs. Private Sector Myths* (New York: Anthem Press, 2013).

10. Rob Larson, *Capitalism vs. Freedom: The Toll Road to Serfdom* (Alresford, UK: Zero Books, 2018), p. 112.

11. "Why US Airports Are So Bad," CNBC, Sept. 30, 2019, https://www.youtube.com/ watch?v=5lL-Y-rgNr4 For a fuller critique of CNBC's arguments on airports, see Nathan J. Robinson, "Beware Arguments for Privatization," *Current Affairs*, Oct. 15, 2019.

12. Hugh Stretton and Lionel Orchard, *Public Goods, Public Enterprise, Public Choice: Theoretical Foundations of the Contemporary Attack on Government* (New York: St. Martin's Press, 1994), noting that in Britain, "Railways, coal, and steel prospered better after their original nationalization than before it . . . [and] when the British-owned private car-makers failed, public owners took them over and put most of them back into profit," p. 118.

13. Ha-Joon Chang, *Bad Samaritans: The Myth of Free Trade and the Secret History of Capitalism* (New York: Bloomsbury, 2008).

14. "Notable and Quotable: Milton Friedman," *Wall Street Journal*, Oct. 6, 2015, https://www .wsj.com/articles/notable-quotable-milton-friedman-1444169267.

15. Max Colchester and Joanna Sugden, "U.K.'s Rapid Covid-19 Vaccination Campaign Shows Early Signs of Success," *Wall Street Journal*, Feb. 3, 2021, https://www.wsj.com/articles/u -k-s-rapid-covid-19-vaccination-campaign-shows-early-signs-of-success-11612350120.

16. Thomas Sowell, interview by Peter M. Robinson, *Uncommon Knowledge*, Hoover Institution, July 2, 2009, YouTube video, https://www.youtube.com/watch?v=5GoAGuTIbVY.

17. See Nathan J. Robinson, "Why Private Health Insurance Makes No Sense," *Current Affairs*,

Nov. 21, 2020, https://www.currentaffairs.org/2020/11/why-private-health-insurance
-makes-no-sense.

18. Often, this is obscured by defining *available* to mean "able to be purchased by those with enough money" rather than "actually accessible in practice." But this means that health-care is "available" in the sense that if I don't like Amazon, one "available" option is for me to buy the company. If we define "available" and "accessible" without reference to whether people can, in practice, afford something, we make the words practically meaningless, since they do not tell us anything about whether in the real world it is realistic for people to be able to have the things they ought to have.

19. Nolan D. McCaskill and Matthew Nussbaum, "Trump Signs Executive Order Requiring That for Every One New Regulation, Two Must Be Revoked," *Politico,* Jan. 30, 2017, https://www.politico.com/story/2017/01/trump-signs-executive-order-requiring-that-for
-every-one-new-regulation-two-must-be-revoked-234365.

20. Nathan Goldschlag and Alex Tabarrok, "Is Regulation to Blame for the Decline in American Entrepreneurship?," *Economic Policy* 33, no. 93 (Jan. 2018), pp. 5–44, https://doi.org
/10.1093/epolic/eix019. When Goldschlag and Tabarrok began their study, "they were sure they'd find proof that regulations were dragging down the economy. But they didn't. No matter how they sliced the data, they could find no evidence that federal regulation was bad for business." Rachel Cohen, "The Libertarian Who Accidentally Helped Make the Case for Regulation," *Washington Monthly,* April/May/June 2018, https://washingtonmonthly.com
/magazine/april-may-june-2018/null-hypothesis/.

21. Daniel S. Greenbaum, "The Clean Air Act: Substantial Success and the Challenges Ahead," *Annals of the American Thoracic Society* 15, no. 3 (March 2018), pp. 296–97, https://doi.org
/10.1513/AnnalsATS.201710-763PS.

22. On the Consumer Financial Protection Bureau, see Nathan J. Robinson, "Requiem for an Agency," *Current Affairs,* Jan. 19, 2018, https://www.currentaffairs.org/2018/01/requiem
-for-an-agency. On the way the FAA has worked with airlines to dramatically improve the safety of air travel, see Andy Pasztor, "The Airline Safety Revolution," *Wall Street Journal,* April 16, 2021, https://www.wsj.com/articles/the-airline-safety-revolution-11618585543. For a dramatic story about how bad incentives in the private sector can cause deadly air disasters, see Maureen Tkacik, "Crash Course," *New Republic,* Sept. 18, 2019, https:
//newrepublic.com/article/154944/boeing-737-max-investigation-indonesia-lion-air
-ethiopian-airlines-managerial-revolution.

23. The National Highway Traffic Safety Administration estimates that 50,457 lives were saved by airbags in the period from 1987 to 2017. "Air Bags," National Highway Traffic Safety Administration, https://www.nhtsa.gov/equipment/air-bags.

24. Sari Horwitz et al., "Inside the Opiate Industry's Marketing Machine," *Washington Post,* Dec. 6, 2019, YouTube video, https://www.youtube.com/watch?v=gIlpd40CpT0.

25. Tobacco companies are only required to put small, unobtrusive labels on their products, and the different warnings rotate. Sometimes they mention cancer, but other times they just mention that cigarettes pose a risk to anyone who is pregnant—meaning that, if you're not pregnant, it's possible to buy a pack of cigarettes that does not warn you of *any* negative health repercussions that you personally might experience.

26. For a discussion of the way the for-profit food industry profits off keeping people un-healthy, and a proposal for *more* government involvement in feeding people, see Nathan J. Robinson, "A Public Option for Food," *Current Affairs,* Nov. 6, 2017, https://www
.currentaffairs.org/2017/11/a-public-option-for-food. For an excellent in-depth look at corporate food production, see Mark Bittman, *Animal, Vegetable, Junk: A History of Food, from Sustainable to Suicidal* (New York: Houghton Mifflin Harcourt, 2021).

27. Christie Aschwanden, "Contact Tracing, a Key Way to Slow COVID-19, Is Badly Underused by the U.S.," *Scientific American,* July 21, 2020, https://www.scientificamerican.com/article
/contact-tracing-a-key-way-to-slow-covid-19-is-badly-underused-by-the-u-s/.

28. Todd Pollack et al., "Emerging COVID-19 Success Story: Vietnam's Commitment to Containment," *Our World in Data,* March 5, 2021, https://ourworldindata.org/covid-exemplar
-vietnam; "Cuba Begins Applying Restrictions on Flights, Passengers to Stop Spread of

COVID-19," *Xinhua*, Feb. 7, 2021, http://www.xinhuanet.com/english/2021-02/07/c
_139726817.htm. With the subsequent rise of the Delta variant, both countries experi-
enced greater challenges in containing the virus.

29. Spencer wrote: "If, by saying 'that it is the duty of the State to adopt measures for protecting the health of its subjects,' it is meant (as it is meant by the majority of the medical
profession) that the State should interpose between quacks and those who patronize them,
or between the druggist and the artisan who wants a remedy for his cold . . . then the reply
is, that to do so is directly to violate the moral law. Men's rights are infringed by these,
as much as by all other trade interferences. The invalid is at liberty to buy medicine and
advice from whomsoever he pleases. . . . On no pretext can a barrier be set up between the
two, without the law of equal freedom being broken; and least of all may the Government,
whose office it is to uphold that law, become a transgressor of it."

30. Robert Nozick, *Anarchy, State, and Utopia* (New York: Basic Books, 1974).

31. This does not necessarily mean that there are no good reasons *not* to redistribute wealth.
Someone can believe that from a pure utility maximization perspective, it is good to take
from the rich and give to the poor, but that in practice, doing so would create bad incentives or empower the government too much, and indeed this is what the right will often
begin arguing once you have shown incontrovertibly that a great deal of wealth that is
presently in the hands of the rich would do more good in the hands of the poor. But in
this section I am interested in showing that *even* where there are no "practical" objections,
there are "rights-based" objections that pop up.

32. Nozick did offer a famous example to defend his anti-redistribution view. He asked us to
think of the famous basketball player Wilt Chamberlain. If thousands of basketball fans
each give Wilt Chamberlain twenty-five cents to watch him play basketball, it is hard to
object to any of the individual transactions. Giving someone twenty-five cents is a perfectly legitimate way for wealth to pass from one person to another. But if, at the end of all
the twenty-five-cent transactions, Wilt Chamberlain has become a billionaire because so
many people have come to see him play basketball, we have a highly skewed distribution
of wealth in our society (Wilt, the billionaire, and everyone else, far from a billionaire). But
since all of the wealth was transferred legitimately, how can we then object to the distribution? The answer to this is: no matter how someone *ends up* with far more wealth than
everybody else, there can still be a moral problem in a situation where a pile of private
wealth that could be used to solve social problems is not being used. For example: if I buy
up all of the world's masks and hand sanitizer, and then a pandemic hits, and I refuse to let
anyone touch my stockpile, the fact that I acquired the masks and hand sanitizer through
legitimate unobjectionable transactions does not provide an answer to the question of
whether it is morally permissible to enforce my property rights even if doing so will cause
large numbers of people to die who might otherwise live. For more, see Nathan J. Robinson, "It's Basically Just Immoral to Be Rich," *Current Affairs*, June 14, 2017, https://www
.currentaffairs.org/2017/06/its-basically-just-immoral-to-be-rich.

33. However, the vaccine example is quite a real one. The property rights of pharmaceutical
companies were indeed valued over the lives of those who desperately needed COVID-19
vaccines during the coronavirus pandemic. See Jessica Glenza, "Coronavirus: How
Wealthy Nations Are Creating a 'Vaccine Apartheid,'" *The Guardian*, March 31, 2021,
https://www.theguardian.com/world/2021/mar/30/coronavirus-vaccine-distribution
-global-disparity.

34. Sometimes conservatives argue that rational self-interest will prevent a company from
being environmentally unfriendly. Arlie Russell Hochschild, in *Strangers in Their Own
Land*, quotes a Louisiana Tea Party activist saying of fossil fuel companies: "It's not in
the company's own interest to have a spill or an accident. They try hard . . . so if there's
a spill, it's probably the best the company could do." But this is false. It often pays to be
wasteful, as I show in this article: Nathan J. Robinson, "Why Doing Harm Is Profitable," *
Current Affairs*, July 15, 2019, https://www.currentaffairs.org/2019/07/why-doing-harm-is
-profitable. If regulation doesn't prevent a harm, the media doesn't expose it, and tort laws
don't effectively punish corporations for it, then a company not only has an *incentive* to

commit the harm, but arguably has a *legal duty* to do so—at least if you strictly believe Milton Friedman's theory that the corporation's sole social obligation is profit maximization. A Friedmanite, i.e., sociopathic, company only has incentives not to hurt people to the extent that there are strong external institutions, in the form of government, media, consumer groups, and labor groups, that can create those incentives. If hurting people doesn't cost money, then it isn't in the interest of companies to avoid cheap, risky practices. The "expected return" on a dangerously risky move might be high enough that it is "economically rational" (not to be confused with being "actually rational"). Frequently, conservatives respond to this by pointing out that in many countries that have had powerful state sectors, such as the Soviet Union, there has been a great deal of environmental destruction, because costs to the environment are entirely unpriced. But the fact that governments fail to accomplish goals that they do not set for themselves does not mean they cannot accomplish these goals when they do set them. If the Soviet Union had attempted to be environmentally sustainable and had failed for reasons that were obviously related to being a powerful state, this argument might hold.

35. For an explanation of left anarchism, see Nathan J. Robinson, "The Power of Anarchist Analysis," *Current Affairs*, Dec. 5, 2019, https://www.currentaffairs.org/2019/12/the-power -of-anarchist-analysis.

Chapter 2: Minimum Wages and Rent Control Are Economically Disastrous

1. Allana Akhtar, "NYC's $15 Minimum Wage Hasn't Brought the Restaurant Apocalypse— It's Helped Them Thrive," *Insider*, Aug. 9, 2019, https://www.businessinsider.com/nyc -restaurant-industry-thriving-after-15-dollar-minimum-wage-2019-8.

2. Matthew Zeitlin, "Laboratories of Democracy: What Seattle Learned from Having the Highest Minimum Wage in the Nation," *Vox*, July 22, 2019, https://www.vox.com/the -highlight/2019/7/13/20690266/seattle-minimum-wage-15-dollars.

3. Noah Smith, "Why $15 Minimum Wage Is Pretty Safe," *Noahpinion*, Jan. 15, 2021, https: //noahpinion.substack.com/p/why-15-minimum-wage-is-pretty-safe.

4. Whenever someone invokes "Econ 101" principles to justify a free-market policy, it's best to ask them why they didn't make it past 101. The most simplistic, and wrong, models of economic activity are the ones lumped together as Econ 101; professional economists are often much more sophisticated and realistic. The monopsony argument showing that raising minimum wages can actually increase employment rates is much less intuitive than the argument that minimum wages lower employment.

5. For more on how empirical studies destroyed the free-market fundamentalist position, see David Card and Alan B. Krueger, *Myth and Measurement: The New Economics of the Minimum Wage*, rev. ed. (1995; repr., Princeton, NJ: Princeton University Press, 2015).

6. Yannet Lathrop, "Impact of the Fight for $15: $68 Billion in Raises, 22 Million Workers," National Employment Law Project, Nov. 29, 2018, https://www.nelp.org/publication /impact-fight-for-15-2018/.

7. Jeff Stein, "Georgia Republican Candidate: 'I Do Not Support a Livable Wage,'" *Vox*, June 7, 2017, https://www.vox.com/policy-and-politics/2017/6/7/15753432/georgia-republican -livable-wage.

8. J. W. Mason, "Considerations on Rent Control," *J. W. Mason* (blog), Nov. 14, 2019, https: //jwmason.org/slackwire/considerations-on-rent-control/.

9. Richard Arnott, "Time for Revisionism on Rent Control?," *Journal of Economic Perspectives* 9, no. 1 (Winter 1995), pp. 99–120, https://pubs.aeaweb.org/doi/pdfplus/10.1257 /jep.9.1.99.

10. For a review of this book, see Nathan J. Robinson, "Everything You Love Will Be Eaten Alive," *Current Affairs*, Feb. 9, 2018, https://www.currentaffairs.org/2018/02/everything -you-love-will-be-eaten-alive.

11. For an introduction to socialist housing policy in the contemporary U.S., see Galen Herz, "Social Housing Is Becoming a Mainstream Policy Goal in the US," *Jacobin*, Feb. 21, 2021, https://jacobinmag.com/2021/02/social-housing-public-affordable-california -maryland.

Chapter 3: Taxation Is Theft and/or Slavery

1. Mark Stoval, "Taxation, Slavery, the State, and Robert Nozick," *On the Mark* (blog), April 2, 2013, https://markstoval.wordpress.com/2013/04/02/taxation-slavery-the-state-and -robert-nozick/.

2. For a more detailed explanation, see Matt Bruenig, "Land as Soil and Land as Space," *MattBruenig.com* (blog), Nov. 9, 2017, https://mattbruenig.com/2017/11/09/land-as-soil -and-land-as-space/.

3. To further illustrate the point, Bruenig wrote a charming Socratic dialogue between an ordinary rational person and a delusional maniac who thinks you can come to own something by "mixing" your labor with it. Matt Bruenig, "Initial Appropriation: A Dialogue," *MattBruenig.com* (blog), Feb. 4, 2014, http://mattbruenig.com/2014/02/04/initial -appropriation-a-dialogue/.

4. Robert Nozick, *Anarchy, State, and Utopia* (New York: Basic Books, 1974).

5. "Neither slavery nor involuntary servitude, except as a punishment for crime whereof the party shall have been duly convicted, shall exist within the United States, or any place subject to their jurisdiction." That unfortunate little caveat allowed for the creation of a brutal "convict leasing" system in the South after the Civil War that ended up resembling slavery in many crucial respects. See Douglas A. Blackmon, *Slavery by Another Name* (New York: Anchor Books, 2009).

6. "Capitalism vs. Socialism Debate—LibertyCon 2018," Institute for Humane Studies, March 19, 2018, YouTube video, https://www.youtube.com/watch?v=SE711kjGnrg&t =43m12s. The relevant exchanges go as follows:

> **BRUENIG:** How does a thing come to be yours?
> **CAPLAN:** How does a thing come to be yours?
> **BRUENIG:** In the state of nature, how do I acquire something and it becomes absolutely my property?
> **CAPLAN:** Right, good question. So, first of all, I would never say "absolutely." Absolutely never say absolutely. So if my baseball is required to save the universe, then it's not absolute. How do things normally come to be yours—?
> **BRUENIG:** Wait, why wouldn't it be absolutely yours if it was required to save the universe?
> **CAPLAN:** Pardon?
> **BRUENIG:** Why wouldn't it be yours if it was required to save the universe?
> **CAPLAN:** Uh . . . so . . . uh . . . so . . .
> **MODERATOR:** Let's let him answer the first question that you posed.
> **CAPLAN:** So, on that here's what I would say. There's a general moral principle that there's a presumption in favor of leaving people and their stuff alone, and if you need to save the universe that's strong enough to overcome the presumption.

The moderator appeared to believe that Caplan was struggling because he had been posed two questions at once. Perhaps. But an alternative explanation is that Caplan, who is intelligent, realized that the moment he admitted that the "general" principle in favor of property rights can be "overcome" in cases where a lot of people's interests would be served by violating property rights, he would be inviting an obvious follow-up question: Why is "saving the universe" a case in which property rights cease to matter, but "saving thousands of lives" is not? If property rights are *not* absolute, but can be violated in cases where the property holder's desire to keep their property is outweighed by the needs of the many (e.g., the fact that you like your baseball does not mean you are allowed to keep it when it is needed to help save the universe), then how do we determine when property rights are insufficiently compelling and can be trampled on to serve society? Seizing a rich person's seventh McMansion and giving it to a homeless person so they do not die of exposure might not be *quite* the same as seizing a baseball to save the universe, but it is similarly a case where a person's right to continued possession of their wealth is not morally compelling next to the alternate uses to which that wealth could be put if it were seized to serve the good of others. For an explanation of why Caplan's answer to the question of how unowned things become owned in the first place was similarly unsatisfying, see

Matt Bruenig, "How Did Private Property Start?," *Jacobin,* March 16, 2018, https://www.jacobinmag.com/2018/03/libertarian-property-ownership-capitalism.

7. For more on the morality of possessing large amounts of wealth, see Nathan J. Robinson, "It's Basically Just Immoral to Be Rich," *Current Affairs,* June 14, 2017, https://www.currentaffairs.org/2017/06/its-basically-just-immoral-to-be-rich.

8. Julia Glum, "The Median Amazon Employee's Salary Is $28,000. Jeff Bezos Makes More Than That in 10 Seconds," *Money,* May 2, 2018, https://money.com/amazon-employee-median-salary-jeff-bezos/.

9. Bram Sable-Smith, "Insulin's High Cost Leads to Lethal Rationing," *NPR,* Sept. 1, 2018, https://www.npr.org/sections/health-shots/2018/09/01/641615877/insulins-high-cost-leads-to-lethal-rationing.

10. Elizabeth Anderson, *Private Government: How Employers Rule Our Lives (and Why We Don't Talk about It)* (Princeton, NJ: Princeton University Press, 2017). For an interview I did with Anderson in which she goes over some of the basics, see Nathan J. Robinson, "Professor Elizabeth Anderson on Workplace Democracy and Feminist Philosophy," *Current Affairs,* Jan. 31, 2021, https://www.currentaffairs.org/2021/01/interview-professor-elizabeth-anderson-on-workplace-democracy-and-feminist-philosophy.

11. Graham Lanktree, "More Rich Americans Are Giving Up Their Citizenship to Avoid Taxes," *Newsweek,* Nov. 2, 2017, https://www.newsweek.com/more-rich-americans-are-giving-their-citizenship-avoid-taxes-699247.

Chapter 4: Capitalism Rewards Innovation and Gives People What They Deserve

1. For a description of what a plausible market socialist society might look like, see David Schweickart, *After Capitalism,* 2nd ed. (Lanham, MD: Rowman and Littlefield Publishers, 2011).

2. I say "economically speaking" because there is more to socialism than collective ownership. See Nathan J. Robinson, "Socialism as a Set of Principles," *Current Affairs,* March 12, 2018, https://www.currentaffairs.org/2018/03/socialism-as-a-set-of-principles. I expand on this in my book *Why You Should Be a Socialist* (New York: All Points Books, 2019).

3. Paul K. Piff et al., "Higher Social Class Predicts Increased Unethical Behavior," *Proceedings of the National Academy of Sciences* 109, no. 11 (March 2012), pp. 4086–4091, https://doi.org/10.1073/pnas.1118373109.

4. Thiel: "You're the smartest physicist of the twentieth century . . . you don't get to be a billionaire, you don't even get to be a millionaire." "Peter Thiel—Competition Is for Losers," posted by Joel Moxley, April 12, 2009, YouTube video, https://www.youtube.com/watch?v=gQPlhycLmMk.

5. F. A. Hayek, *The Constitution of Liberty,* rev. ed. (1960; repr., Abingdon, UK: Routledge, 2014), p. 82.

6. Dinesh D'Souza, *United States of Socialism: Who's Behind It. Why It's Evil. How to Stop It.* (New York: All Points Books, 2020).

7. Nicole Fallert, "CEO Who Raised Company Minimum Wage to 70K Says Revenue Has Tripled," *Newsweek,* April 14, 2021, https://www.newsweek.com/ceo-who-raised-company-minimum-wage-70k-says-revenue-has-tripled-1583610.

8. Doris Taylor, "Rush Limbaugh Calls CEO 'a Socialist and Communist' for Plan to Pay Employees $70,000 Minimum," *WKTR.com,* Aug. 4, 2015, https://www.wtkr.com/2015/08/04/rush-limbaugh-calls-ceo-a-socialist-and-communist-for-plan-to-pay-employees-70000-minimum/.

9. Alicia Adamczyk, "Full-Time Minimum Wage Workers Can't Afford Rent Anywhere in the US, According to a New Report," *CNBC,* July 24, 2021, https://www.cnbc.com/2021/07/14/full-time-minimum-wage-workers-cant-afford-rent-anywhere-in-the-us.html.

10. Edward Bernays, *Propaganda* (1928; repr., Brooklyn, NY: IG Publishing, 2005).

11. Emily Elert, "Why You Can't Stop Eating Cheetos," *Popular Science,* Feb. 26, 2013, https://www.popsci.com/science/article/2013-02/why-you-cant-stop-eating-junk-food/.

12. Frederick Douglass, "Address to the People of the United States," in *Frederick Douglass: Selected Speeches and Writings,* edited by Philip S. Foner, abridged and adapted by Yuval

Taylor (Chicago: Lawrence Hill Books, 1999). Douglass also gave a speech in 1888 called "I Denounce the So-Called Emancipation as a Stupendous Fraud," in which he explained that because of the way exploitation could still occur even under free-market conditions, emancipated Black people in the South were still being tyrannized over by white people despite not being formally enslaved. Douglass explained that the concentration of economic power in the hands of a white ownership class, and Black laborers' dependence on receiving wages from that class in order to survive, meant that Black people were systematically cheated and kept in poverty despite their "freedom." The passage is an excellent explanation of how libertarian "economic freedom" does not actually guarantee authentic emancipation for workers, and is worth quoting at length:

Do you ask me why the Negro of the plantation has made so little progress, why his cupboard is empty, why he flutters in rags, why his children run naked, and why his wife hides herself behind the hut when a stranger is passing? I will tell you. It is because he is systematically and universally cheated out of his hard earnings. The same class that once extorted his labor under the lash now gets his labor by a mean, sneaking, and fraudulent device. That device is a trucking system which never permits him to see or to save a dollar of his hard earnings. He struggles and struggles, but, like a man in a morass, the more he struggles the deeper he sinks. The highest wages paid him is eight dollars a month, and this he receives only in orders on the store, which, in many cases, is owned by his employer. The scrip has purchasing power on that one store, and that one only. A blind man can see that the laborer is by this arrangement bound hand and foot, and is completely in the power of his employer. He can charge the poor fellow what he pleases and give what kind of goods he pleases, and he does both. His victim cannot go to another store and buy, and this the storekeeper knows. The only security the wretched Negro has under this arrangement is the conscience of the storekeeper—a conscience educated in the school of slavery, where the idea prevailed in theory and practice that the Negro had no rights which white men were bound to respect, an arrangement in which everything in the way of food or clothing, whether tainted meat or damaged cloth, is deemed good enough for the Negro. For these he is often made to pay a double price. . . . The Negro sees himself paid but limited wages—far too limited to support himself and family, and that in worthless scrip—and he is tempted to fight the devil with fire. Finding himself systematically robbed he goes to stealing and as a result finds his liberty—such as it is—taken from him, and himself put to work for a master in a chain gang, and he comes out, if he ever gets out, a ruined man. Every Northern man who visits the old master class, the land owners and landlords of the South, is told by the old slaveholders with a great show of virtue that they are glad that they are rid of slavery and would not have the slave system back if they could; that they are better off than they ever were before, and much more of the same tenor. Thus Northern men come home duped and go on a mission of duping others by telling the same pleasing story. There are very good reasons why these people would not have slavery back if they could—reasons far more creditable to their cunning than to their conscience. With slavery they had some care and responsibility for the physical well-being of their slaves. Now they have as firm a grip on the freedman's labor as when he was a slave and without any burden of caring for his children or himself. The whole arrangement is stamped with fraud and is supported by hypocrisy, and I here and now, on this Emancipation Day: denounce it as a villainous swindle, and invoke the press, the pulpit and the lawmaker to assist in exposing it and blotting it out forever.

13. See Nathan J. Robinson, "Why I Love Mark Zuckerberg and Can Never Say a Word against Him," *Current Affairs*, Jan. 3, 2018, https://www.currentaffairs.org/2018/01/why-i-love-mark-zuckerberg-and-can-never-say-a-word-against-him.
14. See Nathan J. Robinson, "'Preferences,' My Ass," *Current Affairs*, Oct. 24, 2018, https://www.currentaffairs.org/2018/10/preferences-my-ass/. This article is about the way that a corporate chain can undermine local small businesses *even* if customers prefer the small business, and how concentrated economic power can distort the results of "free-market competition" so that the most popular products actually lose out. The point is important in responding to those who insist that it is the consumer, rather than corporations, who have "power to decide" in a market.

15. For more on how the Chinese economy is far less "free market" than propagandists would have you believe, see David Schweickart, "China: Market Socialist or Capitalist?," in *Alternative Globalizations Conference Documents*, ed., Jerry Harris (Chicago: Changemakers Publications, 2007), pp. 162–178.

16. See Ha-Joon Chang and Ilene Grabel, "Reclaiming Development from the Washington Consensus," *Journal of Post Keynesian Economics* 27, no. 2 (Winter, 2004–5), pp. 273–291.

17. For a more detailed refutation of pro-capitalist myths about poverty reduction, see Jason Hickel, *The Divide: A Brief Guide to Global Inequality and Its Solutions* (Portsmouth, NH: Heinemann, 2017). Hickel has also responded carefully to criticisms of his position; see Jason Hickel, "A Letter to Steven Pinker (and Bill Gates, for That Matter) about Global Poverty," *JasonHickel.org* (blog), Feb. 4, 2019, https://www.jasonhickel.org/blog/2019/2/3/pinker-and-global-poverty. A good summary of some of the basic points can be found in Roge Karma, "5 Myths about Global Poverty," *Current Affairs*, July 26, 2019, https://www.currentaffairs.org/2019/07/5-myths-about-global-poverty. Another excellent refutation is: Jeremy Lent, "Steven Pinker's Ideas Are Fatally Flawed. These Eight Graphs Show Why," *openDemocracy*, May 21, 2018, https://www.opendemocracy.net/en/transformation/steven-pinker-s-ideas-are-fatally-flawed-these-eight-graphs-show-why/.

Chapter 5: The United States Is a Force for Good in the World

1. Rob Schmitz, "Poll: Much of the World Sees the U.S. as a Threat to Democracy," *NPR*, May 5, 2021, https://www.npr.org/2021/05/05/993754397/poll-much-of-the-world-sees-the-u-s-as-a-threat-to-democracy.

2. Levin compares this to the electoral interventions conducted by the USSR/Russia and finds that the United States intervenes far more in elections. His conclusion is remarkable:

    Overall, 117 partisan electoral interventions were made by the US and the USSR/Russia between 1 January 1946 and 31 December 2000. Eighty-one (or 69%) of these interventions were done by the US while the other 36 cases (or 31%) were conducted by the USSR/Russia. To put this number in the proper perspective, during the same period 937 competitive national-level executive elections, or plausible targets for an electoral intervention, were conducted within independent countries. Accordingly, 11.3% of these elections, or about one of every nine competitive elections since the end of the Second World War, have been the targets of an electoral intervention.

    Dov H. Levin, "Partisan Electoral Interventions by the Great Powers: Introducing the PEIG Dataset," *Conflict Management and Peace Science* 36, no. 1 (January 2019), pp. 88–106, https://doi.org/10.1177%2F0738894216661190.

3. See Peter Beinart, "The U.S. Needs to Face Up to Its Long History of Election Meddling," *The Atlantic*, July 22, 2018, https://www.theatlantic.com/ideas/archive/2018/07/the-us-has-a-long-history-of-election-meddling/565538/.

4. John M. Broder, "White House Is Quietly Pro-Barak," *New York Times*, May 17, 1999, https://www.nytimes.com/1999/05/17/world/white-house-is-quietly-pro-barak.html.

5. For a good overview, see Lyle Jeremy Rubin, "It's Time for a Little Perspective on Russia," *Current Affairs*, July 20, 2018, https://www.currentaffairs.org/2018/07/its-time-for-a-little-perspective-on-russia.

6. Mark Weisbrot, "Does the US Back the Honduran Coup?," *The Guardian*, July 1, 2009, https://www.theguardian.com/commentisfree/cifamerica/2009/jul/01/honduras-zelaya-coup-obama; Mark Weisbrot, "Hard Choices: Hillary Clinton Admits Role in Honduran Coup Aftermath," *Al Jazeera*, Sept. 29, 2014, http://america.aljazeera.com/opinions/2014/9/hillary-clinton-honduraslatinamericaforeignpolicy.html.

7. Reading newspapers of the time shows how disturbingly unconcerned the American press was with the horrifying atrocities unfolding in Europe, even though ample information about Nazi crimes was available. See Nathan J. Robinson, "How Horrific Things Come to Seem Normal," *Current Affairs*, July 4, 2018, https://www.currentaffairs.org/2018/07/how-horrific-things-come-to-seem-normal.

8. Stuart Taylor Jr., "U.S. Says Army Shielded Barbie, Offers Its 'Regrets' to the French," *New York Times*, Aug. 17, 1983, https://www.nytimes.com/1983/08/17/world/us-says-army

-shielded-barbie-offers-its-regrets-to-the-french.html; "Klaus Barbie: Spy for the U.S.," *Washington Post,* July 2, 1984, https://www.washingtonpost.com/archive/lifestyle/1984/07/02/klaus-barbie-spy-for-the-us/557ad6a4-f233-4f1a-a6e6-f2525f24e9cc/.

9. Even Dwight Eisenhower said of U.S.' use of the bomb, "The Japanese were ready to surrender and it wasn't necessary to hit them with that awful thing." General Douglas MacArthur said he saw "no military justification for the dropping of the bomb." See Nathan J. Robinson, "How to Justify Hiroshima," *Current Affairs,* May 11, 2016, https://www.currentaffairs.org/2016/05/how-to-justify-hiroshima. See also Gar Alperovitz, *The Decision to Use the Atomic Bomb* (New York: Vintage Books, 1996).

10. Stephen Wright, "Files Reveal Details of US Support for Indonesian Massacre," Associated Press, Oct. 17, 2017, https://apnews.com/article/a14d23b403804c548b3c6da3428827fa. The AP details "U.S. government knowledge and support of an Indonesian army extermination campaign that killed several hundred thousand civilians during anti-communist hysteria in the mid-1960s."

11. Max Fisher, "Americans Have Forgotten What We Did to North Korea," *Vox,* Aug. 3, 2015, https://www.vox.com/2015/8/3/9089913/north-korea-us-war-crime. Fisher writes:

    In the early 1950s, during the Korean War, the US dropped more bombs on North Korea than it had dropped in the entire Pacific theater during World War II. This carpet bombing, which included 32,000 tons of napalm, often deliberately targeted civilian as well as military targets, devastating the country far beyond what was necessary to fight the war. Whole cities were destroyed, with many thousands of innocent civilians killed and many more left homeless and hungry. For Americans, the journalist Blaine Harden has written, this bombing was "perhaps the most forgotten part of a forgotten war," even though it was almost certainly "a major war crime." Yet it shows that North Korea's hatred of America "is not all manufactured," he wrote. "It is rooted in a fact-based narrative, one that North Korea obsessively remembers and the United States blithely forgets."

12. Rather than go into details of the entire argument for why the invasion of Vietnam was an indefensible atrocity, I will here direct you to an article in which I have summarized the case: Nathan J. Robinson, "What We Did," *Current Affairs,* July 8, 2018, https://www.currentaffairs.org/2018/07/what-we-did.

13. Padraic Convery, "US bombs Continue to Kill in Laos 50 Years after Vietnam War," *Al Jazeera,* Nov. 21, 2018, https://www.aljazeera.com/features/2018/11/21/us-bombs-continue-to-kill-in-laos-50-years-after-vietnam-war.

14. Fred Kaplan, "America's Flight 17," *Slate,* July 23, 2014, https://slate.com/news-and-politics/2014/07/the-vincennes-downing-of-iran-air-flight-655-the-united-states-tried-to-cover-up-its-own-destruction-of-a-passenger-plane.html.

15. It is now commonly understood that George W. Bush is a war criminal, but the crimes of George H. W. Bush are less universally acknowledged. For an introduction see Nathan J. Robinson, "I'm Sorry but This Is Just Sheer Propaganda," *Current Affairs,* Dec. 9, 2018, https://www.currentaffairs.org/2018/12/im-sorry-but-this-is-just-sheer-propaganda.

16. In *America: Imagine the World Without Her,* directed by Dinesh D'Souza and John Sullivan (Lionsgate Films, 2014).

17. See Institute of Medicine Committee to Review the Health Effects in Vietnam Veterans of Exposure to Herbicides, "The U.S. Military and the Herbicide Program in Vietnam," in *Veterans and Agent Orange: Health Effects of Herbicides Used in Vietnam* (Washington, DC: National Academies Press, 1994).

18. See Robinson, "What We Did."

19. Antonia Juhasz, "Why the War in Iraq Was Fought for Big Oil," *CNN,* April 15, 2013, https://www.cnn.com/2013/03/19/opinion/iraq-war-oil-juhasz/index.html.

20. David Vine, *The United States of War: A Global History of America's Endless Conflicts, from Columbus to the Islamic State* (Berkeley, CA: University of California Press, 2020), pp. xix, 329.

21. Joseph E. Stiglitz and Lori Wallach, "Preserving Intellectual Property Barriers to COVID-19 Vaccines Is Morally Wrong and Foolish," *Washington Post,* April 26, 2021, https://www.washingtonpost.com/opinions/2021/04/26/preserving-intellectual-property-barriers-covid-19-vaccines-is-morally-wrong-foolish/.

Chapter 6: There's No Such Thing as White Privilege

1. Mary C. Daly et al., "Disappointing Facts about the Black-White Wage Gap," Federal Reserve Bank of San Francisco Economic Letter, Sept. 5, 2017, https://www.frbsf.org /economic-research/publications/economic-letter/2017/september/disappointing-facts -about-black-white-wage-gap/.

2. Rakesh Kochhar and Anthony Cilluffo, "How Wealth Inequality Has Changed in the U.S. since the Great Recession, by Race, Ethnicity and Income," Pew Research Center, Nov. 1, 2017, https://www.pewresearch.org/fact-tank/2017/11/01/how-wealth-inequality-has -changed-in-the-u-s-since-the-great-recession-by-race-ethnicity-and-income/.

3. Akilah Johnson, "That Was No Typo: The Median Net Worth of Black Bostonians Really Is $8," *Boston Globe,* Dec. 11, 2017, https://www.bostonglobe.com/metro/2017/12/11/that -was-typo-the-median-net-worth-black-bostonians-really/ze5kxC1jJelx24M3pugFFN /story.html.

4. Dedrick Asante-Muhammed et al., *The Ever-Growing Gap: Without Change, African-American and Latino Families Won't Match White Wealth for Centuries,* Institute for Policy Studies, Aug. 8, 2016, https://ips-dc.org/wp-content/uploads/2016/08/The-Ever-Growing -Gap-CFED_IPS-Final-1.pdf.

5. Michael W. Kraus et al., "The Misperception of Racial Economic Inequality," *Perspectives on Psychological Science* 14, no. 6 (September 2019), pp. 899–921, https://doi.org/10 .1177%2F1745691619863049.

6. Juliana Menasce Horowitz et al., *Race in America 2019,* Pew Research Center, April 9, 2019, https://www.pewresearch.org/social-trends/2019/04/09/race-in-america-2019/. Note that over two-thirds of Black Americans say that we need to pay more attention to race issues. Polling consistently shows that Black people tend to see America as far more racist than white people do, which you might think would make white people wonder whether Black people were noticing or experiencing something that white people were not.

7. Nathan J. Robinson, "Slavery Was Very Recent," *Current Affairs,* Oct. 20, 2016, https:// www.currentaffairs.org/2016/10/slavery-was-very-recent.

8. For more on why reparations to Black Americans for slavery (*and* the subsequent exploitation that occurred under Jim Crow) are morally necessary, see Nathan J. Robinson, "Why Reparations Should Be One of Today's Top Political Demands," *Current Affairs,* June 17, 2020, https://www.currentaffairs.org/2020/06/why-reparations-should-be-one-of-todays -top-political-demands.

9. For a longer discussion of Sam Walton and the conditions under which billionaires accumulate their wealth generally, see Nathan J. Robinson, "How Billionaires See Themselves," *Current Affairs,* Jan. 5, 2021, https://www.currentaffairs.org/2021/01/how-billionaires-see -themselves.

10. Sparky Abraham, "How Student Debt Is Worsening Gender and Racial Injustice," *Current Affairs,* June 26, 2018, https://www.currentaffairs.org/2018/06/how-student-debt-is -worsening-gender-and-racial-injustice.

11. See Arlie Russell Hochschild, "How the White Working Class Is Being Destroyed," *New York Times,* March 17, 2020, https://www.nytimes.com/2020/03/17/books/review/deaths -of-despair-and-the-future-of-capitalism-anne-case-angus-deaton.html. But note that while this is often discussed as a "white working-class problem," there is some evidence that "the same forces of rising suicide rates and the opioid epidemic have been affecting Black and Latino Americans as well." Rob Arthur, "Deaths of Despair Have Surged Among People of Color," *New York* magazine, March 25, 2021, https://nymag.com/intelligencer /2021/03/deaths-of-despair-have-surged-among-people-of-color.html.

Chapter 7: The Left Are Woke Totalitarians Trying to Destroy Free Speech in the Name of "Social Justice"

1. Matt Taibbi, "The American Press Is Destroying Itself," *TK News* (newsletter), June 12, 2020, https://taibbi.substack.com/p/the-news-media-is-destroying-itself. For a response to Taibbi's case in particular, see Nathan J. Robinson, "Has the American Left Lost Its

Mind?," *Current Affairs,* June 15, 2020, https://www.currentaffairs.org/2020/06/has-the-american-left-lost-its-mind.

2. John McWhorter, "The Elect: The Threat to a Progressive America from Anti-Black Antiracists, Serial Excerpt No. 1," *It Bears Mentioning* (newsletter), Jan. 27, 2021, https://johnmcwhorter.substack.com/p/the-elect-neoracists-posing-as-antiracists.

3. "Why Was UMass Lowell's Nursing Dean Removed?," *The Sun* (Lowell, MA), July 12, 2020, https://www.lowellsun.com/2020/07/12/turmoil-in-uml-nursing-school/.

4. Ashley Mowreader, "Seaver Hires Political Science Lecturer Who Quoted Racial Slur in Class at UCLA," *Pepperdine University Graphic,* Nov. 14, 2020, https://pepperdine-graphic.com/seaver-hires-political-science-lecturer-who-used-racial-slur-in-class-at-ucla-2/.

5. Ibid.

6. Conor Friedersdorf, "A Food Fight at Oberlin College," *The Atlantic,* Dec. 21, 2015, https://www.theatlantic.com/politics/archive/2015/12/the-food-fight-at-oberlin-college/421401/.

7. Zack Beauchamp, "One of the Most Famous Incidents of Campus Outrage Was Totally Misrepresented," *Vox,* Nov. 5, 2019, https://www.vox.com/identities/2019/11/5/20944138/oberlin-banh-mi-college-campus-diversity.

8. Clover Linh Tran, "CDS Appropriates Asian Dishes, Students Say," *Oberlin Review,* Nov. 6, 2015, https://oberlinreview.org/9055/news/cds-appropriates-asian-dishes-students-say/.

9. Andrew Stuttaford, "Making a Meal Out of Everything," *National Review,* Dec. 20, 2015, https://www.nationalreview.com/corner/cultural-appropriation-and-oberlin-menu/.

10. Beauchamp, "One of the Most Famous."

11. Bruce Gilley, "How the Hate Mob Tried to Silence Me," *Standpoint,* Nov. 27, 2017, https://standpointmag.co.uk/features-december-17-bruce-gilley-how-the-hate-mob-tried-to-silence-me/.

12. Sahar Khan, "The Case against 'The Case for Colonialism,'" *Duck of Minerva,* Sept. 19, 2017, https://www.duckofminerva.com/2017/09/the-case-against-the-case-for-colonialism.html.

13. Essentially, Gilley tried to defend colonialism through a "cost-benefit analysis" without even acknowledging its true human cost, or dealing with the fact that "cost-benefit analysis" is a poor way of morally evaluating criminal acts. I wrote a lengthy debunking of Gilley's argument. Nathan J. Robinson, "A Quick Reminder of Why Colonialism Was Bad," *Current Affairs,* Sept. 14, 2017, https://www.currentaffairs.org/2017/09/a-quick-reminder-of-why-colonialism-was-bad.

14. Yes, moral values have a place in scholarship. For a long explanation of why, see Nathan J. Robinson, "How Should Values Influence Social Science Research?," *Current Affairs,* July 10, 2020, https://www.currentaffairs.org/2020/07/how-should-values-influence-social-science-research.

15. Helen Pluckrose and James Lindsay, *Cynical Theories: How Activist Scholarship Made Everything about Race, Gender, and Identity—and Why This Harms Everybody* (Durham, NC: Pitchstone, 2020), p.# p. 218.

16. Nathan J. Robinson, "The Stereotypes about College Students and Free Speech Are False," *Current Affairs,* Feb. 1, 2018, https://www.currentaffairs.org/2018/02/why-do-those-college-students-hate-free-speech-so-much.

17. "Lecture by Iconic Activist Cancelled after Pressure from Pro-Israel Students," Middle East Monitor, April 1, 2021, https://www.middleeastmonitor.com/20210401-lecture-by-iconic-activist-cancelled-after-pressure-from-pro-israel-students/.

18. Lee Roop, "Birmingham Civil Rights Institute Cancels Plan to Honor Angela Davis," AL.com, Jan. 5, 2019, https://www.al.com/news/birmingham/2019/01/birmingham-civil-rights-institute-cancels-plan-to-honor-angela-davis.html.

19. Joe Kottke and Vicky Carmenate, "Students for Justice in Palestine Face Fordham in Court Once Again," *Fordham Observer,* Nov. 29, 2020, https://fordhamobserver.com/52547/news/sjp-students-for-justice-in-palestine-face-fordham-in-court-once-again/.

20. Sarah McLaughlin, "Zoom Cancels Another Academic Event with Leila Khaled, Again Raising Questions about Company's Role in the Classroom," Foundation for Individual Rights in Education (FIRE), April 22, 2021, https://www.thefire.org/zoom-cancels

-another-academic-event-with-leila-khaled-again-raising-questions-about-companys
-role-in-the-classroom/.

21. Supporters of Israel do not hesitate to use the law to suppress their critics. See Glenn Greenwald, "A Texas Elementary School Speech Pathologist Refused to Sign a Pro-Israel Oath, Now Mandatory in Many States—so She Lost Her Job," *The Intercept*, Dec. 17, 2018, https://theintercept.com/2018/12/17/israel-texas-anti-bds-law/.

22. For an overview of Yiannopoulos's embarrassing fifteen-minute career, see Nathan J. Robinson, "What We'll Tolerate, and What We Won't," *Current Affairs*, Feb. 21, 2017, https://www.currentaffairs.org/2017/02/what-well-tolerate-and-what-we-wont.

23. See Nathan J. Robinson, "I Don't Care How Good His Paintings Are, He Still Belongs in Prison," *Current Affairs*, April 19, 2017, https://www.currentaffairs.org/2017/04/i-dont-care-how-good-his-paintings-are-he-still-belongs-in-prison.

24. For the full text of the speech I gave, see Nathan J. Robinson, "Text of University of Connecticut Speech," *Current Affairs*, Jan. 26, 2018, https://www.currentaffairs.org/2018/01/text-of-university-of-connecticut-speech.

25. Nathan J. Robinson, "How the Media Cracks Down on Critics of Israel," *Current Affairs*, Feb. 10, 2021, https://www.currentaffairs.org/2021/02/how-the-media-cracks-down-on-critics-of-israel.

26. Roxanne Jones, "Alexi McCammond's Dismissal Isn't the End of This Story," *CNN* (March 26, 2021, https://www.cnn.com/2021/03/26/opinions/alexi-mccammond-teen-vogue-what-comes-next-jones/index.html.

27. Margot Harris, "A College Student Says She Lost Her Internship after Posting a Satirical TikTok Video Criticizing 'All Lives Matter' Statements," *Insider*, July 2, 2020, https://www.insider.com/college-student-deloitte-internship-anti-all-lives-matter-tiktok-2020-7.

28. Associated Press, "Marc Lamont Hill Fired from CNN after His Speech on Israel Draws Outrage," *NBC News*, Nov. 30, 2018, https://www.nbcnews.com/news/us-news/marc-lamont-hill-fired-cnn-after-his-speech-israel-draws-n942151.

29. Brandon J. Dixon and Anna M. Kuritzkes, "Charles Murray Event Draws Protest," *Harvard Crimson*, Sept. 7, 2017, https://www.thecrimson.com/article/2017/9/7/charles-murray-visits-harvard/; Charles Murray, "The Coming Apart Election—Discussion with Dr. Charles Murray" (lecture, Yale University, Oct. 5, 2016). If "white supremacist pseudo-scholar" seems too harsh a term, see Nathan J. Robinson, "Why Is Charles Murray Odious?," *Current Affairs*, July 17, 2017, https://www.currentaffairs.org/2017/07/why-is-charles-murray-odious. In this article I comprehensively review Murray's work and show why it is fair to call him a racist.

30. Osita Nwanevu, "The 'Cancel Culture' Con," *New Republic*, Sept. 23, 2019, https://newrepublic.com/article/155141/cancel-culture-con-dave-chappelle-shane-gillis.

31. For an example of the kind of story that gets too little attention, see this powerful essay by Cassandra Greer-Lee, whose husband died of COVID-19 in a Chicago jail: Cassandra Greer-Lee, "COVID-19 Killed My Husband in Jail. So Did Democrats' Indifference," *Current Affairs*, Feb. 7, 2021, https://www.currentaffairs.org/2021/02/covid-19-killed-my-husband-in-jail-so-did-democrats-indifference. When we published this essay in *Current Affairs*, I was saddened that it did not get more readers, but far more people are interested in articles about cancel culture than in serious discussions of depressing but important topics.

32. For a discussion of how the media devalues the lives of non-Americans and thus reinforces U.S. indifference to the suffering of people outside its national borders, see Nathan J. Robinson, "There Is No Justification for the Media's Hierarchy of Victims," *Current Affairs*, July 24, 2017, https://www.currentaffairs.org/2017/07/there-is-no-justification-for-the-medias-hierarchy-of-victims.

33. See Nathan J. Robinson, "The 'Microaggression' Concept," *Current Affairs*, Feb. 17, 2018, https://www.currentaffairs.org/2018/02/the-microaggression-concept.

34. Tom Cotton, "Cotton Introduces Bill to Combat Racist Training in the Military," March 25, 2021, https://www.cotton.senate.gov/news/press-releases/cotton-introduces-bill-to-combat-racist-training-in-the-military.

35. If you would like such a discussion, however, I have written a long article explaining the basics

of critical race theory and making the case for teaching it widely: Nathan J. Robinson, "Why Critical Race Theory Should Be Taught in Schools," *Current Affairs*, July 27, 2021, https://www.currentaffairs.org/2021/07/why-critical-race-theory-should-be-taught-in-schools.

36. For more, see the *Current Affairs* YouTube video: "Safe Spaces Are a Perfectly Reasonable Concept," Jan. 24, 2020, https://www.youtube.com/watch?v=DNsnqKv9Ekc.

37. For a good introductory discussion of what social justice is and why it's an important concept, see Brian Barry, *Why Social Justice Matters* (Malden, MA: Polity Press, 2005).

38. Tim Hains, "Jordan Peterson on Identity Politics, Race Protests: 'Drop Your Cult-Like Affiliations' and Sort Out Your Own Life First," *RealClearPolitics*, Aug. 20, 2017, https://www.realclearpolitics.com/video/2017/08/20/jordan_peterson_if_the_right_degenerates_into_identity_politics_the_left_wins.html.

39. Martin Luther King Jr., "Remaining Awake through a Great Revolution" (sermon, National Cathedral, March 31, 1968).

40. Jonah Goldberg, *Suicide of the West: How the Rebirth of Tribalism, Populism, Nationalism, and Identity Politics Is Destroying American Democracy* (New York: Crown Forum, 2018), p. 64.

Chapter 8: Socialized Medicine Will Kill Your Grandmother

1. If you are fortunate enough to have been spared personal exposure to the extortionate pricing of U.S. medical services, you can learn a great deal about it from the excellent work of journalist Sarah Kliff of the *New York Times*. For a primer, see Sarah Kliff, "Why I'm Obsessed with Patients' Medical Bills," *New York Times*, Aug. 7, 2020, https://www.nytimes.com/2020/08/07/insider/coronavirus-medical-bills.html; Sarah Kliff, "I Read 1,182 Emergency Room Bills This Year. Here's What I Learned," *Vox*, Dec. 18, 2018, https://www.vox.com/health-care/2018/12/18/18134825/emergency-room-bills-health-care-costs-america. I also recommend the newsletter *Sick Note* by Libby Watson: https://www.sicknote.co/.

2. Margot Sanger-Katz, "1,495 Americans Describe the Financial Reality of Being Really Sick," *New York Times*, Oct. 17, 2018, https://www.nytimes.com/2018/10/17/upshot/health-insurance-severely-ill-financial-toxicity-.html.

3. Abdul El-Sayed and Micah Johnson, *Medicare for All: A Citizen's Guide* (New York: Oxford University Press, 2021). This book is *extremely* useful for combatting right-wing talking points on single-payer healthcare and well worth picking up. I have written a review that summarizes its essentials: Nathan J. Robinson, "The Definitive Case for 'Medicare for All,'" *Current Affairs*, Feb. 3, 2021, https://www.currentaffairs.org/2021/02/the-definitive-case-for-medicare-for-all. El-Sayed and Johnson have also written a short but compelling response to an anti-M4A op-ed Donald Trump published in *USA Today*: Abdul El-Sayed and Micah Johnson, "Caring for All," *Current Affairs*, Oct. 15, 2018, https://www.currentaffairs.org/2018/10/caring-for-all.

4. Elisabeth Rosenthal, *An American Sickness: How Healthcare Became Big Business and How You Can Take It Back* (New York: Penguin Books, 2017).

5. For more on the relative simplicity and ease-of-use in the British system, see Nathan J. Robinson, "The Health Care System You Could Have," *Current Affairs*, Jan. 10, 2018, https://www.currentaffairs.org/2018/01/the-health-care-system-you-could-have. For a look at how this system actually makes people more free rather than less, see Aisling McCrea, "Freedom-Loving Americans Should Demand Universal Healthcare," *Current Affairs*, May 9, 2019, https://www.currentaffairs.org/2019/05/freedom-loving-americans-should-demand-universal-healthcare. For some of the backstory to how a highly class-stratified society like Britain got a socialist healthcare system, see Nathan J. Robinson, "How Britain Got Its NHS," *Current Affairs*, Feb. 10, 2020, https://www.currentaffairs.org/2020/02/how-britain-got-its-nhs/.

6. Melissa Healy, "U.S. Health System Costs Four Times More to Run Than Canada's Single-Payer System," *Los Angeles Times*, Jan. 7, 2020, https://www.latimes.com/science/story/2020-01-07/u-s-health-system-costs-four-times-more-than-canadas-single-payer-system. Healy cites a study that "concluded that if the U.S. healthcare system could trim its administrative bloat to bring it in line with Canada's, Americans could save $628 billion a year while getting the same healthcare."

7. Eric C. Schneider et al., *Mirror, Mirror 2017: International Comparison Reflects Flaws*

and Opportunities for Better U.S. Health Care, Commonwealth Fund, July 2017, https://interactives.commonwealthfund.org/2017/july/mirror-mirror/. The report contains the answer to a conservative objection raised by Kevin D. Williamson in *The Politically Incorrect Guide to Socialism.* Williamson writes: "It is true, unquestionably, that the United States spends more as a share of its economy on healthcare than do most other countries. Why is that inherently problematic? The United States spends more on lots of goods and services than do other countries" (p. 238). The answer, of course, is that we spend more *but do not get a better healthcare system.* We waste money on bureaucratic administration and pay a lot more for the exact same services. We are *ripped off.*

8. Interestingly, right-wing congressman Dan Crenshaw had an encounter with Joe Rogan that illustrated the difficulty that conservatives have in responding to this point. Rogan asked Crenshaw why having a Medicare for All system would be different to having a fire department. Crenshaw clearly couldn't think of why it would be different, and struggled to find an answer. The exchange is worth examining:

ROGAN: The human right issue . . . the idea that [medical care is] different than the fire department or the police department.

CRENSHAW: Well, it's not a right either. The fire department's not necessarily a "right."

ROGAN: But it's a public service that's provided to everyone.

CRENSHAW: It is, but understand, let's call it a public service, and let's call doctor healthcare a public service as well, if we were to do Medicare for All.

ROGAN: Wouldn't the result be the same, if it's provided for everyone?

CRENSHAW: Um, not from a practical standpoint, just because it's much easier—again, you could add 100,000 people more to your city and the fire department would have marginally more work to do. You know, compared to like a doctor, for instance. Does that make sense? You just, it doesn't, I think if we're trying to compare them in that sense, that non-rival attribute matters quite a bit, if I'm describing that correctly.

ROGAN: So what you're saying is because competition is necessary with medical innovation and also doctors profit off being exceptional, they have an incentive to be exceptional?

CRENSHAW: No, no, what I'm saying is if you have ten doctors that are serving a community, every time that doctor is serving someone it means someone else can't see them.

ROGAN: Well, isn't that just a signal that we need more doctors and more hospitals? They're understaffed?

CRENSHAW: It is. It would be, yes. But I'm saying that's how it's different from a fire department. Which is sort of lying in wait for a fire to occur.

ROGAN: Well, if there was more fires . . .

CRENSHAW: Which is unlikely. I just, I'm trying to distinguish why those aren't very comparable things. Why one is more a public service that we see to work while the other wouldn't necessarily be.

Crenshaw is indeed *trying* to find a distinction, and the distinction he comes up with is that while fire departments wait for fires to be put out, doctors have to see patients all the time. But this is about as sound an argument as saying that firefighters drive big trucks that make noise, while doctors do not. Rogan is correct to point out that if there were more fires, so that firefighters were putting out fires all the time just as doctors are treating the sick, it wouldn't affect whether public funding could be used to meet the public's needs. Crenshaw later makes the classic conservative argument that "socialism" lacks all-important "price signals" and thus medicine would be calamitous if funded by the government. But the point remains: we do not have to buy firefighting services in a free market. There are no price signals. And yet it turns out that the government can simply recruit, train, and pay a group of skilled workers to do a task and they can do it quite well. The question of why the government can successfully train soldiers, police officers, and firefighters and give their services to the public *gratis* but not doctors or nurses is the one that needs to be answered (and isn't) by the right. Conservatives struggle especially when you point out the huge number of places around the world in which this is already done successfully, because the plausibility of right-wing arguments often depends on forgetting that the world outside the United States exists.

9. For more on the fire department analogy, see Nathan J. Robinson, "A Way to Think Clearly about 'Medicare for All' Debates," *Current Affairs*, Dec. 18, 2019, https://www.currentaffairs.org/2019/12/a-way-to-think-clearly-about-medicare-for-all-debates.

10. Wendell Potter, "Wendell Potter on How the Health Insurance Industry Manipulates Public Opinion," interview by Nathan J. Robinson, *Current Affairs*, Oct. 26, 2020, https://www.currentaffairs.org/2020/10/interview-wendell-potter-on-how-the-health-insurance-industry-manipulates-public-opinion.

11. Tess Bonn, "Former Health Insurance Executive: Buttigieg Uses Industry Talking Points against Progressive Health Care Policy," *The Hill*, Dec. 24, 2019, https://thehill.com/hilltv/rising/475844-former-health-insurance-executive-says-buttigieg-uses-industry-talking-points-against-progressive-health-care-policy; Ben Palmquist, "Why the Argument that Medicare for All Will Curtail 'Freedom' Is So, So Wrong," *In These Times*, Oct. 15, 2019, https://inthesetimes.com/article/medicare-for-all-joe-biden-bernie-sanders-democratic-debate-2020.

12. See Nathan J. Robinson, "Why Private Health Insurance Makes No Sense," *Current Affairs*, Nov. 21, 2020, https://www.currentaffairs.org/2020/11/why-private-health-insurance-makes-no-sense.

13. For more, see Matt Bruenig, "Universal Health Care Might Cost You Less Than You Think," *New York Times*, April 29, 2019, https://www.nytimes.com/2019/04/29/opinion/medicare-for-all-cost.html.

Chapter 9: Scandinavian Social Democracy Won't Work in the United States

1. Pete Hegseth, *American Crusade: Our Fight to Stay Free* (New York: Center Street, 2020).

2. Matt Bruenig, "Family Fun Pack," People's Policy Project, Feb. 19, 2019, https://www.peoplespolicyproject.org/projects/family-fun-pack/. Bruenig demolishes conservative objections to the proposal in a subsequent post: Matt Bruenig, "The Conservative Objection to the Family Fun Pack," People's Policy Project, Feb. 27, 2019, https://www.peoplespolicyproject.org/2019/02/27/the-conservative-objection-to-the-family-fun-pack/.

3. Lillian Mongeau, "Why Oklahoma's Public Preschools Are Some of the Best in the Country," *Hechinger Report*, Feb. 2, 2016, https://hechingerreport.org/why-oklahomas-public-preschools-are-some-of-the-best-in-the-country/.

4. Kevin D. Williamson, *The Politically Incorrect Guide to Socialism* (Washington, DC: Regnery Publishing, Inc., 2011), p. 102.

5. For instance, thanks in part to China's "state-owned rail engineering colossus," it has "created an entire high-speed rail network on an unprecedented scale." Ben Jones, "Past, Present and Future: The Evolution of China's Incredible High-Speed Rail Network," *CNN*, December 27, 2021, https://www.cnn.com/travel/article/china-high-speed-rail-cmd/index.html.

6. Note: There is an extremely tedious argument about Scandinavian countries as to whether they are "socialist" or "capitalist." Some conservatives (Hegseth, D'Souza) argue that Scandinavian countries are socialist, but that they are failures, or that we cannot have their model here. Some conservatives argue that they are capitalist countries, and cite random facts like the nonexistence of a minimum wage or the ease of starting a small business. You can counter these facts with others, like their greater union density. But it is best to try to avoid this horrible argument, with its predictable talking points, and instead get down to the more important question of what these countries do, whether it works, and whether we should do it here. For a spoof of the conservative tendency to treat Scandinavia as capitalist one moment and socialist the next, based purely on convenience, see "Ben Shapiro," "Why Nordic 'Socialism' Won't Work in the U.S.," *Current Affairs*, Aug. 21, 2018, https://www.currentaffairs.org/2018/08/why-the-nordic-model-wont-work-in-the-u-s.

Chapter 10: The Welfare State Will Lead Us Down the "Road to Serfdom"

1. Sunder Katwala, "The NHS: Even More Cherished Than the Monarchy and the Army," *New Statesman*, Jan. 14, 2013, https://www.newstatesman.com/politics/2013/01/nhs-even-more-cherished-monarchy-and-army.

2. See Aisling McCrea, "Freedom-Loving Americans Should Demand Universal Healthcare," *Current Affairs,* May 9, 2019, https://www.currentaffairs.org/2019/05/freedom-loving -americans-should-demand-universal-healthcare.

3. Francis Fukuyama, "Friedrich A. Hayek, Big Government Skeptic," *New York Times,* May 6, 2011, https://www.nytimes.com/2011/05/08/books/review/f-a-hayek-big-government -skeptic.html.

4. "New Poll Shows Canadians Overwhelmingly Support Public Health Care," Healthcare-NOW!, Aug. 17, 2009, https://www.healthcare-now.org/blog/new-poll-shows-canadians -overwhelmingly-support-public-health-care/.

5. Luke Savage, "Tommy Douglas, Canada's Great Prairie Socialist, Wasn't Always So Beloved," *Jacobin,* June 5, 2019, https://jacobinmag.com/2019/06/tommy-douglas-ndp-ccf -socialist-medicare.

Chapter 11: The Nazis Were Socialists

1. Quoted in F. L. Carsten, *The Rise of Fascism* (London: Batsford, 1967), p. 137.

2. I have written a comprehensive review of this book demolishing all of its central claims. Nathan J. Robinson, "Does 'The Case against Socialism' Hold Up?," *Current Affairs,* May 18, 2020, https://www.currentaffairs.org/2020/05/does-the-case-against-socialism-hold-up.

3. Jeff Cox, "JP Morgan CEO Jamie Dimon Takes on Socialism, Says It Will Lead to an 'Eroding Society,'" *CNBC,* Jan. 22, 2020, https://www.cnbc.com/2020/01/22/jp-morgan-ceo -jamie-dimon-takes-on-socialism-says-it-will-lead-to-an-eroding-society.html.

4. George Reisman, "Why Nazism Was Socialism and Why Socialism Is Totalitarian," Mises Institute, Oct. 1, 2021, https://mises.org/library/why-nazism-was-socialism-and-why -socialism-totalitarian.

5. Nick Warino, "The Data Show That Socialism Works," *Current Affairs,* Dec. 7, 2019, https: //www.currentaffairs.org/2019/12/the-data-show-that-socialism-works.

6. Nathan J. Robinson, "Beware Arguments for Privatization," *Current Affairs,* Oct. 15, 2019, https://www.currentaffairs.org/2019/10/beware-arguments-for-privatization. In this article I rebut claims that United States airports are poor quality because they are government-run. In fact, some of the best airports (and even airlines) in the world are owned by states.

7. Nathan J. Robinson, "We Must Save and Strengthen Our Precious Public Assets," *Current Affairs,* Jan. 13, 2020, https://www.currentaffairs.org/2020/01/we-must-save-and-strengthen -our-precious-public-assets.

8. If every corporation was a worker-owned cooperative rather than a dictatorship, socialists would have less to object to about corporations.

9. For more on how Nazi healthcare is used as a cudgel against social democracy, see Michael Scott Moore, "Nazis and Health Care," *Pacific Standard,* May 3, 2017, https://psmag.com /news/nazis-and-health-care-3483.

10. In fact, one reason that the government can enforce economic mandates without much totalitarianism is that the government is so important to the functioning of the marketplace to begin with. The state doesn't need to throw anyone in jail for violating its requirements: it could just decline to enforce their property rights. Corporations only exist because the state has granted them a charter and agreed to enforce their rights in court, meaning that the state would have quite a lot of coercive power over them even if it had no ability to put anyone in prison.

11. Defenders of Mises insist the quote was taken out of context. It wasn't. Ludwig von Mises, *Liberalism* (1927), p. 51.

Chapter 12: Feminism Hurts Both Men and Women

1. Matt Bruenig, "The Gender Pay Gap Is Bigger Than You Thought," *Jacobin,* April 17, 2018, https://www.jacobinmag.com/2018/04/gender-pay-gap-statistics-national-womens-law -center.

2. Charlotte Higgins, "The Age of Patriarchy: How an Unfashionable Idea Became a Rallying Cry for Feminism Today," *The Guardian,* June 22, 2018, https://www.theguardian.com

/news/2018/jun/22/the-age-of-patriarchy-how-an-unfashionable-idea-became-a-rallying
-cry-for-feminism-today.

3. David Gelles, "C.E.O. Pay Remains Stratospheric, Even at Companies Battered by Pandemic," *New York Times,* April 24, 2021, https://www.nytimes.com/2021/04/24/business /ceos-pandemic-compensation.html. The top-paid CEO in the United States is Paycom's Chad Richison, which sounds like the name of an evil businessman from a children's movie.

4. See Bruenig, "The Gender Pay Gap Is Bigger Than You Thought."

5. Leila Idliby, "Glenn Greenwald Says 'Whole Me Too Movement Was about Destroying People,'" *Mediaite,* April 23, 2021, https://www.mediaite.com/podcasts/glenn-greenwald -says-whole-me-too-movement-was-about-destroying-people/.

Chapter 13: Price Gouging, Child Labor, and Sweatshops Are Good

1. Block's *Defending the Undefendable* (1976) is a libertarian defense of a number of classes of people Block believes are unfairly stigmatized by moralists. Each chapter looks at a particular stigmatized occupation and explains why, on a free-market theory of justice, the person in it is actually doing good for the world. Chapters include: "The Pimp," "The Drug Pusher," "The Blackmailer," "The Slanderer," "The Ticket Scalper," "The Dishonest Cop," "The Miser," "The Slumlord," "The Strip Miner," "The Litterer," "The Scab," "The Fat Capitalist Pig Employer," "The Employer of Child Labor," among others. Block mounts a persuasive case that on libertarian premises, each of these can be defended, the logic always being roughly the same: they engage in "voluntary transactions," and all voluntary transactions are made because they make people better off. But what Block sees as a defense of these individuals, we can instead see as a highly persuasive *indictment* of libertarianism. If a world full of litter, slums, blackmail, sexual exploitation, stinginess, lying police, and child labor is unable to be condemned by a worldview that perceives "whatever the market throws up" as synonymous with justice, then clearly the worldview is faulty. Block's book is one of the most extreme works in the libertarian canon, but it is actually very useful because it is willing to be honest about the absurdities that flow from placing excessive emphasis on "nonaggression" as the criterion for judging society. Interestingly, and in case one is inclined to dismiss Block's perspective as fringe, the book contains a short foreword from Nobel Prize–winning economist (and strong intellectual influence on Reagan and Thatcher) Friedrich von Hayek, who commends the work for its economic reasoning and its shattering of "stereotypes" and "prejudices."

2. Kristof is not a conservative himself but his column articulates clearly the laissez-faire view of sweatshops.

3. Michael Munger, "Three Undeniable Problems with Anti-Gouging Laws," American Institute for Economic Research, Sept. 15, 2018, https://www.aier.org/article/three-undeniable -problems-with-anti-gouging-laws/.

4. Steve Patterson, "Thank Goodness for Price Gougers," Foundation for Economic Education, Jan. 14, 2016, https://fee.org/articles/thank-goodness-for-price-gougers/.

5. John Stossel, "Prices Should Rise," *Townhall,* Sept. 19, 2018, https://townhall.com /columnists/johnstossel/2018/09/19/prices-should-rise-n2520198.

6. Giulia McDonnell Nieto del Rio et al., "His Lights Stayed On during Texas' Storm. Now He Owes $16,752," *New York Times,* March 1, 2021, https://www.nytimes.com/2021/02/20 /us/texas-storm-electric-bills.html.

7. Dan Cancian, "Jerry Jones Profits from Texas Power Outages as Gas Prices Skyrocket," *Newsweek,* Feb. 18, 2021, https://www.newsweek.com/jerry-jones-profits-texas-power -outages-gas-prices-skyrocket-1570176.

8. Ted Cruz (@tedcruz), "This is WRONG," Twitter, Feb. 21, 2021, 11:41 a.m., https://twitter .com/tedcruz/status/1363529410268319747.

9. Ted Cruz, "Full transcript: POLITICO's Glenn Thrush Interviews Ted Cruz," interview by Glenn Thrush, *Politico,* July 18, 2016, https://www.politico.com/story/2016/07/off -message-transcript-ted-cruz-225655.

10. Meryl Kornfield, "Cruz Is Trying to Repair His Public Image after His Cancún Trip. He's

Still Feeling the Heat," *Washington Post,* Feb. 21, 2021, https://www.washingtonpost.com /politics/2021/02/21/ted-cruz-texas-storm-response/.

11. For more on why right-wing arguments in favor of price gouging do not work, see Nathan J. Robinson, "Do Economists Actually Know What Money Is?," *Current Affairs,* Oct. 27, 2016, https://www.currentaffairs.org/2016/10/do-economists-actually-know-what -money-is. In this article I critique a piece by former Bush economic adviser and economics textbook author N. Gregory Mankiw, who defends price gouging by pointing to an instance in which he was able to obtain *Hamilton* tickets at the last minute by forking over a giant pile of money. I note that his example proves the anti–price gouging case by showing that what gouging mainly does is make sure the rich are the ones whose access to a scarce good is never compromised. In a follow-up piece, I respond to the argument that even if gouging creates an unfair distribution at the start, it also creates incentives to create more of a scarce good. Nathan J. Robinson, "Incentives and Price Gouging," *Current Affairs,* Oct. 28, 2016, https://www.currentaffairs.org/2016/10/incentives-and-price-gouging.

12. This distinction is often blurred by free-market economists, who treat ability to pay as an appropriate measure of "desire" and thus reach perverse conclusions, like seeing the market's production of grotesque McMansions for the rich and too few doctors for the poor as reflective of the public's desires when it is, in fact, merely a reflection of the unequal distribution of wealth.

13. Jack Nicas, "He Has 17,700 Bottles of Hand Sanitizer and Nowhere to Sell Them," *New York Times,* March 14, 2020, https://www.nytimes.com/2020/03/14/technology/coronavirus -purell-wipes-amazon-sellers.html. The pandemic profiteer featured in the article does not think of himself as parasitic or self-interested, because he has accepted conservative arguments that price gougers are actually helping people. He says he is fixing "inefficiencies in the market place" and "helping send the supply toward the demand." When asked about the fact that he is trying to make a windfall profit, he says: "I honestly feel like it's a public service. I'm being paid for my public service." Due to online retailers' crackdowns on gougers, this particular entrepreneur ended up with a giant stockpile of sanitizer he could not unload, but the *Times* features another who made nearly $40,000 by selling $20 boxes of face masks for between $80 and $125. There is no public benefit from these men's actions, because all of the masks *would* have ended up getting worn, and the hand sanitizer used, even if they had not acted. They were only addressing an "inefficiency" on the theory that those willing to pay the most for something are the ones who most deserve to have it, but the main effect of these men's actions is not to improve public health but simply to transfer wealth from other people's pockets to their own due to their monopolization of something people desperately need. This should be obvious, but conservative arguments have allowed them to justify their unethical conduct as being good. (A great deal of conservative argumentation is meant to show how things that are obviously bad and motivated by greed, like raising poor people's rent or flattening a historic neighborhood to build luxury condos, are actually good and help us all.)

14. Quoted in Nathan J. Robinson, "Texas Republicans Discover the True Meaning of Free Markets," *Current Affairs,* Feb. 28, 2021, https://www.currentaffairs.org/2021/02/texas -republicans-discover-the-true-meaning-of-free-markets. Interestingly, while this quote appeared in the *Wall Street Journal*'s print edition, it disappeared from the online version of the article.

15. Bryan Caplan, *The Case against Education: Why the Education System Is a Waste of Time and Money* (Princeton, NJ: Princeton University Press, 2018).

16. Chelsea Follett, "Why You Shouldn't Knock 'Sweatshops' If You Care about Women's Empowerment," Cato Institute, July 19, 2017, https://www.cato.org/commentary/why-you -shouldnt-knock-sweatshops-you-care-about-womens-empowerment.

17. For more on how feminist rhetoric is used to justify the miserable conditions of sweatshops, see Hester Eisenstein, "The Sweatshop Feminists," *Jacobin,* June 17, 2015, https: //www.jacobinmag.com/2015/06/kristof-globalization-development-third-world/.

18. I earlier quoted Frederick Douglass's assessment on this system. Douglass was so critical

that he believed the very notion that Black people had been "emancipated" by the end of slavery to be a "fraud."

19. See Nathan J. Robinson, "Better Does Not Mean Good," *Current Affairs*, June 5, 2018, https://www.currentaffairs.org/2018/06/better-does-not-mean-good. This may seem like a minor point, but it is important to learn to notice the conflation of "better than some horrible alternative" and "actually good" because it is frequently used in conservative argumentation. For instance, the horrors of Northern industrial work were used to show that the Southern slave system was good for Black people because slavers, unlike private industrialists, had a financial incentive to keep their workers alive. A sensible human being can see that both systems are exploitative.

20. Margaret Wurth, "More US Child Workers Die in Agriculture Than in Any Other Industry," Human Rights Watch, Dec. 4, 2018, https://www.hrw.org/news/2018/12/04/more-us -child-workers-die-agriculture-any-other-industry.

21. I always thought school was the most boring place you could possibly be, until I had my first experience of a workplace.

22. In a review of Caplan's book, I and my coauthor, Sparky Abraham, have suggested a few ways in which school could be made better. Our review responds to the libertarian view that public school is a waste of time by arguing for a better way of doing public school rather than getting rid of it. Nathan J. Robinson and Sparky Abraham, "What Is Education For?," *Current Affairs*, Aug. 11, 2018, https://www.currentaffairs.org/2018/08/what-is-education-for.

Chapter 14: We Don't Need a Green New Deal

1. Shellenberger and Lomborg do not self-identify as political conservatives (in fact, they identify as environmentalists), but their books are direct attacks on left-wing climate politics.

2. Michael Shellenberger (@ShellenbergerMD), "2M acres of California have burned so far this year," Twitter, Sept. 8, 2020, 4:07 p.m., https://twitter.com/shellenbergermd/status /1303424670398439424.

3. A. P. Williams, et al. "Observed impacts of anthropogenic climate change on wildfire in California," *Earth's Future* (2019), pp. 892–910.

4. Michael Goss et al., "Climate Change Is Increasing the Likelihood of Extreme Autumn Wildfire Conditions across California," *Environmental Research Letters* 15, no. 9 (2020), https://iopscience.iop.org/article/10.1088/1748-9326/ab83a7.

5. Anne C. Mulkern, "Climate Change Has Doubled Riskiest Fire Days in California," *Scientific American*, April 3, 2020, https://www.scientificamerican.com/article/climate-change -has-doubled-riskiest-fire-days-in-california/.

6. James Temple, "Yes, Climate Change Is Almost Certainly Fueling California's Massive Fires," *MIT Technology Review*, Aug. 20, 2020, https://www.technologyreview.com/2020 /08/20/1007478/california-wildfires-climate-change-heatwaves/.

7. Darryl Fears et al., "Heat Is Turbocharging Fires, Drought and Tropical Storms This Summer," *Washington Post*, Aug. 21, 2020, https://www.washingtonpost.com/climate -environment/2020/08/21/heat-climate-change-weather/.

8. This is precisely what was done by "skeptical environmentalist" Bjorn Lomborg, in *False Alarm: How Climate Change Panic Costs Us Trillions, Hurts the Poor, and Fails to Fix the Planet.* See Bob Ward, "A Closer Examination of the Fantastical Numbers in Bjorn Lomborg's New Book," Grantham Research Institute on Climate Change and the Environment, Aug. 10, 2020, https://www.lse.ac.uk/granthaminstitute/news/a-closer-examination-of -the-fantastical-numbers-in-bjorn-lomborgs-new-book/. Lomborg has long been a favorite on the right, because while he is not a climate change denier, he insists that panic over climate change is unwarranted and the costs of addressing it in the way progressives want are too high to be worth it. As this review shows, Lomborg does this by underestimating the damage that climate catastrophes will cause (he thinks it will be a small, manageable hit to GDP) and exaggerating the costs of transitioning to renewable energy. Book publishers do not fact-check, and Lomborg is a *very* skilled manipulator whose deceptions

can be difficult to spot, so he has become one of the most insidiously harmful pundits on the issue. The eminent biologist E. O. Wilson lamented Lomborg's presence in the discourse thusly: "We will always have contrarians like Lomborg whose sallies are characterized by willful ignorance, selective quotations, disregard for communication with genuine experts, and destructive campaigning to attract the attention of the media rather than scientists." E. O. Wilson, "On Bjorn Lomborg and Extinction," *Grist,* Dec. 12, 2001, https://grist.org/article/point/.

9. Dinesh D'Souza (@DineshDSouza), "Hahaha! It's 2020 and the glaciers are still here. If all of this is 'settled science,' how come it can't make a single valid prediction?," Twitter, Jan. 8, 2020, 11:23 p.m., https://twitter.com/DineshDSouza/status/1215126884494778373.

10. If you would like to see the most common forms of bullshit debunked, this video is helpful: "13 Misconceptions about Global Warming," posted by Veritasium, Sept. 22, 2014, YouTube video, https://www.youtube.com/watch?v=OWXoRSIxyIU.

11. Mark Lynas et al., "Greater Than 99% Consensus on Human Caused Climate Change in the Peer-Reviewed Scientific Literature," *Environmental Research Letters* 16, no. 11 (2021), https://iopscience.iop.org/article/10.1088/1748-9326/ac2966.

12. Mark R. Levin, *American Marxism* (New York: Threshold Editions, 2021), p. 172.

13. Jeremy Schulman, "Every Insane Thing Donald Trump Has Said about Global Warming," *Mother Jones,* Dec. 12, 2018, https://www.motherjones.com/environment/2016/12/trump-climate-timeline/.

14. I am quoting here from the following article summarizing the report, not the report itself. Brady Dennis and Chris Mooney, "Major Trump Administration Climate Report Says Damage Is 'Intensifying Across the Country,'" *Washington Post,* Nov. 23, 2018, https://www.washingtonpost.com/energy-environment/2018/11/23/major-trump-administration-climate-report-says-damages-are-intensifying-across-country/.

15. "Our Climate Target," Shell, https://www.shell.com/energy-and-innovation/the-energy-future/our-climate-target; "BP Sets Ambition for Net Zero by 2050, Fundamentally Changing Organisation to Deliver," BP, Feb. 12, 2020, https://www.bp.com/en/global/corporate/news-and-insights/press-releases/bernard-looney-announces-new-ambition-for-bp.html. ExxonMobil, too, has a portion of its website devoted to convincing the public that it cares about climate change, as well as a long series of denials that it covered up its knowledge of climate change and misled the public. (Which it absolutely 100 percent did. See Shannon Hall, "Exxon Knew about Climate Change Almost 40 Years Ago," *Scientific American,* Oct. 26, 2015, https://www.scientificamerican.com/article/exxon-knew-about-climate-change-almost-40-years-ago/.)

16. Ben Shapiro, *Bullies: How the Left's Culture of Fear and Intimidation Silences Americans* (New York: Threshold Editions, 2013), p. 204.

17. James P. Kossin et al., "Global Increase in Major Tropical Cyclone Exceedance Probability over the Past Four Decades," *Proceedings of the National Academy of Sciences of the United States* 117, no. 22 (June 2020), pp. 11975–11980, https://doi.org/10.1073/pnas.1920849117.

18. Dana Nuccitelli, "Why the Mail on Sunday Was Wrong to Claim Global Warming Has Stopped," *The Guardian,* Oct. 16, 2012, https://www.theguardian.com/environment/2012/oct/16/daily-mail-global-warming-stopped-wrong.

19. For a rebuttal to Svensmark, see "Henrik Svensmark," OSS, http://ossfoundation.us/projects/environment/global-warming/myths/henrik-svensmark.

20. Benjamin Zycher, "The Green New Deal: Economics and Policy Analysis (One Pager)," American Enterprise Institute (2019). https://www.aei.org/wp-content/uploads/2019/03/Green_New_Deal_One-Pager_Zycher.pdf.

21. Adrian Foong, "Of Yellow Vests and Green Policies," Climate Diplomacy, April 18, 2019, https://climate-diplomacy.org/magazine/cooperation/yellow-vests-and-green-policies.

22. Specifically, Gates told *Wired*: "I'm enough of a centrist to look at the Green New Deal and say, what world do you people live in that you're going to give everyone a job, and you stuck that in a climate bill? You must not be serious about climate. You must be singing the theme song of the Internationale and reading Marx." Bill Gates, "Bill Gates Is Upbeat on Climate, Capitalism, and Even Politics," interview by Steven Levy, *Wired,* March 18, 2021, https://

www.wired.com/story/bill-gates-is-upbeat-on-climate-capitalism-and-even-politics/. Gates does not understand the basic theory of why it's important to make sure climate policies are designed to address people's economic concerns as well so that there will be mass support for climate policy. Because he is a technocrat, Gates prefers to focus narrowly on technological solutions for climate change and shows little understanding of the political realities of solving the problem. For example, in the same interview, he says that he believes Republicans should be in power sometimes, because it is important not to have one party always in charge. But he does not consider the implications of Republican rule, namely that *any* further governance by Republicans forecloses the possibility of doing anything about climate catastrophe. To want Republicans in charge is to want climate change to go unaddressed. Gates appears to see the Green New Deal and Republican climate denialism as equally pernicious, which they are not. Gates appears to be advocating something sensible—bipartisanship—but is really advocating something insane—the preclusion of meaningful climate action. For a longer critique of Gates in particular, see Nathan J. Robinson and Rob Larson, "Humanity Does Not Need Bill Gates," *Current Affairs*, May 4, 2021, https://www.currentaffairs.org/2021/05/humanity-does-not-need-bill-gates.

23. Rhiana Gunn-Wright has given a clear and persuasive answer to the question of why it is necessary to include more than just explicit climate policy in the Green New Deal: "I [keep] seeing a lot of these arguments about how this is too big because it includes inequity, because we're trying to deal with justice, it should just focus on climate, why doesn't it just focus on climate, so on and so forth. And I think there's a few reasons for that. The first one is that the two are intertwined. We know that the folks who are the most at risk of basically living through the worst effects of climate change are people of color, especially low-income people of color. . . . So an example of that would be Detroit, which has shed a lot of its population, and now the residents who are left don't have as much money, are stuck trying to pay for the cost of this big, aging system. And you could see something like this happening in say, a coastal community, where as climate change gets worse, the people who can afford to move will move, and the people that will be left there are people who can't afford to move. . . . So the cause could be climate change, but it's going to appear as a municipal finance problem. It's going to appear as a city going bankrupt, because their tax base is eroding. And then you add on top of that, they're going to have to adapt to the effects of climate change, and this goes across the whole nation, with the heavier storms. So, for instance, imagine a city like Detroit, that now desperately needs to make updates to its stormwater system so that it can handle these heavy rains. And so, to me and everyone else who is working on the GND, why not address those together? Because in fact, that is a climate issue, and if you do have things like Medicare for All, where you're unlinking employment from health insurance, if you are having a jobs guarantee program, that means that people can be mobile. That means that people who are stuck in that community can now move to places where we need them to move, in order for them to do certain types of work. Or, they can stay, and still be earning a living wage, and have that money going back into their communities, and into their tax coffers, so that places have a better chance of actually being able to afford the adaptations that they need, and to support themselves in the midst of the sort of changing climate. That's one of the reasons. Another is that people don't experience things as climate change, right? They experience them as economic loss: of a job, of a home, of savings. So we need to also be able to communicate what the transition will mean to them, and the benefits for them of transitioning to a green economy, and similarly, personal terms, in terms of jobs, in terms of equity, in terms of reinvestment in their community, because right now, it's kind of separated. People understand that climate change will cost them something, and that a transition away from fossil fuels, or whatever else, will change the way that they live, but then, we'll communicate about the benefits in a very national way, or a global way. We talk about emissions going down, we talk about us being able to keep warming at 1.5 degrees Celsius. But that's not telling anybody what they actually stand to gain for themselves as we transition. So I think it's also a political move, in the sense that for people to really act on climate change, or to feel empowered to do it, we also have to give them a vision of what their lives will look like after this transi-

tion, which we have to communicate in economic terms." Rhiana Gunn-Wright, "Rhiana Gunn-Wright on Insurgent Left Policy-Making," interview by Nathan J. Robinson, *Current Affairs*, June 5, 2020, https://www.currentaffairs.org/2020/06/rhiana-gunn-wright-on -insurgent-left-policy-making.

24. Ibid.

Chapter 15: Academia Is a Radical Indoctrination Factory

1. Nathan J. Robinson, "Value of AAAS Should Not Be Undermined," *The Justice*, April 28, 2009, https://www.thejustice.org/article/2009/04/value-of-aaas-should-not-be -undermined. This is an op-ed from the Brandeis student newspaper in which I protested against the proposal to dismantle the department. It was shocking to me as an undergraduate that the university could so casually attack an important discipline, but it should be remembered that it took aggressive and courageous action by Black scholars to establish Black studies departments in the first place. Far from being embraced by the "radical" university system, ethnic- and gender-studies departments have often struggled to survive. See Corey Williams, "Experts: Black Studies Programs Face Campus Challenges," Associated Press, Nov. 20, 2015, https://www.detroitnews.com/story/news /michigan/2015/11/20/missouri-oglesby-michigan-black-studies-protests/76147988/.

2. Ali Trachta, "The Most Popular College Majors," *Niche*, posted on June 18, 2019, updated on Jan. 9, 2021, https://www.niche.com/blog/the-most-popular-college-majors/.

3. Bryan Caplan, "The Prevalence of Marxism in Academia," *The Library of Economics and Liberty (Econlib)*, (March 31, 2015), https://www.econlib.org/archives/2015/03/the _prevalence_1.html.

4. Schumpeter is known for his defense of capitalism's powers of "creative destruction," so readers of his *Capitalism, Socialism, and Democracy* (1942) may be surprised by the amount of praise Schumpeter gives Marx as a sociologist and economist. Schumpeter calls Marx a genius and a highly capable economic analyst, and argues that his ideas need to be seriously grappled with.

5. Corey Robin, "The Limits of Liberalism at Harvard," *Current Affairs*, Oct. 27, 2016, https: //www.currentaffairs.org/2016/10/the-limits-of-liberalism-at-harvard. Robin is scathing of Harvard professors who oppose Donald Trump but decline to publicly support efforts to modestly improve the wages of the workers in their own dining halls.

6. Helen Pluckrose and James Lindsay, *Cynical Theories: How Activist Scholarship Made Everything about Race, Gender, and Identity—and Why This Harms Everybody* (Durham, NC: Pitchstone, 2020), p. 13.

7. For very detailed looks at how defenders of "Enlightenment rationality" and "science" are actually neither rational nor scientific, see my deconstructions of the arguments of Charles Murray, Steven Pinker, and Sam Harris (the latter cowritten with Eli Massey). These men think that the left rejects reason itself because they think their own viewpoints are Reason Itself. Nathan J. Robinson, "Why Is Charles Murray Odious?," *Current Affairs*, July 17, 2017, https://www.currentaffairs.org/2017/07/why-is-charles-murray-odious; Nathan J. Robinson, "The World's Most Annoying Man," *Current Affairs*, May 29, 2019, https://www.currentaffairs.org/2019/05/the-worlds-most-annoying-man; Eli Massey and Nathan J. Robinson, "Being Mr. Reasonable," *Current Affairs*, Oct. 12, 2018, https://www .currentaffairs.org/2018/10/being-mr-reasonable.

Chapter 16: There Is a War on Cops When We Need to Be Tougher on Crime

1. Wendy Sawyer and Peter Wagner, "Mass Incarceration: The Whole Pie 2020," Prison Policy Initiative, March 24, 2020, https://www.prisonpolicy.org/reports/pie2020.html.

2. Atul Gawande, "Hellhole," *New Yorker*, March 23, 2009, https://www.newyorker.com /magazine/2009/03/30/hellhole; Gali Katznelson and J. Wesley Boyd, "Solitary Confinement: Torture, Pure and Simple," *Psychology Today*, Jan. 15, 2018, https://www.psychologytoday .com/us/blog/almost-addicted/201801/solitary-confinement-torture-pure-and-simple.

3. David Shichor and Dale K. Sechrest, eds., *Three Strikes and You're Out: Vengeance as Public Policy* (Thousand Oaks, CA: Sage Publications Inc., 1996).

4. Branden A. Bell, "Not for Human Consumption: Vague Laws, Uninformed Plea Bargains, and the Trial Penalty," *Federal Sentencing Reporter* 31, no. 4–5 (April/June 2019), pp. 226–33, https://doi.org/10.1525/fsr.2019.31.4-5.226.

5. Stephen B. Bright and Sia M. Sanneh, "Fifty Years of Defiance and Resistance after *Gideon v. Wainwright*," *Yale Law Journal* 122, no. 8 (June 2013), pp. 2150–74, https://www.yalelawjournal.org/essay/fifty-years-of-defiance-and-resistance-after-gideon-v-wainwright.

6. Nathan J. Robinson and Oren Nimni, "There's a New Entry on the List of Reasons Why Police Can Shoot You If You're Black," *Current Affairs*, July 21, 2016, https://www.currentaffairs.org/2016/07/theres-a-new-entry-on-the-list-of-reasons-why-police-can-shoot-you-if-youre-black.

7. *Investigation of the Chicago Police Department*, United States Department of Justice Civil Rights Division and United States Attorney's Office Northern District of Illinois, Jan. 13, 2017, https://www.justice.gov/opa/file/925846/download.

8. *Investigation of the Ferguson Police Department*, United States Department of Justice Civil Rights Division, March 4, 2015, https://www.justice.gov/sites/default/files/opa/press-releases/attachments/2015/03/04/ferguson_police_department_report.pdf. The report shows how ordinary residents of Ferguson, ensnared in its punishment system, had exorbitant fines extracted from them and wound up in jail if they didn't comply. It also shows how racial bias, rather than "crime rates," influenced police conduct.

9. Note that I am restricting myself here to a few snippets from a couple of reports on a couple of police departments. We have not even begun to discuss the abuses that occur in the prison system. Have a look, for example, at the DOJ's 2019 report on Alabama's state prisons for men, which reveals truly horrific conditions that should shock the conscience of everyone in the United States. But of course, because prisoners are ignored or treated as deserving what they get, these crimes against humanity are given little attention in the press, and zero attention by the conservative right. *Investigation of Alabama's State Prisons for Men*, United States Department of Justice Civil Rights Division, April 2, 2019, https://www.justice.gov/crt/case-document/file/1149971/download.

10. "Poll: 7 in 10 Black Americans Say They Have Experienced Incidents of Discrimination or Police Mistreatment in Their Lifetime, Including Nearly Half Who Felt Their Lives Were in Danger," Kaiser Family Foundation, June 18, 2020, https://www.kff.org/racial-equity-and-health-policy/press-release/poll-7-in-10-black-americans-say-they-have-experienced-incidents-of-discrimination-or-police-mistreatment-in-lifetime-including-nearly-half-who-felt-lives-were-in-danger/.

11. Camille Lloyd, "For Black Americans, 41% of Police Encounters Not Positive," *Gallup*, July 30, 2020, https://news.gallup.com/poll/316247/black-americans-police-encounters-not-positive.aspx.

12. "Vision for Black Lives," Movement for Black Lives, https://m4bl.org/policy-platforms/. To those curious about the substance of the BLM agenda, I would recommend diving into this detailed set of proposals.

13. *Report to the United Nations on Racial Disparities in the U.S. Criminal Justice System*, The Sentencing Project, April 19, 2018, https://www.sentencingproject.org/publications/un-report-on-racial-disparities/.

14. *Stop and Frisk: The Human Impact—the Stories behind the Numbers, the Effects on Our Communities*, Center for Constitutional Rights, July 2012, https://ccrjustice.org/sites/default/files/attach/2015/08/the-human-impact-report.pdf. For a briefer look, see Reina Sultan, "6 People Describe Being Stopped and Frisked when Bloomberg Was Mayor of NYC," *VICE*, Feb. 21, 2020, https://www.vice.com/en/article/3a85nn/stop-and-frisk-mayor-bloomberg-nyc-personal-stories.

15. Coleman Hughes, "Stories and Data: Reflections on Race, Riots, and Police," *City Journal*, June 14, 2020, https://www.city-journal.org/reflections-on-race-riots-and-police.

16. "Retraction for Johnson et al., Officer Characteristics and Racial Disparities in Fatal Officer-Involved Shootings," *Proceedings of the National Academy of Sciences* 117, no. 30 (July 2020), p. 18130, https://doi.org/10.1073/pnas.2014148117. The authors write in a note that "our work has continued to be cited as providing support for the idea that there

are no racial biases in fatal shootings, or policing in general. To be clear, our work does not speak to these issues and should not be used to support such statements."

17. Members of Race A agree that for the vast majority of the history of the country, this wealth gap was the result of a regime of racial terrorism and discrimination, but they insist that about forty years ago, when formal legal barriers to the advancement of Race B were removed, the whole situation changed and now lingering disparities must be the result of the cultural and/or genetic dysfunction of Race B.

18. There are other possibilities, too. It could be that officers are not biased in their decisions as to whether or not to *shoot* a person they confront, but they are biased in their decisions about whom to confront. For a discussion of the statistical debate here, see Andrew Gelman, "It's All about the Denominator: Rajiv Sethi and Sendhil Mullainathan in a Statistical Debate on Racial Bias in Police Killings," *Statistical Modeling, Causal Inference, and Social Science,* Oct. 21, 2015, https://statmodeling.stat.columbia.edu/2015/10/21/its-all-about -the-denominator-and-rajiv-sethi-and-sendhil-mullainathan-in-a-statistical-debate-on -racial-bias-in-police-killings/.

19. Quoctrung Bui and Amanda Cox, "Surprising New Evidence Shows Bias in Police Use of Force but Not in Shootings," *New York Times,* July 11, 2016, https://www.nytimes.com /2016/07/12/upshot/surprising-new-evidence-shows-bias-in-police-use-of-force-but-not -in-shootings.html.

20. Justin M. Feldman, "Roland Fryer Is Wrong: There Is Racial Bias in Shootings by Police," Harvard FXB Center for Health and Human Rights, blog, July 12, 2016, https://scholar .harvard.edu/jfeldman/blog/roland-fryer-wrong-there-racial-bias-shootings-police. A team of Princeton researchers showed that Fryer's methods "can severely underestimate levels of racially biased policing or mask discrimination entirely." Dean Knox et al., "Administrative Records Mask Racially Biased Policing," *American Political Science Review* 114, no. 3 (August 2020): 619–637, https://doi.org/10.1017/S0003055420000039.

21. Radley Balko, "Why It's Impossible to Calculate the Percentage of Police Shootings That Are Legitimate," *Washington Post,* July 14, 2016, https://www.washingtonpost.com/news /the-watch/wp/2016/07/14/why-its-impossible-to-calculate-the-percentage-of-police -shootings-that-are-legitimate/.

22. Conservative statistical arguments on police shootings are frequently dubious. For debunkings of several others, see Nathan J. Robinson, "How Conservatives Use Made-Up and/or Misleading Nonsense to Justify Police Killings," *Current Affairs,* June 26, 2018, https://www.currentaffairs.org/2018/06/how-conservatives-use-made-up-nonsense-to -justify-police-killings/; Nathan J. Robinson, "Examining the Conservative Defense of Police Shootings," *Current Affairs,* Dec. 30, 2015, https://www.currentaffairs.org/2015/12 /examining-the-conservative-defense-of-police-violence.

23. Joe Neel, "Poll: 6 in 10 Black Americans Say Police Unfairly Stopped Them or a Relative," *NPR,* Oct. 30, 2017, https://www.npr.org/sections/codeswitch/2017/10/30/560382301 /poll-6-in-10-black-americans-say-theyve-been-unfairly-stopped-by-police. The right will often cite highly selective polling data purporting to show that Black people want more, rather than less, policing. In fact, the polling reveals that Black people are extremely dissatisfied with police, and while they want safer communities, it is a gross misrepresentation to portray Black Americans as approving of the existing policing system. As Aaron Ross Coleman explains in a deep dive into the polling data:

Polling does capture black people's discontent with police racism and impunity. According to a 2019 Pew survey, "84% of black adults said that, in dealing with police, blacks are generally treated less fairly than whites; 63% of whites said the same." The survey also found that "Black adults are about five times as likely as whites to say they've been unfairly stopped by police because of their race or ethnicity (44% vs. 9%)."

Similarly, a 2016 Pew survey found that "Black Americans are far less likely than whites to give high police marks for the way they do their jobs." In the poll, "only about a third of Black adults said that police in their community did an 'excellent' or 'good' job in using the right amount of force (33%, compared with 75% of whites), treating racial and ethnic groups equally (35% vs. 75%), and holding officers accountable for misconduct (31% vs. 70%)."

Last year, the Black Census Project polled more than 30,000 Black people (likely the largest poll of Black people since Reconstruction) and found similar results. "The vast majority of Black Census respondents see the excessive use of force by police officers (83 percent) and police officers killing Black people (87 percent) as problems in the community," the study read. Aaron Ross Coleman, "How Black People Really Feel about the Police, Explained," *Vox,* June 17, 2020, https://www.vox.com/2020/6/17/21292046/black-people -abolish-defund-dismantle-police-george-floyd-breonna-taylor-black-lives-matter-protest. There is evidence that among students, police officers make the majority of white students feel safer but not the majority of Black students. Claire Bryan, "Police Don't Make Most Black Students Feel Safer, Survey Shows," *Chalkbeat,* June 8, 2020, https://www.chalkbeat.org /2020/6/8/21284538/police-security-guards-schools-black-white-students-racism.

24. This is not a good defense. It is often used to justify stop-and-frisk policies and other forms of racial profiling, the idea being that discrimination *does* occur but that it is "rational" because the person's demographic characteristics are associated with crime. Note that it fully admits the police are racist in the most literal sense of the word—viewing someone's race as implying something negative about them is likely to be true—but says that racism is okay in the pursuit of a certain end. What it leaves out is that following this path leads to a nightmarish regime for every individual of a certain race, in which they are constantly a suspect no matter what they do. This is why, no matter *what* the statistical demographics of criminal perpetrators are, racist policing is foul. It means that an individual has no way to escape the stigma of racism and must constantly be singled out for discrimination even if there is no evidence against them beyond their race. It is unbelievable to me that some people can justify this.

25. Tim Scott, "I've Choked on Fear When Stopped by Police. We Need the JUSTICE Act," *USA Today,* June 18, 2020, https://www.usatoday.com/story/opinion/2020/06/18/police -still-stop-me-pass-justice-act-senator-tim-scott-column/3214395001/.

26. Nathan J. Robinson, "The Faults of American Criminal Justice Run Deeper than Race," *New Politics,* Dec. 15, 2014, https://newpol.org/faults-american-criminal-justice-run-deeper -race/. One of the most disturbing cases of police misconduct in the last ten years was the killing of Robert Saylor, a man with Down syndrome who was wrestled to the ground and choked to death in a movie theater after he tried to watch a movie a second time without paying. I confess I do not understand the mentality of the kind of person who can be more upset by the movement for police accountability than by the actions of the cops who murdered Robert Saylor. David M. Perry, "Justice for Down Syndrome Man Who Died in Movie Theater," *CNN,* Aug. 29, 2013, https://www.cnn.com/2013/08/29/opinion/perry -down-syndrome-death/index.html.

27. Michael R. Sisak, "NYPD Officer Says He Inflated Charge against Eric Garner," Associated Press, May 21, 2019, https://apnews.com/article/ce589240fb884eceab7eaba2bfdff9e2.

28. Jack Dutton, "Daunte Wright's Mother Says Son Killed Over Air Freshener in Car," *Newsweek,* April 12, 2021, https://www.newsweek.com/daunte-wrights-mother-says-son-killed -over-car-air-freshener-1582776. The police insisted Wright had been pulled over for having expired plates, and the illegal air freshener was noticed after the fact. Either way, Wright is dead.

29. Mariame Kaba, "Yes, We Mean Literally Abolish the Police," *New York Times,* June 12, 2020, https://www.nytimes.com/2020/06/12/opinion/sunday/floyd-abolish-defund-police.html. It is important to note that even Kaba, who is among the most radical on the left in her anti-police stance, is not talking about just eliminating police departments and letting people fend for themselves against violence, and emphasizes that the core of the idea is to build a society where murder, rape, and robbery do not happen, rather than one in which they do happen but are responded to with state force. She writes:

When people, especially white people, consider a world without the police, they envision a society as violent as our current one, merely without law enforcement—and they shudder. As a society, we have been so indoctrinated with the idea that we solve problems by policing and caging people that many cannot imagine anything other than prisons and the police as solutions to violence and harm. People like me who want to abolish prisons and police, however, have a vision of a different society, built on cooperation instead of individualism, on mutual aid instead of self-preservation. What would the country look like if it had billions of extra dollars to spend on housing, food and education for all?

Even those who disagree with Kaba on policing should take her vision seriously. See also Mariame Kaba, *We Do This 'Til We Free Us: Abolitionist Organizing and Transforming Justice* (Chicago: Haymarket Books, 2021).

30. For an example of this type of argument, see Matthew Yglesias, "The End of Policing Left Me Convinced We Still Need Policing," *Vox*, June 18, 2020, https://www.vox.com/2020/6/18/21293784/alex-vitale-end-of-policing-review. For a response to this particular piece, see Alec Karakatsanis, "Why 'Crime' Isn't the Question and Police Aren't the Answer," *Current Affairs*, Aug. 10, 2020, https://www.currentaffairs.org/2020/08/why-crime-isnt-the-question-and-police-arent-the-answer.

31. Roscoe Scarborough, "Want to Reform America's Police? Look to Firefighters," *The Conversation*, Sept. 11, 2019, https://theconversation.com/want-to-reform-americas-police-look-to-firefighters-120573.

32. Many communities have sparse ambulance services, in part because in the United States ambulances are often operated for profit, and serving the poor isn't especially profitable. In fact, in many places, ambulances aren't even legally classified as essential services, meaning that local governments aren't required to provide them. Redirecting bloated police budgets to the provision of essential medical care would help solve this. Ali Watkins, "Rural Ambulance Crews Have Run Out of Money and Volunteers," *New York Times*, April 30, 2021, https://www.nytimes.com/2021/04/25/us/rural-ambulance-coronavirus.html.

33. Forman's book is a good complement to Alexander's bestseller, both affirming and critiquing parts of *The New Jim Crow*'s analysis. See also James Forman, Jr. "Racial Critiques of Mass Incarceration: Beyond the New Jim Crow." *New York University Law Review*, vol. 87, no. 1 (2012), pp. 21–69.

Chapter 17: Labor Unions Hurt Workers

1. German Lopez, "I Was Skeptical of Unions. Then I Joined One," *Vox*, Aug. 19, 2019, https://www.vox.com/policy-and-politics/2019/8/19/20727283/unions-good-income-inequality-wealth.

2. Ibid.

3. Matthew Walters and Lawrence Michel, "How Unions Help All Workers," Economic Policy Institute, Aug. 26, 2003, https://www.epi.org/publication/briefingpapers_bp143/.

4. "Statement from the New Republic Union on Company's Reversal," NewsGuild of New York, April 1, 2021, https://www.nyguild.org/post/statement-from-the-new-republic-union-on-companys-reversal.

5. Amazon lied about this when they were called out on it. See Nathan J. Robinson, "Amazon Is Caught in a Brazen Lie about Its Exploitative Practices," *Current Affairs*, March 29, 2021, https://www.currentaffairs.org/2021/03/amazon-is-caught-in-a-brazen-lie-about-its-exploitative-practices.

6. Kate Taylor and Avery Hartmans, "Amazon Drivers Say They Had to Poop in Bags and Struggled to Change Menstrual Pads in Addition to Peeing in Bottles," *Business Insider*, March 26, 2021, https://www.businessinsider.com/amazon-drivers-say-pooped-in-bags-changed-pads-pee-bottles-2021-3.

7. Will Evans, "Ruthless Quotas at Amazon Are Maiming Employees," *The Atlantic*, Nov. 25, 2019, https://www.theatlantic.com/technology/archive/2019/11/amazon-warehouse-reports-show-worker-injuries/602530/. This report not only documents poor safety practices at Amazon but shows how the company is essentially above the law and escapes punishment for violations of workplace safety standards.

8. Sarah Krouse, "The New Ways Your Boss Is Spying on You," *Wall Street Journal*, July 19, 2019, https://www.wsj.com/articles/the-new-ways-your-boss-is-spying-on-you-11563528604.

9. For more on the coercive power of employers, see Chris Bertram et al., "Let It Bleed: Libertarianism and the Workplace," *Crooked Timber*, July 1, 2012, https://crookedtimber.org/2012/07/01/let-it-bleed-libertarianism-and-the-workplace/. This piece cites many

real-world examples and powerfully undermines the argument that libertarian ideology creates meaningful freedom for people who do not have much money.

10. Elizabeth Anderson, *Private Government: How Employers Rule Our Lives (and Why We Don't Talk about It)*, (Princeton, NJ: Princeton University Press, 2017).

11. For an explanation of why all the specific points made in Ben Shapiro's union video are wrong, see Nathan J. Robinson, "Everything Ben Shapiro Says Is Still Worthless," *Current Affairs*, June 30, 2021, https://www.currentaffairs.org/2021/06/everything-ben-shapiro-says-is-still-worthless. I also address his arguments on minimum wages and "transgender ideology."

12. Erling Barth et al., "Union Density Effects on Productivity and Wages," *Economic Journal* 130, no. 631 (October 2020): 1898–1936, https://doi.org/10.1093/ej/ueaa048.

13. Morgan O. Reynolds, "Labor Unions," *Library of Economics and Liberty*, https://www.econlib.org/library/Enc/LaborUnions.html.

14. James Sherk, "What Unions Do: How Labor Unions Affect Jobs and the Economy," Heritage Foundation, May 21, 2009, https://www.heritage.org/jobs-and-labor/report/what-unions-do-how-labor-unions-affect-jobs-and-the-economy.

15. Barth et al., "Union Density Effects on Productivity and Wages."

16. Lopez, "I Was Skeptical of Unions."

17. If you would like a refutation of the argument in favor of "right to work" laws, see Nathan J. Robinson, "How Expanding the Right to Contract Can Limit Rights," *Current Affairs*, May 23, 2018, https://www.currentaffairs.org/2018/05/why-expansions-of-the-right-to-contract-are-limitations-on-rights. These are laws that prohibit employers from requiring union membership as a condition of employment, ostensibly on the grounds that this "coerces" employees into doing something they don't want to do. The reason this argument makes no sense is that conservatives *do not* object to employers requiring an endless number of other highly objectionable things as conditions of employment, on the grounds that if employees don't like it, they are "free to choose" to work somewhere else. Why, all of a sudden, when it's *union membership* being required, are they concerned about protecting workers from having to agree to things they don't want? Workers might not want to have to, say, wear a uniform or take a drug test or work on a weekend, but these types of contractual obligations are unobjectionable to the right. It's clear that the "freedom" argument for right-to-work laws is not principled, and they actually just come from a dislike of unions. (Milton Friedman, who was actually consistent, opposed right-to-work laws because he believed an employer's power to impose objectionable conditions on employees should be virtually limitless.)

18. Quoted in Allana Akhtar, "Martin Luther King Jr. Was as Vocal about Union Power as He Was about Racial Injustice—but No One Remembers It," *Insider*, Jan. 20, 2020, https://www.businessinsider.com/martin-luther-king-jrs-thoughts-on-the-labor-movement-unions.

Chapter 18: Transgender People Are Delusional and a Threat

1. Deirdre N. McCloskey, *Crossing: A Memoir* (Chicago: University of Chicago Press, 1999), pp. 175–76.

2. Julia Serano, *Whipping Girl: A Transsexual Woman on Sexism and the Scapegoating of Femininity* (Emeryville, CA: Seal Press, 2007), pp. 51–52.

3. "Pronouns," ContraPoints, Nov. 2, 2018, YouTube video, https://www.youtube.com/watch?v=9bbINLWtMKI.

4. Scott Alexander, "The Categories Were Made for Man, Not Man for the Categories," *Slate Star Codex* (blog), Nov. 21, 2014, https://slatestarcodex.com/2014/11/21/the-categories-were-made-for-man-not-man-for-the-categories/.

5. Anthony J. F. Griffiths et al., "Historical Development of the Chromosome Theory," in *An Introduction to Genetic Analysis*, 7th ed. (New York: W. H. Freeman and Company, 2000).

6. For more on why gender is hard to discuss and that's okay, see my colleague Adrian Rennix's excellent essay "The Peculiarity of Gender," *Current Affairs*, June 25, 2020, https://www.currentaffairs.org/2020/06/the-peculiarity-of-gender.

7. Katie Herzog, "Where Have All the Lesbians Gone?," *Weekly Dish* (newsletter), Nov. 27, 2020, https://andrewsullivan.substack.com/p/where-have-all-the-lesbians-gone-0a7.

8. Amira Hasenbush et al., "Gender Identity Nondiscrimination Laws in Public Accommo-dations: A Review of Evidence Regarding Safety and Privacy in Public Restrooms, Locker Rooms, and Changing Rooms," *Sexuality Research and Social Policy* 16 (March 2019), pp. 70–83, https://doi.org/10.1007/s13178-018-0335-z. The study "finds that reports of privacy and safety violations in public restrooms, locker rooms, and changing rooms are exceedingly rare" and "provides evidence that fears of increased safety and privacy viola-tions as a result of nondiscrimination laws are not empirically grounded."

9. Samantha Schmidt, "1 in 6 Gen Z Adults Are LGBT. And This Number Could Continue to Grow," *Washington Post,* Feb. 24, 2021, https://www.washingtonpost.com/dc-md-va/2021/02/24/gen-z-lgbt/.

10. The parents Shrier profiles don't have very good reasons for objecting to their children being trans, and often show an extreme discomfort with their children's choices without making any effort to empathize with them.

11. While more young people are choosing to identify as trans, the evidence does not support the conservative narrative about a "trans contagion" in which peer pressure is causing children to turn trans. For a much more detailed refutation of the conservative "trans panic" arguments as articulated by Shrier and others, and an explanation of why these myths are harmful, see Nathan J. Robinson, "Why the Panic over Trans Kids?," *Current Affairs,* April 30, 2021, https://www.currentaffairs.org/2021/04/why-the-panic-over-trans-kids. For a look at claims made about trans women in sports, see Nathan J. Robinson, "The Arguments against Trans Athletes Are Bigoted and Irrational," *Current Affairs,* May 31, 2021, https://www.currentaffairs.org/2021/05/the-arguments-against-trans-athletes-are-bigoted-and-irrational. For a look at the arguments made by J. K. Rowling, see Na-than J. Robinson, "J. K. Rowling and the Limits of Imagination," *Current Affairs,* July 23, 2020, https://www.currentaffairs.org/2020/07/jk-rowling-and-the-limits-of-imagination.

12. See Roanne K. Jalopy, "Transgender Trouble: 40 Years of Gender Essentialism and Gatekeep-ing," *Current Affairs,* Dec. 29, 2020, https://www.currentaffairs.org/2020/12/transgender-trouble-40-years-of-gender-essentialism-and-gatekeeping.

Chapter 19: Abortion Is Murder

1. When pressed on what this meant, Williamson indicated he believed in "hanging" as pun-ishment for abortions. This was evidently meant quite seriously, and Williamson later lost a job as a writer at *The Atlantic* over the comments.

2. Karen Swallow Prior, "Texas' Abortion Law Should Force America to Change Its Ways," *New York Times,* Sept. 9, 2021, https://www.nytimes.com/2021/09/09/opinion/texas-abortion-pro-life.html.

3. Robert H. Bork, *A Time to Speak: Selected Writings and Arguments* (Wilmington, DE: ISI Books, 2008), p. 352.

4. The exception being *National Review* columnist Kevin D. Williamson, who said that for conservatives to be consistent, women who had abortions should be hanged. Williamson's remarks were appalling, but he is one of the rare people on the right to openly admit the horrifying logical conclusion of right-wing rhetoric on abortion. We can be grate-ful that fellow conservatives did not second Williamson's proposal, but the fact that they didn't shows that most pro-lifers *do* perceive some kind of difference with other cases of "murder." Jacqueline Thomsen, "*The Atlantic* Fires Conservative Writer after Audio Re-veals He Called for Death Penalty for Women Who Get Abortion," *The Hill,* April 5, 2018, https://thehill.com/homenews/media/381823-the-atlantic-fires-conservative-writer-after-audio-reveals-he-called-for-death.

5. Sarah Kliff, "Abortion Rates in North America and Europe Are Now at 30-Year Lows," *Vox,* May 11, 2016, https://www.vox.com/2016/5/11/11657174/abortion-rates-falling.

6. Gretchen Livingston and Deja Thomas, "Among 41 Countries, Only U.S. Lacks Paid Pa-rental Leave," Pew Research Center, Dec. 16, 2019, https://www.pewresearch.org/fact-tank/2019/12/16/u-s-lacks-mandated-paid-parental-leave/.

7. See Michelle Oberman, *Her Body, Our Laws: On the Front Lines of the Abortion War, from El Salvador to Oklahoma* (Boston, MA: Beacon Press, 2018). Oberman's book is excellent

in showing how the lives of women, especially poor women, are affected by changes to abortion laws. Reporting from places where abortion is already criminalized, Oberman shows that many of the consequences of criminalized abortion are heinous. Women are falsely accused of abortions and jailed, and rich women are able to leave the country to have the procedure while poor women risk jail sentences.

8. For a longer discussion of the abortion issue, and why legalized abortion is necessary regardless of where one comes down on the philosophical issue, see Adrian Rennix and Nathan J. Robinson, "Abortion and the Left," *Current Affairs*, Aug. 30, 2018, https://www .currentaffairs.org/2018/08/abortion-and-the-left. For an explanation of why it's important to aggressively defend abortion rights, see Cate Root and Lyta Gold, "We Just Have to Fight," *Current Affairs*, Aug. 13, 2019, https://www.currentaffairs.org/2019/08/we-just -have-to-fight.

Chapter 20: There Is a War on Christianity

1. Daniel Cox and Amelia Thomson-DeVeaux, "Millennials Are Leaving Religion and Not Coming Back," *FiveThirtyEight*, Dec. 12, 2019, https://fivethirtyeight.com/features /millennials-are-leaving-religion-and-not-coming-back/.

2. I do not have space here to go through and refute all of Christianity, but if interested in responses to its creationist aspects in particular, the TalkOrigins Archive is a useful compendium: http://www.talkorigins.org/.

3. Mary Ziegler, "Texas Has Cleared a Path to the End of Roe v. Wade," *New York Times*, Aug. 26, 2021, https://www.nytimes.com/2021/08/26/opinion/abortion-supreme-court.html.

4. The legal controversy is ongoing, however. Lauren M. Johnson, "Colorado Judge Finds Christian Baker Broke State Discrimination Law by Refusing to Bake a Birthday Cake for a Trans Woman," *CNN*, June 18, 2021, https://www.cnn.com/2021/06/18/us/jack-phillips -colorado-baker-discrimination-trnd/index.html.

Chapter 21: We Must Respect the Constitution and the Founding Fathers

1. Colin G. Calloway, *The Indian World of George Washington: The First President, the First Americans, and the Birth of the Nation* (New York: Oxford University Press, 2018), p. 378.

2. Gillian Brockell, "George Washington Owned Slaves and Ordered Indians Killed. Will a Mural of That History Be Hidden?," *Washington Post*, Aug. 25, 2019, https://www .washingtonpost.com/history/2019/08/25/george-washington-owned-slaves-ordered -indians-killed-will-mural-that-history-be-hidden/.

3. "To Thomas Jefferson from Benjamin Banneker, 19 August 1791," *Founders Online*, National Archives, https://founders.archives.gov/documents/Jefferson/01-22-02-0049.

4. "Abigail Adams to John Adams, 31 March 1776," *Founders Online*, National Archives, https://founders.archives.gov/documents/Adams/04-01-02-0241.

5. "John Adams to Abigail Adams, 14 April 1776," *Founders Online*, National Archives, https: //founders.archives.gov/documents/Adams/04-01-02-0248.

6. "Abigail Adams to John Adams, 31 March 1776," *Founders Online*.

7. "Term of the Senate, [26 June] 1787," *Founders Online*, National Archives, https://founders .archives.gov/documents/Madison/01-10-02-0044.

8. I put "universal" in quotes because it is not universal. Prisoners, children, and noncitizens cannot vote. This may seem "self-evidently" rational, but it is not. I know many noncitizen residents who have spent their lives here and are just as connected to the country as any citizen, but cannot vote. For the case in favor of prisoner voting, see Nathan J. Robinson, "Why Can't Prisoners Vote?," *Current Affairs*, May 8, 2018, https://www.currentaffairs.org /2018/05/why-cant-prisoners-vote.

9. Garrett Epps, "The Founders' Great Mistake," *The Atlantic*, Jan./Feb. 2009, https://www .theatlantic.com/magazine/archive/2009/01/the-founders-great-mistake/307210/.

10. Nathan J. Robinson, "Why Ginsburg Didn't Retire," *Current Affairs*, Sept. 23, 2020, https: //www.currentaffairs.org/2020/09/why-ginsburg-didnt-retire.

11. Some conservatives suggest that the Electoral College system makes sense because it forces candidates to "campaign in every state" and not neglect smaller states. In fact, the opposite

is the case. Without the Electoral College system, it would make sense for a Democrat to campaign in a red state, because any votes amassed there would still help the Democrat. With the Electoral College, there is no reason whatsoever for Democrats to want to get votes in a reliably red state. Eliminating the Electoral College would create an incentive for candidates to go to states they currently do not visit.

12. For the most part. It is still the case that George W. Bush owes his entire political career to the fact that his father was a president.

13. "U.S. Supreme Court Justices Antonin Scalia & Stephen Breyer Conversation on the Constitution," James E. Rogers College of Law, Jan. 24, 2019, YouTube video, https://www.youtube.com/watch?v=jmv5Tz7w5pk.

14. I have written much more on the role of value judgments in the law and the way judges disguise their own political preferences as "originalism" or "textualism." See Nathan J. Robinson, "How the Supreme Court Pretends to Be Reasonable," *Current Affairs*, June 29, 2018, https://www.currentaffairs.org/2018/06/how-the-supreme-court-pretends-to-be-reasonable. I have also written long analyses of the jurisprudence of Amy Coney Barrett and Brett Kavanaugh in particular, showing the ways in which, despite professing to merely *apply* the law, both smuggle in conservative values. See Nathan J. Robinson, "Why Everyone Should Oppose Brett Kavanaugh's Confirmation," *Current Affairs*, Aug. 6, 2018, https://www.currentaffairs.org/2018/08/why-everyone-should-oppose-brett-kavanaughs-confirmation; Nathan J. Robinson, "Why Amy Coney Barrett Should Not Be on the Supreme Court," *Current Affairs*, Sept. 27, 2020, https://www.currentaffairs.org/2020/09/why-amy-coney-barrett-should-not-be-on-the-supreme-court.

Chapter 22: People Should "Pull Themselves Up by Their Bootstraps" and Not Need "Handouts"

1. See Nathan J. Robinson, "The Cool Kid's Philosopher," *Current Affairs*, Dec. 1, 2017, https://static.currentaffairs.org/2017/12/the-cool-kids-philosopher.

2. Isabel V. Sawhill and Ron Haskins, *Work and Marriage: The Way to End Poverty and Welfare*, Brookings Institution, Sept. 1, 2003, https://www.brookings.edu/research/work-and-marriage-the-way-to-end-poverty-and-welfare/.

3. George F. Will, "Listen Up, Millennials. There's Sequence to Success," *Washington Post*, July 5, 2017, https://www.washingtonpost.com/opinions/listen-up-millenials-theres-sequence-to-success/2017/07/05/5a4a8350-6011-11e7-a4f7-af34fc1d9d39_story.html; Wendy Wang, "'The Sequence' Is the Secret to Success," *Wall Street Journal*, March 27, 2018, https://www.wsj.com/articles/the-sequence-is-the-secret-to-success-1522189894.

4. *The State of America's Children® 2020*, Children's Defense Fund, https://www.childrensdefense.org/the-state-of-americas-children-2020/.

5. George F. Will, "Listen Up, Millennials."

6. Richard V. Burkhauser et al., "Evaluating the Success of President Johnson's War on Poverty: Revisiting the Historical Record Using a Full-Income Poverty Measure," Institute of Labor Economics, IZA Discussion Papers, no. 12855 (Dec. 2019), https://www.iza.org/publications/dp/12855/evaluating-the-success-of-president-johnsons-war-on-poverty-revisiting-the-historical-record-using-a-full-income-poverty-measure.

Chapter 23: Immigration Is Harmful

1. Note that in this passage, Cooke is not actually endorsing the conservative position but merely stating it.

2. Erik Wemple, "Fox News's Bill O'Reilly Embraces Activism with 'Kate's Law,'" *Washington Post*, July 14, 2015, https://www.washingtonpost.com/blogs/erik-wemple/wp/2015/07/14/fox-newss-bill-oreilly-embraces-activism-with-kates-law/.

3. See Nathan J. Robinson, "The Case against Deporting Criminal Aliens," *Current Affairs*, Oct. 15, 2015, https://www.currentaffairs.org/2015/10/the-case-against-deporting-criminal-aliens. In this article, I go into more detail about the fact that deporting aliens who commit crimes does not necessarily save lives, but merely makes sure that the lives taken are non-

American rather than American. This is only a moral improvement if we believe that people outside this country matter less than people in it, which I do not believe is the case.

4. Noah Smith, "Why Immigration Doesn't Reduce Wages," *Noahpinion* (newsletter), Dec. 29, 2020, https://noahpinion.substack.com/p/why-immigration-doesnt-reduce-wages. Smith shows that immigration restrictionists have no good responses to the argument that immigration is economically positive, and constantly cite the same unpersuasive studies by a single contrarian economist, George Borjas. One common tendency on the right is to ignore almost all of the existing academic literature on a subject and cite the one study they find that supports their position.

5. Donald Trump Jr., *Triggered: How the Left Thrives on Hate and Wants to Silence Us* (New York: Center Street, 2019).

6. A quote from this FAIR's founder: ""One of my prime concerns is about the decline of folks who look like you and me. . . . For European-American society and culture to persist requires a European-American majority, and a clear one at that." Quoted in Jason DeParle, "The Anti-Immigration Crusader," *New York Times*, April 17, 2011, https://www.nytimes.com/2011/04/17/us/17immig.html.

7. Alex Nowrasteh, "FAIR's 'Fiscal Burden of Illegal Immigration' Study Is Fatally Flawed," Cato Institute, Sept. 29, 2017, https://www.cato.org/blog/fairs-fiscal-burden-illegal -immigration-study-fatally-flawed. One thing that has to be said for the free-market libertarians, as opposed to the traditionalist conservatives, is that they generally have a good understanding of the economics of immigration.

8. Jack Citrin et al., "Testing Huntington: Is Hispanic Immigration a Threat to American Identity?," *Perspectives on Politics* 5, no. 1 (March 2007): 31–48, doi:10.1017/S15375927 07070041.

9. Elliot Hannon, "U.S. Deported a Detroit Man to Iraq, Where He'd Never Been and Didn't Speak the Language. He Died on the Streets," *Slate*, Aug. 8, 2019, https://slate.com/news -and-politics/2019/08/detroit-michigan-man-deported-died-iraq-diabetic-homeless .html. See also Nathan J. Robinson, "The Descent into Cruelty," *Current Affairs*, Aug. 9, 2019, https://www.currentaffairs.org/2019/08/the-descent-into-cruelty.

10. For example, "As President Trump says time and time again, 'If you don't have borders, you don't have a country.' . . . No country can survive without enforceable borders and empowered law enforcement enforcing the law equally." Pete Hegseth, *American Crusade: Our Fight to Stay Free* (New York: Center Street, 2020), p. 57.

11. For a longer response to critics of open borders, see Adrian Rennix and Nathan J. Robinson, "Responding to 'The Left Case against Open Borders,'" *Current Affairs*, Nov. 29, 2018, https: //www.currentaffairs.org/2018/11/responding-to-the-left-case-against-open-borders.

12. I use quotes to draw attention to the fact that while we accept the phrase "detention facility" as normal and neutral, it is, in truth, an Orwellian euphemism for what amounts to a prison.

13. Ronald Brownstein, "Places with the Fewest Immigrants Push Back Hardest against Immigration," *CNN*, Aug. 22, 2017, https://www.cnn.com/2017/08/22/politics/immigration -trump-arizona/index.html.

14. Phillip Connor and Jens Manuel Krogstad, "Many Worldwide Oppose More Migration— Both Into and Out of Their Countries," Pew Research Center, Dec. 10, 2018, https://www .pewresearch.org/fact-tank/2018/12/10/many-worldwide-oppose-more-migration-both -into-and-out-of-their-countries/.

15. "Immigration," Gallup, In Depth: Topics A to Z, https://news.gallup.com/poll/1660 /immigration.aspx.

16. "Voter Enthusiasm at Record High in Nationalized Midterm Environment," Pew Research Center, Sept. 26, 2018, https://www.pewresearch.org/politics/2018/09/26/voter -enthusiasm-at-record-high-in-nationalized-midterm-environment/.

17. Anna Merlan, "Here's Tucker Carlson Doing a Racist, Poop-Fixated Segment on 'Gypsies' Overtaking a Pennsylvania Town," *Jezebel*, July 18, 2017, https://jezebel.com/heres-tucker -carlson-doing-a-racist-poop-fixated-segme-1797020246.

18. Hegseth, *American Crusade*, p. 101.

19. Victor Davis Hanson, "The Diversity of Illegal Immigration," Hoover Institution, Aug. 23, 2018, https://www.hoover.org/research/diversity-illegal-immigration.

20. Andy Ngo, "A Visit to Islamic England," *Wall Street Journal,* Aug. 29, 2018, https://www.wsj.com/articles/a-visit-to-islamic-england-1535581583.

21. "Tucker Carlson: Iraqis Are 'Semiliterate Primitive Monkeys,'" *Daily Beast,* March 11, 2019, https://www.thedailybeast.com/tucker-carlson-iraqis-are-semiliterate-primitive-monkeys.

22. Quoted in Nathan J. Robinson, "What the Left Must Fight Against," *Current Affairs,* Nov. 10, 2018, https://www.currentaffairs.org/2018/11/what-the-left-must-fight-against. In this long article I go through Tucker Carlson's book *Ship of Fools* to explain why I find his rhetoric so dangerous. I also show, in a different article, the chilling similarities between Carlson's anti-diversity rhetoric and racist murderers: Nathan J. Robinson, "Guess Who Said It: Tucker Carlson or a Far-Right Shooter," *The Guardian,* Aug. 10, 2019, https://www.theguardian.com/commentisfree/2019/aug/10/tucker-carlson-fox-news-united-states-race.

23. If Antiziganism was taken as seriously as it should be, it would not be controversial to call such a segment fascist. Imagine "Jews: Coming to America." Let us remember, too, how many Roma people perished in the Holocaust.

24. It does, in fact, make sense. Why would someone who has broken immigration laws be less likely to commit other kinds of crimes? Because the penalty for committing other crimes is much higher if you're an unauthorized immigrant, since you risk deportation. Carlson wants us to think it's intuitively implausible that undocumented people would have lower crime rates, but there is a perfectly reasonable theory for why it would be the case.

25. You can see the Carlson clips and a slightly more detailed response in this video I produced: "Exposing Tucker Carlson's Immigration Ignorance," *Current Affairs,* Sept. 18, 2018, YouTube video, https://www.youtube.com/watch?v=7hRpWZe0lbw.

26. Quoted in Alex Nowrasteh, "Illegal Immigrants and Crime—Assessing the Evidence," *Cato at Liberty* (blog), March 4, 2019, https://www.cato.org/blog/illegal-immigrants-crime-assessing-evidence.

Chapter 24: Inequality Is Fine

1. Thomas Sowell argues that it is a mistake even to talk of "redistribution" because it suggests that the government has a legitimate role in deciding who should get what. Because Sowell is a libertarian, he believes that whatever "distribution" the market produces is ultimately just because it is the product of voluntary transactions between people, and the government is an interloper with no right to second-guess this result. This theory can sound persuasive, but its implications are so extreme that few people would be willing to accept them. If a portion of the population is literally starving to death, and another portion of the population is living in opulence, the theory would say that it is illegitimate for the government to tax the opulent portion of the population—that is, *even* if the rich have so much wealth that they *would not even notice the difference.* This means that we would view it as an illegitimate imposition of our moral views to prevent Person A from starving to death by causing minor inconvenience to Person B. This conflicts so deeply with basic human moral instinct that I do not think it would be accepted in practice by any but the most extreme adherents to the belief that property rights trump all other forms of human rights, such as the right to life.

I should also add that my discussion here assumes the view that government spending should be conceived of as the government taking from some people to give to others. This view has been challenged by economists from the school known as Modern Monetary Theory, which argues that government spending creates money rather than "redistributes" it. On an MMT view, there is no "fixed pie," either, but there is also no one-to-one "redistribution," i.e., giving Peter food stamps does not require taking money from Paul. For an overview, see Stephanie Kelton, *The Deficit Myth: Modern Monetary Theory and the Birth of the People's Economy* (New York: PublicAffairs, 2020).

2. The usual response here is that redistribution creates an "incentives" problem because if wealth is taken away, people won't work as hard, and thus the pie won't grow, etc. But the effects of redistribution on productivity are something to be studied empirically, not merely

theorized. In reality, the existing evidence, as former World Bank chief economist François Bourguignon writes, suggests "the redistribution of income might achieve not only greater equality but also faster growth and, for developing economies, faster poverty reduction." François Bourguignon, "Spreading the Wealth," *Finance & Development* 55, no. 1 (March 2018), https://www.imf.org/external/pubs/ft/fandd/2018/03/bourguignon.htm.

3. Some libertarians argue that Robin Hood was a libertarian because he detested the state. I have no interest in litigating the question of what the politics of a fictional character whose actions preceded our current ideological terminology "was" or "was not." I will only defend the position that taking from the rich to give to the poor is an objectively good thing. See Maura Pennington, "Robin Hood Has Always Been a Libertarian Hero," *Forbes*, March 26, 2012, https://www.forbes.com/sites/maurapennington/2012/03/26/robin-hood -has-always-been-a-libertarian-hero/?sh=542d980d7cd3.

4. Leticia Miranda et al., "Here Are the Most Outrageous Incentives Cities Offered Amazon in Their HQ2 Bids," *BuzzFeed News*, Nov. 14, 2018, https://www.buzzfeednews.com /article/leticiamiranda/amazon-hq2-finalist-cities-incentives-airport-lounge.

5. I do despise the rich, but there is empirical evidence that they are objectively worse people, so this is pure rationality on my part. See Paul K. Piff et al., "Higher Social Class Predicts Increased Unethical Behavior," *Proceedings of the National Academy of Sciences* 109, no. 11 (March 2012), pp. 4086–4091, https://doi.org/10.1073/pnas.1118373109.

6. Nathan J. Robinson, "A Speech on Socialism at Andover," *Current Affairs*, Feb. 12, 2019, https://www.currentaffairs.org/2019/02/a-speech-on-socialism-at-andover.

7. "The 50 Best Private Elementary Schools in the U.S.," *TheBestSchools.org*, Jan. 6, 2022, https://thebestschools.org/rankings/k-12/best-private-elementary-schools/.

8. Laura Meckler, "Report Finds $23 Billion Racial Funding Gap for Schools," *Washington Post*, Feb. 26, 2019, https://www.washingtonpost.com/local/education/report-finds -23-billion-racial-funding-gap-for-schools/2019/02/25/d562b704-3915-11e9-a06c -3ec8ed509d15_story.html.

9. Jonah Goldberg, *Suicide of the West: How the Rebirth of Tribalism, Populism, Nationalism, and Identity Politics Is Destroying American Democracy* (New York: Crown Forum, 2018), p. 54. If you are interested in a more thorough discussion of Goldberg's book and its arguments, see this review: Nathan J. Robinson, "'Never Trump' Conservatives Won't Save Us," *Washington Monthly*, April 8, 2018, https://washingtonmonthly.com/2018/04/08 /never-trump-conservatives-wont-save-us/.

Chapter 25: Democracy Is Overrated

1. More precisely, "except for all those other forms that have been tried from time to time," which is slightly less pithy than the commonly heard version.

2. Ryan Cooper, "The Cynic's Case for Democracy," *The Week*, April 9, 2021, https://theweek .com/articles/976287/cynics-case-democracy.

3. Jonathan Chait, "Ted Cruz and the Death of Conservatism," *New York* magazine, Sept. 18, 2018, https://nymag.com/intelligencer/2018/09/republican-memo-admits-voters-oppose -republican-policies.html.

4. "Most Americans Favor the Death Penalty despite Concerns about Its Administration," Pew Research Center, June 2, 2021, https://www.pewresearch.org/politics/2021/06/02 /most-americans-favor-the-death-penalty-despite-concerns-about-its-administration/.

5. The civil rights movement succeeded in many things, but it had to succeed in persuading white people. *Brown v. Board of Education* was decided by an all-white court, Lyndon B. Johnson signed the Civil Rights Act and Voting Rights Act. If Black freedom had been up to Black people, of course, it would have been granted from the country's earliest days. But it wasn't, meaning that a huge political struggle had to be waged over centuries.

6. Some might say that by talking of representation here, I am referring to a republic, not a democracy, but I don't use the terms the way Madison does. I believe our representative system is best referred to as a democratic republic, with a "direct democracy" being the term for the kind of system in which everyone participates directly in decision-making.

7. I have written before about the way the Democratic Socialists of America has tried to create an internally democratic organization, with imperfect but impressive results. See Nathan J. Robinson, "A Gathering of Comrades," *Current Affairs,* Aug. 7, 2019, https://www.currentaffairs.org/2019/08/a-gathering-of-comrades.

8. We still do not have universal suffrage, of course. See Nathan J. Robinson, "Why Can't Prisoners Vote?," *Current Affairs,* May 8, 2018, https://www.currentaffairs.org/2018/05/why-cant-prisoners-vote.

Conclusion

1. For more on the socialist Orwell, see Nick Slater, "Taking Orwell's Name in Vain," *Current Affairs,* Oct. 11, 2017, https://www.currentaffairs.org/2017/10/taking-orwells-name-in-vain.

2. More on this subject can be found in my book *Why You Should Be a Socialist* (New York: All Points Books, 2019).

3. For an excellent review of the book and demolition of its arguments, see Adrian Rennix, "The Cruelties of Coulter," *Current Affairs,* March 11, 2018, https://www.currentaffairs.org/2018/03/the-cruelties-of-coulter.

4. I am grateful to the creator of this Twitter thread for pointing me to this horrifying document: Neoliberal (@ne0liberal), "I don't think it gets enough play how insane some state Republican parties are," Twitter, July 22, 2021, 8:34 p.m., https://twitter.com/ne0liberal/status/1418368987600142337.

5. It would take at least one additional full-length book for me to go through the entire Texas GOP platform and argue against each of its proposals. I am, for the moment, going to have to simply assume that you are capable of seeing why a world in which these ideas are implemented is not one anyone should want to live in.

6. This is genuinely a position that has been defended in the *Wall Street Journal* multiple times. See Phil Gramm and Mike Solon, "In Defense of Scrooge, Whose Thrift Blessed the World," *Wall Street Journal,* Dec. 23, 2020, https://www.wsj.com/articles/in-defense-of-scrooge-whose-thrift-blessed-the-world-11608762986; Rob Long, "In Defense of Scrooge," *Wall Street Journal,* Dec. 18, 2015, https://www.wsj.com/articles/in-defense-of-scrooge-1450455523. Scrooge, you see, made productive contributions to the GDP, and a person's moral worth is measured by their economic output.

7. This topsy-turvy land can really give you a headache sometimes. Dinesh D'Souza's book *The Big Lie,* for instance, argues that while the left calls the right fascist, it is, in fact, the classic tendency of fascists to call the non-fascists fascists, and the real fascists are the ones called the anti-fascists. As a leftist, I think the opposite is the case, but it's easy to get muddled when everyone is pointing their finger at the other and yelling, "Fascist!" This helps to explain why live debates often do not go well, even if you come well-prepared, and may be best avoided. See Aisling McCrea, "Resolved: Debate Is Stupid," *The Outline,* Nov. 28, 2018, https://theoutline.com/post/6709/debate-is-stupid.

8. Mill clarified that "I did not mean that Conservatives are generally stupid; I meant, that stupid people are generally Conservative." John Stuart Mill, "Speech on May 31, 1866," *Public and Parliamentary Speeches: November 1850–November 1868,* eds., John M. Robson and Bruce L. Kinzer, vol. XXVIII (New York: Taylor & Francis, 1996), p. 83.

9. One of my problems with Barack Obama is that too often, he spoke as if it were the case that "red America" and "blue America" had only superficial disagreements, the result of misunderstanding one another. I don't think this is true. For a critique of Obama's view, see Luke Savage and Nathan J. Robinson, "The Fraudulent Universalism of Barack Obama," *Current Affairs,* Dec. 23, 2020, https://www.currentaffairs.org/2020/12/the-fraudulent-universalism-of-barack-obama.

Index

About the Author

Brandon Baudier

NATHAN J. ROBINSON is a leading voice of millennial left politics. He is the editor of *Current Affairs*. His work has appeared in *The New York Times, The Washington Post, The New Republic, The Nation, Salon, The Guardian,* and elsewhere. He is a graduate of Yale Law School and holds a PhD from Harvard University. He is the author of *Why You Should Be a Socialist.*